FROM DUST THEY CAME

NORTH AMERICAN RELIGIONS

Series Editors: Tracy Fessenden (Arizona State University), Laura Levitt (Temple University), and David Harrington Watt (Haverford College).

Since its inception, the North American Religions book series has steadily disseminated gracefully written, pathbreaking explorations of religion in North America. Books in the series move among the discourses of ethnographic, textual, and historical analysis and across a range of topics, including sound, story, food, nature, healing, crime, and pilgrimage. In so doing they bring religion into view as a style and form of belonging, a set of tools for living with and in relations of power, a mode of cultural production and reproduction, and a vast repertory of the imagination. Whatever their focus, books in the series remain attentive to the shifting and contingent ways in which religious phenomena are named, organized, and contested. They bring fluency in the best of contemporary theoretical and historical scholarship to bear on the study of religion in North America. The series focuses primarily, but not exclusively, on religion in the United States in the twentieth and twenty-first centuries.

Books in the series

Ava Chamberlain, *The Notorious Elizabeth Tuttle: Marriage, Murder, and Madness in the Family of Jonathan Edwards*

Terry Rey and Alex Stepick, *Crossing the Water and Keeping the Faith: Haitian Religion in Miami*

Isaac Weiner, *Religion Out Loud: Religious Sound, Public Space, and American Pluralism*

Hillary Kaell, *Walking Where Jesus Walked: American Christians and Holy Land Pilgrimage*

Brett Hendrickson, *Border Medicine: A Transcultural History of Mexican American Curanderismo*

Jodi Eichler-Levine, *Suffer the Little Children: Uses of the Past in Jewish and African American Children's Literature*

Annie Blazer, *Playing for God: Evangelical Women and the Unintended Consequences of Sports Ministry*

Elizabeth Pérez, *Religion in the Kitchen: Cooking, Talking, and the Making of Black Atlantic Traditions*

Kerry Mitchell, *Spirituality and the State: Managing Nature and Experience in America's National Parks*

Finbarr Curtis, *The Production of American Religious Freedom*

M. Cooper Harriss, *Ralph Ellison's Invisible Theology*

Ari Y. Kelman, *Shout to the Lord: Making Worship Music in Evangelical America*

Joshua Dubler and Isaac Weiner, *Religion, Law, USA*

Shari Rabin, *Jews on the Frontier: Religion and Mobility in Nineteenth Century America*

Elizabeth Fenton, *Old Canaan in a New World: Native Americans and the Lost Tribes of Israel*

Alyssa Maldonado-Estrada, *Lifeblood of the Parish: Masculinity and Catholic Devotion in Williamsburg, Brooklyn*

Caleb Iyer Elfenbein, *Fear in Our Hearts: What Islamophobia Tells Us about America*

Rachel B. Gross, *Beyond the Synagogue: Jewish Nostalgia as Religious Practice*

Jenna Supp-Montgomerie, *When the Medium Was the Mission: The Religious Origins of Network Culture*

Philippa Koch, *The Course of God's Providence: Religion, Health, and the Body in Early America*

Jennifer Scheper Hughes, *The Church of the Dead: The Epidemic of 1576 and the Birth of Christianity in the Americas*

Sylvester Johnson and Tisa Wenger, *On Imperial Grounds: New Histories of Religion and US Empire*

Deborah Dash Moore, *Vernacular Religion: Collected Essays of Leonard Primiano*

Katrina Daly Thompson, *Muslims on the Margins: Creating Queer Religious Community in North America*

Jonathan H. Ebel, *From Dust They Came: Government Camps and the Religion of Reform in New Deal California*

From Dust They Came

Government Camps and the Religion of Reform in New Deal California

Jonathan H. Ebel

NEW YORK UNIVERSITY PRESS
New York

NEW YORK UNIVERSITY PRESS
New York
www.nyupress.org

© 2023 by New York University
All rights reserved
Please contact the Library of Congress for Cataloging-in-Publication data.
ISBN: 9781479823635 (hardback)
ISBN: 9781479823673 (library ebook)
ISBN: 9781479823666 (consumer ebook)

This book is printed on acid-free paper, and its binding materials are chosen for strength and durability. We strive to use environmentally responsible suppliers and materials to the greatest extent possible in publishing our books.

Manufactured in the United States of America

10 9 8 7 6 5 4 3 2 1

Also available as an ebook

"The Government Camp"
Hurrah! Hurrah for the Government Camp
We all came here flat broke and lank
Mr. Ross takes us in and gives us a tent
And all he requires is three Dollars rent,
Then some will say I don't think it fare
To clean the labortories is more than my share
But when they bring in a bunch of old clothes
Then in pokes everbodys nose.

The Welfare ladys they do their best
Trying to satisfy all the rest
If we would only think it over rite
To live in this world is a pretty hard fight
But we ought to be thankful for this place to stay
And put all those foolish ideas away
We could make this camp a beautiful town
If wed only give a smile instead of a frown
And theres only one way this thing to do
Do unto other as you'd have them do unto you.

—Rosetta Spoehward, Arvin Camp, Weedpatch, California, 1939

CONTENTS

Introduction: The Camp, Imagined — 1

1. The Gate — 31
2. The Office — 80
3. The Tent Platform — 129
4. The Sanitary Unit — 182
5. The Community Center — 227
6. The Paper — 274
7. The Gate, Revisited — 329

Epilogue: The Camp, Reimagined — 375

Acknowledgments — 381

Notes — 385

Bibliography — 407

Index — 413

About the Author — 431

Introduction

The Camp, Imagined

If J. A. Wall was a praying man in 1931, he likely spent many nights asking God for help. A second full year of drought was again wiping out any hope he had of finding profit somewhere on his 140 acres in Cherokee, Oklahoma. If J. A. Wall was a praying man, he may have wondered if anyone was listening.

Perhaps, though, Wall was predisposed to see the Lord's hand not just in those prayers that seemed to be answered but in unanswered prayers as well, and so could find meaning in the withering crops and the poverty that deepened with each passing month. And he may have seen it as a blessing that he could at least feed his family.

By the time the calendar turned to 1934, praying man or not, J. A. Wall was on his knees. For four straight years his farm had earned him nothing. Foreclosure was imminent. So Wall moved his family of seven east to Arkansas, where they rented a farm. He worked that land for a year, but the results were identical. Conditions were every bit as bad. The drought persisted. He earned no money.

Due to forces that Wall surely understood but was powerless to control, Oklahoma and Arkansas had become a kind of biblical Egypt, turning his thoughts more and more frequently to exodus. Perhaps something like a promised land lay to the west.

If he was a praying man, J. A. Wall might have asked God to bless his family's decision to head for California, and to watch over them along the way.

By March of 1936, the seven members of the Wall family were living in the Arvin Migratory Farm Labor Camp, located in Kern County in California's San Joaquin Valley. This camp and others like it were built by the federal government to meet the basic needs of migrant farm workers and their families. The Arvin camp, operated by the Resettlement

Administration and managed by Thomas Collins, was likely less than J. A. Wall had hoped for, but it provided a place where a family gutted by their struggle against farm consolidation, collapsing prices, persistent drought, and a devilish wind could find its bearings and, perhaps, a shred of hope.

The Walls set up their tent on a platform located on Lot 22 of Unit 2 in the Arvin camp. Working for "various farmers" around Kern County brightened the family's financial picture somewhat, but the 250 dollars Wall earned in 1935 had to buy groceries for seven and gas to move them around.

With nothing more to his name than a car valued at fifty dollars and possessions worth thirty-five, J. A. Wall spoke to camp manager Collins about his circumstances. He stated bluntly, "Drought burned me out until I had no money.... My farm of 140 acres was foreclosed. Drought broke me." He still dreamt of getting "a small place of my own to be self-supporting" and of picking up occasional work "during harvest seasons." But at fifty-five years of age, it was an open question how viable that dream was.

If J. A. Wall was a praying man in 1936, he might have offered thanks to God for the respite he and his family found in the Arvin camp, for the protection the camp afforded from vigilante violence, for the raised platform on Lot 22 of Unit 2 on which they made a home, for the clean water, the showers, and the flush toilets. He might also have asked God what in Jesus's name he had done to deserve the past five years.[1]

Drought had broken J. A. Wall financially. It had broken him with five consecutive years of no income and the resulting loss of his Oklahoma farm. Yet the migratory farm labor camp where he was living when he told his story to Tom Collins was part of a program that believed Wall and those like him were broken in other ways as well. Indeed, beyond simply offering a helping hand with shelter and sanitation, New Deal reformers used these government camps as mission sites in which to civilize and modernize white migratory farm laborers.

This book tells the story of the religious dynamics at work in these migratory farm labor camps, which the federal government operated in rural California between 1935 and 1943. For roughly eight years, successive New Deal administrations, the Resettlement Administration (RA), and the Farm Security Administration (FSA) designed, built, managed, and maintained the migrant camps as an intervention into California's rural economies and, most important, into the dissolving lives of thousands of mostly white farm laborers and their families. The government camps—fifteen fixed sites and three mobile units—formed temporary communities of and for migratory farm laborers while also providing them with facilities offering shelter, sanitation, medical attention, and social order.

The camps also formed environments in and through which New Deal officials could engage in long-term projects to redeem Dust Bowl migrants from life patterns and cultural practices—some recently developed, others deeply ingrained—that progressive reformers believed were incompatible with human flourishing in the modernizing world. Put another way, the camps offered migrants an implicit exchange: take refuge from the depredations of life at the mercy of the elements, greedy growers, and extortionate private camps, and gain a foothold on the crumbling façade of American capitalism, but agree to live in the midst of a program designed to reform you and your kind.

These efforts to convert migrant farm laborers to worldviews and practices imagined as more secular and more modern inevitably encountered resistance from migrant women and men who often embraced conservative Protestant theologies and ecstatic, revivalistic Protestant practices. Some migrants, inspired by the reformers' efforts and animated by their own aspirations, pursued the redemption that the New Deal offered them. Others found in their own Protestant doctrines, practices, and communities ways to reassert their worth on terms that reformers within the camp system were reluctant to accept as valid.

*　*　*

On April 30, 1935, President Franklin D. Roosevelt signed an executive order creating the Resettlement Administration and appointing Rexford Tugwell, undersecretary of agriculture, as its administrator. Harry Drobish, director of rural relief for the state of California, kept a copy of the executive order in his files. Though Drobish didn't know exactly how just yet, this bureaucratic genesis would figure significantly in his plan to assist hundreds of thousands of migrant farm workers trying to survive in Depression-era California.

President Roosevelt created the Resettlement Administration to save American agriculture from itself. Up and down the bureaucracy, Resettlement Administration employees re-imagined land-use practices, developed programs to keep small-scale farming viable, and intervened directly in the lives of America's poorest, most vulnerable agricultural workers.

Roosevelt included among the new agency's three "functions and duties": "To administer approved projects involving resettlement of destitute or low-income families from rural and urban area[s], including the establishment, maintenance, and operation, in such connection, of communities in rural and suburban areas." The Resettlement Administration would also attempt to address environmental problems: "soil erosion, stream pollution, seacoast erosion, reforestation . . . and flood control," and oversee the lending of money "to finance, in whole or in part, the purchase of farm lands and necessary equipment by farmers, farm tenants, croppers, and farm laborers."[2] But the chief concern for Drobish was the destitute people he saw wandering through California's agricultural interior. The language of Roosevelt's executive order was far from ideal, but it nonetheless gave him hope that the federal government might see and address their needs.

As far as Harry Drobish and rural relief in California were concerned, the trouble with President Roosevelt's order began at the beginning. The very name of the agency, "Resettlement," made it an ambiguous blessing. To resettle farm laborers in agricultural California, to permanently reestablish them on the land, was to challenge the very nature of how agriculture worked in the state. An alliance of large growers, larger banks, and myriad interlocking industries involved in the cultivation and shipping of California's agricultural bounty, had long since made farming in the state an industrial undertaking. The whole wealth-generating endeavor relied on workers who were unsettled, both domestically and psychologically. They had to be domestically unsettled to follow the seasonal harvests, to arrive when the crops were ready and to leave once the crops were in. They also needed to be psychologically unsettled, on the edge of desperation, in order for the backbreaking work and the piece- or pound-rate pay to be attractive.

"Resettlement" was a charged word in other ways as well. While California agriculture resisted settlement and stability for its lowest paid workers, *re*settlement was even worse. Resettlement implied that outsiders would be entering rural communities, drawing on their resources, and introducing difference. It also implied that they would be staying and settling. Still, Harry Drobish saw the Resettlement Administration as the most promising source of support yet for a program he had been hoping to build.

Three days before President Roosevelt wrote the agency into existence, Harry Drobish and his colleagues produced a document titled "Tentative Program of the Division of Rural Rehabilitation, California." It opens, "It is conservatively estimated that 255,000 rural persons were dependent upon relief in California in February, 1935, or 33% of the entire relief load of the state.... The total of persons on relief and eligible to rural rehabilitation, of course, greatly exceeds the figures presented in this necessarily rough approximation."

In the rest of the report's seventeen pages, Drobish engaged head-on the problem of resettlement in agricultural California and what he called the "basic dissimilarities" between the agricultural economy of California and that of other regions and states. These dissimilarities, the document argues, "must modify to an appropriate pattern the program of rural rehabilitation in California."[3] One such modification, titled "Rural Rehabilitation Camps for Migrants," appears on page eight.

> These camps are designed as an integral and essential part of the rehabilitation program.... The camps will provide for minimum facilities necessary to health and decency, healthful camp sites, pure water in pipes, hot and cold showers and laundry facilities, garbage disposal, and emergency hospitalization.... Under present conditions a large percentage of the migrants are entirely homeless and the whole family travels with the breadwinners and lives a wandering life.[4]

Drobish had in mind a network of "45 migrant camps" that would begin to replace what he referred to as "the menacing squatter camps." These filthy, chaotic, semi-permanent "agricultural slums" were, he believed, an affront to the decency of the migrant. Budgets, economics, and political resistance would eventually whittle Drobish's dream from forty-five camps down to eighteen. But after a visit in October of 1935 from Rexford Tugwell, the head of the agency and a close confidant of President Roosevelt, Drobish won the significant victory of federal approval of and support for his plan.

This approval allowed the migratory farm labor camp program time to take root in Depression-era California. And with those roots well established, the program weathered both intense local resistance and the inevitable departures of its early leaders and visionaries, including Drobish himself. The camp program endured as the Resettlement Administration became the Farm Security Administration in 1937. It continued to shelter migrant farm workers through the early years of World War II, while managers, nurses, administrators, and bureaucrats, like the seasons and the crops, came and went.[5]

And though the migratory farm labor camps attracted starving families, altruistic reformers, and local outrage, they have not attracted much interest from historians of religion in the United States. Indeed, those with an interest in American religious history will find few familiar names in these pages. The social forces and the religious movements running through this story, however, are well known: poverty, displacement, migration; domesticity, purity, community; modernity, secularism, liberalism; missions, evangelism, conversion. Preachers and revivals, scripture and prayer, apocalyptic prophecies and visions of Jesus also figure in this narrative.

But this is also a story of spaces and places not immediately identifiable as religious: the federal migrant camps and the structures that defined them. These government camps—planned, intentionally communal spaces—stand in a long history of mission communities in North America, spaces established by powerful institutions for the religious and cultural conversion of people perceived as marginal, problematic, uncivilized. This history reaches back to the colonial period, to European encounters with indigenous people and to Spanish Catholic missions and English Puritan praying towns. These colonial missionary spaces, though different in many ways, were connected by the belief that native people were culturally and socially and, therefore, religiously, deficient, and also that they needed to be settled, re-clothed, re-educated, and converted to truly be reformed. Mission priests and Protestant missionaries claimed to care about the souls of Native Americans. They cared equally, perhaps more, about their ways of living.[6]

As migrant camp managers and program staff traveled through California's agricultural valleys and saw how Dust Bowl refugees were living, and as they accepted migrants into federal camps and observed and interacted with them, they reacted with a mix of horror, awe, frustration, compassion, and resolve. These ways of being are uncivilized, they wrote, these people have returned to the jungle. Something had to be done to save them, and that something, one reformer wrote, had to be "more than a palliative."[7] White migrants had to come out of the dark, musty past and into the light of civilization and modernity, both in how they lived and in how they believed.

Federal migrant camps were not affiliated with a denomination, but they were most certainly spaces for evangelism, developed and operated for the education and redemption of a people. The camp managers did not wear vestments or clerical collars, but they were called to embody virtue, and to encourage and exhort migrants to follow their example. The regulations governing camp life were shot through with judgments about good conduct and bad conduct, proper and improper dress, and appropriate and inappropriate ways of having sex, raising children, structuring families, and building communities. The encounters between a supposedly secular federal program and an unapologetically Protestant people are best understood as encounters between (at least) two religious populations, one thoroughly down on its luck and struggling to make sense of dislocation and destitution, the other powerful and well-educated by comparison, and also convinced that their efforts and their truths would lead the others to salvation.

Not surprisingly, camp managers and their staff could be quite condescending toward the expressions of Protestantism they encountered among the migrants. This was and remains a common posture adopted by the educated and employed when looking across lines of class, race, and region. Regardless of their own religious backgrounds, the women and men employed by the Resettlement Administration in California were far more likely than the migrants to approach religion from an intellectual perspective and to think of revivalistic, body-centered worship as belonging to some previous evolutionary stage.[8] Whether or not they saw "religion" as incompatible with a modern, scientific mindset, reformers certainly saw the religious style of migrants as retrograde, and they preached against it in direct and indirect ways.

Numerous recent books have complicated the juxtaposition of secularism and religion. This one further muddies that distinction and draws on voices from within the camp program to argue that secular evangelism and missionary modernity, far from oxymoronic, were central to this government intervention. Language suggestive of the religious is present throughout the archives of the camp system. A particularly evocative instance comes from a report to the camp program's San Francisco office, filed in December of 1940. In it, camp manager Ray Mork wrote, "a successful camp manager must be a cross between three different persons. A missionary, a politician, and a hard boiled officer. He must have the tact and ken of a politician, the soul and perseverance of a missionary, the disciplinary firmness of [a] military officer, the measure of each in the mixture depending on the particular situation to be met."[9] Historians of the Dust Bowl migration have largely viewed the migrant camps as secular endeavors. I see things differently.

I also see things differently than did Clarence Glacken, who became a renowned environmental historian but, in 1936, was working for the Resettlement Administration in California. Reporting on a visit to the government camp in Arvin—near Bakersfield in Kern County—Glacken led with the sentence, "The physical set-up in the Arvin camp is not important."[10] It is not surprising to find such a categorical dismissal of the importance of space from the pen of this energetic reformer. When Glacken looked at the camps, he saw a program built of people and relationships, a program where beliefs and commitments were made present through education, example, and other forms of persuasion. He was not wrong. But the program was also, quite crucially, about spaces and places—camps that the government built, buildings and layouts that migrants came to know. These structures and buildings and systems—the architecture of missionary intervention—organized lives visually and kinetically, and were no small part of the migratory farm workers' worlds.

The structure of this book, first suggested to me by Professor Angie Heo, anthropologist of religion at the University of Chicago Divinity School, reflects the structure of the camps. Each of the following chapters focuses on a prominent element of the camp and its religious significance to camp officials and to camp residents. I have ordered the chapters to match the order in which most migrant families would have encountered these structures. Not all camps were laid out in the same way, but the built environments were very much alike in their critical elements and the roles those elements were designed to play in the lives of camp residents. These were spaces designed to shelter, to clean up, to educate, and to change the trajectory of a people. In this program, structures and the environment were suffused by religious sensibilities.

My decision to organize the book this way reflects my beliefs, first, that space matters both for the ways it structures our lives and for the subtle catechesis in which it engages, and second, that the specific missionary program undertaken by camp officials is easier to see and to understand when we look closely at its spatial dimensions. From the gate through which they passed to the flush toilets they learned to use, the stuff of religion surrounded migrants and New Dealers alike.

The fifteen fixed-site camps that dotted California's agricultural interior from Winters in the north to Brawley in the south shared certain key elements that shaped migrants' movements each day and that made the camp system's values visible and tangible in their lives. These elements included the gate, the office, the tent platform, the sanitary unit, the community center, and, eventually, the newspaper. The gate was the point of entry into and exit from the camp. It was a threshold, a point of crossing between the marginality and hostility of life in California's agricultural-industrial complex, and the protection and concern found in the government camp. The office of the camp manager was the center of the camp's executive authority, and also the place where data about the camp and its residents flowed up and out to the camp system and its headquarters, located first in Berkeley and then in San Francisco. The office gave structure to an epistemology of data collection, analysis, and preservation, and created ritual space for authoring reports, maintaining inventories, and submitting requests.

Camps had tent platforms on which migrants sought to reconstruct domestic spaces, and sanitary units where camp residents found toilets, showers, sinks, and laundry facilities, which they used and cleaned communally. These spaces were stages on which migrants rehearsed and performed the domestic and hygienic choreography of modern civilization for an audience of their neighbors and, most importantly, for the camp manager and his staff, who saw these performances as evidence of a migrant family's righteousness and worthiness. Camps also had communal spaces designated for activities ranging from meetings of the camp council and labor organizations, to amateur music nights, dances, movie showings, and worship services. In scheduling and using the community

A sanitary unit in the Arvin Camp, Kern County, 1936.
Photograph by Dorothea Lange. *View of Kern migrant camp showing one of three sanitary units. California*. Kern County, California, November 1936. Courtesy of Library of Congress. https://www.loc.gov/item/2017763234/.

center, migrants participated in a program meant to expand social connection and to restrict the reach of Protestant worship.

These structural features expressed the program architects' thoughts regarding the migrants' most pressing needs and also their sense of how best to modernize and civilize camp residents. The idea was to separate them from the dehumanizing circumstances outside the gate and, for the length of their stay, to provide them with the basics of modern community life and with guidance as to how to use them. These spaces were not, however, the entirety of the camp. Camps also published weekly newspapers, portable spaces in which migrants conveyed their understanding of what was going on in the world around them and camp officials argued for compliance with the camp's program of redemption.

The chapters that make up this book discuss the religious meaning of the camp and its features. They also describe more recognizably religious discourse and practice in the camps and locate them in and around these elements. The "what" of these Protestant discourses and practices mattered a great deal. The "where" mattered also for the message it sent to camp residents about the permissible and the impermissible, the suitably public and the preferably private. The final chapter, which returns to the meaning of the gate, explores the actions and the motives of migrants who, though they lived in the camps and lived at least adjacent to its cultural evangelism, sought religious sustenance and community outside of the gate.

Religion, America, and the Great Depression

Historians of religion in America have not taken the full measure of the Great Depression's effects on religions as lived, practiced, and institutionalized in the United States. The Depression appears in some works as historical context, a decade that birthed particular devotional practices or that favored religious actors of a certain type.[11] In 1959, historian Robert Handy spoke and wrote of a "religious depression," that preceded economic collapse and persisted into the 1930s. But Handy focused his analysis on urban religious elites and their feelings of irrelevance in the roaring twenties and the early thirties.[12] Few have revised or continued his work.

One challenge in writing a religious history of the Great Depression, though, is that the Great Depression was not one thing. The crisis was felt differently in different parts of the country. Destitution looked one way in industrial Detroit and another in the rural Delta. Homelessness in Worcester, Massachusetts was not the same as homelessness in Wasco, California. Institutional responses to human suffering were shaped by these differences. Both the Great Depression and the New Deal could look very different depending on where in the United States one stood.

The same can be said of religious traditions and communities in the Depression and, for that matter, in general. Terms like Protestant, Catholic and Jew; Baptist, Methodist, and Presbyterian; fundamentalist, modernist, and pentecostal—all convey important truths about lineages and traditions and institutions, feelings of affinity and affiliation. But the experience of being one of those terms, living it, filling it with one's own past, present, and future, was and always will be different from person to person and from place to place. The different ways that economic and religious factors interacted from region to region in America's Great Depression call for multiple monographs.¹³

This book builds on the work of journalist and activist Carey McWilliams, and historians Walter Stein and James Gregory on the subject of (to borrow Stein's title) California and the Dust Bowl Migration.¹⁴ These authors noted religion as an important aspect of migrants' experiences and, occasionally, as a shaping force in their interactions with federal authorities and California growers. They did not, however, make it the focus of their studies. Historian Alison Greene did, in her book on religion and the Great Depression in Memphis and the Mississippi Delta, and the results are breathtaking. I am following in her footsteps, though across a much different landscape and through a set of problems that strike me as meaningfully distinct. A quick survey of the contextual differences suggests why a regional approach to the religious history of the Great Depression is both fruitful and important.¹⁵

Memphis and the Delta, the geographical setting of Greene's 2016 study *No Depression in Heaven*, presented a different social and religious ecosystem than did California's interior valleys. For one thing, the dominant social structures in California were newer. Much of the development that shaped life for settled residents and migrants alike was less than thirty years old when the Depression hit, and the agricultural patterns that were both phenomenally lucrative and relentlessly exploitative had been in place for barely a half century. Without romanticizing California as endlessly new and in motion, and without losing sight of its deep Spanish colonial and indigenous histories, it is important to note that, circa 1935 and relative to Memphis and the Mississippi Delta, California as an agricultural powerhouse was new and in motion.

Two additional differences set California apart: its sheer agricultural diversity and its eye-popping profitability. In contrast to the one-legged stool that was the Delta cotton economy, California growers diversified, and then diversified their diversity. Writing in the early days of World War II, an expert on the Sacramento and San Joaquin Valleys by the name of Roland Curran noted,

> Among the kinds of crops produced in quantity can be listed peaches, wine grapes, figs, prunes, apricots, raisins, table grapes, nuts, plums, olives, oranges, melons, alfalfa, sugar beets, rice, flax, hops, cotton,

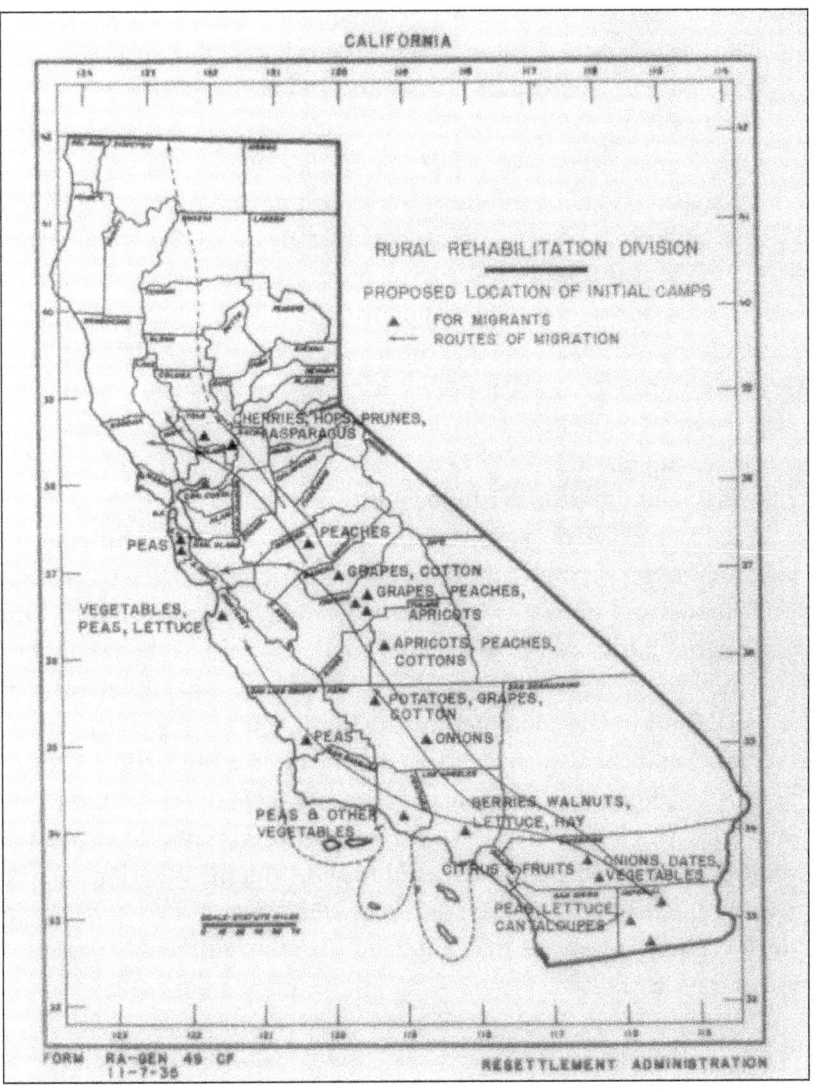

Map of California by the Rural Rehabilitation Division showing areas where different crops are grown, proposed location of initial camps for migrants, and routes of migration. Courtesy of Library of Congress. LC-USZ6–1018.

grain, asparagus, potatoes, beans, peas, tomatoes, and many others. One million head of cattle, 1,725,000 sheep, 245,000 hogs, 4,500,000 chickens, and 400,000 turkeys approximates the annual production of livestock.[16]

And this accounted for just two of California's interior valleys.

The state's agriculture industry was certainly not immune to the adverse economic conditions that ravaged much of the US after the Great War and through the early 1940s, but neither was it ruined, in large part because it was not a monolith. When drought and poor land-management practices brought crop failures to the Great Plains and the Delta, California growers and their irrigated ranches could step in to meet the need. Failed cotton crops in the Southeast were a tragedy for a regional population. They were a boon for the cotton growers who bulked large in California's San Joaquin Valley.

To become America's produce aisle and to contribute meaningfully to America's cotton supply, California needed myriad additional industries, connections, and networks to bear the load. There is far too little rain in the agricultural valleys to support anything close to the amount of food they yield. As of the early 1940s, there were 3.5 million acres of irrigated land in the Sacramento and San Joaquin Valleys, the dams, reservoirs, and canals being the conditions of possibility for the entire industry. Without the diversion and canalization of the Colorado River, California's Imperial Valley, the most productive agricultural area in the world, could produce salt, cacti, and little else. But the watering and the growing and the harvesting are only part of the story of the networks on which California growers relied. Roland Curran continued his description of the Central Valley:

> Three transcontinental railroads, thousands of miles of paved highway, national bus and airlines, river packet and barge service and intercoastal steamship lines serve the valley with means of transportation. Operating in many of the valley's eighty-three cities and towns . . . are many industries such as canneries, creameries, wineries, processing plants, lumber and paper mills, oil and sugar refineries and numerous others.

The agricultural juggernaut that is California's interior both drove and required these supporting and transporting industries. "More than

90,000 cars of fresh fruits and vegetables," Curran wrote, "are shipped outside the state every year from the Central Valley with 75 percent of these going to markets more than 2,000 miles away."[17]

There were many religious continuities between rural California and the rural / urban Delta in the Depression era. Both featured Protestant and Catholic communities; both religious cultures were shaped by class and race; both knew well revivalistic and more liturgically-inclined congregations, not to mention divisions between economically and politically conservative churches and those that were progressive and social-justice oriented. But here, too, there were differences. The variations begin with the size and ethnic makeup of rural California's Catholic population, which combined Mexican, Spanish, Portuguese, and Filipino practitioners as well as Irish, German, Polish, and Italian. California lacked a clearly dominant evangelical Protestant establishment that, Greene writes, was "at the peak of [its] power" in Memphis and the Delta as the Depression took hold. California Protestants had energy and some had fame, but they lacked the institutional and political focus that characterized their southern kin.[18]

Moreover, racial, ethnic, and religious diversity was more complex in agricultural California than in the Delta or perhaps any other rural area in North America. This diversity, fed by immigration from Mexico, Japan, China, and the Punjab, while not the focus of this book, was an important part of an atmosphere into which hundreds of thousands of white migrants flowed during the Depression.[19] Whiteness in rural California meant something different than "not Blackness." The state's racial, ethnic, and religious diversity forced a more complicated definition.

Because of these many differences, and because her work demonstrates it time after time, I share Alison Greene's convictions, first, that the Depression matters as a religious event, and second, that we see most clearly how it matters by focusing on regional effects and responses to them.

This book also aligns with Colleen McDannell's 2004 *Picturing Faith: Photography and the Great Depression* in examining the intersection of Americans' religious lives and Depression-era efforts to shape American self-understanding. The Historical Section of the RA/FSA, which McDannell describes so compellingly, employed photographers and used actual images to contribute to a figurative, civil religious image of the

United States. The work done by those involved in the project remains moving and era-defining.

Describing the challenge that FSA photographers faced, McDannell writes, "[They] were asked to portray the nightmare of poverty but not to represent it as so horrible that people would turn their faces from the images. The pictures had to show the inhumanity of economic hardship without destroying the humanity of the poor or directly attacking capitalism. . . . Photographing religious practices, spaces, and objects helped the photographers achieve their goals by presenting faith as an integral but circumscribed part of the culture of average Americans."[20] McDannell's story of the effort and of the images it produced is one of the great works on the religious history of twentieth-century America.

This book is different from McDannell's both in the intensity of its focus (one federal program's efforts in one state) and in the nature of the program it examines. Federal migrant camp managers and their staff were working to rebuild and reshape Americans' understandings of themselves, but they directed their work at white, displaced, destitute agricultural workers. And the tools they used were not cameras (though the archives do contain some pictures) but structures and arguments and social pressure. Their goal was not to depict practice and to picture faith; it was to change both. The power of the photographic image is indisputable. But officials of the migrant camp system exercised a different and more directly palpable kind of power, the effects of which they hoped would be both immediate and lasting.

What *Picturing Faith* and this book also show is the interaction that can exist among medium, method, and a historical study. In both McDannell's book and this one, the way that New Deal reformers approached their work and captured the religious lives of their subjects is itself a major part of the story. Technology, be it a camera or triplicate paper and a file folder, is intrinsic to the production and the expression of knowledge and, therefore, shapes the way historians tell their stories. It is important that our histories acknowledge and explain the knowledge-producing technologies to which they are indebted.

Understanding the Government Camp

This book began as an attempt to describe the theological impact of poverty and displacement on people shaken loose from the Great Plains by the Depression. The search for that story led me to this story of religions, declared and undeclared, obvious and hidden, and the way that those religions mixed in spaces established and maintained by the federal government.

Almost as soon as I realized that Record Group 96 at the National Archive and Records Administration in San Bruno, California would be the source of most of the material for this book, I knew that this was not going to be a straightforward history of lay theologies in the midst of economic catastrophe and dislocation. The sources themselves were not going to allow that. They held multiple levels of meaning, all of which were important to this story.

There was the archive itself and the bureaucracy to which it pointed. There were the tissue-thin papers held in the archive, produced in duplicate or triplicate, and the sensibility toward which that thin paper pointed. There were the locations in California's interior that first came into my view as names on file folders stuffed with records: Marysville, Arvin, Brawley, Indio, Shafter, Yuba City, Winters, Thornton, Firebaugh—and the thick communities and economies connected to those places. There were the ideas expressed on the pages, the people who expressed those ideas, the people whose lives were being described and cataloged. Along with all of this, there was extensive reporting and commentary on Protestant practices in the camps. The archive presented the equivalent of a set of Russian dolls, each element distinctive and worthy of attention, but also fitting within the others. And the individual dolls didn't just fit together, they completed each other.

The challenge in writing this book has never been a lack of material. The challenge has been deciding what story to tell and what stories to leave for others, which spaces to draw forward and which to leave in the background. The lesson that emerged, no matter where I looked, is that there was no space where the migrants did not engage religious sensibilities and, on the flip side, no corner of a federal migratory farm labor camp that was devoid of catechetical purpose. As much as modern life trains our eye to see religion in specific spaces and at designated times, close attention to the realities of the migrants' lives (and our lives as well) reduces such distinctions to near meaninglessness.[21]

Readers will most likely be familiar with the general outlines of the three main subjects of this book. The Great Depression, most history students learn, began with the Great Crash of October 1929 and lasted through the decade of the 1930s, ending with the United States entering World War II in December of 1941. Not surprisingly, the story is far more complicated than that, particularly when one does not accept Wall Street as the sole barometer of America's economic health and war as America's savior. Nonetheless, most of the story this book tells took place within this simplified chronological frame.

Dust Bowl migrants, stunned by the one-two punch of plunging commodity prices and unrelenting drought, stumbled away from the worlds they had built in Oklahoma, Arkansas, Texas, Kansas, and Colorado, and headed west to California. Rosetta Spoehward, author of "The Government Camp," the poem that is the epigraph of this book, and J. A. Wall were but two of hundreds of thousands who fit this general description. And while it is impossible to capture the experiences of them all, a survey of 6655 "migrant households in California" conducted by the Farm Security Administration in the course of its direct grant program provides some useful detail.

The report found that seventy-five percent of the migrant families in California came from four states: Oklahoma, Texas, Arkansas, and Missouri. They were young, white, and generally unskilled. They had, on average, one child per family, and they did not make a bee-line for California. Migrant families took an average of seven months to get there, and were, as of 1938, spending about as much time looking for work as they spent working. To nobody's surprise, they gravitated toward agriculture.

The Farm Security Administration studied exactly 6655 migrant households. Their report says exactly zero about religion. Had FSA employees asked, they would likely have found that the group was overwhelmingly Protestant and affiliated with theologically conservative denominations, movements, and churches. They would have found large numbers of Southern Baptists, southern Methodists, and Nazarenes, adherents of the Church of Christ, the Assemblies of God, and also of independent holiness and pentecostal ministries too numerous to name.

More important than these identities, which changed over time and in response to diverse influences, were their preferred religious style and what historian Grant Wacker has called their "temperament." The former was, generally speaking, revivalistic. The latter tended toward exclusivism, evangelism, and a sense of urgency about matters religious. Historian Darren Dochuk has described this "plain folk" evangelical Protestantism as suffused with a sense of national mission. "Plain folk pioneers," he explained, "became pilgrims burdened with the responsibility of evangelizing and civilizing." Even in the bleak period that this book examines, this responsibility to get religion right and to give it to as many of the lost and wandering as possible, shaped migrants' actions and the tenor of their interactions.[22]

Of the many varieties of Protestantism that migrants embraced, pentecostalism claimed the most energetic and persistent membership. A relative newcomer to America's religious landscape in the 1930s, pentecostalism derived much of its urgency from the belief that the end times were upon the world and that, without baptism in the Holy Spirit and the resulting sign of speaking in tongues, a person's journey to salvation was incomplete. Pentecostals won converts and detractors with their message and with their ecstatic worship services, which often featured attempts at faith healing along with eruptions of speaking in tongues.[23]

Readers will also recognize the shadow of the third subject, New Deal reformers, but the individuals who collectively cast that shadow are mostly strangers. Harry Drobish, Millie Delp, Jonathan Garst, Opal Butts, Mary Sears, Clarence Glacken, Harvey Coverley, Ray Mork, Fred Ross, Spencer Bisby, Guy Griset, and the ubiquitous Tom Collins, to name just a few, worked, at different times and in different capacities, for the Resettlement Administration and/or the Farm Security Administration. They were the women and men who gave life to the idea at the heart of this agency's work in California, that the federal government had to do something to address the shattering of rural lives and the systemic dehumanization of labor that seemed part and parcel of industrial agriculture in California.

Because these women and men were, on the whole, well-educated and deeply committed to the rituals of record-keeping and archiving, their voices come through loudly and clearly in this book. Their pens and typewriters often did the work of recording migrant voices and offering commentary on migrant lives. The strong presence of reformers in the sources provides an opportunity to reflect on the norms of the federal camp system and the ways that these norms shaped, for better and for worse, interpersonal relations and cross-cultural understanding. Their words and actions also allow us to see and reflect upon the ongoing influence of liberal, social-reformist Protestantism in the peculiar, often double-edged, benevolence of government interventions. Though the trend of professionalization in social work and its disarticulation from religious institutions was gathering steam in the 1930s, the patterns of judgmental interaction and the calls for conversion had certainly not ceased. New Deal reformers' own words and migrants' reactions to them demonstrate this truth time and again.

That said, in the course of my research and writing, I developed a profound respect not just for the reformers' belief in the responsibility of government to lift up the downtrodden, feed the hungry, and shelter those who wander, but also for their courage in turning those beliefs into action. They were flawed people, some of whom had strong racial, religious, and class prejudices. These prejudices are part of this story. So too are their efforts, undertaken with their own hands, to address a problem of undeniable seriousness.

The migrants too were a group irreducible to one narrative, one family structure, one set of political and religious inclinations. They did have in common the experience of displacement, homelessness, hunger, and uncertainty, and they shared some degree of determination to make good on the American dream. But each was distinct in the home and the land they couldn't keep, the history they tried to keep alive, the precise shape of the circumstances that brought them to California's Imperial Valley, for instance, and that kept them getting up every morning.

It is with the meeting of these two groups that this book unfolds. One group trying to make a place for the other; one group trying to find a way forward; one embarking on a program of reform and redemption, the other wondering what the hell had become of their place in the world; one group desperate for help, the other eager to provide it, though not unconditionally.

The religious tendrils woven into this story are none too simple to trace, particularly as they wend their way through the lives of New Deal progressives. Those tendrils are, however, present and meaningful. The women and men who imagined, built, and managed the federal migrant camps were involved in a missionary program, an effort to convert and redeem the migrant and, at their most ambitious, to reform the agricultural industrial complex.

The life story of camp manager Thomas Collins offers an especially intriguing and colorful picture of the ways that religions were present in the migrant camp program. Collins, the closest thing to a celebrity to emerge from the federal effort, was a key figure in the founding of the camp program, serving as the manager of the program's first camp at Marysville in Yuba County before moving south to Arvin, near Bakersfield in Kern County, to open the second camp. He then served as a manager-at-large in the system, traveling from far-southern Brawley in Imperial County to Winters in northern Yolo County to train new managers, assist with opening new camps, advocate on behalf of the program, and serve the migrants as best he could.

Collins's superiors in the Resettlement Administration hierarchy, Harry Drobish, Irving Wood, Walter Packard, and Jonathan Garst, all agreed that his work in the camps was "absolutely standard forming," and that his example should influence the work of all other camp managers in the system.[24] One of his superiors wrote in August of 1936, "I can think of no possibility of setting up a desirable camp program for migratory workers anywhere which ignores the basic principles that govern Collins's work, and I hope it will be possible to use him widely in opening up the other camps, especially in areas, such as the Imperial Valley, where we shall receive no cordial welcome by the dominating group."[25]

Tom Collins has drawn significant attention from scholars of John Steinbeck's life and work for the role he played in guiding Steinbeck through the migrants' worlds, and the crucial source material he provided. Steinbeck dedicated his Pulitzer-Prize-winning novel *The Grapes of Wrath* to his own wife Carol and "to Tom [Collins], who lived it." Collins was the inspiration for Jim Rawley, a character in Steinbeck's novel, manager of the fictionalized Weedpatch Camp, and also served as a production advisor on John Ford's widely-acclaimed 1940 film adaptation of the novel. Hundreds of millions of people have read Collins's name in the novel's dedication and the film's opening credits.

Tom Collins with a migrant mother and child, Arvin Camp, Kern County, 1936. Photograph by Dorothea Lange. *Tom Collins, manager of Kern migrant camp, with drought refugee family. California.* November 1936. Courtesy of Library of Congress. https://www.loc.gov/item/2017763224/.

But these moments of influence—within the program he helped create, within literature and film—were moments of uncharacteristic clarity and transparency in Tom Collins's life. What came before is considerably harder to narrate. More importantly, Collins's life before his New Deal involvements is suggestive of the complex humanity and tangled motivations of other reformers drawn to the program, and what it was in their religious lives and experiences that brought them to California between 1935 and 1943.[26]

Like the migratory farm workers with whom he worked, Tom Collins knew something about life at the margins. He spent the first fourteen years of his life in a Catholic orphanage in the Baltimore area. His mother, Annie Hopkins, gave him up shortly after she gave birth to him on September 6, 1895. The record of Collins's birth indicates that Hopkins was Caucasian, most likely an Irish domestic. His father, George Collins, a stable boy and horse tender, is listed as "colored." The infant Thomas Collins was thus announced to the world as "colored" as well. Dr. Whitfield Winsey, who attended at the birth, was a prominent African American physician in the Baltimore area whose practice was restricted by the racism of the day to African American patients.[27]

These are, however, the last indications of African American identity in Collins's biography. Indeed, it seems likely that Collins was unaware of his racial background. His birth is the only documented moment of his life until his matriculation in 1909 in a "preparatory seminary" called St. Charles College near Ellicott City, Maryland. He excelled as a pre-seminary student until his studies were halted by tuberculosis, which necessitated a move to a sanatorium in Sabillasville, Maryland.

What could have been a mere rest stop on the highway to the Catholic priesthood became an off-ramp when Collins married Edith Bentzel in 1915. By the time Collins completed a draft registration card for the Great War in 1917, his bureaucratic profile looked very different. The son of an African American stable hand and an Irish woman, abandoned in infancy, reported being married, a father, and a teacher in Wolfsville, Maryland. He also reported that he was Caucasian.[28]

Collins chose not to devote himself to the priesthood. He also chose not to devote himself to Edith and their two children. After roughly five years of marriage, he left them and ran off with a young woman named Nancy Duvall Means, then just sixteen years old. And what a run it was. The couple, pursued by private investigators hired by Means's irate father, traveled from Maryland to Puerto Rico, where they were married, and then continued south to Venezuela, hoping their pursuers would give up. They didn't. The couple made their way across South America, back north to the western United States, and eventually, thanks to liberties that Collins took with his credentials, to Guam, where he was hired as superintendent of schools. While living on Guam, the fugitive couple had two daughters, one of whom survived.

This third act of Collins's life ended less dramatically and less definitively than the second. It appears that parental justice finally caught up with Tom and Nancy on their return to the United States. It appears too that Collins had no stomach for the fight, and therefore again chose flight, abandoning his wife and young daughter. Perhaps he just gave up. Perhaps he was concerned that the Means family would pull back the curtain on a background from which he clearly wanted some distance. Single again and drawn increasingly to drink, Collins used his record of success in education to secure positions with a series of relief agencies, and then, in 1935, accepted the job in rural relief that would lead to a position managing migratory farm labor camps in the Resettlement Administration. His subsequent work in the camps left lasting impressions on the lives of countless thousands of agricultural migrants.

Collins life before 1935 raises myriad questions for those interested in his life after 1935. How was he shaped by his childhood in a Catholic orphanage? How was he shaped by the Catholicism that he learned, saw, and practiced? What should we make of abandonment, movement, and education as forces in his life? Is there a chance that he was "passing" as white? There are few straightforward answers to these questions. It seems likely, though, that spending his formative years living in community with other parentless children under the watchful eye of nuns cultivated in him sensibilities that inclined him toward a blend of discipline and compassion, toward a Christianity made visible through ritual and through caring for the poor and the marginal.[29]

And though Collins's work ran parallel to that of some Catholic reformers, it seems less likely that he was operating consciously in harmony with Catholic social teaching as he helped build federal missions for the desperately poor throughout California. He may have found inspiration in Dorothy Day, Peter Maurin, and their Catholic Worker movement. He may have embraced the program for economic justice and social improvement laid out by Bishop John Ryan or the more locally relevant radio sermons of Father Charles Philipps from the Archdiocese of San Francisco.[30] It seems more likely, though, that he saw his own movement away from regular Catholic practice and identifiable Catholic community as the correct path for enlightened, liberated, modern Americans to follow, and that he was satisfied with his limited involvement with the church as an adult: three Catholic weddings (he married again while working in the camp program) and, ultimately, a Catholic funeral.

Indeed, his reflections in August of 1936 on the struggle between the migratory workers and California's growers—represented by the

Tom Collins with a migrant woman, Arvin Camp, Kern County, 1936. Photograph by Dorothea Lange. *Tom Collins, manager of Kern migrant camp, talking with one of the members. California.* Kern County, California, November 1936. Courtesy of Library of Congress. https://www.loc.gov/item/2017763225/.

notorious "ASSociated Farmers" [sic]—took what might seem a surprising theological turn.

> The ASSociated Farmers . . . formation of an unholy infantry is a damnable attempt to besmirch that vast army of orphans—orphans of the Act of God—that cruelest and most heartless of all parents—who in his wrath, poured down the wiltering [sic] heat and parched the life giving fruits of the harvests—withered and shrunk the bellies of children and the hearts and souls of hard working men and women. In their search for a haven—the opportunity to start anew—they have arrived from scorched homesteads, hearts alive with hope, souls overflowing with faith, demanding work, seeking work, praying for work. Little do they know that about them stalks the ghostly dirge of the machine gun in the hands of mental aborigines of selfishness and greed.[31]

Though his language and stridency might come as a surprise, the fact that Tom Collins, given up by his parents, would feel a connection to a "vast army of orphans" and would call God to account for abusing and then abandoning them makes perfect sense. Collins's passion for intervening and assisting and working to save migrants, seems here to be fueled not by Catholicism but by a righteous fury at damaging social and economic forces, and at the cruel God who hurt him as a child and who continued to break hopeful hearts, punish faithful souls, and ignore those who prayed for work.

There are many ironies in Collins's story. That a person with his tumultuous adult life would be so central to a program that held up domestic stability, geographic fixity, financial responsibility, and sobriety as ideals seems unlikely. These were not values that he embodied. Yet Collins would not be the first person who encouraged others to act in ways that he could not, who recognized the virtue of a particular life but was, like Saint Augustine, unable to choose it, or who attempted to compensate for carelessness in his personal life with principled compassion in his work. Whatever the contours of his motivations, Collins also demonstrates the situatedness of the people in this book in both large- and small-scale histories, their lives shaped by economic collapse, by American racism, by American Catholicism, by secularism, but also by an orphanage in Baltimore, a tenacious disease, an impulse to help the poor, and a baffling tendency to run from the ones he should have held closest.

We can also see in Tom Collins's life the common, perhaps universal, unpredictability of being human in the modernizing world. His life before joining the Resettlement Administration combined Catholicism (the orphanage, preparatory seminary, the Catholic weddings), abandonments (his birth parents' of him, his of two families), and the embrace of education (as a student, teacher, and administrator). All of these experiences contributed to his being in California and being equipped, in an unorthodox and uncredentialled way, to be the heart of the migratory farm labor camp program. Few people who encountered Tom Collins had a single bad word to say about him. Those who did, the higher-ups in the program toward the end of Collins's service, complained most strenuously when he stepped out of line and gave the go-ahead for a massive Christmas party for migrants in and around the Brawley camp without proper approvals—a bureaucratic sin for which he did not care to atone.

Perhaps the greatest value of Collins's story to this one is that it is a reminder of the complex humanity of everyone who crosses this stage, from the migrant pentecostal preacher Georgie Nunn, a.k.a. "Reverend Georgie," to the forceful camp manager Ray Mork—and the puzzles they present to us as, I imagine, they did to themselves.

The Secular and America's Great Depression

The archive and the voices and the moment that this book engages will not support a straightforward portrayal of one set of actors in this narrative as religious and the other as secular. Every person who appears in these pages inhabited a secular age.[32] They breathed in a culture and moved across a landscape in which religion—Protestantism, for the most part—either presented itself as a choice, or was shaped by the awareness that *some people* were acting as if religion were a choice. Yet even among those who saw their Protestant identity as one choice among others, some chose more aggressively and decisively than others.

But we should pause briefly to think about how those choices—to pursue grace; to view economic crisis through a scriptural lens; to embrace more scientific ways of knowing—might affect the way that we think about modernity, and about two of its central concepts: "the religious" and "the secular." The encounter between an ascendant liberal state and downwardly mobile, displaced agricultural workers found New Deal officials—self-proclaimed secular actors—preaching faith in America, in capitalism, and in modernity; it found Dust Bowl migrants—men and women immersed in the culture of biblical literalism and ecstatic worship—ordering and affirming their lives through work, recreation, and the maintenance of domestic spaces. To look closely at this moment in American religious history, so often characterized—then and now—as one of the disentangling of secular and religious worldviews, is to see instead their utter inextricability.

The migrant camps at the center of this book were conceived out of benevolence. Camp officials insisted, often in the face of ferocious counterarguments from growers and townspeople, that the migrants were fully American and deserved government assistance. Yet always present in these pleas, as text and as subtext, was the belief that the agricultural refugees were not fully civilized and, without proper practical and spiritual guidance, would devolve into primitivism and savagery. Camp managers throughout California wrote repeatedly that before migrants could be reattached to the American civic and economic body, they had to wash off years of accumulated dirt, let go of antique worldviews and ecstatic worship practices, and embrace modernity.

Modernity is hardly a universal concept, much less a religiously or morally neutral one. Those who describe and adjudicate the modern, especially those who work to convert others to it, do so with normative stances and religious investments obscured by their appeals to reason, science, and progress. The work of convincing a person to clean and maintain her body in a modern way begins with an effort to convince her that the old ways leave her both physically and morally unclean; the modern reflex to consult a doctor when one is sick begins with the assumption, far from universal in Depression-era America, that healing is a matter of science, not faith. The federal migrant camp program was thus committed to a deeply normative civilizational evangelism and to actions that had clear religious implications and real consequences for families who chose to move out of rural slums and into government camps.[33]

Seen in context of the New Deal's hundreds of programs, the camp program in agricultural California was quite limited. However, the very limits of this program help reveal the dynamics with which this book is concerned. Within the camps' limits, abstractions became embodied realities. The "migrant problem," widely discussed by camp program representatives, became particular individuals: Rosetta Spoehward, Vester Pickle, and O. V. Owens, women and men with histories, aspirations, and beliefs. Likewise, "the New Deal" was embodied in camp staff like Tom Collins, Ray Mork, Millie Delp, Mary K. Davies, people capable of heroic compassion and fiery advocacy, who relied on appeals to morality, pride, and Americanism to implement their program of reform. The relationships that developed among these actors are at the heart of this story of religion, secularism, tradition, and modernity. In them we see how truly interwoven these categories are with the lives and bodies and interests of individuals and communities.

Studying migrants and New Deal officials in close quarters also reveals their shared vulnerabilities and reliance upon faith. The migrants' vulnerabilities were extreme. They were hungry, impoverished, and often sick. They begged employment from men who despised them only slightly less than they needed them. In this atmosphere of vulnerability, the most banal daily acts were acts of faith: faith in a god who would heal and sustain them, faith in a nation and a system that might, eventually, have room for them.

The New Dealers' vulnerabilities, in contrast, were the product of emotional and philosophical investments in a fragile vision of American society. The America they hoped for was democratic, meritocratic, and bureaucratic; a community of men and women who valued cleanliness, order, cooperation, and the insights of modern science. Camp program officials sought to create this America in miniature within the camps, but found themselves defending the program from hostile publics, proud camp residents, and their own paternalistic tendencies and subtle condescensions. These vulnerabilities prompted camp managers and program officials to preach about their vision for modern America, to develop programs of catechesis for the migrants, and to justify both of these repeatedly, as expressions of faith in America as a modern capitalist democracy. This story of the back-and-forth between a government agency and a wandering people demonstrates that characterizations of the 1930s as a time of "religious depression" and advancing secularism depend for their coherence on terms that cannot withstand the historical specifics they seek to explain.

These pages and the historical moment they attempt to describe are haunted by these spirits of modernity. This book is haunted, too, by (to borrow from Bruce Springsteen and, in a sense, from Woody Guthrie) "The Ghost of Tom Joad." The story of displacement, death, struggle, awakening, and precariousness told so powerfully and so famously by John Steinbeck in *The Grapes of Wrath*, set expectations for the type of people one might encounter in California's agricultural valleys during the Great Depression. An old generation of tenant farmers was passing away and being replaced by younger generations who, like Steinbeck's Tom Joad, were able to see beyond a tired plot of land or a refreshing river to something grand and collective and intentional, who, like Ma Joad, embraced a peoplehood characterized by awareness of shared interests and resistance to the dehumanizing effects of industrial agriculture.

Steinbeck's heroes, redeemed and redeemers, were those who contributed to this project of peoplehood. Those who could not or would not, he moved to the margins of the world he wrote into being.

Without diminishing Steinbeck's heroism in helping to nationalize the "Okie Problem," his vision for resolving the problem was not without its costs for the displaced and for the stories we tell about them. *The Grapes of Wrath* established and solidified categories of worthy migrant and unworthy migrant, pouring into the former all the hopes of the migratory farm labor camp program, including its hopes for a change in migrant Protestantism, and leaving the latter to be occupied by those who lived and believed differently from Tom Joad, Jim Casy, and Ma.

Worthy migrants practiced "good religion." Unworthy migrants—invasive revivalists, harassing moralists like his character Lizbeth Sandry—practiced "bad religion." It is not insignificant that Steinbeck's heroic, self-sacrificing labor organizer Jim Casy is a former revivalist preacher, a one-time pentecostal performer who has lost the spirit, who hesitates to pray, and who is looking for a different, truer Truth. It is no accident that Ma Joad repeatedly pushes back against pentecostal intrusions into Joad family life.

John Steinbeck found the charismatic Protestantism of many Dust Bowl refugees problematic. His era-defining novel insists that the reforms undertaken in the government camps should address the excesses of the migrants' anti-modern Protestantism. Tom Joad's ghost also drifts through a 1944 dissertation written about the religious leaders and organizations operating in California's Central Valley, and through historian Walter Stein's 1972 book on the Dust Bowl migration. It is not an especially menacing spirit, but we do well to be aware of its origins in a particular set of political and religious aspirations, and to understand that its message need not be ours.

This is not, in the end, a story of a perfectly executed humanitarian intervention. Neither does it describe an act of governmental condescension marred throughout by overreach and misjudgment. The camps, instead, present us with a story of encounter, of adaptation, of connections made and missed, of the ongoing struggle to understand one another, and of the complexity of religious lives in modern America.

1

The Gate

This story of government camps and the religion of reform in New Deal California opens forty miles north of Sacramento, in the town of Marysville. In the late spring and early summer of 1935, roughly twelve hundred migrants had taken up residence in a squatters' camp just outside of town. This mass of people was living in flagrant squalor, looking to all the world as if they were in full retreat from civilization.

Marysville is also the place where a handful of California-based reformers working first for California's State Emergency Relief Administration (SERA) and then for the New Deal's Resettlement Administration (RA) established California's first federally-supported camp for migratory farm laborers and their families "on a thirty-acre tract on the outskirts of the city."[1] Marysville marked the initial point of intersection between California's destitute migratory farm labor force and a New Deal program to shelter and restore them. The work of building the Marysville camp began in July. The official dedication took place on October 12, 1935.

By the time Tom Collins, manager of the Marysville Migratory Farm Labor Camp, and the leadership of the Resettlement Administration staged a public ritual to mark the establishment of the camp and to explain its significance, the women and men living within its boundaries had surely formulated their own answers to questions of the meaning of the place. But the surrounding community and the thousands of migrants who would, at some point in its life, call the Marysville camp home, may well have wondered: What does it mean to enter the government camp? How does living there influence a migrant's sense of place and worth? How will the camp shape the lives migrants live and the faiths that sustain them?

The beginnings of answers to these questions came through in the Marysville camp's ceremonial opening—the dedication—and were also expressed in its physical opening—the gate. The gate to a federal

The gate to the Arvin camp, Kern County, 1936.
Photograph by Dorothea Lange. *Entrance and view of Kern migrant camp. California.* November 1936. Courtesy of Library of Congress. https://www.loc.gov/item/2017763238/.

migratory farm labor camp was more than an object, more than "a forty-foot entrance arch of hand adzed square logs and a rustic gate to match" as an inspector described the Arvin camp's main gate in 1936. The gate, through which camp residents passed to reach their tents, the sanitary facilities, the community center, and some measure of personal and communal stability, created two worlds. These worlds, the inside and the outside, were governed by different powers, and different truths. They were driven by different visions of who the migrants were and where they belonged.

The gate to a government camp was a tangible invitation to those who wandered and were oppressed, to come inside. The "inside" that migrants encountered when they passed through the gate had been created in direct response to a perceived crisis "outside." Lawless, squalid, dehumanizing conditions, noticed and named, drove reformers in California to create an "inside," to develop and shape their program, their approach, and their goals. At the same time, the existence of the inside helped migrants to see the outside not simply as the dehumanizing reality of industrial agriculture in Kern, Yuba, or Imperial County, but as something from which they could separate themselves physically and intellectually. The outside and the inside created each other, and challenged both reformers and reformed to rebuild lives that made sense in and of these two worlds.

By moving spatially from outside to inside the camp and chronologically from an agricultural California before the federal camp system to one in which that system was functioning, if not always familiar, it is possible to trace the conditions to which the camp system responded and the developing contours of that response. We can also understand more fully why camp program officials placed so much hope in the power of example. The system of federally-funded migrant camps in California grew slowly. Long after the camp system was a reality and camp gates were open to migrants in Yuba County (the Marysville camp) and Kern County (the Arvin camp) federal camps remained unavailable to workers everywhere else in the state. Constrained in their ability to intervene directly in California's agricultural system writ large, Resettlement Administration representatives held their work up as exemplary, a compelling built argument, they hoped, for a reformed approach to migrant labor. They wanted California and the nation to see the benefits that came to all when growers and communities invested in higher quality facilities and treated migrants like humans. In so doing, reformers drew on the tradition of evangelism by example, familiar from numerous missionary contexts, from the colonial era forward.

The migrant men, women, and children who passed through the camp gate gained much that mattered to their restoration, not to mention their survival. Enjoyment of these gains was, however, predicated on acceptance of a social and religious order established by men and women eager to reshape migrants' practices and values to fit what they saw as a more modern, more sophisticated understanding of community, of knowledge, and of faith.[2]

Marysville, California: October 12, 1935

After years of concern about the punishing lives lived by migrant farm workers in agricultural California, months of research into possible solutions, and with the prospect of funding and support from the newly-established Resettlement Administration, officials from the State Emergency Relief Administration chose the town of Marysville, California to launch their intervention into a desperate situation. They began their work of rescue and reform before the new government camp was ready for occupancy, getting to know the migrants who were living in the massive squatters' camp.³ The reformers initiated this phase of their mission in July of 1935.

A public ceremony held on October 12 made official the opening of the Marysville Migratory Farm Labor Camp and helped the surrounding community, as well as those who would inhabit the camp, understand the significance of this new project. As described in the event program, the dedication began with a thirty-minute concert capped by the "singing of 'America.'" Reverend Lynn T. White, Dean of San Francisco Theological Seminary, then gave a benediction. After Reverend White said "amen," Leo Smith, mayor of Marysville, offered his words of welcome.⁴

Marysville, located forty miles north of Sacramento, is the seat of Yuba County, and many of the area's leading lights were present that October day. The printed program from the dedication includes three full pages of dignitaries, representing thirty-one organizations. The governor sent a representative to the ceremony, as did the Department of Public Health and the University of California's College of Agriculture. Representatives of the Farm Bureau and the American Legion were on hand, as were members of the Chamber of Commerce, the State Agricultural Council, and the State Federation of Labor. Men and women from the Yuba County Board of Supervisors, the Citizens Advisory Committee, and the Welfare Department attended, alongside representatives of the state League of Women Voters, the Marysville Relief Society, the Northern District Women's Club, the Home Owned Business Association, and the National Reemployment Service. Ceremony organizers deemed fifty-eight individuals important enough to list individually.

This long list of organizations offers one clue as to the range of possible meanings that various communities and jurisdictions (Marysville,

Yuba City, Yuba County, California) attached to the Marysville camp and to the camps that came after it. The Department of Public Health cared about the potential health risks the migrants and their living situations posed to residents of settled communities, and also about the physical well-being of the migrants themselves. To these officials, the camp was another step in the long, slow process of extracting migrants from filthy living conditions, managing their waste more effectively, and mitigating the risk of such devastating diseases as smallpox, measles, malaria, and tuberculosis. These diseases were common and, as historian Walter Stein rightly noted, did not ask if a child was a migrant or not before striking.[5]

The Farm Bureau, Chamber of Commerce, and Home Owned Business Association were interested in the economic effects of the new camp and how those who came to live in it might help or hinder local farmers in their efforts to get crops out of the field and to market. California growers had never complained about a labor surplus, but they did worry, sometimes loudly, about the attitudes of pickers and the inverse relationship that they perceived between the availability of relief and the desire to work.

The American Legion was infamously explicit in its concern about the radicalization of the migrant population and the perceived Communist sympathies of those who advocated for better wages and living conditions. In his passionately pro-labor history of agricultural labor in California, Carey McWilliams presented the Legion as the most reliable and reliably vicious source of anti-migrant violence up and down the valleys. They had not come to Marysville that October day to cheer.[6]

With their names in the program and their bodies in the crowd, all these groups made it clear that they were interested in the Resettlement Administration camp program. Some were indeed present to support the endeavor and to celebrate the improvement it would bring both for camp residents and for those living in nearby towns. Others were keeping a watchful eye on an unwelcome population and an equally unwelcome federal intervention in the industrial dynamics of California agriculture.

Leaders of California's arm of the Resettlement Administration, many of whom had worked previously in state-level relief, were also present that day. These reformers had brought the camp gates into being for migrants to contemplate, to move toward, and perhaps to move through.

How did these architects of the camp and the camp program see the world of California agriculture? What were their goals in building a camp and bringing migrants through its gate? In order to see what the Resettlement Administration was dedicating in Marysville, California on October 12, 1935, and to see what they hoped the gate would mean, we need to first erase the entire camp and take stock of the situation for migratory farm workers in California in the early years of the Depression.

By the time the Great Depression began in 1929, agriculture in California had long looked and acted much more like the large industries characteristic of America's urban centers than like the family-owned farms of the Midwest and the Great Plains.[7] Since the late 1800s, California growers had been producing melon, citrus, nuts, lettuce, apples, cotton, and hundreds more crops, not for their families and communities, but for national distribution and for as much profit as they could extract. These growers depended on thousands of pickers and packers to get their product out of the field and on its way to market. In pursuit of the highest possible profit, they sought to maximize yields and to minimize the one cost in their equation over which they had the most control: the cost of labor.

With the goal of keeping costs as low as possible, growers employed the already impoverished, invested as little as possible in housing, and encouraged a surplus of workers. If a picker decided that wages were too low or conditions too foul, another was always ready to take his or her place.[8] Industrial agriculture depended on the near poverty of farm laborers to make the work and the living they offered appealing. For the better part of six decades, the system worked with Chinese, Japanese, South Asian, Filipino, and Mexican laborers following the crops around California's interior, accepting the pay that was offered, and spending slack months in semi-permanent neighborhoods on the wrong side of the tracks.

This system was unjust in fundamental ways. It was predicated on poverty and propped up by coercion, harassment, and violence. It did not acknowledge, much less properly value, the status of the worker as an indispensable link in the chain of production. To put it another way, the growers and their supporters acknowledged the value of the worker when they beat him, kicked him, and jailed him in response to his demands for higher wages. The growers' worst nightmare, realized frequently in the Depression years, was a strike that coincided with the harvest. And rather than acknowledge the causes of this nightmare and try to address them, they hid their dependencies and their vulnerabilities behind a wall of vigilante justice.

The reformers who contributed to the Resettlement Administration's mission, many of whom were students of California agriculture, were aware of this dependency and described it publicly many times. They were also aware of the power organized labor could have to bring California's system, dependent as it was on human hands for the harvest, to a screeching halt. Their files document the struggle between growers and pickers in the early- to mid-1930s, the years in which state-level debates began about whether and how to assist the workers. Two clashes documented in Resettlement Administration files show clearly that the reformers who created the migratory farm labor camp system were aware of the systemic problems of industrialized agriculture and of the way violence shaped the workers' world.

When these reformers spoke of the threat to California agriculture posed by inattention to the deplorable conditions in which migrants lived, they were not speaking abstractly. When they envisioned greatly-improved housing for migrants and a gate that separated them from those who would exploit them, they had recent experiences in mind. Among these experiences was what Carey McWilliams referred to as "The Cotton Strike," which took place in Kern County in the fall of 1933. Irving Wood, the first director of the camp program, transcribed coverage of the strike from *The Fresno Bee* and kept those reports in his files. The story they tell is brief but grim.[9]

As the picking season approached in the fall of 1933, San Joaquin Valley cotton growers gathered and set a valley-wide pay rate of sixty cents (roughly thirteen dollars in 2022) per hundred pounds. Pickers in the valley refused to work at that rate, demanding instead one dollar (or about twenty-two dollars today) per hundred. In early October, unable to reach an agreement with growers, cotton pickers called a strike, the reach of which was impressive. *The Fresno Bee* describes the mayhem that ensued when, on October 10, striking pickers gathered in the towns of Pixley and Arvin to picket and protest.

"We had been holding a meeting near the railroad tracks here in Pixley," a twenty-three-year-old picker named William Thomas told the paper. "Thirty or forty farmers with rifles, shot guns, and an automatic came up to our meeting. They didn't say much of anything." When the speaker, strike leader Pat Chambers, decided to move the meeting to strike headquarters, "the farmers followed us, two of them in the lead, one with a pistol and one with a rifle." E. G. Kruger, whom *The Fresno Bee* identified as both the "leader of the ranchers" and "a special deputy sheriff of Kern County," noted that Chambers had launched a "harangue against the growers" in which he "call[ed] us robbers and dogs." Shortly thereafter, Kruger continued, shots were fired and fighting broke out.[10]

When the smoke cleared, the paper reported, two strikers were dead and the strike headquarters in Pixley was "bespattered with bullet marks . . . a mute warning of possible trouble to come." Kruger and his fellow growers insisted that "the trouble started when a shot was fired from the direction of strike headquarters," and that though they were present at the scene, they had not seen anyone of their number holding a gun, much less firing one. Eleven growers were arrested and charged with murder after the violence in Pixley. McWilliams added, "Their trial was a delightful farce and they were promptly acquitted despite positive identification of their participation in the Pixley murders." The murdered pickers, Delfino Davila and Dolores Hernandez, both of Mexican origin, had lived in California for a combined twenty-seven years.

A similar scene unfolded in Arvin when two hundred striking pickers attempted to block a road. One of the pickers, Pedro Subia, was shot to death there and three growers were injured. Alonzo Andrews, a picker who joined the strike, was charged with Subia's murder. Police reported Andrews had mistakenly shot Subia while trying to snipe a deputy sheriff deploying tear gas. Reporting in the *Fresno Bee* noted that numerous strikers were arrested and that three "prominent Kern men" sustained injuries in the "battle." The extensive additional injuries that strikers suffered from gunshots and beatings did not make the paper.[11]

One year later, in 1934, farm workers organized and struck in the Imperial Valley, just north of the Mexican border. This case also drew the attention of camp program director Irving Wood, who kept two accounts of the strike in his files, one penned by retired Brigadier General Pelham Glassford in his capacity as an arbitrator between growers and laborers, the other by Simon J. Lubin, representing the National Labor Board. Glassford wrote in June of 1934, describing the poverty and exploitation affecting the mostly "Mexican Indian" workforce. But the "deplorable conditions" that Glassford paid the most attention to were the abuses of law and authority that were a regular feature of grower-worker relations in and around the Imperial County towns of Brawley, El Centro, Calipatria, and Niland. His report reads, in part:

> After more than two months of observation and investigation in Imperial Valley, it is my conviction that a group of growers have exploited a "communist" hysteria for the advancement of their own interests; that they have welcomed labor agitation, which they could brand as "red," as a means of sustaining supremacy by mob rule, thereby preserving what is so essential to their profits—cheap labor: that they have succeeded in drawing into their conspiracy certain county officials who have become the principal tools of their machine.[12]

The conspiracy against which Glassford urged action pitted local authorities and business interests against farm workers. Their goal, he argued, was to keep laborers dependent, off-balance, and unorganized.

A separate report, submitted in early 1934 to the National Labor Relations Board by Simon J. Lubin, former chairman of California's Housing and Immigration Commission, described the Imperial County machine in action.[13] "On January 21st a representative of the American Civil Liberties Union made formal request upon the Sherriff of Imperial County and the Chief of Police of Brawley for permission to hold a meeting at Azteca Hall on the evening of January 23rd." Although the exact reasons for the meeting are not detailed in the report, the agenda surely included a discussion of the issues facing workers and how to address them collectively. The initial request was denied. But on the morning of January 23, 1934, the federal government issued an injunction forbidding local officials from "interfering with the meeting in any manner."[14] County and town authorities may have felt bound by this injunction in their official capacities. A group of town residents felt differently.

> At 7:15 that evening, the person announced as chairman of the meeting was abducted from the Planters Hotel in Brawley by a large mob, and threatened, and then left in the desert about twenty miles from the point

of abduction. Later, after he found his way back to El Centro, he was escorted out of the County of San Diego by peace officers.[15]

Farm laborers in Imperial County were surely vulnerable. So too were those who had a mind to help them in any way—lawyers, advocates, union organizers. Anyone who sought to correct the balance of power even slightly made themselves the target of a ruthless coalition of growers, county officials, law enforcement, and unapologetic vigilantes.

Local clergy, too, were subjected to marginalization and intimidation if they stuck their noses where they did not belong. Glassford described the travails of Brawley's Reverend Gerald Harvey, witness to what Glassford called a "lawless and brutal assault" that took place on Harvey's own front lawn. The victim was a lawyer named William Breeden. Reverend Harvey did what most citizens would do and filed a complaint against the assailant, W. L. Montgomery. He then withdrew the complaint fearing some form of "reprisal." Then, after steeling himself to work for justice, the reverend filed a second complaint, only to withdraw that one too.

After W. L. Montgomery attacked another attorney and a warrant was issued for his arrest, General Glassford himself urged Reverend Harvey to refile the complaint against the menacing vigilante. At this point Harvey's flock gathered to offer its shepherd some advice. Glassford recounted, "The same evening a group of Mr. Harvey's parishioners (including Clyde Jack, Philo Jones, and C. E. Boylston) met at his residence and persuaded him to withdraw the complaint."[16]

How did the members of Reverend Harvey's church persuade him to back off? Did they label the roughed-up attorneys "outside agitators" who only wanted to divide the community? Did they argue that W. L. Montgomery was a good man standing up for what was right? Did they replay the old, threadbare argument that churches should stay out of politics and worry about saving souls? Or did they threaten Reverend Harvey, warning him that if he did not withdraw the complaint, they would withdraw their membership in his church and withhold their contributions? Whatever their means, these citizens made it clear that appeals to the rule of law, not to mention prophetic calls for reform, were unwelcome when migrants stood to benefit. Religious leaders had a place, and it was best for everyone who actually belonged in the community if they remembered that place and stayed in it.

In his report, General Glassford described the injustice of agricultural poverty in Imperial County. He was appalled at what he saw. "On one ranch where melon pickers were employed," he wrote, "I found that their average daily earnings amounted to less than $1.50 a day." Melon picking is short-term work, ten days to two weeks. In Imperial County in 1934, melon picking was usually the province of Mexican migrants. None of this diluted Glassford's indignation. "It may be that alien Mexicans receive higher wages and live better in Imperial Valley than they do in their own country, but this cannot constitute an excuse for countenancing poverty and squalor in the United States."[17] The brigadier general believed that America had to be better than the lowest wage and the barest existence that dark-skinned migrants would accept.

Along with wage disputes, extra-legal violence, and grower impunity, the strikes in Kern County and Imperial County highlighted the vulnerability of pickers in the places where they lived. There was no security for migrant workers and families even in times of labor harmony. They could try to protect themselves in times of conflict, but with the mechanisms of local government and the force of law resolutely protecting settled citizens, migrants were all but powerless to stop attacks on their camps or to seek redress when what little they had was destroyed or left behind in a desperate flight from violence.

The outlines of the injustice and the developing humanitarian crisis were clear before a camp gate existed behind which migrant families could find refuge. Migratory farm workers were without power or means of defense against the greed of growers. Strikes could have temporary effects, but poverty, starvation, and exposure, ills that stalked the migrants constantly, were strong inducements to accept the work and the wages offered. Housing and health conditions were perennially deplorable. Those who dared speak on behalf of the destitute, whether politicians, lawyers, or clergy, faced the threat of violence.

There was little that was new in the 1930s about filth, poverty, sickness, and wage suppression among those who harvested California's crops. The state's veritable army of agricultural laborers had been living physically and economically precarious lives before state and federal officials and California-based activists began a coordinated effort to study and improve their living conditions. Participation in migratory farm labor makes conventional housing and recognizable forms of community difficult to establish, much less maintain and protect. This was business as usual throughout much of California's interior.

Business as usual took an alarming turn in the early 1930s as those brutalized and marginalized by the system became less Mexican, Filipino, Japanese, and Punjabi, and rather suddenly and undeniably more white. The whitening of California's migratory farm labor force made visible and problematic the dehumanizing conditions that industrialized agriculture engendered and defended, and was one reason that, on a state and national scale, agricultural migrants became "the migrant problem," and "the migrant problem" became something that the federal government cared to solve.

As historian Walter Stein wrote in his 1973 study of Dust Bowl migrants in California, "Until the coming of the Okies, race had differentiated California's Mexican, Filipino, or Oriental field hand from the white population of inland towns. . . . The Okies posed a problem that the social system had to resolve: they were white, old-stock Americans, but they were also field hands. . . . The future unfolding of the migrant problem hinged upon whether the Okie's whiteness or his role as field worker took priority in the perception of the Californians."[18]

The whitening of California's farm labor force, though not the absolute beginning of concern for migratory farm workers in California, did push state and federal authorities to act, and thus reveals another layer of meaning in the camp gate. The gate was a symbol of an official desire to address the vulnerability and the "savage" living conditions among the women and men whose bodies were crucial to the survival of industrial agriculture; but this desire only became a solution when the exploited laborers no longer fit long-held assumptions about racial hierarchies. American civilization was only "collapsing" when white Americans bodies could be found in the rubble.

Camp system records make clear that the whiteness of the camps was no accident. Writing in 1936 of the proposed location for a government camp in the Imperial County town of Brawley, Resettlement Administration employee Clarence Glacken stated, "The camp site itself is not near the Mexican quarters of the town. Since the Mexicans remain segregated from the whites, both by volition and custom and because there is virtually no racial intermixture, the camp in practice will house exclusively white itinerant field labor."[19]

The camps were established for and served an overwhelmingly white agricultural labor force. Nevertheless, the plan to establish federal camps to redeem the migrants also reflected reformers' long-standing and more general concerns about the exploitative nature of California's agricultural system. Harry Drobish, who served as California's director of rural relief and continued in a similar capacity in the Resettlement Administration, had a good bit to say about the crises in which he and his staff had been intervening. In the memorandum that he wrote in May of 1935 requesting funding for "rural rehabilitation camps for migrants," he underscored the extent to which their problems—problems of poverty and housing—were problems for an entire system, not just its most disadvantaged participants.

> These laborers stand at the foot of the socio-economic scale in our state. They constitute numerically the major element among our rural relief clients. To a high degree they are, as a class, either on relief during slack season or on the verge of relief. Their only means of vocalizing their plight is through strikes. During the past two years they have struck approximately fifty times, practically always appealing to decent housing. These are the "forgotten men, women, and children" of rural California but on these people the crops of California depend.[20]

Without serious and sustained attention to the well-being of the migratory farm laborer, the entire agricultural economy of California would remain vulnerable to disruption from labor unrest. Approval of the camp program could not wait. As Drobish put it, "This need is urgent. Immediate action is necessary if camps are to be ready this year. The harvest season is now upon us."[21]

Drobish made a similar point in an analysis prepared in August of 1935 for Walter Packard, second-in-command in the Resettlement Administration's western region, Region IX.[22] Though he harbored concerns that the purpose of government camps in California would not be resettlement, per se, Drobish argued again that peril to migrant families was peril to the entire system of California agriculture. "The administration of camps is an experiment directed at a major rural problem in California," he wrote. "More than half of those gainfully employed in California agriculture are laborers. Failure to provide clean living conditions for migrants is an important cause of jeopardy in which California's most valuable harvests have been placed during the past three years."

And lest anyone in Washington or Sacramento get the impression that the "migrant problem" could be obscured by the veil of racial difference, Drobish offered an update. "The [squatter] camps have become more extensive and a greater menace to public health and morals and to industrial peace with each succeeding year. Increasingly they are occupied by white Americans, many of whom are drought and depression refugees from the Great Plains." Drobish did not contest the characterization of migrants and their camps as threats to health, morals, and peace. That was a battle for another day. But he let Packard know that the demographics of agricultural exploitation and destitution were changing, that the victims were whitening and the crisis was spreading.[23]

In theory, the gate to an RA/FSA camp was open to all migrant farm laborers in need. In practice, it was less open to migrants of color than it was to white migrants. While some Hispanic and African American farm laborers lived in the camps and the official policy was one of non-discrimination, camp gates functioned quietly but meaningfully to maintain something approaching racial homogeneity.

* * *

In the first years of the migrant camp program, correspondence poured into the Resettlement Administration's offices from throughout the state's agricultural interior. As the long-standing practices of California agriculture came to be seen as a problem to be solved, and as awareness of the Resettlement Administration's work in this direction spread, some residents of California's agricultural communities expressed a desire to see a camp built near them. Whether writing from Kern County in the San Joaquin Valley or from Contra Costa County near the San Francisco Bay, they argued that migrants, victimized by circumstance and exploited by industry, should be taken in and sheltered so that they could be made whole.

Kern County was at the center of the conflict over exploitation and abuse of the migrants. Its fields would become the backdrop for many Americans' understandings of California's struggles when John Steinbeck wrote the Joad family into American history in 1939. Before Joad became a household name and before Kern County residents recoiled at Steinbeck's depiction of them, some county residents were sounding

Human Habitation, Oasis, California, March 2, 1935.
Photograph by Dorothea Lange. Courtesy of Library of Congress. Image LC-DIG-ppmsca-19156, https://www.loc.gov/pictures/item/2004678009/.

alarms about the living conditions of farm workers in their district. A February 1937 letter from W. L. Smith of Buttonwillow, chairman of Kern County's farm debt committee, offered Jonathan Garst, director of the Resettlement Administration's Region IX, a terse summary. Smith wrote, "Our district is badly in need of better housing facilities for our migratory help.... This is a cotton district.... The housing facilities are very poor, and as I understand it, is classed as the second poorest in the valley.... Something needs to be done to provide us better housing and better sanitary conditions."[24]

By the time Smith wrote, something had been done. Garst and his agency had opened camps in the Kern County towns of Arvin and Shafter. But the labor-intensive nature of the county's cotton crop made the migrant problem large and persistent. Garst sent regrets within a week—the budget was not sufficient to meet the request—but before the year was out he heard again from Buttonwillow, this time from John Thomson, secretary of the local Chamber of Commerce. The Chamber was not usually a friend of the migrant and Thomson was careful to praise Kern County's growers. But what he saw around him could not go unreported.

Thomson began by describing the crop situation for 1937–38: "15,000 acres planted to cotton this year and the cotton pickers have been listed as high as 3000 during the peak." He wrote of local efforts to do the right thing: "the bulk of the cotton farmers have good camps." This was not, to Thomson's eye, a case of grower negligence. Rather, the problem was the scale of the "influx of pickers" and the hovels built out of desperation from whatever materials could be found.

> Many pickers who have been unable to get into the camps are squatted out here and there on waste ground without any sanitary conditions what-so-ever and the health authorities have been condemning these places and ordering the occupants to move on. Probably the most pitiful part is the fact that some of these people are living in tents, some in improvised shelters made of cardboard . . . and burlap and anything else that can be picked up in the junk pile, and in such places as these women and children are sleeping on the ground.

Thomson noted that these suffering families were trapped. It did not matter that "county health officers [had] . . . condemned this unsightly camping ground." Migrants needed shelter, condemned or not. "The poor transients have no place to go . . . so are just sticking." A federal camp would change their circumstances immediately.[25]

Two dispatches from Imperial County describe different aspects of the "problems" present in areas without federal camps. A 1936 survey of the situation in the town of Brawley, characterized the conditions for workers and their families as "deplorable." The survey's author was aware that the agricultural economy of the Imperial Valley was rigged to benefit those with massive land holdings and to exploit the labor of a permanently impoverished, historically Mexican labor force. He was, however, writing at a moment when the face of the picker was changing. He focused a section of his report on the problems that could arise if white Dust Bowl migrants lived alongside Mexican workers.

"The standards of resident workers of this region is [*sic*] low," he wrote, "partly due to the predominance of foreign workers. Ninety percent of the stoop labor is supplied by Mexican Indians whose standard of living shows little improvement from year to year."[26] These immigrant laborers established themselves in make-shift but durable residences in Brawley's poorer neighborhoods and tended to resist the efforts of "civic groups and churches . . . to better [their] living conditions."[27] The author continued, "[the] predominance of foreign labor in the Imperial Valley has been a serious problem," but the outlook was brighter now that federal policy was affecting demographic change. He explained, "a marked improvement is to be expected in the immediate future because Mexican immigration is now a thing of the past and an improvement may be noticed in the county's efforts toward the betterment of conditions." Resident Mexican laborers could persist in their substandard living conditions. A federal camp would shelter the increasingly white migratory labor force in more ways than one.

Two years later and thirty miles away, conditions around the pea fields of Calipatria undermined racial explanations for poverty and homelessness. The white migrant work force that was encamped in the northern reaches of Imperial County was in dire straits. Charles Barry, manager of the new Brawley Migratory Farm Labor Camp, drove out to the Calipatria area to get a sense of the situation and to provide some direct financial relief. Settled county residents had asked for a camp in Calipatria many times. Federal officials built one in nearby Brawley instead, but many migrants needed to be closer to the fields and opted to squat in Calipatria. Barry described the scene in a March 17, 1938 letter to the agency's economist, Omer Mills.

> Very few people have left the Calipatria area. The situation here, in this county, as far as migratory workers are concerned, is deplorable. Starvation and filth prevail throughout the Holtville, Calipatria, Calexico, and Westmoreland areas. . . . There is a great deal of disease and illness among the workers. In other words, they are stranded.

"Squatters camp in the brush, near Thermal. March 1, 1935."
Photograph by Dorothea Lange. Courtesy of Library of Congress. Image LC-DIG-ppmsca-19156.

Barry reported that he and his staff had processed relief checks for 700 families, which had eased the suffering somewhat, but the scale and intractability of the problem were truly daunting. The Brawley camp was already full. Barry was certain that even if he could double the camp's capacity, there still wouldn't be enough room.[28]

The problem that New Dealers throughout California's agricultural counties were trying to solve was too big. Moreover, the "problem" of poor, transient farm labor was not incidental to industrial-scale agriculture as practiced in California. The harshest aspects of the system, from extra-legal violence and exploitation to demonization and blind-eyes turned to need, would not be solved without a complete and completely impossible reimagining of California agriculture.

Harry Drobish heard the voices of those around him who were calling for a root-and-branch tear-out of the current system in favor of something more equitable and humane. He was sympathetic to such a revolution. The migratory farm labor camps were but a modest solution. But perhaps there was something to be said for building these camps, with their gates through which migrants could pass into some degree of protection and cleanliness and stability. Drobish reflected on the situation in his personal notes, concluding that

> ... under [the current] circumstances the man who has definite convictions about what constitutes a successful [program] has one of two alternatives. Agree with the superiors and say yes yes [and] sacrifice your own soul [and] the respect of your friends in agriculture or try to modify the program [and] eventually lose one's goal to meet the needs as you see them. The latter course was decided upon.[29]

And though he may not have been fully satisfied, Drobish was at least pleased to see that his work was "meeting a recognized need ... of the homeless laborers needing a place to live" and that the "migrant camp program" was "spreading across the country." Criticism would come that the camps were a subsidy to growers and were letting industrial agriculture off the hook.[30] But the camps and their gates were also demonstrating that the federal government cared about the rural poor, and Drobish hoped that this model would encourage imitators.

The Government Camp and the City on a Hill

The name of Claude V. Biggs, editor and publisher of the *Yuba City Herald*, appears nowhere in the program for the dedication of the Marysville camp, but Biggs surely had his eye on the proceedings. Yuba City is adjacent to Marysville, and became the site of a government camp when floods forced evacuation of the Marysville camp in the winter of 1938.

Editor Biggs fancied himself a field commander in the war against domestic radicalism, and used his position at the *Yuba City Herald* to rally local troops against the camp and its residents. His animosity was rooted in the conviction that "Reds [are] using the camp as their headquarters to foment strikes in the orchards." In this, Biggs was building on a fifty-year trend, intensified in the wake of the Great War, of seeing Communism in every attempt to organize workers for better wages and working conditions. To label a person or a group "communist" was to reject their Americanness and to authorize violence against them.

Claude Biggs thumped his chest in his young newspaper, describing violence against organized laborers as sport. "I do get just as much enjoyment out of hunting reds," he wrote, "as some people get out of hunting deer." To Biggs and, presumably, to a subset of his readership, the Marysville camp was a symbol of foreignness, interference, and disruption. He shook his fist at the gate, furious that the camp gave its residents an "inside" in which they could belong and, by belonging, contest the hegemony of entrenched industrial agriculture.

The gate was both a real limit on the growers' power and a symbolic limit on Claude Biggs's power to dictate the terms of community membership. Which is perhaps why, in the autumn of 1935, rather than simply report on the camp's opening, he predicted its destruction. If "reds" continued to agitate from behind the gate, he wrote, "ranchers will level [the camp] to the ground."[31]

Prompted by these threats, Frank Weller, an attorney for the Resettlement Administration, wrote to California's Attorney General, to call his attention to the "irresponsible charges . . . contained in the *Yuba City Herald*" and to Biggs's threats of mob violence. Weller reminded the attorney general that the Marysville camp was serving a population, "bonafide migratory agricultural workers," on whom California agriculture depended: "In order to avail themselves of the facilities for decent living provided in these camps, those who are admitted must show that they desire to support themselves by their earnings as farm laborers, that they are qualified to perform farm labor and that they will perform such labor whenever jobs are offered." The camp gate would not be closed to migrants based on "political or religious beliefs, or on their purely private and personal beliefs, the free exercise of which is guaranteed them by the Constitution."

The camps were as symbolic to camp program personnel as they were to Claude Biggs. But for New Deal reformers, they symbolized respect for the humanity and the citizenship rights of migrants, and a partial fulfillment of America's promise, directed at an especially vulnerable group within its agricultural economy.[32]

A camp's symbolic function was essential to the broader camp program. The migratory farm labor force in California—estimated at 150,000 in 1935 and growing rapidly—was beyond the program's capacity to shelter. At its most extensive—fifteen fixed-site and three mobile camps—the system could accommodate no more than fifteen thousand people. What, then, was the point? The answer was that, in addition to providing much-needed refuge for migrants, the camps could also provide examples to communities and to growers. The camps argued forcefully for public and private investment in clean, orderly, properly-equipped housing for agricultural workers. The Resettlement Administration's California leadership made this point repeatedly. The camps were small cities on a hill, examples for surrounding communities to notice and emulate.

Indeed, when Harry Drobish wrote to George Nickel, director of relief in Kern County, he sounded very much like John Winthrop describing the Massachusetts Bay Colony more than three centuries earlier. Winthrop famously declared the colony "a city upon a hill," a model for proper Christian living that he hoped would prompt fellow European Protestants to "say of succeeding plantations: the Lord make it like that of New England." Drobish wrote on June 11, 1935 that the camp program's mission was to show California how to house and reform migrant workers.

> We know you feel as we do . . . that it is regrettable this work could not have started some time ago, but now we should center all of our efforts

to set up the best camp possible with the money available, for this will be considered a demonstration camp, the success of which will be watched with interest by other counties in the state considering the need for better camping facilities for migratory workers.[33]

Resettlement Administration personnel hoped that private citizens, growers, and land owners would take note too. In their request for federal funding to expand the camp program, Jonathan Garst and Harry Drobish wrote that "the conditions under which the migrants are forced to live . . . constitute a serious health and social menace . . . [c]amps provided by individual farmers have thus far not been much better." Their hopes for the Marysville and Arvin camps and for the system more generally were that they would "not only operate so as to elevate the standard of living of these people but will also stimulate growers to establish better camps themselves in order to attract workers to their farms."[34] Not only was it the right and humane thing to do. Providing camps like those the federal government was building would bring workers and, therefore, profits to the region without the usual "menace."

Jonathan Garst, director of the Resettlement Administration for the West Coast region, also wrote of the symbolic power of the camps when replying to a letter from John Thomson of the Buttonwillow Chamber of Commerce. Despite a convincing case from the Buttonwillow district, there simply wasn't enough money to support a permanent camp there. Garst explained further why the program had established camps in places like Gridley, Winters, Westley, and Visalia, but not in Buttonwillow. "Since the Farm Security Administration camps are regarded as demonstrational, that is, indicating to the communities in which they are placed the desirability of having satisfactory sanitary conditions, we have naturally tried to get some dispersion throughout the state so that as many communities as possible will be able to judge their effects."[35]

These voices express a position, widespread in the camp program, that the best way to change corrupt, fallen, or heathenish practices was to model virtue. Making values physically present was the most effective way to convince others not just to adopt those values, but to accept the broader cultural system of which they were a part. On this point of evangelism by example, the government camp program built on a long North American legacy that included Jesuit missions to indigenous tribes, John Winthrop's description of the Massachusetts Bay Colony, the Puritan concept of visible sainthood, the "disinterested benevolence" of Protestants in the early national period, settlement houses in American cities, and countless literary accounts of righteous lives and martyrs' deaths. These American expressions of evangelism by example connect with a much broader religious history of attributing missionary power to properly ordered communities and righteously lived lives.

In some cases, California's unconverted could encounter these examples and learn from them directly. In others, those who knew the models best went forth to describe them. Indeed, beginning in 1935, Resettlement Administration personnel fanned out across the state to make the case that the camp program could redeem individual migrants and, perhaps, California agriculture as well. They went to churches, local voluntary associations, university classes, ladies' auxiliaries, and civic clubs to argue that tens of thousands of impoverished and homeless families on the move were "California's big agricultural problem."[36] To encourage migrants to pass through the gates was to give them an opportunity to get back on their feet and to force agricultural industrialists to confront the humanity of their workforce.

This was the essence of Harry Drobish's remarks before the Commonwealth Club of California in March of 1936. He argued that the Resettlement Administration camp program was both necessary to the farm laborer and necessarily operated by the government. He and his colleagues had a vision for remaking the farm labor system using a population that was anchored; "people with homes," he said, who could travel out to pick and travel back to "a home and garden, possibly a cow and some chickens."

That was the goal. But on the way to that goal there was a lot of suffering and desperation to alleviate. The agricultural system in California needed these workers, Drobish noted, but growers had neither the wherewithal nor the incentive to help them more than was minimally necessary. Workers, he said, often arrive "a week or two" in advance of a job. "But the man who owns the peaches does not want those laborers until the peaches are ripe to pick. Where is the migratory laborer going to stay in the meantime?" The answer, Drobish continued, was a federal camp where "he can stay, wash up his clothes, and get ready for the next job."[37]

It was March when Drobish spoke, a time of comparatively low demand for farm labor. "We are using about one-fourth as many migratory workers as are employed in the summer. What happens to the other workers?" he asked, "Where are they going to go?" Those who traveled through agricultural areas with their eyes open could see. "They have to go to the river bottoms, the ditch banks and the shanty towns."

Drobish did not imagine an immediate change of attitudes toward the workers, but he sensed a shift in thinking. "There is talk now about the responsibility of farmers, groups of farmers, and counties to establish migratory camps," he said. "I hope that out of this interest there will develop a real campaign to establish more decent housing . . . on individual farms." Perhaps the Resettlement Administration's model of housing migrants in clean, sanitary, community-oriented camps would spread, but the obstacles were many. Growers wanted to maximize profits. The general public knew little about the migrants in 1936, and not surprisingly, most settled citizens of California were prone to latch onto stereotypes and caricatures. Drobish offered the Commonwealth Club some thoughts on this unfortunate tendency.

> The time the public becomes concerned is when it reads in the paper that a strike has been declared, or that disease has broken out at a squatter camp or bad moral conditions created in schools in the vicinity. It is then that we become interested in this problem which concerns over half of our agricultural population, for, according to the 1930 census, over half of those gainfully employed in California agriculture are . . . not owners or tenants or share croppers or ranchers, but farm laborers.

You may have heard, he said, that "growers have excellent houses" for their workers. Some did. But many, many more did not and relied instead on "river bottoms . . . ditch banks . . . and the road side" to shelter their workers. You may have heard, he continued, "that some of these people belong to the lowest order of society" and will not appreciate any good thing they receive. This might be true for some, Drobish conceded, "but a large percentage are good folk. They are poor, but aspire to better living, just as you and I."

On that March night, in front of that audience, Drobish was in no mood to let growers off the hook for the crisis to which they contributed and from which they profited. Invoking the specter of slavery and perhaps purposefully touching a racial nerve, he compared California growers unfavorably to plantation owners in the antebellum South. "Even in the slave days of the South, houses were provided for the slaves, and the slaves did not go hungry." In California in 1936, farm workers were both homeless and starving. "It is definitely a responsibility of the farmer to care for these laborers," he said, though he also encouraged his audience to "recognize that the farmers have been going through a depression which dates back to the war days," and which had made it difficult for even the well-intentioned to do right by laborers.

Harry Drobish was a smart and accomplished man. Born in Illinois in 1893, he moved to California at the age of twelve and spent his adult life studying and practicing agriculture there.[38] He knew the migrant situation in California from a statistical and economic standpoint, and from the human side as well. He was nothing short of intrepid in his field work in 1934 and 1935. More than any one person, he deserves credit for making the idea of government camps for migratory farm workers into a proposal and, finally, into a federal program. In the course of studying the problem of farm labor in California he encountered land owners, growers, and fully-in-the-pocket local authorities who were ready at the first mention of government assistance to shout that any worker who accepted it preferred the dole to hard work.

The foil for the lazy, freeloading migrant in this mythology was the self-reliant grower who, through hard work and determination, had made the desert bloom, made his fortunes swell, and made it possible to feed the nation. Worshippers of the mythologized farmer were quick to protest the use of government funds to support migrants, whose problems, they argued, were the result of character flaws. Drobish did not appreciate this line of reasoning and addressed it head on.

> Like businessmen generally, farm owners have become used to receiving assistance from the Government, through A. A. A. [the Agriculture Adjustment Administration], the seed and feed loan program, the buying up of farm surplus for relief purposes, the Farm Credit Administration and the like. But just two things have been done for [farm laborers], representing over half our agricultural population . . . direct relief and work relief. How can these people be placed on a higher plane of living?[39]

Don't come to me complaining about government aid for workers when your business model is predicated on government aid, Drobish warned. The camp program was the right thing to do to relieve suffering. He also noted that to pass through the camp gate was hardly to enter some government-funded paradise. Drobish explained that the two camps that were open at the time of his address—Marysville and Arvin—"provide minimum facilities: A good camp ground, proper sanitary facilities, flush toilets with adequate sewage disposal through septic tanks, hot and cold water for showers, and facilities for campers to wash their clothes. This is about all we supply besides supervision and an educational program."

While Drobish was addressing the Commonwealth Club in March of 1936, Tom Collins was managing the Arvin Migratory Farm Labor Camp, which had been open for three months. Collins had moved to Arvin from Marysville to ensure an orderly opening and to welcome migrants to their new community. But Drobish took the audience back to Collins's work at Marysville to explain what it meant to build and operate a camp. The work began among the squatters, he said, and was made successful by the right "supervisor," Collins, "who was trained in handling this type of people." Drobish then recounted more comprehensively Collins's approach and the redemptive effects of it.

> He did not strut around with a star on his lapel and a club at his side. He strove to get the campers to work out matters with him. He organized a local camp committee to assist him in managing the camp. If any trouble developed, if men came in drunk and got disorderly, the members of that committee took care of the drunks and got them out of camp without calling up the assistance of the camp supervisor.[40]

This was, in other words, an orderly community interested in and capable of self-governing. There was no need for external authority or the vicious shows of law-and-order barbarism of deputies and mercenaries. And those conditions of filth in which growers forced migrants to live? Those, Drobish pointed out, were gone once the campers passed through the gate. "Few public latrines are kept cleaner than the Marysville sanitary units. The sanitary units scrubbed out with hot water daily by the campers themselves." The migrants, he seemed to be saying, could be just like you and me.

In conclusion, Drobish noted that two camps were in operation and that funds had been requested for fifteen more, but that the migratory labor population was far larger than he could dream of accommodating. "All we can do in the Resettlement Administration," he said, "is simply to stage a demonstration," and to encourage, "whatever effort is made to provide proper living conditions for this large group of our people."

There was meaningful redemptive work to be done in the camps as migrants entered, came together, and halted their slide into something like "savagery." With the right personnel preaching the right message, they became recognizably American stock shortly after passing through the gate. But as Drobish also made clear, the goal was a broader redemption: the redemption of America's agricultural economy from the rapacious industrial forces that had convinced so many that the laborers on whom the system depended were enemies to be subdued and controlled. He hoped to move society toward the recognition that the interests of workers and growers were bound together, both as participants in the world's most productive agricultural economy and as citizens.

Perhaps the broader awakening could begin with the simple recognition of the migrant farm worker as a fellow human, a fellow American. The processes carried out inside the gate were aimed at sparking just such a recognition.

A Faithful Narrative of the Surprising Work of Tom

The dedication of the Marysville Migratory Farm Labor Camp on October 12, 1935 provided the Marysville and Yuba County communities with a ritual introduction to the idea of a federally-managed camp for migratory farm labor. The architects of the RA/FSA camp system used the ceremony to describe these benefits of life inside the gate and the process by which residents would be transformed. On that October day, the job of explaining the work being done inside the camp fell to camp manager Tom Collins.[41] In a talk titled, "The Human Side in the Operation of a Migrants Camp," Collins gave his account of the conversions happening inside the gate and described the process by which the camp environs, migrant sensibilities, and social pressures worked together to mend the migrants' brokenness.

This narrative of conversions reveals much about the religiousness of the government camp program. At the program's core was a normative position as to what a good American looked like, how he approached the world, in what and in whom he placed faith. The reason to bring migrants through the gates was to restore them physically and to redeem their worldviews; to move them from physical chaos to order, and from a predisposition to suspicion, through a state of bewilderment, and finally to an attitude of confidence.

Before looking at the details of Collins's narrative, it is important to make note of these intended changes in outlook and the assumptions that accompanied them. Because while Collins applied words like "suspicion" in a general way, seeming to refer to a way of perceiving rather than a specific response to a person or object, he was not out to convert all types of suspicion into confidence. There were certain kinds of confidence toward which Collins and the camp program more broadly were quite hostile. There were types of suspicion that they nurtured.

What Collins tried to inculcate inside the gate was confidence in modern, secular actors, institutions, and ways of knowing, along with a related suspicion of people, practices, and explanations that he saw as anti-modern or antique. Within the gates, migrants could be exposed to the grace of an orderly and modern community and the possibility of a rekindled faith in a rapidly modernizing America. But the journey from misplaced suspicion to proper confidence, and from misplaced confidence to proper suspicion, would be neither easy nor immediate. Migrants would almost surely have to spend time "bewildered," in a state of betwixt and between, after they encountered modern instruments and modern ways but before they made sense of, much less adopted or embraced, them.[42] Collins saw it as his job to guide the migrants through their bewilderment as he attempted to equip them for civilized, modern living.

Tom Collins opened his address by taking his audience back a few months in time, to the "Migrant Colony on the outskirts of the city of Marysville," where in the spring of 1935, nearly 1200 people were living in haphazard community. "Here was a small city, a city without order, a city of neglected souls." As some of Marysville's residents could surely attest, the disorderliness of the space had been all encompassing. "So great was the demand for space that tents were pitched wall against wall. Here and there a 'lean-to' . . . dotted the acreage, while on the outer fringe of it all many had thrown their mattresses or bedding in the dirt . . . having abandoned all thought or hope of privacy."

In this "city of neglected souls," domestic space dissolved into a too-exposed, too-intimate jumble of bodies and canvas, bedding and dirt. There was nothing in the colony that resembled civilization, nothing built that gestured toward order. More hellish still was the condition of the bodies that dwelled there. They were unwashed, filthy, and living in sanitary conditions that compounded filth and made its infectious dangers more present. Collins continued, "The only sanitary facilities available were two rough pit-type privies. The only water supply was furnished by a broken hand pump." Even those who aspired to something better could do no more than aspire. There was no visible path to redemption.[43]

To read Collins's words is to get a sense of the reformers' perplexity. He and his colleagues were aware of the scale of the problem in and beyond Marysville. "These people," he explained to the attendees, "part of an estimated 150,000 farm workers who follow the crops . . . had been making their homes under such circumstances for many years." They were one part of a group of the lost, and their number was growing. "This year," he told the audience, "many were newcomers who were forced [into] migratory labor . . . through circumstances beyond their control and in an effort to keep off the relief rolls."

As a theologian of the crisis, Collins was subtle but insistent on the question of culpability. The migrants—the newly migratory at least—were not in this situation because of some unatoned-for sinfulness. The structures of industrial agriculture, the misfortune of drought, the relentlessness of wind, the rapacity of wealthy men, these were the factors that had them backpedaling, grasping for some kind of hold. They are not parasitic in their essence or their actions, Collins insisted. They do not want something for nothing. They wander to avoid relief, not to find it.

Collins recalled that he and his associates, like evangelists looking out on a town draped in spiritual slumber, were overwhelmed by the problem before them: How would they achieve the needed awakening?

Where would they begin? The first step, Collins decided, was to work "through the children."

> We found there were in the colony, 127 children between the ages of four and twelve years. . . . Within a few days we organized a playground, fully equipped with those little things which are the joy and rightful heritage of every American child. We eagerly watched the results. Children came, gaped wild-eyed, tempted, but went away. They returned with other children. There was more gaping, more wild eyes, but not a child responded to the temptation.[44]

The playground equipment beckoned to the youngest migrants, coaxing them out of states of suspicion and into bewilderment, evidenced by their expressions of amazement. They did not immediately reach confidence, the state in which they would use and enjoy the playground, but it seemed only a matter of time. The "tiny tots," Collins reported, were the first ones "bold enough to venture on the ground." Quickly their inhibitions melted away and "screams of delight" filled the air. The first sparks of revival among the squatters came from the children.

Those sparks, however, did not ignite the community. Not all children took an interest in the playground. And the children's parents remained unmoved, stuck in the mire of suspicion. Collins and his team decided to walk around the squatters' camp searching for holdouts, young and old. "On the third day we visited a number of mothers to find out why their children did not go to the playground. From them we learned there was a general air of suspicion throughout the camp."

Some mothers were worried that they would have to pay a fee for sending their little ones to the playground. Others expressed a more general worry that there must be a "ketch." One migrant shared a rumor that the playground was a ploy "to take our kids from us caus we ain't able to keer for em." It was not unreasonable for a destitute, abandoned people to worry that the shiny object ahead was a mirage or, worse, a trap. Collins met these suspicions with assurances that the playground was simply a playground—a debatable claim—and that the government's purposes in establishing the camp were benevolent.

His assurances led to more questions about the contours of the government camp, questions that indicated progress from suspicion to bewilderment. One woman finally asked, "Is it true we is getting hot baths and laundries with hot water?" Collins recounted for the audience that he confirmed this rumor, which prompted another migrant woman to comment, "Gee, we's being noticed at last—we can be human bein's onct agin." He then summarized the developments of those early days, "So through the children and the playground we made our first step forward, and the suspicion we encountered soon changed to bewilderment, bewilderment in the knowledge someone was taking an interest in them and their welfare."

A realization was dawning among some migrants that they might not be alone in their struggles, that there might be some help on the way. Months or years of suffering, deprivation, wandering, and invisibility had obliterated their confidence in people and institutions. But those trials had brought them to Marysville, California where, as the migrant woman noted, they were "being noticed at last."

For some the experience of bewilderment was a prelude to a blessing. Others, however, recoiled from the government camp and persisted in their suspicion. In his address, Collins explained that nearly half of those living in the Hooverville hit the road as "a second exodus of the Egyptians," rather than pass through the gate. He described the scene: "We stood by as broken down cars, house cars, trailers, trucks, men with packs on their backs, deserted the camp.... Tramps, 'bundle stiffs,' [sic], pan handlers, loafers, realizing at last that the camp was to be supervised and administered for the migratory workers, had made a hasty retreat to the four winds."

Collins saw the flight of these undesirables not as a failure on the part of the Resettlement Administration and not as an indication that his approach to working among the migrants might be flawed. Rather, he described the mass departure as occasion for faith in the camp program. "This proves most conclusively that the Resettlement Administration Migrants Camp will be given the 'go by' by that class which will not work and which prefers to remain as aloof as possible from the conventions of a well-regulated and ordered community." In other words, the irredeemably suspicious would avoid the camp. In Collins's estimation, those who passed through the gate had, at the very least, the potential to achieve confidence.

With the departure of more than five hundred souls, Collins and his colleagues directed their efforts toward the roughly seven hundred who remained. The quality of life for children remained an important focus of the staff's efforts, but they were also concerned about personal hygiene and public sanitation among squatters of all ages.

Rather than preach fire-and-brimstone, Collins hoped to convert the migrants to more orderly ways of living by showing them that some of their own already embraced the virtues of cleanliness and order. He wanted to convert them by example. "We selected several of the better men and women, encouraged them to keep themselves and their tents orderly and clean as demonstrations for the other hundred in camp." Just as the migrant city on a hill would shine forth as an example to the communities outside the gate, so too would exemplary migrants demonstrate to those inside the gate what it meant to live rightly. Collins continued, "This group went about their tasks in fear and trembling. When all was ready for the first step, they backed out on us." This first group of reluctant exemplars was followed by a second, also chosen by Collins. When the time came for them to stand in public as representatives of a new and virtuous way, they too backed down.

Collins's evangelism among the poverty-weary adults was hampered, it seems, by the migrants' self-consciousness, and perhaps by a desire to not be perceived as "exemplary." The migrants knew at least as well as Collins that many factors had brought them to homeless life in California's agricultural interior. They knew, too, that the road back to normalcy would be harder to travel if jealousies and grievances were aimed at them from within the community.

Asking women and men at the bottom of the social and economic ladder to put themselves forward as models of cleanliness and charity was a gamble, and it didn't pay off. According to Collins a jealousy- and gossip-filled rift developed between the two exemplary groups. In fact, he observed, the gossip engaged in by the first group spread so widely and built such a "following" against the second group that it gave him an idea for refining his method. He told the audience,

> We again solicited the cooperation of four women of the first trained group, the four best gossipers. We complimented them for their interest in the women of the camp and their neighborly spirit. We again made known to them our plans for cleaning up the camp and again solicited their cooperation. We suggested they broach the subjects very much

along these lines when they visited a tent . . . "your kids must keep you awfully busy keeping them clean out in this dirt. Let us help you clean up your tent and the grounds about your tent while you go and bathe and dress the kids."

The anthropologist in Collins combined with the reformer and the evangelist to develop new measures to spread a gospel grounded in "a well-regulated and orderly community." The sin of gossip could generate social pressure toward the virtue of cleanliness. "There is tremendous horsepower or marepower [sic] in gossip," he wrote. "We harnessed it and it served a good purpose, and thus . . . bewilderment gave way to confidence."

Collins informed those gathered for the dedication ceremony that outward signs of a new season of confidence suffused the camp after just two weeks. Families started to clean their bedding and cover used pots to keep flies and vermin at bay. Women "appeared in clean print dresses, or slacks," and domestic cleaning and laundry happened regularly. The children, with whom the whole revival began, "appeared after the evening meal clean of body and cleanly dressed."

The true victory, though, was the transformation of the evangelized into evangelists. As new families passed through the gate and into the camp community, they crossed into a life where "the good neighbor idea"—helping each other clean up and stay clean—held sway. Those who headed out through the gate and into the world, having "been trained" into this approach to orderly living, carried the gospel with them "to other fields." The fruits of all this, Collins told the Marysville crowd, were that "our problems of child hygiene, personal hygiene, and public sanitation were, to a great degree, solved." This proclamation of victory was premature, but it points to a persistent connection in Collins's eyes and in the entire camp system, between attitudes and physical appearances. Confidence and suspicion were not just interior states. They were evident in the presentation of community, home, and body.

To enter into the migrant camp community was to assent to standards of physical and spatial order that contrasted dramatically with the standards that prevailed outside of the gates. It was also to participate in a broader program of restoration that included taking responsibility for self-government and the rule of law. Having made noticeable progress toward a clean, orderly, and confident community, Collins and his coworkers moved to the "next step" of ensuring that the collective would be "well-regulated."

After repurposing gossip to improve the migrants' hygiene and self-presentation, Collins looked again to popular authority and formed "a committee of campers to assist the management in the proper conduct of the camp." Collins turned to the women of the camp to set tents in order and to clean bodies. He turned to the men to establish and enforce laws. "For this committee we selected five men, considered leaders of various groups," he explained. "This experiment was successful from its inception, so much so that to date it has not been necessary to refer to the peace authorities to make an arrest, quell a disturbance or any other cause. This committee handled every problem of discipline with the exception of family squabbles."

In order to get a community of displaced and destitute Americans back on its feet and feeling somewhat whole, the Resettlement Administration was going to rely on migrant women to set and enforce domestic standards, migrant men to address the "problems of community life," and leaders like Collins who "had a keen understanding of human problems." Each of these three prongs, described by Collins and endorsed by the program hierarchy, was essential to what Collins referred to as "the gospel of the good neighbor." Camp managers and camp spaces spread this gospel. Camp residents who embraced it became proof, both to program staff and to attentive Californians, that the gospel could save.

Looking back on the early days of this federal mission, Collins told those present at the dedication ceremony that the essence of the program was to lift up the downtrodden souls and to be gentle in the lifting.

> To many of these migratory workers a camp such as this one . . . is their only intimate contact with self respect. It lifts them out of the dust heap and from the banks of stagnant streams where they made their homes for many years, and enables them to walk among their fellowmen [sic], clean of body and cleanly dressed. And cleanliness helps lift one's head, braces the spirits, and fortifies the morale of the laborer.

In the eyes and the words of Tom Collins, the most influential camp manager in the migratory farm labor camp program, this is what it meant to cross from outside the camp to inside: to accept the possibility of walking, clean in body and confident in spirit, among one's fellow Americans. It meant letting the kids loose on a playground without suspicion of being charged a hidden fee, or worrying that the whole thing was a way for the government to lure kids away and seize them. It meant leaving behind the dark clouds and stooped postures of suspicion and moving toward the salvation of a confident life. It meant perseverance in that confidence, expressed in the establishment of self-government and the maintenance of a properly governed self.

In a set of personal notes dated July 1936, Harry Drobish sketched an account of a migrant conversion like those described by Collins. The subject was a man named "Baughn" who was trying to scratch out a living in Kern County. Along with his wife and a newborn, Baughn had been living in a grower-administered camp on the Hoover Ranch (owned by the family of former President Herbert Hoover), until they were forced to leave their cabin "on one day's notice."[45]

Drobish narrated in short bursts of prose. "Had nothing when arrived at Migrant Camp. Discouraged and down and out. Collins helped." What Collins did, according to the notes, was introduce Baughn to other campers and get him involved in a game of checkers. This cheered him up and convinced him to come through the camp gate for good. Baughn and his young family were without a tent, so Collins let them sleep on the floor of one of the buildings.

Life continued to throw challenges at Baughn and his wife—their "rattley Ford" got wrecked, forcing him to walk to the fields or to hitch rides with other campers—but a check-up showed that their infant was a "perfect baby," and the once "discouraged" Baughn became a "happy member of [the] camp." He found work again at the Hoover Ranch, but after less conscientious camp residents made him late one day, he decided to walk the seven miles to work his twelve-hour shift in irrigation. He refused to buy a car because "[he] had to pay for baby's bed and some furniture first." This transformation, worked out inside the gates, carried over into Baughn's life outside the gates.

Reflecting on Baughn's story, Drobish proclaimed, "This is a migrant with spunk. A man Hoover ranch wanted to dump out of a shack on one day's notice, despite the fact his wife had a two-weeks old baby." He came through the gate. He joined the community. He bought a tent and some furniture.

And with Collins's encouragement, he set himself on a path to restoration. To borrow from Collins, his head was up, his spirit was braced, and his morale was fortified. Baughn was, in short, a convert to confidence.[46]

Migrants at the Gate

Toward the end of the lengthy printed program for the Marysville camp dedication, just after the promise that the band would play a second set, an item reads:

> Talk—Mrs. A dy, a camper—"What camps mean to the campers."

It is the only item in the program to promise a migrant's perspective, and the title is barely a title. "What camps mean to the campers" reads more like an essay assignment given to a migrant by a camp staff member than a talk imagined independently. "Mrs. A dy," the name recorded in the program, is either incomplete (Mrs. Andy? Mrs. Addy? Mrs. Aidy?) or improperly spaced (Mrs. Ady). This migrant woman has a place in the program, just as Miss Mary Hutchinson from the League of Women Voters, and is just as visible to history. But her place is marred, her name mishandled.

I have no record of what "Mrs. A dy" said, what exactly she told the representatives of thirty-one organizations, the fifty-eight dignitaries, and the audience of God-knows-how-many about what "camps" meant to "the campers." It is, moreover, an open question how much those present cared about the migrants' perspectives. Other interpretations of the meaning of the camp were front and center that day.

Yet Mrs. A dy's simultaneous presence and silence are provocative. They remind us that this project of reform was not abstract, that it involved people who were often lost and in pain. Mrs. A dy also prompts us to recognize that the government camps did not mean any one thing to all campers, or one constant thing to any one camper. The paths migrants had traveled to the gate were different, as were the lives they left behind and those they hoped to build. Moreover, migrants were not uniformly eager to enter the camps, nor were they uniformly accepting of the program Tom Collins described. Experiences outside the gate and inside changed migrants' perceptions of the camps and the sanctuary they provided.

Entrance to the Shafter Camp, 1938.
Photograph by Dorothea Lange. *Shafter camp for migratory agricultural workers, Farm Security Administration. Entrance and office.* November 1938. Courtesy of Library of Congress. https://www.loc.gov/item/2017770855/.

The migrant woman whom Collins quoted exclaiming that the new camp would let her be a human being once again engaged in a process of reflection (I am human; poverty and destitution have forced me to live in a sub-human way; the government camp will allow me to recover my humanity) for which some migrants had neither the energy nor the distance from their own tragedies. The thoughts of migrants who approached and passed through the gate at Marysville, Arvin, Indio, or any of the other fixed-site camps were not always so lofty.

Accounts of migrants' arrivals often describe needs so intense that they likely narrowed a family's focus to basics: water, food, and shelter. In light of such want, the question as to why some migrants passed through the gates of a Resettlement Administration camp all but answers itself: they were desperate for help. Collins's report for the week of April 18, 1936 told of a family that entered the Arvin camp starving, disintegrating. Two of their children had to be hospitalized. One child had worms. An infant, still nursing, was diagnosed with pneumonia and struggled to get milk from the mother. It had a fever of 104 degrees and was, "a miserable sight, emaciated, filthy, ill and in much pain." The mother, undone by her inability to nurse, suffered a breakdown. Collins continued, "We have had many such cases at Marysville and here [Arvin]. We merely stress the point that this is the most wretched case we have as yet handled."[47]

Just over a month later, with the Arvin camp population at 339, almost triple what it had been in mid-April, Collins noted that an influx of new campers had come from a "notorious" Hooverville in Bakersfield. The effects of living in that environment were deeply distressing. "May you never witness the terrible sights, the filthy, human derelicts such as chugged to the camp from that hell hole." He continued, "Our own campers were amazed at the condition of these people. It was difficult to tell whether the newcomers were white or Black."[48] One can imagine the camp residents' amazement being amplified by the realization that those filthy, derelict, racially ambiguous newcomers were reflections of their former selves.

In January of 1936, Charles Eddy, who succeeded Collins as the manager of the Marysville Camp, noted in a weekly report that thirteen new arrivals had brought the total camp population to a respectable off-season total of fifty-four. He then offered brief profiles of a few who had passed through the gate. "Mr. Parks, single man, out of work and can not get any, applied for aid to SERA refused, can not get on WPA, very low on funds. Hard up. 60 years old." State and federal aid programs had failed Mr. Parks. Perhaps the prospect of some form of community and a warm shower drew him in. Eddy then turned his attention to one of the four families that had arrived that week.

> Mr. Bartlett, wife and six children ages 3 to 13, moved in on the 16th and are very hard up. They applied for aid to the SERA and was [sic]

Entrance to the Yuba City Camp, 1940.
Photograph by Russell Lee. *Sign at entrance to the Yuba City FSA Farm Security Administration farm workers' camp. Yuba City, California.* December 1940. Courtesy of Library of Congress. https://www.loc.gov/item/2017788512/.

turned over to WPA. He refused WPA work at $44.00 per mo. The wife is going on WPA sewing next week. He refused to send the children to school. He said the government owed him a living and he was going to get it. I asked him how and he said he would find a way, he always had.[49]

The camp was not a first option for Mr. Bartlett and his family. He had clearly tried other avenues to support his family but had been either turned away or unwilling to accept the wages. Charles Eddy's assessment that Mr. Bartlett was "very bitter against the SERA, the WPA, and the government in general," is no doubt accurate. Mr. Bartlett was used to finding his way through hard times. Having failed to "find a way" and failed to find a government program that would help him on terms that he judged fair, he threw up his hands in frustration. Meanwhile, his wife put her hands to work sewing. Proud and hopeful before he arrived at his state of bitterness, perhaps Mr. Bartlett saw the camp as assistance—the living that the government owed him—and not as relief, which signaled a deeper dependency.[50]

Mr. Bartlett was not alone in resisting "relief" but accepting residency in the camp. Writing just a week later from the Arvin camp, Tom Collins noted that many residents refused direct financial relief. "The mere thought of asking for relief seems to be an unpleasant thought for all of them. To quote them, 'It ain't relief we's after it's wuk. We ain't had no relief fer over a year.'"[51] Collins had expanded on this idea while addressing the audience at the Marysville dedication four months prior: "We are astounded at [the migrants'] independence," he confessed, "*The real migratory worker* abhors relief. He wants to pay his own way. He is not a loafer."[52]

The basic contours of these narratives of desperation are similar to the story told in his own words by migrant husband and father William Mercer. His circumstances were different though. Mercer's reflections on the meaning of his entry into the Brawley Migratory Farm Labor Camp, written in a letter to camp program officials, came as his fellow campers sought to evict him and his family. The Mercer children fought incessantly with other children in the camp, and their mother Nova's tendency to curse a blue streak and to threaten other campers was too much for the community to take.

William, Nova, and their six children were living in the Brawley camp, William wrote, not "because we wish to be but because we were without funds and needed a home." The Brawley camp met a need and, according to William Mercer, met it well. "We have found the conditions here a godsend to poor migrating needful travelers for which we are grateful to the federal government as well as the citicens [sic] of California and other states; however this is the first one that we have ever been in in any state." We are not camp hoppers, Mercer insisted. And we are not ungrateful.

Mercer then described his work history in detail: two stints in the military, many years of farming, jobs in construction, oil work, painting, carpentry, automobile repair, and unnamed "other jobs that a human could learn and do." He was neither lazy nor a freeloader, he insisted. Things had only gotten "so cayotic," Mercer explained, because of the "unemployment situation," which left millions of people "hard up," not just him.

Mercer made clear that he and his family appreciated the camp and everything that it was providing for them. "The facultys [sic] of this camp have been a great asset to us as a place to call home and the utility house has been a great help to us to keep our family clean." The social environment left much to be desired, he continued, but he and his family were good people and the camp had been good for them.[53]

A migrant's entry into the camp was a petition for help. While pride or independence or stubbornness could stop the word "relief" from crossing a migrant's lips, persistent need pushed them through the gate. Crossing this threshold reoriented a person's relationship to the federal government, making much more explicit the fact that a family needed some government support. As Harry Drobish had pointed out to the Commonwealth Club in March of 1936, the fact that migrants received federal assistance hardly set them apart from other participants in California's colossal agricultural economy. What made them different was the visible form in which their aid came. One had to scan federal budgets and dig through balance sheets to see a grower's dependence on government aid. To see a migrant's dependence, one only had to watch the gate.

Many migrants would surely have preferred to avoid aid or to receive it in some more discreet way. But discretion in such matters was a privilege enjoyed by the powerful few. Which meant that many proud and hesitant migrants—Baughn, Bartlett, Mercer—eventually had to relent and to move not just themselves but their families through the camp gate.

The camps seem to have appealed to migrants as oases in a troubled landscape. Over a period of eight years—1935 to 1943—tens of thousands of migratory farm workers passed through the gates and, with varying degrees of energy, joined their communities, served on committees, celebrated holidays, wrote to camp newspapers, and cheered for camp baseball teams. A question to ponder, given the size of the migratory farm labor population and the conveniences provided in the camps, is why every migrant didn't at least attempt to enter a camp. Why was each and every camp not full from the first moment it opened? Was the need for housing not acute enough? Was the appeal of a clean and comparatively stable living space not sufficient to bring thousands of migrants through the gates every month of every year?

The need was indeed great. The appeal was strong. And yet camp occupancy was often below capacity. Some of this was due to the normal flow of workers around and through California's agricultural interior. Workers follow the crops. It makes no sense to stay somewhere where there is nothing to pick, pack, or prune.

Still, the question hung in the air. It occurred to Collins in December of 1935 as he was opening the Arvin camp. The previous summer he had witnessed the "second Exodus of the Egyptians" from the Marysville site and interpreted it as a preference among a certain class of destitute migrants for a lower type of life. Circumstances at Arvin were different. The Arvin camp was not being built as a replacement for a specific squatters' camp, as the Marysville camp had been. It was going up as an alternative to all of the roadside camps, ditch bank camps, and the filthy camps run by neglectful growers. And still there were those who would not come in. Five years later, Harvey Coverley, assistant director of the FSA's Region IX, wrote to J. C. Henderson, chief of its migratory labor section, "There is one thing that puzzles me. If the housing situation among low-income farm workers at Brawley is as acute as Mr. Brunton pointed out, why is it that our free camp is not more fully occupied."[54]

The answers that Collins reported to the Resettlement Administration hierarchy on December 28, 1935, a mere two weeks after the Arvin camp opened, were closely tied to the Protestant commitments of the migrants and their perceptions of the challenges that life inside the gate posed to those commitments. As he wrote,

> It was interesting to learn from some of the migrants just why they have been so slow moving in. It seems that the "Full Gospel" followers (Holy Rollers) had the impression the camp would be over run with "Free Methodists." The "Free Methodists" were under the impression the camp would be over run with "Full Gospelites." There is some breach between the two. Both factions wanted to know if it would be possible to be off to one section of one of the sanitary units away from the other.[55]

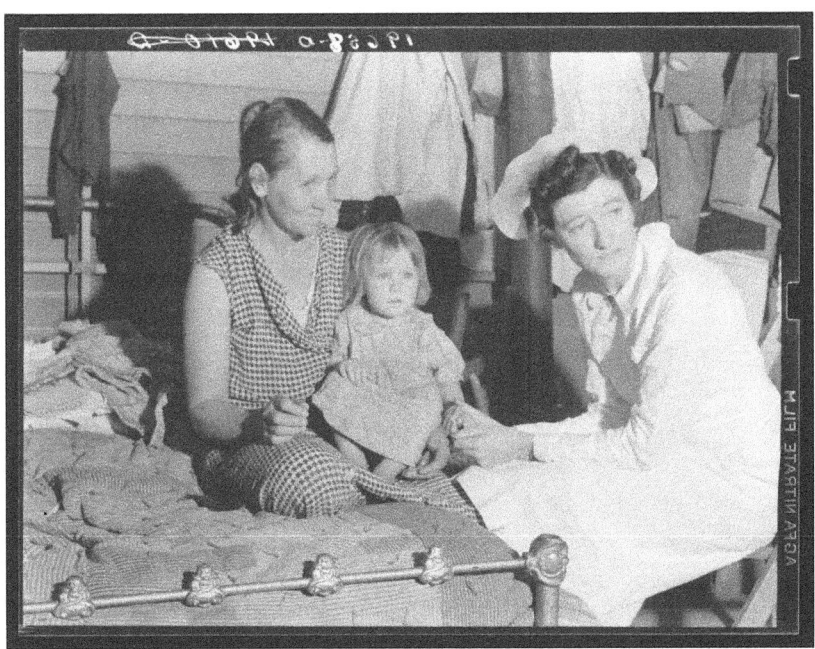

Camp nurse with migrant mother and child, Farmersville Camp, 1939. Photograph by Dorothea Lange. *Untitled photo: Farm Security Administration FSA camp for migratory agricultural workers at Farmersville. Nurse of Agricultural Workers' Health and Medical Association FSA is assigned to the camp.* Tulare County, California, May 1939. Courtesy of Library of Congress. https://www.loc.gov/item/2017772053/.

For these groups, passing through the gate involved an immediate cost. To enter the federal camp was to be forced into community with people whose theologies and practices were an offense to God. By passing through the gate, these migrants would trade away uniformity of religious identity for government protection and modern conveniences. Much to the frustration of camp personnel, this was a trade that some migrants were unwilling to make.

Collins also encountered migrants who were mostly unfazed by Protestant diversity, but were suspicious of camp policies regarding health care and healing. As one migrant asked, "When me and the missus get sick does we HAVE to have a doctor if we comes here? We ain't got no faith in doctors. We just prays because sickness and sin is the same thing." Collins reflected in December of 1935, "As quite a few migrants down here have this same belief, it will require constant vigilance in the daily health check to prevent the spread of disease or infection."[56]

Both the camp policy urging residents to report illness and seek medical treatment, and the migrant husband's concern were well-founded. Given the number of infectious diseases present among the migrants and the close quarters in which they lived in the camps, the possibility for outbreaks was high. And Collins and other managers did all that they could to steer residents toward medical interventions when they were ill. Campers within the gates found ways around these efforts, but the efforts were real and involved pressures and confrontations that one could avoid more easily outside the gate.

While surveying a squatter camp at the nearby Frick Ranch a few weeks later, Collins encountered another group, "a religious group conducted on the old patriarchal family system," led by a man named Farmer. Collins wrote of "squalor, filth, and other abuses" at the Frick Ranch and noted many times that Frick was both a strident critic of the Arvin camp and a relentless exploiter of the migrants. Some living on Frick's property wanted to leave, but their Protestant commitments held them back. "The younger group of families desires to move to the Kern Migrants Camp [Arvin] but Farmer will not permit account of religious reasons. . . . It is understood they will not enter the [camp] for fear physicians will be called in case of sickness."

This same group had lost a child to illness the previous spring when their prayers for healing were not answered. Neighbors called a physician but he arrived too late to save the child's life. Farmer framed his insistence that his followers stay out of the government camp not as a rejection of modern medicine, but as an expression of independence. "We ain't goin to have anything to do with the government or anything the government has to do with."[57]

Some migrants who preferred prayer to medical treatment, including a group of Farmer's faithful, judged the security and sanitation of the camp worth trying. In passing through the gate they brought camp officials new faiths to observe and new problems to solve. Religious differences could create tension between individuals or groups, as well as between migrants and camp officials. The migrants' tendency to avoid health checks and medical professionals brought them into regular conflict with those charged with administering the camp's program of education and modernization. Collins and others usually treated tensions over religious matters as legitimate, but they also remained insistent that the practice of faith healing was fueled by "false fears and superstitions regarding health," and should be navigated around or, better yet, educated away.[58]

In late January of 1936, reflecting on the presence of an "old-fashioned revivalist" in the town of Arvin and his experiences with religious conflict between groups of migrants, Collins wrote extensively on "the religious problem" inside the gate. He had been staying up late, he wrote to program headquarters, "since rival religious groups, when worked to a high degree of religious fervor, easily cause dissention in the camp." The dissention was due to denominational rivalry and to noise. "It is a common thing for some of these people to awake at midnight and start a wailing cry to Jehovah and thus disturb the camp." The noise was disruptive. The opposition of "such religious groups" to "physicians and medicine" was possibly dangerous. "That has always been a delicate problem for camp management for, or rather because, such groups will not report sickness, thus leaving epidemics hanging over us and general contaminations." Collins felt he had to tread lightly to avoid confirming migrants' worst suspicions about life inside the gate. "Care is essential to prevent interfering with the individual or group privilege of freedom of thought and worship."[59]

To demonstrate what he meant, Collins described a recent case. It began with an uneventful health inspection, a daily routine in which he walked through the camp, talked to migrants, asked them about their health and casually looked them over for signs of sickness. He hadn't found any. But following the inspection, "quite a number of campers" from "one of our more fervent religious groups" had gathered in and around one of the migrant's tents. The situation looked suspicious, so Collins approached the "lead of that family" to ask what was going on. He answered, "We always prays fer to cure sickness by bringin' the saints.... Yet the ol' woman ain't no better. Whatya think?"

The migrant husband was experiencing exactly the kind of bewilderment Collins intended. The failure of anti-modern practices to address sickness or injury was experienced differently when modern practices were close at hand. Collins called the county nurse. She arrived and diagnosed the "ol' woman" with pneumonia.[60]

There is no clear moment of conversion in this story, no dramatic scene in which the husband decisively transfers his wife's care from one type of healer to another. But in his question to Collins, "Whatya think?" there is an expression of faith in Collins's ability to assess and begin to remedy the situation, an opening of a door just wide enough for the practice of modern medicine to make its way in. And with a county nurse on the case, diagnosing and treating effectively, Collins's preferred modes of evangelization: word of mouth, example, and experience, could do the rest. "We have been informed by some of these groups that from now on they will use both prayer and the services of the nurse and physician," he wrote. "For this we are glad."

The vestiges of suspicion that remained, in this case prayers for healing, were of little concern. Collins could see clearly the development of confidence in the modern.

* * *

Writing of Catholic women's experiences of medicine and hospitalization in the middle decades of the twentieth century, scholar of religion Robert Orsi notes that the modernization of medicine was a mixed blessing for those who needed treatment or hospitalization. It wasn't just that diagnostic advances moved more quickly than advances in treating illness and managing suffering, that doctors could tell a patient what was wrong before they could do much of anything about it. It was also that, increasingly, to be sick in modernizing America also meant to be alone and vulnerable.[61]

Orsi's artful account of Catholic women and their investments in St. Jude in times of precariousness can help us to understand, at least partially, migrants' hesitations when confronted with more "modern" ways of thinking about sickness and treatment. For many of them physical illness was an occasion to gather the saints, to constitute community, to be surrounded by and filled up with prayer. Once inside the gate, illness and suffering—realities that essentially defined migratory farm work—became cause for suspicion, dispersal, and isolation.

At this meeting point of ways of believing and ways of healing, migrants could be reluctant to trade their relationship with the Great Physician for a consultation with a competent nurse. They were suspicious of modernizing medicine and its ability to help them navigate the challenges of human frailty, which were made all the more intractable by poverty, hunger, and exposure.

In addition to challenging theologies of healing and the body, camp gates functioned to limit migrants' exposure to certain types of religious leaders, especially those who cultivated the wrong types of suspicion and who nurtured the wrong type of confidence. In his report from Marysville for the week of April 18, 1936, Charles Eddy included a list of "Campers denied entrance and reasons." His account of "1 group of three women" surely caught the eye of the headquarters staff in San Francisco. They were not disrespectful or drunk, but they were potentially disruptive. "They are traveling evangelists," he wrote, "and requested permission to camp and hold open air revival meetings in the grove. Their request was denied."[62]

Eddy did not expand on the reason for barring them entry. He could have done so on vocational grounds. The camps were for the exclusive use of agricultural workers, though it is possible that the evangelists had multiple vocations. They would not have been the first to combine work in the fields with work in the fields of the Lord. Eddy could also have refused them entry out of concern for communal harmony, since religious intensity and tension between campers were correlated in the eyes of Tom Collins, who trained Charles Eddy.

It is likely, though, that turning the female evangelists away was, in Resettlement Administration terminology, a demonstration: an action that officials hoped migrants would see, admire, and repeat. As accommodating as Collins and Eddy and others could be toward migrant religiosity, they most certainly hoped that migrants would reevaluate their confidence in preachers who emphasized Holy Spirit baptism and who fostered apparently chaotic worship services. They hoped migrants would become enduringly suspicious of the charismatic faiths and revivalistic practices that so often guided them. Within the gate, camp officials resisted the expansive role that religion often played in the lives of migrants. They believed that the migrants' confidence in their faiths and practices was misplaced and that those who cultivated this religiosity should, when possible, be kept out.

Writing from the Arvin camp in mid-summer 1936, Collins described the uncanny ability of traveling evangelists to perceive a downturn in economic prospects and, precisely at that moment, to circulate among the desperate migrants offering comfort. One evangelist couple stood out particularly vividly to Collins. "He possessed a Packard, 1935 sedan. He himself was dressed expensively. His wife could have passed for an urban society leader en route to a cocktail party." The back of their new Packard bore a sign that read, "Jesus Is Here!" Collins did not hide his disdain. "These birds of prey (rather than pray) purvey bootleg 'gospels' and drain the last penny from the laborers, after which they go to some other hunting ground."

From Collins's perspective, the coming together of evangelistic opportunism and migrant credulity functioned only to keep the migrants down.[63] Put differently, the problem with these "transient preachers" was not primarily theological. It was, rather, the blind confidence that migrants placed in them and, in this case, the lack of concern for the migrants' economic well-being shown by the "birds of prey." According to Collins's report, his perceptions were confirmed in conversation with the unnamed evangelist. Upon seeing the comforts of life within the gate and hearing of migrant self-rule, the evangelist remarked, "I cannot imagine these people . . . thinking for themselves. . . . I have always been under the impression they had to have someone to think for them and show them the LIGHT."

By the model of the Arvin camp, though, the people to whom he condescended also held the keys to the gate. He could not hold services in camp without their approval, which was not immediately forthcoming. In Collins's eyes this wasn't just a delightful comeuppance for a gasbag evangelist. It was progress toward suspicion and confidence properly placed. Collins explained,

> Our campers visit churches in Weed Patch and Arvin. When we first opened the camp the campers were in semi-destitute circumstances and looked for these roving evangelists. They give them a wide berth now and prefer the village churches. Resettlement has pulled the farm laborer from the dung hill, scrubbed him down and enabled him to put a clean foot forward. Precious pennies formerly wasted on mendicants of all types now go to a more holy cause—to keep away the wrinkles from the little bellies of children.[64]

For the time being, the migrants had closed the gate on a merchant of bad religion, whose business model monetized and increased human suffering. For the time being, the migrants had shown themselves properly suspicious of the "dung" that was transient preachers and their boot-leg gospels, and had embraced the more polite, or at least the more settled, "village churches."

Writing of himself in the plural, as was his tendency, Collins closed the report to Resettlement Administration headquarters with some condescension of his own. "Should hard times return next winter we wonder whether the laborers will call in the roving and raving evangelists." Would they backslide into a longing for the ecstatic, volatile practices and the otherworldly orientations that robbed them blind and left them hungry? How long would it be before they forgot the difference between being prayed for and being preyed upon? Collins was keenly aware that there were those outside the gate who would exploit migrants eagerly and unapologetically. The inside existed to break the grip of exploitation, to cultivate a sense of self-worth and community value unrelated to piece- and pound-rate compensation, and, to borrow a phrase from the notorious evangelist whom Collins labeled a bird of prey, to give reform-minded New Dealers the opportunity to "think for [the migrants] and show them the LIGHT."

The records show that hard times persisted. The records also suggest that "roving and raving" religion remained a concern of camp officials and a draw to migratory farm workers, and that efforts to change migrants' religious inclinations and to discredit so-called "birds of prey" continued. Once migrants and their faiths were inside the gate, the camp manager became a central figure in this effort, a mission priest for New Deal modernity.

2

The Office

The gate created an inside in which migrants found sanctuary. Every day, migrants living in a government camp moved through and around spaces conceived to repair their presupposed brokenness. The office of the camp manager coordinated that program of repair and redemption in ways both visible and invisible to the migrants. Given the camp manager's central role in running the camp and documenting its successes and its failures, it is crucial to examine the religion of the camp manager's office, the embodiment of the office religion in the camp manager, and the camp office's role in producing knowledge about migrants' religious lives.[1]

The documents generated in the camp office almost always served multiple purposes. A single report sent by a camp manager to the program headquarters in San Francisco might contain a request for supplies (grass seed, paint, fencing), a question about a speaking invitation, a description of camp politics, an update on wages for cotton picking, and a transcription of a migrant's poem. The mixed contents were matched by mixed sentiments: admiration for the migrants side-by-side with condescension toward some aspect of their lives; expressions of kinship and connection combined with descriptions of profound and troubling differences.

Dry, mundane, routinized correspondence, part and parcel of the bureaucratic ways of knowing that operated within the Resettlement Administration and the Farm Security Administration, too easily hides the program's biases and polemics. That is, explicit and ritualized adherence to data collection and reporting requirements gives scientific cover and the legitimacy of objective observation to negative portrayals of camp residents. Also obscured by the bureaucratic process and the immense archive it produced is the theological nature of the RA/FSA program in agricultural California. Officials within the camp program's hierarchy not only practiced a faith, they contributed to unflattering portrayals of

Entrance to Indio Camp and Camp Office, 1939.
Photograph by Dorothea Lange. *Entering Farm Security Administration FSA camp for migratory laborers at Indio. Coachella Valley, California.* February 1939. Courtesy of Library of Congress. https://www.loc.gov/item/2017771737/.

the migrants' faiths and, especially though not exclusively through John Steinbeck's era-defining 1939 novel *The Grapes of Wrath*, shaped perceptions of the migrants beyond the official channels through which their memos and reports flowed.

The camp office was the bureaucratic node of the migrant camp. The immense and expanding bureaucratic authority of the federal government in New Deal America was concentrated in the camp office as in no other place inside the gate. Additionally, the camp office was the place where each individual camp connected most clearly to the central office of the Resettlement Administration and the Farm Security Administration in California. The office was therefore also the place where the camp was most clearly and traceably part of a camp *system*. With the bureaucratic heart beating in the Bay Area, information flowed to and returned from the camp offices. The left ventricle of that heart pumped guidance and regulations, decisions and explanations, public relations materials and money to the camp office. The pull of required weekly and monthly reports, inventories, accountings, and requests for permission drew information back to the heart's right atrium, from which it circulated through the main office and was processed, aggregated, filed, and sometimes pumped back out through the system.

This circulatory system and its associated files and folders, drawers and offices kept the camp program alive and working. Blood was paper and paper was blood. An incident or a person or a need became real within the system when the camp manager committed it to paper. For example, a report from the Arvin camp dated May 29, 1937 brought grim news to the attention of the central office. "We had two deaths during the week, in both cases the deaths were children one a two-year old and the other only a few weeks old, both died at the County Hospital. The small baby suffered from a congenital stomach defect and the two-year old boy died of diarrhea." Two weeks later, data entered under the heading "Number Cases Illness and Injury" made visible the health challenges facing camp residents.

> Sunburn—1; Chicken Pox—2; Whooping Cough—7; Ring Worm—1; Syphilis—3; Impetigo—2; San Joaquin Fever—1; 2 were hospitalized, one for malaria and one for appendectomy.[2]

Without reports like this, deaths and illnesses remained officially invisible. At the same time that paper made bodies and blood part of the record, paper was also the blood that kept the camp program alive. Paper carried the information that justified the existence of the camp program. Without records of migrants' comings and goings, their struggles and losses; without evidence of camp staff accountability, without measurements of progress, the argument for the camp program and for additional support would be far harder, perhaps impossible, to make.

The camp office was also a node for a type of charismatic authority. Sociologist Max Weber described charismatic authority as based on "a certain quality of an individual personality by virtue of which he is considered extraordinary and treated as endowed with supernatural, superhuman, or at least specifically exceptional powers or qualities... not

Tom Collins with migrant family, Arvin Camp, 1936.
Photograph by Dorothea Lange. *Tom Collins, manager of Kern migrant camp talking with drought refugee and her four sons. California.* November 1936. Courtesy of Library of Congress. https://www.loc.gov/item/2017763223/.

accessible to the ordinary person," and differentiated it from the institutional, rational, legal authority of "the bureau." But in the government camp, bureaucratic and charismatic authority often came together in the camp manager, the officially recognized executive responsible for the migrants living in the camp and the prophet of modern ways of being.[3]

As we have seen in Tom Collins's self-presentation and in descriptions of his work by other officials of the Resettlement Administration, camp managers could radiate charismatic authority. Collins understood that charismatic authority was his most important tool. Those around him agreed. Harry Drobish's praise for Collins at the Commonwealth Club in March of 1936 focused on his particular type of charisma. "He did not strut around with a star on his lapel and a club at his side. He strove to get the campers to work out matters with him." Collins got things done in camp and mended frayed and weary people through subtle persuasion, example, and sympathy. The Resettlement Administration and the Farm Security Administration asked for and cultivated charisma in camp managers out of the belief that the manager's leadership was key to restoring and redeeming the migrants. The managers thus became mission priests for the vision of the RA/FSA: working inside the gate to show migrants the way forward out of destitution and suspicion; working outside the gate to convince locals that the camp program's mission was both intrinsically good and good for California agriculture.[4]

The office in each camp operated on bureaucratic and charismatic authority. Nobody outside of the Resettlement Administration hierarchy could legitimately challenge the bureaucratic authority of the office and of the camp manager. This authority flowed in channels that were largely inaccessible to migrants and locals alike. The manager's charismatic authority was more vulnerable, especially among a people with demonstrated affinities for revivalistic Protestantism. In his capacity as New Deal mission priest, the camp manager had to locate and navigate around other forms of charisma, to convince migrants that *his* way was *the* way and that they should follow him. In some instances, this meant keeping religious leaders outside the gate or at arm's length. In others, it meant holding them surprisingly close.

* * *

A major theme winding its way through this discussion of the camp office is the production and dissemination of knowledge within the camp system. Religion, defined as the beliefs and practices of a people who situate themselves within a tradition of supernatural discourse and intentional community, is present here as part of the knowledge produced about migrants. Information about the migrants' religion was collected and described alongside information about their race, state of origin, former profession, and the make, model, and license plate number of their car. Religion, understood as a set of meaning-making practices tied to a belief that the world works in a particular way and that men and women are better off if they accept that way as right and true, is present here in the religion of the office, the system-wide commitment to producing and disseminating knowledge. It is present in employees of the camp system living up to that commitment, and in their ritualized writing and sending and filing of correspondence and reports.

The reflections of Ms. Hazel K. Peterson at a Farm Security Administration conference in 1938 help make this religion of the office visible. Her topic for the late-September gathering of FSA office personnel was "Office Procedure, Routine and Forms." As a "clerk stenographer" in the Merced, California FSA office, Peterson surely knew her topic well. She spoke of the communal spirit of the ideal office and how it could lift up the downtrodden and strengthen the failing. "Many of us have never discovered our reserve stores of ability because we have formed the habit of becoming easily discouraged," she said. But then she urged conference attendees to abandon their anxiety. "If there is complete cooperation among employees of an office the work and general atmosphere and outlook of the employees should and will be much brighter and more interesting." Peterson then turned to the stuff with which the office worked so often and so well: paper. "Now just a little about Regional Office forms."

> We all think sometimes there are too many forms, but as each and every one was made for a special purpose, we should try to use them to the best of our knowledge. With the many necessary revisions and supplements frequently being made in regard to instructions, we sometimes wonder which one to follow. The best policy which I have found is to study the original instruction. By so doing, you have all basic information in mind and any additions and changes can then be easily applied.[5]

Peterson closed her presentation with an exhortation to the form-filling faithful. "The employee who is interested in his work and delights in it will find that working for the Farm Security Administration is never a burden." The psalmist could not have said it any better.

Hazel Peterson's views on the communal spirit of the office and the meaningfulness of forms, and her faith in the creator(s) of the forms and instructions, are uncommon in their clarity. She was likely chosen to speak because her attitudes were known to be exemplary. The burden of having been chosen almost certainly influenced her to compose a talk that would be received as exemplary.

Religions are, however, dwelling places of exemplars and ideals. Ideals obscure more complicated realities, but also establish important norms to which people can aspire. Peterson addressed her colleagues after the Resettlement Administration had been remade as the Farm Security

Administration. But the values and practices she described had been present in the system from the very beginning.

Instructions and Control

In the eyes of the New Deal officials who planned and ran them, migratory farm labor camps were both sites for sheltering and restoring migrants and sites for studying them. They were part of a bureaucratic system that, in addition to managing properties and administering an aid program, was gathering and saving information, sometimes using that information to show success, learn from failure, and inform decisions; sometimes filing it away as a record of an event that happened, a purchase that was made.

The location in each camp where this gathering and filing and submitting took place was the office of the camp manager. It was also that office and the man who occupied it on whom, according to all accounts, the success of the entire program depended. There would be little reason to come through the gate and no reason to stay if the person in the office were a despot, or a weakling, or a snob, or an ingrate. The man in the office had to approach his job in such a way that he won the trust of the migrants and showed that he would work for their interests within the framework of the camp system.

In August of 1935, Irving Wood, director of the camp program, signed a confidential document titled "Instructions to Camp Managers." In it he laid out the Resettlement Administration's expectations for camp managers and for the office in which they worked. The "Instructions" open with a statement of purpose, followed by two and a half pages devoted to issues that might be described as cultural or atmospheric. What kind of place should the camp manager strive to create for the migrants? Where is the line between encouraged behavior and the merely allowable? How should the camp manager encourage, discourage, and forbid? In short, how should the manager approach the work of managing the camp? The document read in part:

> Your camp is established primarily for the purpose of providing sanitary camp facilities for migratory farm workers. . . . There shall be no distinction as to race, nationality, creed or political affiliation, etc. All

individuals must conduct themselves in a lawful, peaceful, and orderly manner and comply with the rules and regulations of the camp. Individuals or groups who fail or refuse to comply with the rules and regulations, those guilty of unlawful acts . . . or conduct destructive to the peace and order of the community, and those constituting a continuing nuisance from a sanitary, social or legal standpoint, shall not be permitted the use of the camp facilities and may be discharged from the camp.[6]

Of all the sentiments conveyed in this opening statement, the one present in its first word, "Your," is the most important. Irving Wood and the authority present in the Resettlement Administration's Region IX pressed upon the camp manager the responsibility of custody, bordering on ownership, of the federal migrant camp. With the second person possessive, Wood made one man responsible for establishing and maintaining peace, order, and compliance with rules and regulations throughout the camp. In the next literary breath, he instructed managers to remove from the camp those who could not or would not respect and observe the "sanitary, social or legal" standards of an orderly society. This is your camp, Wood instructs, let everyone in. Set the standards for orderly living. Expel those who do not live up to, or at least live toward the standard.

To remove any ambiguity as to the importance of the camp manager to the success of the camp, the "Instructions" circled back on the topic multiple times. Wood wrote, "the harmonious and successful conduct of the camp will depend not so much on its equipment and services as it will upon the Camp Manager." He then added. "In his capacity as a leader and officer, the Camp Manager must exercise tact, consideration, sympathetic understanding, infinite patience, good humor, absolute impartiality and even-handed justice. Discretion and good judgment will dictate the proper course to cope with any situation."[7]

The reasons to emphasize sympathy, humor, even-handedness, and discretion were both to call the manager back to cool reason should his passions begin to overheat, and to remind him that he should aspire to make the camp a partnership. As Wood explained, "It is believed most problems of control and management will be solved in a more expeditious and satisfactory manner through the leadership of the Camp Manager and his enlistment of the support and cooperation of the camp community, rather than by reliance upon the exercise of his authority." Wood wanted his managers to resist the authoritarian impulses that might rise in them, and to remember that they had been put in the camps "by the Administration 'to help workers help themselves.'"[8]

There is a faith pulsing through both these statements and the Resettlement Administration's more general understanding of managerial excellence. It is a Victorian faith in the power of proper speech, dispassionate intellect, and self-control to steer a man through any storm.[9] It also includes an Enlightenment faith in the possibility of impartiality and evenhanded justice. A man who navigates by these stars will be able quickly to diagnose problems with individuals, families, and the migrant community in the camp, and to move them toward resolution. The camp manager was supposed to be the incarnation of this faith among the migrants.

Yet, at the same time that the camp belonged to the camp manager, it was supposed to belong, as much as possible, to the migrants. By coming through the gate to stay, they had not given away their rights as Americans. To the contrary, they had begun the process of reclaiming those rights. The second section of Irving Wood's 1935 "Instructions," titled "Camp Organization and Government," makes this point clearly. "Camps for migratory agricultural workers should be so conducted as to be regarded by the workers as communities in which they can establish and maintain their homes with the same freedom, rights, duties and privileges enjoyed by American workers dwelling in town and city homes."

It was incumbent upon the camp manager to create the proper environment, to sustain the circumstances under which migrants would "regard" this federal camp as a community like any other community in a "town or city." Wood wrote further, "Therefore, insofar as a rapidly changing population will permit, the camps are to be organized on a self-governing, democratically controlled basis." The instructions called the camp manager to select a Camp Committee or, better, to hold elections, and then to work with that representative body "to enforce camp rules and regulations." He was to empower the migrants to organize "social, educational, and recreational activities." According to the "Instructions," the camp manager was to be "the campers' guide, counselor and friend." His relationship with the migrants was to be built on a foundation of shared purpose and shared responsibility.[10]

The camp manager's relationship to the Resettlement Administration, the power that placed him in the camp, was harder to see and was suf-

Ray Mork addresses a group of migrants in Batavia, New York, 1942. Mork managed the Indio and Shafter camps from 1938 to 1941.
Photograph by John Collier, Jr. *Batavia, New York. Elba FSA Farm Security Administration farm labor camp. Ray Mork, FSA official, addressing West Virginia migrants on the night of their arrival.* September 1942. Courtesy of Library of Congress. https://www.loc.gov/item/2017824059/.

fused with a different sensibility. Though seldom completely inflexible, there was little that was truly negotiable in the bureaucratic partnership between the central office and the camp office. The former required and the latter submitted. The camp manager was instructed to keep records and to file regular reports with the hierarchy. The same confidential "Instructions" that expressed faith in the exemplary, rational gentleman, laid out the guidelines for the documenting, processing, and filing of the migrants' very presence in the camp.

To pass through the gate, whether joining the community or leaving it for good, was to encounter immediately the camp office. Irving Wood described this bit of camp choreography in two paragraphs labeled "Registration." "Individuals and heads of parties or families must register with the Camp Manager before setting up camp. Notice of departure," he added, "must also be given." Wood understood that many legitimate reasons could keep a head of family from filling out a registration card immediately upon entry, so he qualified the requirement, "If impracticable to complete registration fully upon admittance of camper the card should be completed on the day of entry."[11] Campers' arrivals and departures were to be documented and filed as data.

The "Instructions" give three reasons for gathering this information. "The purposes for acquiring the data comprehended by the Registration Forms are: 1) to assist the Camp Manager in the operation of the camp." Wood did not describe in any more detail how the information would be used to assist the camp manager, but we can imagine that names and ages and family composition would be useful as he sought to be more welcoming himself and sought to direct camp welcoming committees and support resources more effectively. This data would also give the manager a clearer sense of occupancy patterns and waxing or waning needs for supplies. No amount of data could make an inept manager into an effective one, but in the hands of the right (tactful, sympathetic, patient) man, registration data could make a challenging job more manageable.

The information was also intended to flow from the camp office back to the bureaucratic heart of the program, "2) to supply the Administration with statistical and social data necessary to the formulation of its program and policies." This level of collection, collation, and analysis might lead to conclusions about the flow of migrants around the state or regional employment patterns. A big-picture view like that could be used to support arguments for a new camp location, for expansion of the program, or to inform program officials in their discussions with, for example, local health departments or school authorities concerned about migrants stretching their resources. Similarly, it might lead to changes in program staffing or alterations to the maximum time a migrant family could reside in a camp. The camp program's approach to knowledge put faith in these statistics and their ability to inform and guide.[12]

The final enumerated purpose for collecting registration data was "3.) [to] benefit the migratory workers through the information . . . acquired from them in this manner." The gathering, analysis, contemplation and storage of their information was, in other words, for the migrants' own good. It is a hard sentiment to dispute. To the extent that the camp manager was able to know the migrants better and to make more informed decisions about running their community, the camp would likely be more responsive to their needs. And to the extent that the hierarchy over the camp manager could lobby more effectively, plan more responsibly, operate more efficiently, and answer concerns outside the gate with data from the front lines of this struggle, migratory workers in the camp, and perhaps outside the camps as well, would benefit. It was a negligible price to pay—one's personal information and a thumbnail biography—to enter and, in a virtually unnoticeable way, to support the Resettlement Administration.

Irving Wood's "Instructions to Camp Managers" made clear, though, that registration cards filled out by entering migrants were to be handled with care, that the information present in and flowing through the camp office, the central office, and the camp system was not for all to consume. Nowhere was this point made more forcefully than in the instructions for registering new camp residents. The precise timing of registration was negotiable based on the arriving migrants' circumstances. Access to the registration file, however, was not. "Registration cards must be executed in duplicate and the duplicate forwarded to the Director of the Camp Program when camper checks out; [registration cards] are strictly confidential and [are] not to be shown to anyone, not even a US Marshall or Department of Justice representative without express authority."

The Resettlement Administration was gathering information. Its leaders in California wanted to impress upon camp managers the value of this information and the need to safeguard it. It was not to be turned over to anyone who might either use it against the migrants or try to undermine their confidence in the camp.[13] And by "anyone" Wood meant anyone. Just because a person wore a badge did not mean they could be trusted. Thousands of migrants knew all too well the twin myths of the rule of law and blind justice in agricultural California. Wood repeated the order.

> The data entered upon Registration forms is to be held strictly confidential in every detail and in no event will access to the Registration Card file

in your custody be given to anyone, except on the express authority of the Director of the Camp Program. This ruling applies to local, state, and federal law enforcement officers, as well as all others.[14]

The protection of registration cards from actors outside of the camp system was fundamental to managing a government camp.

This was not information security for its own sake, a wanton expression of bureaucratic anal retentiveness. In fact, it was the very foundation of a migrant's possible faith in the camp system. The currents of legal and political power flowed fast and strong around the migrant. Civil society was deeply uncivil to him or her when incivility served the interests of growers, politicians, civic leaders, or the settled population more generally. If a record of the names and ages and family composition of camp residents made its way into the hands of a powerful grower or a sheriff's deputy or the publisher of a hostile newspaper, that record could be weaponized against those migrants both directly—in their search for work—and indirectly—as a seed of suspicion planted among the migrant population. *Have confidence in the office and in the federal government*, the lesson might go, *and you will pay dearly*. Anything that fed suspicion of government actions could hinder the Resettlement Administration's efforts to bring migrants into camps. The program and its managers needed migrants to have faith in them. Valuing and protecting names and personal information could encourage that faith.

This is not to say that information derived from migrants' registration cards stayed only in the camp office. Indeed, the longest and most specific single section of the "Instructions" is the section describing "reports that must be sent to Central Office." It fills an entire page of the six-page document and is, therefore, longer than the sections on "Camp Organization and Government," the "Policy with Respect to Meetings at which Labor Conditions May Be Discussed," and the section on "Sanitation." The items to be covered in the weekly report included:

> Daily report of camp population showing total number of families or groups at camp; total number of individuals.
> Number cases of communicable disease;
> Number cases illness
> Number destitute persons;

Number dismissed from camp and reasons;
Number referred to other agencies;
Number employed;
Number unemployed;
Number of children at camp; (boys) (girls)[15]

The list goes on. But even this truncated version reveals a bureaucratic need to aggregate statistics from the registration cards and, just below the surface, a charismatic justification as well. The registration cards could give a camp manager a daily tally of the camp population, assuming that migrants leaving the camp had announced their departures, as was required. The number of children in the camp was also knowable through registration information. The manager and the rest of the camp would have known, too, the numbers of campers dismissed and the reasons. Any pencil-pushing bureaucrat could have collected and reported these numbers without leaving the office.

The other numbers, though, required interaction with each migrant family on a daily or a weekly basis. They required a certain kind of interaction, one that involved greetings and conversations, observations and questions, and then tabulation. The camp manager was instructed to be a "counsellor and a friend," but also a quantifier of the counseled and a classifier of friendships. He was both a guide for the migrants and an informant in their midst.

Through the stated requirement in the "Instructions," the heart of the Resettlement Administration drew information gathered by the camp manager to itself weekly. Central office personnel wanted numerical data, but they also wanted descriptions of "local labor conditions" and "happenings of interest pertaining to the camp." They appreciated stories of migrant interactions with the camp manager and with each other. They needed to know this information every week. And they depended on the camp manager and the camp office to collect it.

The flow of information was not always weekly. For instance, the "Instructions" required that a strike be reported immediately, but only asked for equipment inventories "on the last day of the month." Faith in the camp manager was not absolute. The program director had to approve expenditures and words spoken publicly on behalf of the program. Bureaucracy mattered. But there can be no question that the camp manager was the key to the program's success at a local and personal level. Requiring and processing and circulating his knowledge benefitted the camp system as a whole and it also provided a way to manage the manager.[16]

When the system worked as designed, when the call-and-response of requirement and report filled leaders' in-boxes with paper and with data, the central office was pleased. We can see Irving Wood's satisfaction in his letter of February 5, 1936, "Dear Mr. Collins, This is to acknowledge receipt of your report for the week ending February 1, 1936. In every respect your report is most excellent, and I wish you to know that I am very highly pleased with it." Collins was more than living up to expectations set in the "Instructions." But Wood had subsequently seen the need for a refinement, and so proposed a change. "In order that we may have a current census of the number of children in the camp, I have asked Mr. Eddy [then camp manager at Marysville] and I now request of you that you include on page one of your report, following the statistics on the number of families or groups at camp, an item as follows." He continued.

> Number of children in camp
> Then, to the right of this the following classifications:
> Up to 4 years old;
> From 4 to 12 years old;
> From 12 to 18 years old;
>
> I think you will agree with me that this is very valuable information which we should have tabulated.[17]

Wood added more commentary on the contents of Collins's report to the back-end of this request, expressing his pleasure that "the camp population continues to increase and that there are no cases of disease, illness, or destitution, and that it has been unnecessary to dismiss anyone from camp." Later in the letter, Wood noted that the inventory Collins had sent "came at a propitious moment as the custodian for the Corporation has just called upon us for a complete inventory as of the first of the month." The only problem Wood saw was that Collins had neglected to sign the copies of the inventories, which is why they were being sent back to him in triplicate.

Wood wrote to Collins again on May 29, 1936, acknowledging "receipt of . . . weekly reports for the weeks ending May 16th and May 23rd." Again, he was happy. "They were most excellent and I found the newspaper clippings of great immediate value." Wood noted that he was returning with thanks the negatives of "camp pictures" that Collins had provided, and that he appreciated "Miss Ima Migrant," which seems to have been either a doll or a drawing, conceived as a tool for encouraging donations of "old clothes, magazines, etc."[18]

Camp managers and central office staff repeated this pattern systemwide for the life of the program, though as the system grew, so too did the timeline for filing reports, from weekly to monthly, and acknowledgements of reports received became fewer and further between. Nobody complained about this shift, which seems to have sprung from an awareness of the volume of work confronting offices both in the camps and in San Francisco.

Occasionally the information generated by the camp manager flowed further upstream than the central office. On May 28, 1936, Regional Director Jonathan Garst wrote to Rexford Tugwell, head of the Resettlement Administration in Washington, DC, in response to a query about Collins's reports. Tugwell needed help finding some information that Collins had reported. "Mr. Irving Wood has just received word from Dr. Paul Taylor that you have been unable to locate in Thomas Collins Camp Reports [sic] a description of the Camp Government Organization instituted in the Arvin Camp."

That report had become famous within the California hierarchy. Wood didn't have the file in front of him, but he described it to Garst, who described it to Tugwell. "The report covering this matter . . . is illustrated by a number of photographs, this particular report being the report best known in this office as the 52 page weekly report, which broke all records thus far for size." Due to the continued movement of information between camps and the central office, and the retention of that information, Garst was able to provide his boss with something directly from the hand of Tom Collins. "I am enclosing herewith," he wrote, "data relative to camp organization which was just received by Mr. Wood from the Arvin Camp, which develops this particular subject in more detail. I know you will find it most interesting."

The exact reason for Tugwell's request was not stated, but in response to it he received a page describing the various camp committees and their responsibilities. If anyone in Washington, DC doubted that migrants could be rehabilitated under the right conditions, Tugwell could produce testimony from the field that spoke strongly to the contrary.[19]

The need for this data and for managing its flow was existential. To make the case for the existence or the expansion of the camp program, the Director and his staff had to have data that demonstrated and validated their work. They were constantly under fire from adversaries in and beyond California, some of whom resented the "relief" the camps provided to migrants, some of whom resented the "subsidy" the camps provided to growers, and some of whom argued that the camps were not engaged in "resettlement" at all.[20]

There is, though, something else in these requirements to record and report. It is a belief that the efforts of the camp manager and the regulation and guidance of him by the camp program hierarchy would ultimately redound to the benefit of the program and therefore the migrant. It is a progressive, modern faith connected to a generally scientific approach to knowledge. Collecting data, both narrative and numeric, will help us learn about the subjects with whom we are engaged, the dynamics shaping their worlds, their responses to those dynamics, and the effectiveness of our intervention. Through persistent observation, collection, and analysis, this data will become knowledge—knowledge about California agriculture, about its migratory labor force, and about migrants' often non-progressive faiths. The camp manager and his office embodied and enshrined the faith of the government camp program.

The guidelines for embodiment, set forward in the "Instructions," were clear but not draconian. A manager's priorities could vary from day to day, crisis to crisis. The ritual regularity of reporting did not equate to micro-management of the camps. But the light that shined from the camp office was the light of modern rationality and modern ways of knowing.

The camp manager's place in the migratory farm labor program could not have been more axial. The entire system relied on and revolved around the manager and his office. This is not to imply that all managers were equally adept. They were not. It is to argue that the faith of the migrant camp system was concentrated in one particular space and one local male body, and that the image projected from these two was critical to the entire endeavor. The manager gave life to the ideals of the office. The office gave the manager the authority to walk among the migrants attempting to change them. And as the manager gave flesh to a bureaucratic religion, he and his office observed, recorded, and reported on the religions of the migrants. His words described their faiths. His commentary framed their practices. His sense of what was good and right and true colored descriptions of migrants' understandings of what was good and right and true.

Inspecting the Office

It is because of Tom Collins, his office, and the responsibility he felt to the migrants and to the camp program that we know as much as we do about his interactions with camp residents. His history, personal affinities, and sense of his place in the world shaped his depictions of the program and of the migrants. Collins set a standard for narrative presentation of events in the camp that no other manager approached.[21] He also used his office to advocate for the program and the migrants more forcefully than any other manager or, for that matter, any other representative of the camp program hierarchy. Even in his internal reports, filed more or less according to the "Instructions," his devotion to the program is clear. Describing election day for the Camp Committee in the same report requested by Rexford Tugwell (dated February 29, 1936), Collins wrote of the migrants:

> Knocked from one hog wallow to another they have been the forgotten men and women of the State of California,—American citizens exiled to the distant corners of the [growers' worlds] in an effort . . . to create in California a class of peons, uncouth, uncared for, semi-starved, cowed and without ambition to fight the battle of their very existence. With the Resettlement camp raising the morale of the migratory men, women, and children, is there any wonder we hear from migrants such statements as—'a this camp I is a free 'Merican citzn' . . . 'sum one is a noticin us alast and it had ter bee Uncle Sam.' Men and women at the Resettlement camps now hold up their heads.[22]

The Resettlement Administration had helped move these people from shame and servitude to the respectability of franchise-exercising American citizens, Collins wrote, and those associated with the program should be proud.

From the office of a busy Arvin camp with full employment of male migrants and a thirty-cents-an-hour wage in the cotton, Collins reflected on the privilege of working where he worked.

> To those of us fortunate enough to be working with these people, we know our Administration as 'Resettlement.' To those with whom we work, the migratory laborers, it is not 'Resettlement,' it is re-birth, re-living, the rebuilding of hope . . . it is also the rehumanizing of neglected children so long cast adrift on the ditch banks of prairies to wallow around in inhuman and inhumane conditions.[23]

Tom Collins was invested in the government camp program not as a landlord or as a custodian of government property, though he fulfilled those functions dutifully. He was invested as a mission priest, the leader of a community of redemption for a wayward people.

Two confidential reports from Resettlement Administration inspections of the Arvin Migratory Farm Labor Camp help show how the model of relying on the excellence of one man worked both with Collins as manager and with a successor, Robert Hardie. The investigation division of the Resettlement Administration carried out these inspections in June and July of 1936 and then again in February of 1937. The reports were sent to Jonathan Garst, Director of the Resettlement Administration, Region IX. In preparing the first report, Special Agent Herbert H. Mensing drew on a seven-day visit, during which he took stock of the physical plant and placed the program as executed by Tom Collins in the context of guidelines for the camp program and the opinions of Kern County residents.

Special Agent Mensing began his sixteen-page report with a description of the camp's forty-acre plot of land and the story of its acquisition and construction. "The property on which this camp is situated is now held under lease from the County of Kern, California . . . for a period of five years with an option to purchase the property at any time during that period for eight thousand forty eight dollars." After a brief summary of the camp program, he turned his attention to Collins. "The Camp Manager, Mr. Thomas Collins, appears to be extremely competent and by nature ideally suited to supervise the operation of the camp. He is held in very high regard by persons on the project and is ready and willing at all times to assist." Special Agent Mensing noted further that Collins was being helped with the work of the camp by a recreational specialist and a stenographer from the Works Progress Administration. It was a small staff but because migrant self-government was so successful, it was adequate.[24]

Mensing then described the scene for his reader, Director Garst. The camp sat on 40.24 acres of land "seventeen miles southeast of the city of Bakersfield, one and one half miles south of the village of Weedpatch, and five miles west of the town of Arvin, California."[25] There were nicely paved roads providing access to the site and a small bus that could carry a handful of camp residents the seventeen miles to Bakersfield. Landscaping had not yet begun, but there were abundant cottonwood trees on the grounds.

After entering the camp through "a forty foot entrance arch of hand adzed square logs and a rustic gate to match," an arriving migrant family would immediately pass the office. "From the entrance the roadway veers to the right to pass directly in front of the camp office and then divides into two parallel roadways." In most cases new arrivals would spend some of their first hours in camp sitting in that office, filling out the tightly-held registration forms. As Mensing described the interaction.

> Upon arrival at the camp each family is registered upon a form containing the following information—name, number in party, date of arrival, race, origin, probable destination, previous occupation, type of automobile, relationship of others in the party to its head, condition of equipment, and upon employment being found whether transportation to and from work is furnished by the campers themselves or by their employers.[26]

In exchange for this information, Collins would then give the head of the party a camp permit, which "contains twelve reasonable regulations designed to insure proper use of camp facilities and the maintenance of peaceful and orderly relationships among the campers." Mensing included a copy of the camp permit and rules in his report as "Exhibit C."

Just below the spaces where the manager would enter the name of the camp, the name of the head of the migrant party, and the lot to which he assigned them, there is a brief paragraph. "This camp is maintained for your comfort and convenience. With your cooperation we will endeavor to make your stay with us pleasant and advantageous." Then come the rules.

> We request that you—
> Freely consult the manager for advice, assistance or information;
> Report sickness, accident or infection to the manager at once;
> Occupy the lot assigned for your use;
> Keep your tent, lot, and camp grounds orderly and clear . . .
> Turn off water to prevent waste;
> Make proper use of toilets and baths;
> Be orderly and peaceful and a good neighbor;
> Bring no intoxicating liquors or narcotics into camp . . .

It was a compact ritual, to be sure, and one can imagine that given the events and encounters that many migrants endured prior to coming through the gate, it escaped the notice of many. But in this act of exchange the migrant family officially joined the camp community and was, literally, counted as part of it.

At the time of his inspection, Special Agent Mensing found fifty-eight families and "a total of three hundred forty-five (345) campers" living in the Arvin camp. Some quick math gave him an average family size of "approximately six persons." Digging deeper into the demographics, he found 141 children "under eighteen years of age . . . of these seventy-seven are boys and sixty-four girls." There were 139 adult men living in the camp, all of whom had work at the time of his visit. Mensing counted sixty-five women, nineteen of whom were engaged in part-time agricultural work.

In June and July of 1936, the population of the Arvin camp was, he noted, "all of the white race" and as for their original, never-quite-forgotten homes, forty families of the fifty-eight came from the Southwest: Oklahoma, Texas, and Arkansas. Another six called California home, though it isn't clear whether this was because they had once owned or rented homes in California and sent their children to local schools, or because by June of 1936 they had been wandering and squatting so long in California that the meaning of being "from" someplace had changed.²⁷

In addition to whiteness and regional origin, religious tendencies united a large number of the 345 residents of the camp. Here Special Agent Mensing drew on the insight of the camp manager, "Mr. Collins stated that the majority of persons were of the revivalist type, deeply religious and unshakeable in their belief that a beneficent yet vengeful God completely governs even the most minor detail of their lives." To worship this beneficent, vengeful God, a large number of the camp residents were traveling a mile and a half outside the camp to "a Full Gospel Tabernacle . . . at the village of Weedpatch."

It is a terse description of religiousness, gesturing to the migrants' preferred practices but focused primarily on belief. Reading Collins through Mensing for the moment, we see an emphasis on the persistence of migrant belief—"deeply religious"; "unshakeable"—and on the all-suffusing, all-controlling nature of their god. The inspection report seems to point to the migrants' religion as something that was abnormal and that made the migrants different from fully-civilized, modern Americans. The report also conveys a concern that the migrants' omniscient, omnipotent, omnipresent God left precious little space for the necessary work of rehabilitation.²⁸

The concerns implicit in Collins's characterization of migrant religion appear more clearly when placed in the context of the registration ritual that Special Agent Mensing described in the inspection report. It turns out that Collins also used camp registration as an opportunity to provide migrants with wide-ranging guidance, if not to govern "the most minor detail of their lives." After new arrivals filled out their registration forms and received a camp permit and tent platform assignment, Collins presented them with some additional reading materials. According to Mensing,

> "Mr. Collins furnishes each family with a series of booklets which have been virtuously supplied by the Metropolitan Life Insurance Company. These include a cook book and other information regarding health and food. The following titles are typical: (1) 'The Baby' (2) 'Good Posture and Foot Health' (3) 'Tonsils and Adenoids' (4) 'Overweight and

Underweight' (5) 'Good Habits for Children' (6) 'The Family Food Supply' (7) 'Tuberculosis, How to Prevent and Cure It' (8) 'Colds, Influenza, and Pneumonia' (9) 'What is Rheumatism?' (10) 'Out of Babyhood, Into Childhood.' Included in this set of booklets is a publication from the Children's Bureau of the United States Department of Labor entitled 'Infant Care.'"[29]

Collins reflected on this practice in a weekly report submitted to the camp program's main office in January of 1936. He noted that "many of these pamphlets are beautifully illustrated. The language is simple, and the type of a size to make reading very easy." He created packets of booklets for each family and affixed a note explaining that "your camp committee and the camp manager believe you will like these little books."

Collins was using the authority of his position and the prose of the Metropolitan Life Insurance Company, "the United States Department of Labor, Children's Bureau, and the United States Public Health Service," to encourage migrants to see their bodies through the lens of science and, perhaps, to dislodge their vengeful God from terrain that He had no business occupying. If there were any question as to whose authority ought to matter most on questions of diet, foot health, and growing up, a few minutes with one of the publications mentioned by Mensing would have provided the answer. Collins was a welcoming manager and a respected leader of the community. He was also a determined, if subtle, catechist.[30]

The migrants do not seem to have experienced the Met Life healthy living brochures as an assault on their God or an offense to their religious worldview. If they did, they certainly did not hold it against Collins. In fact, Mensing found again and again that Collins was trusted and admired by the migrants. One camp resident, Thomas Maudlin, had been living in the camp for roughly a month but "wished such a camp had been available long ago." He planned to live in the camp for as long as there was work in Kern County, both because he found the camp to be "a wonderful thing" and because "he realized the benefits from the standpoint of health." Maudlin had high praise specifically for Collins. As Mensing recorded, "In his opinion, no better man could have been selected for that position and . . . he felt certain all other persons in the camp were of a similar opinion." Special Agent Mensing couldn't verify that all persons in the camp admired Collins, but he did get corroboration from Mrs. Charles Hunter, Mr. R. L. Titsworth, Mr. A. A. Hooser, Mrs. J. H. Dunham, Mr. Sherman Eastton, Mr. Jess Stephens, Mr. Walter Collins, and Mr. James Nunn.[31]

Thomas Collins identified Walter Collins (no relation) to Special Agent Mensing as "a typical example of what the camp has done to rehabilitate these people." The Walter Collins who spoke to Mensing in the summer of 1936 was a changed man from the Walter Collins who had come through the gate. In general terms, his "self respect" and desire for "decent standards of living" had been restored. More specifically, though, Thomas Collins told Mensing "when Walter Collins arrived at the camp he was an irresponsible, shiftless individual having little concern for his wife and young child." Collins, embodying the ethic described in the "Instructions for Camp Managers," used "patient suggestion and quiet example" to induce Walter "to straighten himself out." He now had a job "earning four dollars per day" in a nearby town and had moved out of the camp but came back regularly because he "apparently felt such a deep debt of gratitude and realized what the camp had done for him." Perhaps more than any other data he could gather, the story of Walter Collins demonstrated that, as Mensing concluded, the camp project "most certainly makes sense as a federal effort."

Seven months after Special Agent Mensing filed his report on the Arvin camp, the investigation division of the Resettlement Administration was back for another look. The camp was now being managed by Robert Hardie and by an assistant manager, Norman Corse. Special Agent Joe E. Schoales was on site from February 3 through February 6, 1937, and then again on February 15, talking, as his predecessor had, with the staff and residents, as well as members of the surrounding community.

Schoales also spent significant time looking through the records in the office, checking up—in ways Special Agent Mensing had not—on the functioning of the office as an office. It had somehow escaped comment from Mensing that the camp manager's office was in the community building and "[did] not afford the privacy necessary for his office (which is contrary to AO 66, dated 10-1-35, paragraph 3 j I.)" It is unclear whether Hardie and Corse raised this concern themselves, or whether it arose from Schoales's experiences inspecting the camp's files while a parade of migrants interrupted his work. The troubling upshot of the location, in Schoales's eyes, was that "the occupants of the camp more or less made a run way out of the Manager's office."[32]

The camp population had grown since the last inspection. Schoales counted eighty families and four hundred and thirty-two campers. Of these, 137 were men over the age of eighteen, ninety-six were women over eighteen. Of the 199 children in camp, 101 were boys and the rest were girls. Schoales reported further on camp demographics, "All of them are of the white race, and all the adults are married." Of the eighty families in camp, forty-five were from Oklahoma, ten were from Texas, seven were from Arkansas, and six were from California. Four families each called Arizona and Missouri home. "At the time of the last inspection, July 1936," Schoales reminded Director Garst and any additional readers, "there were more families in the Camp from Oklahoma than any other state. The same is true at present, the number from Oklahoma having increased from 27 in July to 45 now."

When Special Agent Schoales described the entry of these families into the camp, he focused not on the registration procedure that had drawn the attention of Special Agent Mensing, but rather on how camp residents interacted with the new arrivals.

> Mr. Hardie explained that the occupants of the Camp are not given a medical examination upon arrival, but the Good Neighbor Committee, which consists of a woman representative from each of the three camp units, takes the newly arrived women and girls to the showers to help them bathe and at that time, if the representative . . . observes any condition needing medical attention, she persuades the woman or child needing medical attention to obtain the same from the Camp Nurse, or doctor.

Schoales did not record whether this process was effective at catching illnesses or not, and what, if anything, was done for, with, or by newly arrived men and boys. He did, however, note some troubling data on cleanliness outside the gate: "many of the women and girls coming to the camp . . . have not bathed for periods of six to eight months."[33]

Like Special Agent Mensing, Schoales devoted a great deal of space in his inspection report to the state of the camp's physical plant. In the context of the "Instructions to Camp Managers" and the burden of ownership that document placed on the manager, Schoales's analysis reads like a running commentary on the manager's effectiveness. He noted that insufficient grading of the land led to the camp flooding in heavy rains. He also reported that "In Sanitary Unit No. 3 there are two toilet seats missing."[34]

Beginning on page ten of the report, under the heading "Management Conditions of the Project," Schoales became more direct in his assessment of the degree to which Robert Hardie was fulfilling the letter of the "Instructions." "Mr. Hardie, Manager of the Camp, stated that he tries to let the Occupants of the Camp manage the Camp as far as possible through a representative governing body." This approach was working "very well," according to Hardie, as elections had successfully given willing migrants responsibility for running the Camp Central Committee, the Recreational Committee, the Good Neighbors Committee, and the Child Welfare Committee.

Special Agent Schoales asked Sherman Eastton, the chairman of the Camp Central Committee, for his evaluation of the "Management Conditions." Eastton responded that "Mr. Hardie has proven very capable, but his assistant Norman I. Corse is handicapped by the fact that he is not a good mixer." Four other camp residents spoke "very complimentarily of the present camp management."[35]

Schoales next addressed the state of the office files maintained by Manager Hardie and his assistant. Though their records were not perfect, they were capturing most of the required information and had reasonable explanations for the occasional gap. "The Camp Manager does not keep a copy of Form RR-CF-163, dated 7-6-36, a weekly report of occupants, but the information recorded therein is kept on plain paper in the office."[36]

The registration card file, to which Special Agent Schoales was granted access, was in good shape, though it too wasn't flawless. Out of the fifty forms that he inspected, ten "showed that these parties had come to camp in either a car or a truck but the license number was not recorded." The majority of the deficient registration forms had been filled out by Norman Corse. Corse explained that when migrants came through the gate, they would often get their camp lot assignment, drive to it, and walk back to the office to complete their paperwork while the rest of the family unpacked and set up. Schoales explained further that "they do not remember their [license plate] number at the time of registration, and in these [eight] cases he [Corse] neglected to look after the matter."

This pattern continued when Schoales examined the forms for "parties checked out of the camp." Three of the thirty that he inspected—the forms of Clifford Morgan, James McKenzie, and Sam Dykes, were missing the "date of check out and the destination" that the departing party had in mind. In all of these cases, Assistant Manager Corse had been responsible for the check out. There were, in other words, some blemishes in the records of the office, but most were directly attributable to the assistant, whose record keeping Schoales characterized elsewhere in the report as "negligent."[37]

When it came to inventories of property, however, camp records were nearly perfect. Form RA-BM-49, which was an inventory of all Resettlement Administration (federal) property in the camp, had been filled out and dated December 30, 1936. Hardie and Corse had completed a second inventory on December 31 accounting for "all Corporation (state-owned) property on the project." Both were checked over by Schoales and deemed "correct." Perhaps the blessing of the spotless inventories counterbalanced the evidence of Corse's negligence. In the end, Schoales reported "The camp to date appears to be a successful venture and with the exceptions noted above is being operated in a proper manner."[38]

Put another way, the camp office was working. There were some flaws in record keeping, some departures from procedure, and some less than perfect personalities in the office, but migrants were coming through the gate and were staying. And, in many cases, they were looking after each other and taking charge of the community as far as they were able. The camp system was working too. The flow of data was robust. The office was generating numbers and narratives to be either stored, circulated, or both. The collection, reporting, and aggregation of data on religion and so many other aspects of migrant life and camp operation was itself a religious practice and the camp managers of the Arvin camp, though not identical, were acceptable models of devotion.

Returning briefly to Tom Collins's description and *sotto voce* critique of the faith of his camp's residents, particularly his assessment that the migrants believed in a God who controlled even the minutest details of their lives, we can recall that the inspection reports described above are hybrid documents. They hold many different types of data and fulfill diverse purposes, one of which was to exert control. They require processes. They demand certain virtues. They give evidence of sins of commission and omission. They say in their very creation that the camp manager is being observed and held accountable.

Special Agents Mensing and Schoales were not New Deal Jeremiahs lamenting the decline of a chosen people, but it was their job to know the law (the "Instructions" are one example) and to take the measure of a person and his community in light of it. It does not seem to have occurred to Collins or to anyone else in the camp system hierarchy that the all-controlling God of the migrants and the report-demanding bureaucracy made present in the office might be mirror images of each other.

The Camp Office and Religion as a Bridge

On March 13, 1937, a month after Special Agent Schoales filed his inspection report, Assistant Regional Director Eric Thomsen wrote to Robert Hardie at the Arvin camp. Thomsen wanted numbers. Perhaps the report of occasionally negligent record keeping gave him cause for concern. Perhaps he needed the latest data to prepare for a season of talking to Californians about migrants and rural relief. "Dear Bob," the brief request reads, "Please let me know at the earliest possible moment how many families have passed through camp since we first began operations, giving the dates from which your earliest records begin." There is no indication of the use to which this data will be put, no attempt to identify who is asking, just an expanding statistical wish list. "Also the number of families who have spent more than six months in camp, the number of such families who are still in camp, the average length of residence of all families now in camp and all families who have been in camp."[39]

This request from a senior administrator in Region IX sent Bob Hardie to the camp office and the files he maintained there. He researched. He compiled. He tabulated. And then, on March 18, he responded. "Dear Mr. Thomsen, With regard to information asked for in your letter of the 13th, please be advised of the following."

> Total number of families through the camp since we began operations—364

Date of formal opening—December 12, 1935
Date of first arrival—December 12, 1935
Number of families with more than six months residence—45
Number of families with more than six months residence still in camp—37
Average length of residence of families now in camp—6.36 months
Average length of all families who have been in camp—1.86 months

Hardie closed with an apology. Thomsen had also been interested in statistics regarding the number of families receiving medical care. "It is impossible even to estimate," he wrote, "our only records are weekly reports, and none of Tom's are on file in this office. Sorry that we could not be of more assistance in this respect."[40]

The system worked as it should, generating data in response to a request. Now Thomsen could convert that data into knowledge, truths about the migrants, their circumstances, and the federal camp program that could shape attitudes and actions within and beyond the Resettlement Administration hierarchy.

Using data from the Arvin camp, Assistant Director Thomsen could tell many different stories to many different audiences. He could begin by offering context. The camp had been operating for sixteen months, but only one cotton crop had come in in that time, and when it came to drawing migrants to Kern County and employing them, cotton was king. In terms of the cycles of Kern County agriculture, it was early to be judging the effectiveness of the camp. He could also remind an audience that he had received the data from his camp manager in March, and that it would be four months before late summer harvests brought another peak in the employment cycle. In other words, the occupancy rate was quite good given the availability of work.

If Thomsen were speaking to a church group or any group of concerned citizens, he could then tell them that for every month the camp had been in operation, twenty-six families had moved from ditch-banks, roadsides, and filthy grower-operated camps to the safer, cleaner, more hospitable environs created by the Resettlement Administration. He could argue from numbers that as migrants became more accustomed to the idea of a federally-managed camp and its communal elements, they were choosing to stay longer. Of the forty-five families who had stayed in the camp six months or more, thirty-seven of them were in the camp currently.

He could also point to the spike in average length of residency and speak to the absolutely critical role that the camp was playing in giving migrant families refuge during the slack, hungry months after the cotton harvest. The migrants had chosen to ride out the cold, wet winter in the government camp, rather than try their luck on the road. Was this statistical support for the view that the white migrants were different than their Mexican and Filipino counterparts? Evidence that they were more domestically inclined? Less eager to follow the crops? Or was the gate serving as a barrier to undesirables, as Tom Collins suggested it would? Was the camp attracting a higher type of migrant, less suspicious, more communally inclined?[41]

Whatever the case, Thomsen could conclude that there was something more than financial incentive holding migrants in the camp; that these families were looking to work, to earn, and to eat, but that they were also looking for some stability and for a home, however modest. Assistant Director Thomsen would have to concede that the Resettlement Administration was not revolutionizing California agriculture. But he could certainly argue that his agency was restoring dignity to some of the region's most vulnerable workers.

This is the kind of knowledge Thomsen could produce from camp-generated data. Indeed, it was the kind of knowledge Thomsen did produce in a lengthy letter to Nellie Porter of Walnut Creek, California on August 14, 1936. Mrs. Porter, who identified herself as a member of a "missionary society," had written to Tom Collins seeking "information on migrant groups in California." She was preparing for the "next meeting" of her missionary group, at which they would be "studying these people."

Mrs. Porter was well aware of the limits of her knowledge and of her biases. Echoing words Harry Drobish spoke to the Commonwealth Club in March of 1936, she wrote, "Newspapers are about the only source of information for those of us on the outside" and the press focused on stories of "strikes and threats of strikes." She wrote on, "Having lived in a farming community the past two years, my sympathies have been on the side of the farmer," but she wanted to hear the other side and was hoping to learn about "the conditions in your camp."

Collins did not answer Mrs. Porter directly. He followed the letter of the "Instructions for Camp Managers" and forwarded her request to Assistant Director Thomsen with the comments, "You will note she would like to have the information by or before August 27," and "You will also note she is a missionary." Thomsen dutifully penned the official response.[42]

"I am particularly happy," Thomsen began, "that, as a church group you should want to study the circumstances which govern migratory labor, the Church has a very distinct contribution to make in this field and, I think, more than a moral obligation to make it." He did not describe further what that contribution was. We are left to guess the meanings of the phrase "more than a moral obligation" and of the label "the Church." Did he mean to imply with the former that it was God's will that church groups assist in the migratory labor situation? When he imagined "the Church," which faiths and classes and races and politics were allowed inside? Thomsen regretted that the members of the missionary society couldn't visit the camp for a few days to get to know the community and its residents. This would have been "the best thing." But with time and travel making a visit difficult, he offered instead to "picture to you briefly what the camp looks like, and then . . . what goes on in it."[43]

Thomsen's picture draws directly on the inspection report authored by Special Agent Mensing. His knowledge, developed from Mensing's data, became Mrs. Porter's knowledge. "As you enter the camp through a nicely made rustic gate, set in an arch of hand-adzed square logs, you have the manager's little home on your left and the office and community building on your right." The community building held not only the camp office, as Special Agent Schoales would later lament, but also storage space, a library, and "a large room for the sewing project the women of the camp have organized." He then directed Mrs. Porter's attention to the presence of a "nursery and first aid building" where you could either find children playing or, if one came on the right day:

> The visiting physician and the camp nurse . . . having one of their frequent clinics intended to give the camp families the medical care and protection which all of us like to take for granted as indispensable means of civilized living. As indeed they are, for unless we somehow manage to

provide the necessary medical care for all who need it, how can we guard against the spread of epidemic disease which may break out anywhere ... and is no respecter of class barriers.

In finishing this portion of the picture, Thomsen drew on the sentiment that Irving Wood had expressed in the opening section of the "Instructions for Camp Managers." "We are very much concerned with setting these camps up at the very least as a means of sanitary living."[44]

To emphasize how seriously they took this mission, Thomsen turned to numbers. If the missionary society were to visit, they would "quickly discover that for every thirty-two families, there is a sanitary unit or utility building with a women's and a men's section. The women's section contains 4 two-compartment cement laundry trays, six showers and dressing rooms, six water closets and one sixteen foot galvanized iron wash sink with double faucets." He continued, "The men's section is similarly equipped to meet the needs of the men and boys in camp." The commitment to sanitary living was codified and quantifiable.

Thomsen devoted another section of his letter to the ways in which the migrants realized the camp program's goal of democratic self-governance, describing in detail the various camp committees and their contributions to community life inside the gate. Though he had surely seen these programs in action, he depended quietly on Collins's reporting for his descriptions, paraphrasing Collins's prose frequently. This dependence became more obvious in Thomsen's description of the camp population as people. Who were they? Where did they come from?

> As I study the weekly camp reports I discover that the group is almost entirely a native, white American group (96%) which mostly hails from Oklahoma, Texas, Arkansas, and California, with a constant sprinkling of citizens of almost every other state in the union, coming one or two at a time as economic necessity has driven them farther and farther west; 86% of them have formerly been either farm owners or tenants, or farm laborers; the remaining 14% though in more recent times working in cities and towns ... are almost invariably country born and bred.

Using numeric and narrative evidence, Thomsen was drawing the migrants and the missionaries closer together. These are white, rural folk like you, he is saying. They have been pushed into this situation by economic circumstance. Even those who haven't come to California directly from a farming community have rural America in their blood. "They do the things and think the thoughts which are characteristic of any number of common folk living in small country towns, especially in the South and Southwest."

Lest any members of the missionary society associate southern country living with violence, filth, or moral depravity, Thomsen described precisely what he meant. "They are usually sober, hard-working, self-respecting, and deeply religious; but equally frequently under-nourished, under-privileged, untutored and very poor in this world's goods." Experience had shown him that their poverty was the result not of character deficiencies or an unchecked sinful nature, but rather of "the barest economic accident." In fact, when it came to character, they were remarkable. He testified, "by sheer elementary virtues of frankness, honesty, simplicity and Christian neighborliness they often put me to shame."[45]

Before closing his letter to Mrs. Porter, Assistant Director Thomsen turned again to statistics, this time to underscore the need for the Resettlement Administration's work in California. For all of their Christian neighborliness and lived commitment to virtue, the migrants' reality in this moment was destitution. "You will not quite appreciate the conditions which govern their living under the provisions of the Resettlement Administration until you know the conditions under which they have so often to live elsewhere."

To appreciate the inside, Porter had to understand something of the outside. Thomsen cited descriptions of unsanitary conditions, of houses made of "wood, tin, paper boxes or such cast off material as can be obtained in the vicinity." He cited accounts of the connection between poor housing conditions and labor unrest. He wanted Mrs. Porter's missionary society to know that the problem California was facing was not small. "The State of California Division of Immigration and Housing reports for 1932–34 that 3543 labor camps were inspected and a total of 141,827 persons were found housed therein." According to those inspection reports, conditions in these labor camps were "primitive in the extreme."[46]

Thomsen ended his letter by expressing the hope that "I have shared with you enough of our knowledge of the conditions under which migratory workers live and work to give your members the incentive to seek the facts which may govern your own immediate locality." Perhaps knowledge would inspire a thirst for more knowledge. After offering to answer any additional questions they might have, he wrote, "And I should likewise be grateful if you would share with me whatever discoveries you make on our own, as they might serve us usefully in trying to meet the needs of the situation."[47]

Though it wasn't required by Resettlement Administration procedure, Thomsen sent a copy of his letter to Nellie Porter to Tom Collins back at the Arvin camp. Collins responded immediately, positively ebullient over Thomsen's account. The letter to Porter, Collins gushed, was too good to be kept in a filing cabinet in the office; there was work that it could do in the world.

> I would strongly suggest that your letter to Mrs. Porter be mimeographed and placed with the Division of Information for general distribution through its regular channels. Frankly, I consider the letter the finest exposition of the work Resettlement is doing for Migratory Laborers. It would be a pity to have that letter rest in Regional files, when it could do so much as an ambassador of sympathetic understanding of the problem with which we are confronted.

Along with such high praise for Thomsen, Collins also sent the "weekly statistical summaries for the periods ending August 8 and August 15," fulfilling his end of the knowledge production covenant. And then he closed with an expression of his love for the work and for the people. "Every day makes me appreciate more deeply the privilege and the honor that is mine—working with these plain, simple, frank and honest American citizens. Truly, we are happy."[48]

Whether Thomsen followed Collins's strong suggestion and sent his letter to Mrs. Porter to Fredrick Soule in the Division of Information for wider dissemination, or whether Collins filed the letter in his office for subsequent camp managers to read, Thomsen's letter to the missionary society was indeed born again. In early 1937, Robert Hardie, manager of the Arvin camp, addressed two chapters of the League of Women Voters, one serving the city of Bakersfield and the other serving Kern County. A reporter from the *Bakersfield Californian* covered the former event and recounted Hardie's description of self-government in the migrant camp and the roles of the various camp committees. Hardie's account drew heavily from Thomsen.

A separate article covering the Kern County event shows that Hardie's reliance on Thomsen, though not complete, was no accident. This second article described Hardie's presentation at the "junior college lecture hall" as "brilliant," and devoted most of the article to direct quotes. Hardie was quite forceful in arguing that the migrants were not invaders, explaining, "migratory workers, whether native Californians or recent arrivals from other states, are here because they are needed."

Hardie also seems to have been eager to position himself and his program as in no way revolutionary. "If most of them did not find work here they would not come. If they did not, on the whole, find wages which they would accept, they would not stay." He then offered an assurance drawn directly from Thomsen's letter.

> Our weekly camp reports will show that we are dealing with a 98 percent native white American group hailing mostly from Oklahoma, Texas, Arkansas, Arizona, and California with a constant sprinkling of citizens from almost every other state in the Union, coming one or two at a time as economic necessity has driven them farther and farther west. By sheer elementary virtues of frankness, honesty, simplicity and Christian neighborliness, they often put us to shame.[49]

Advocating for the nobility and perseverance of the migrants "in the midst of deplorable circumstances which would have surely tried the saints," Hardie brought the intertwined charismatic and bureaucratic authority of his office to bear. He stood before a local audience in Kern County, led "brilliant" discussions, and related narrative data based on personal relations with the migrants. He sought to reframe the "migrant problem" not as an invasion of unwashed, untutored, unworthy poor, but as an expression of California's agricultural economy and the operation of market forces in and around it.

Dr. M. A. Gifford, Chief Health Officer in the Kern County Health Department, attended Hardie's presentation to the Bakersfield League of Women Voters and forwarded a newspaper clipping describing the event to Thomsen. Gifford wrote that he was, "proud of the able way

[Hardie] presented himself. I'm sure you and Mr. Collins would have appreciated hearing him too."⁵⁰

It is hard to imagine that camp program officials would have taken issue with any aspect of the talks when so much of the knowledge conveyed had been produced and processed and approved by Collins, Thomsen, and the bureaucratic apparatus of the Resettlement Administration. The migrants—white, rural Americans—were committed to hard work and, as the records demonstrated, to democracy as well. What was more, they weren't just good Christians, they were better Christians—more neighborly, stronger in the midst of suffering—than the reformers who worked with them and the community members who so often shunned and slandered them. This was, at least, the knowledge that the office produced for the League of Women Voters in early 1937.

Thomsen's letter and Hardie's talks are siblings, if not identical twins. They share genetic material and a general tone toward their subjects. In making the migrants legible to the surrounding community, Thomsen and Hardie relied on demographic data and on accounts of progress within the camp system. They also presented the migrants' religion as modern and largely domesticated. Their Christianity was evident in their kindness and perseverance. Their faith presented no obstacle to the prevention and care of ailments and, though "revivalist," "unshakeable," and deep, it was in no way off-putting.[51]

The Camp Office and Religion as a Wedge

Tom Collins was an energetic producer of knowledge about the theologies and religious practices of the migrants. His upbringing in a Catholic orphanage and his early immersion in Catholic education likely trained his eye for religious subjects. But he also saw building knowledge about migrant religious beliefs and practices as central to his role in the camp system. He wrote in February of 1936, "For proper camp management it is essential that we know their songs, hymns, religious beliefs and acquired peculiarities due to environment."[52] Collins grasped, correctly, that there were deep differences between the religious attitudes of camp officials and the migrants who came through the gate. He also learned that familiarity with migrants' beliefs could help him understand why some migrants acted as they did, and that knowledge of their hymns could give him hints as to what was going on in their worship services.

Collins's reports from the Arvin camp offer extensive descriptions of groups in and around the camp, their beliefs, practices, and prospects for modernization. He was intensely interested in religiously-expressed suspicions of medicine and the alternate approaches that migrants sometimes took to healing. He had encountered this phenomenon at the Marysville camp in 1935, but wrote and reflected on it most extensively as the manager of the Arvin camp.

Collins opened his report for the week ending January 25, 1936 with a practical concern. Because some migrants were coming through the gate in desperate circumstances and with no tent, he requested that the Resettlement Administration offer tents for sale inside the camp, perhaps on an "installment pay" plan. Collins then reflected voluminously on religion among the migrants, writing of himself again in the plural. "From our observations and deductions at Marysville we were able to get some key to the [religious] situation by attending regularly, the services of the various non-organized religious groups, such as the Holy Rollers, Full Gospelites, the Apostles of Paul, etc." He noted that his "experiences at Marysville were verified by . . . experiences here [at Arvin]," and that he could now tell the difference between regular worship and a healing service:

(1) When the singing is "peppy," the voices of the prayers lusty, the harmony outrageous, clapping of hands in keeping with the tunes, and the services lasting from a half hour to hour, that all were well physically and (of course) spiritually. We had nothing to fear from this group.
(2) When the singing is a droll, the voices low and gradually ascending to a long whine, the tent flaps down, and the services intermittent, that someone was quite ill. Yet when we reached the tent we would find no one abed although many would be sitting on the bed. It seems a lookout is on the job to warn of the approach of anyone, be it man or devil, and since the people seldom take off their clothing when they go to bed, the management has consistently failed to locate the person or persons ill.[53]

In case personnel in the central office or elsewhere in the hierarchy were struggling to imagine the scene, Collins added one last auditory detail.

"On a still night, this class of service sounds very much like a dog on a distant hill, baying a mournful ritual at the full moon." Howling dogs were, to say the least, not the most flattering comparison that Collins could have chosen for his campers and their approach to worship.

Collins reported again on migrants' ritual approaches to sickness and healing in early May of 1936. The camp was in the midst of a measles outbreak that happened to coincide with increased cases of the mumps and whooping cough. "Usually, the whole group, under such circumstances, could be expected to congregate in the tents and carry on as all good Jehovaites do—shouting, exhorting, and praying to chase off the devils who brought the measles."[54]

In an attempt to prevent such a gathering and, perhaps, to counter its theological interpretation of illness, Collins had made a garden plot available for the migrants to cultivate. His report indicates that this simple distraction encouraged the worried "Jehovaites" to focus on more earthly matters and, for the time being at least, to leave the healing to the doctors. He addressed the topic again six weeks later with many migrants still suffering from various maladies: four cases of flu, five of tonsillitis, three malaria, four dysentery, nine measles, six mumps, and a miscarriage. The garden plot distraction had only been the beginning of a larger and largely successful conversion effort. As Collins wrote, "Despite the sickness reported, we experienced no general attempts to band together for praying, exhorting, and 'rolling'. We are most thankful such experiences are behind us. It is gratifying to know that our educational program has done much to enlighten the migrants in the value of medical care."[55]

These descriptions of theological tendencies and specific practices have a distinctly anthropological flavor to them. They are studies, albeit brief ones, of the migrants as people. They document attempts by displaced men and women to find order in a disordered world and to name and address failings in their bodies. In observing and recording the activities of the migrants, Collins placed himself in a lineage that connected him to the anthropologists of his day, and also to numerous distant relatives in the Catholic communion who cataloged indigenous religious practices and judged them unsparingly. And as with most anthropological field notes, modern and ancient, Collins's reports reveal a great deal about their author.

Collins's secularizing inclinations figure prominently in his accounts. He is uncomfortable with, and often disdainful of, manifestations of charismatic Protestantism that make broad claims to authority in the realms of the body, morality, social order, and economics. He also possesses a bias, faintly though by no means exclusively Catholic, against disorder in worship, community, and society. Confronted with inversions of social roles, confusion around the sacraments, or a scrambling of epistemological categories, Collins collects data, imparts judgment, and also attempts remedies. Moreover, as he wrote detailed and often quite sympathetic descriptions, Collins made clear to his audiences that he stood apart from, if not over, his subjects.

At the conclusion of his much-discussed fifty-two-page illustrated report for the week ending February 29, 1936, he told a story of migrant appreciation for an act of largesse that brought unexpected food items inside the gate. "Sunday, after the distribution of the fruits, nuts and ice cream," he wrote, "a woman rushed up to the manager." Her excitement at the boon made it a struggle for her to articulate her feelings, so she threw an arm around Collins and "shrieked"

> Jesus lufs us yer kain see
> Tho poor farmer folk we bee
> We has to trafel all ofer the erf
> Ter see if we kain allus gits wuk[56]

Setting aside Collins's rendering of the woman's English, his description of the encounter reveals a wide gulf between him (and his readers in the camp system hierarchy) and the migrant subject (and at least some camp residents). According to Collins, he is the level-headed, competent, benevolent, and somewhat detached informant, the adult in charge, the manager. The migrant woman is the bewildered, disordered, child-like subject. She is overcome with excitement. She is physically too familiar. She shrieks out her gratitude in an ill-rhyming adaptation of a Sunday School song. Collins did not describe the woman as savage or primitive. He may not have thought of her in such terms. But he clearly saw a vast space between the two of them and, it is fair to say, between the two groups they represented.

Collins wrote often of the migrants in general terms, without identifying individuals by name. The files of his office also contain myriad examples of bureaucratic portraiture, pointillist flashes of names and data on rosters and petitions and meeting minutes. But for all his professed interest in "the human side" of working in government camps, his files contain little that might be described even loosely as biography. His discussions of migrant religion, though frequent and detailed, are also imprecise when it comes to particular bodies, names, and families. The howling dogs, the "Jehovaites," the credulous audiences for faith healers and other charlatans, remain anonymous in the files, almost as if there is a confidence Collins wishes to keep, aspersions he will not cast, a hope of reform that he holds out for all.

Tom Collins was deeply interested in the religions he encountered inside and outside of the gate. He was almost never interested in connecting religious identities to particular migrants. A glaring exception to this rule was Georgie Nunn, a young woman evangelist who all but forced herself and her faith into the records of the camp office. Georgie Nunn came to the Arvin camp in April of 1936 with eleven family members, a functioning "autotrailer," and little else. Her family was destitute. They registered upon arrival, presumably received some booklets from the Metropolitan Life Insurance Company, and then, since they had no tent, no money, and little food, George Nunn, head of the party and Georgie's father, asked about relief. They hadn't been in California long enough to be eligible, so Collins referred them to the camp committee. The Nunn's fellow camp residents arranged a five-dollar line of credit at a local store.[57]

The men of the Nunn family did themselves proud and found work almost immediately. With work came earnings and with earnings came the ability to purchase. Harry Drobish wrote of the family's ascent in typically terse prose. "George Nunn arrived about April 15, with 12 in family. No tents. One auto trailer. Today has two tents, a new auto, beds, household furniture, ice box."[58] Papers from the Arvin office contain other bits of data suggestive of the Nunn family's process of acclimation to their new life. Minutes of a camp committee meeting on June 29, 1936 mention "Mr. Nunn" in connection with the Unit 1 Good Neighbors committee. Transcribed minutes from the July 13th meeting include the line, "Recomended That Mr. Nunn be asked by important indivigel to do his camp duties."[59]

Most Nunn family members inhabit the office files like the other camp residents. Georgie Nunn was different. She came to Collins's attention because she was relentlessly gregarious, an avid gossip, and a pentecostal evangelist given to repeating the "clarion call" of "Praise God for Victory." With this mix of attributes in mind and with a reformer's desire to change them, Collins hired Georgie as his housekeeper.

In his report for the weeks of July 11 and July 18, 1936, Collins described the circumstances leading to his decision to hire Georgie. It wasn't that she showed an aptitude for domestic work or had a flair for cooking. These would, in fact, prove to be weaknesses. Rather, he judged her to be a nuisance around camp and hoped to diminish and redirect her energies. "Now for Reverend Georgie," Collins wrote, "She found it difficult to sit still or keep her tongue quiet. She would roam about the camp—in one tent out the other. She soon gathered all the gossip possible and for some weeks she was our camp newspaper. Georgie never missed a crumb of gossip."[60]

Not only was she transgressing domestic boundaries and creating a market for the hidden lives of others, she also talked endlessly with the manager and with anyone who came through the gate. Collins reported that Georgie made herself the unofficial camp greeter and office muse. "As news became scarce, she decided to haunt the camp manager," he wrote. "Many times a day she would go to the office. She would stand by the door and blather away about this and that and these and those. When visitors arrived she would stand by the car and jibber and jabber for many minutes. She soon became a 'camp pest.'" Collins's answer was to offer her a job, which "she gladly accepted." He paid her twenty-five cents per hour out of his own pocket—the same rate that the men in her family were making in the field.[61]

The new role taxed Georgie's talents but had the intended effect of changing her behavior. "She gradually lost her contacts with many of the campers and as a result restricted her visits to her close neighbors." The redrawing of the lines of community in what Collins saw as a more conventional way came with an added benefit. By spending more time with her true neighbors, Georgie came to know a young man named Noah Stephens. Noah had been in the camp since February of 1936,

Georgie Nunn and Noah Stephens, Arvin Camp, 1936. Photographer unknown. Appears in Thomas Collins's "Reports for the weeks ending July 11 and July 18, 1936."

largely keeping to himself, first because he was recovering from jaundice and then because he liked it that way. His personality seems to have been as different from Georgie's as could be, but the two clicked and, in Collins's words, "the Reverend Georgie launched her Ark of Love with Noah as the skipper." By the second week of July, the ark had carried the young couple through courtship and into the safe harbor of marriage, but only after Noah agreed to let Georgie stay on as Collins's housekeeper.

Collins noted that Georgie saw the marriage as key to Noah's salvation. In her eyes, "Noah's virtues" had all been "acquired since she met him—no drinking, got the Faith, baptized, a Christian, goes to church and 'don't treat her rough.'" He continued, "She takes full credit for saving Noah's soul and since she saved it she feels it is her duty to assure Noah continued salvation."[62]

The sailing may have been smooth for Georgie and Noah's Ark of Love, but her work as Collins's housekeeper was considerably more storm-tossed. In his report for the week ending June 6, 1936, Collins documented still more domestic ineptitude. "Our migrant woman preacher, housekeeper is quite an interesting holy soul," he wrote. "She cooked a dinner for us and called us over. After sitting at the table several minutes she brought in the dessert, and coffee. Then followed the soup, stone cold." Confused by the order of presentation, Collins "asked for dinner." Collins described the ensuing conversation.

"S'funny. I done cooked supp'r. At least I thinks I did."
She had put the meat and vegetables in the ice box.
"My mind aint clicked ter day right."
Moral: Never hire a housekeeper with the unusual qualifications—preacher—romancer. The cooking will be far from heavenly.[63]

But in Collins's eye, Georgie's irksome presence in the manager's house was preferable to her unannounced, disruptive, and, presumably, unwelcome presence in the tents of other migrant families. And so the arrangement continued. By the time of his mid-July profile of Georgie and Noah, Collins had realized that she was not going to grow into her job and that her personality was not going to change drastically. He described her priorities:

1) entertaining visitors at manager's house
2) having her husband rock her before he goes to work and for hours after he returns.
3) saving souls through her preaching
4) conducting revival services anywhere, any time
5) TALKING [sic]
6) housekeep[ing][64]

Perhaps it was some consolation to Collins that Noah also suffered because of Georgie's lack of domestic acumen. In early September, a few weeks before he finally let her go, Collins recorded a breakfast conversation with Georgie, "our 'sanctified, saved and salivated' housekeeper," in which she described how Noah had "fhrowed up, fhrowed up, and fhrowed up" the previous night.

When Collins finally "dismissed" Georgie, an act that he described facetiously as "a mortal sin," the reason he gave was her "far from heavenly" cooking. "Despite her holiness and her ability as a preacher and her closeness to the Deity we found ourselves slowly starving to death." He continued, "It got so that the Reverend would fail to show up at all. Then there were times when she would show up all in a bluster of heavenly abandon but without whim and without the urge to prepare us a meal." He closed this account of the termination of Georgie Nunn's employment with her signature phrase, "So one and all let's join in the chorus, 'Praise Gawd Fer Vittery.'"[65]

Tom Collins's reports focused intently on Georgie's struggles to operate in and make sense of the world around her. According to Collins, she needed him (or some modern mentor) to redirect her energies and sculpt her public persona. And in spite of Collins's work with Georgie, and his unquestionable affection for working among the migrants, she fell short of his expectations.

The reason for Georgie's failings can't be reduced to her charismatic Protestantism, but her beliefs and practices serve as a clear marker of her intractable, loopy marginality. Collins's internal reports name her alternately Reverend Georgie, the Reverend Holiness Georgie, and the Reverend Holy One. In a letter of July 7, 1936, Collins told Harry Drobish that Georgie "still sings your praises. You have all the Christian attributes, she believes. She does have some doubts as to whether you have as yet had the tongues.'"[66] The myriad ways in which she departed, laughably, from the social, intellectual, and religious norms for which Collins and those around him advocated became part of the Resettlement Administration's knowledge about Georgie and her people.

This knowledge might have stayed within the circulatory system of the Resettlement Administration, moments of condescension filed alongside accounts of redemption and noble struggle. But John Steinbeck came through the gate of the Arvin camp in 1936. He was hoping to tell the story of Dust Bowl migrants in agricultural California.

The Office, *The Grapes*, and Migrant Protestantism

John Steinbeck's novel *The Grapes of Wrath*, published in 1939, is inextricably intertwined with Tom Collins and with the bureaucratic workings of his office. On assignment from the *San Francisco News* to write a series of articles on the Okie migration and California agriculture, Steinbeck visited Collins several times between 1936 and 1938. The two men developed a friendship and a substantial correspondence.

Steinbeck spent weeks reading through Collins's reports and other papers, seeking out stories, characters, and turns of phrase, work that added to the deep realism of the novel and made the articles successful precursors to it. Steinbeck and Collins also traveled through the San Joaquin Valley together, offering direct relief to squatters during the bitter winter rains and floods of 1938. In his writings on the struggles of migratory farm workers, Steinbeck relied heavily on Collins's files.[67]

The Grapes of Wrath is not a novel about Oklahoma per se. It is a novel about Oklahomans and other agricultural migrants trapped between long-accepted but increasingly obsolete and destructive patterns of land use and the dehumanizing practices of industrial farming on California's vast plantations. Steinbeck knew this terrain quite well. Nevertheless, his reliance on documents produced by the camp office was real and is traceable. He lifted the lives of men and women from Tom Collins's files and re-formed those lives to amplify the othering force of Okie Protestantism and to convince readers that some migrants' beliefs and practices were, at best, primitive.[68]

Not surprisingly, given Collins's fascination with Georgie Nunn, she and her faith are woven into *The Grapes of Wrath*, though neither is immediately recognizable. Far from the young, quirky, evangelist, Steinbeck's incarnations of Georgie, which he signaled linguistically, behaviorally, and religiously, are either dying or wholly unlikable. Three examples are especially salient. Early in the novel, a voice like Georgie's rises from the aged Granma Joad, who upon Tom's return from prison, "bleated her terrible war cry: 'Pu-raise Gawd fur vittory.'"[69] Steinbeck's word choice is telling. Granma Joad bleats like an animal. Her words of praise are a "war cry." Not sure whether to classify her as animal or savage, Steinbeck chose to do both.

Georgie later inhabits the body of a female "Jehovaite" who describes herself and her companions as "in Holiness." "Jehovaites" were among the most disruptive Protestant groups in camp, according to Collins, who described the sounds of their religious services as akin to "a dog on a distant hill." Like Georgie, the nameless woman in Steinbeck's novel praises God for "vittory" and violates "domestic" space when she comes uninvited to Granma Joad's make-shift deathbed. As Steinbeck imagined the scene, "Her eyes were bleared and indefinite, and the skin sagged to her jowls and hung down in little flaps. Her lips were loose, so that the upper lip hung like a curtain over her teeth and her lower lip, by its weight, folded outward." The woman imposes herself on Ma Joad offering to "hol' a meetin—a prayer an' grace" to bring the "sweet breath of Jesus" to the dying woman. Ma refuses but must listen as the revival gets going in a nearby tent. Steinbeck picked up Collins's canine analogy and ran with it. In his treatment the sweet breath of Jesus becomes the hot breath of dogs.[70]

> The sentences of exhortation shortened, grew sharper, like commands... in the middle of a response one woman's voice went up and up in a wailing cry, wild and fierce, like the cry of a beast; and a deeper woman's voice rose up beside it, a baying voice, and a man's voice traveled up the scale in the howl of a wolf. The exhortation stopped, and only the feral howling came from the tent, and with it a thudding sound on the earth.

Steinbeck then describes the "gabbling screams of a hyena" and, in the revival's aftermath, "whining, like that of a litter of puppies at a food dish."[71] The Protestantism ricocheting around the inside of that tent reveals that its practitioners live their lives balanced precariously between human and animal existence.

But the character in *The Grapes of Wrath* who bears the closest relationship to Georgie Nunn in terms of her theology and the space she occupies, enters the story on the exact terrain where Collins and Reverend Georgie interacted for nearly seven months: "Weedpatch Camp," a fictionalized version of the Arvin camp. In the novel, the Weedpatch camp gives the Joad family a glimpse of paradise, as only normalcy in the midst of catastrophe can. It is clean and orderly with hot showers and flush toilets. The camp is suffused by a spirit of neighborliness.

But this New Deal Eden houses a pentecostal serpent named Lizbeth Sandry, a "stocky woman" with a brown face, black eyes, and a penchant for intrusiveness. The racially vexing Lizbeth Sandry appears first to a pregnant and depressed Rose of Sharon Joad and reads the government camp against the grain. "They's scandalous things goes on in this here camp," she announces, "They ain't but a few deep down Jesus-lovers lef'." The problem, she explains, is the "hug dancin'" and the "stage plays," which are an offense to a strict, judging God. As proof of divine displeasure, Sandry tells of two women who suffered miscarriages after they acted in plays and danced too close to their partners. She then enjoins Rose of Sharon to "take heed a that pore chile in your belly an keep outa sin."[72]

In a second encounter, Sandry tells Ma Joad, "They's wicketness all around about wicket goins on that a lamb'-blood Christian jes can't hardly stan'." Ma, enraged at this intrusive evangelist, moves to strike her with a stick, but the Spirit strikes Sandry first.

> For a moment the woman backed away and then suddenly she threw back her head and howled. Her eyes rolled up, her shoulders and arms flopped loosely at her side, and a string of thick ropy saliva ran from the corner of her mouth. She howled again and again, long, deep animal howls. Slowly the woman sank to her knees and the howls sank to a shuddering, bubbling moan."[73]

Lizbeth Sandry is an extremely angular character in the government camp as depicted by Steinbeck. He painted her mind and body as equally troubling. She shifts back and forth between the human and the animal while espousing a theology and a social ethic appropriate to her retrograde state. Her shape-shifting disrupts the progressive spirit of the camp and contests the religion of the office with a come-outer spirit, counter-modern views, and a suspicion that the camp manager is in league with Satan. Faceless mobs of thugs and Legionnaires besiege, exploit, and murder migrants outside the gate. Sandry and her transgressive Protestantism resist and threaten their redemption from within.

The creative, imaginative process in which Collins and Steinbeck both engaged made for powerful, indeed transformative fiction. But that power was not abstract in its origins or its object. In fact, it seems to have been directed toward the project of re-forming and modernizing migrant faith. The re-forming of Georgie's faith in *The Grapes of Wrath* implicates the camp office in a particular kind of knowledge production. Collins and Steinbeck used the substantial authority of that office to force a stereotype and, with it, a choice upon the migrants. Either they could turn from expressions of Protestantism that New Deal reformers found jarring, or they could write themselves permanently to the margins of American society.

One way to explain Steinbeck's depiction of Georgie and her Protestantism is to focus on the relationship between Steinbeck and Collins and their inclinations toward religion. Steinbeck the public intellectual was eager to see traditional religious expressions in his rearview mirror. In Thomas Collins he found a camp manager whose accounts of religion he could read and, with his skilled novelist's hand, re-narrate and re-form. He also found a post-Catholic reformer, a man who, like Steinbeck's martyred hero Jim Casy, had lived a religious life, indulged his libido, and chosen to embrace the cause of humankind. In Georgie Nunn and others empowered by spirit-filled Protestantism to contest and counter the modernism of 1930s reformers, Collins and Steinbeck found people and ideas and experiences that threatened their reformist faith. Steinbeck, using Collins's reports, wrote the Okies' struggles into the American consciousness for a price. I will present you as quintessentially American, Steinbeck seems to say, but you must lose your animalistic, retrograde faith.

A second explanation focuses on the dehumanizing effects of the office and the bureaucratic literature on which Steinbeck's novel relied. Steinbeck's fun-house distortions of a young woman committed to Pentecostal evangelism into three old women—one dying, one howling, and the other drooling—express the dark side of categorization, analysis, and problem-solving using ink and papers and files. Steinbeck cut Georgie up like a subprime mortgage and bundled her with toxic assets: ropes of saliva, hyena laughter, the smell of death, because in collecting and reporting and categorizing, those who are human but different become that which we wish would "go away." This is one thing that many twentieth-century bureaucracies did, rather infamously.

A third explanation returns to questions of authority and the mixed moral and religious legacies of New Deal bureaucracies. The "stuff" of those bureaucracies—reports, files, papers—are in the blood of Steinbeck's novel. The passion of a reformer is there as well. Much of what Tom Collins and the migrant camp program accomplished in the agricultural valleys of California was truly heroic. They healed. They fed. They documented.

Steinbeck participated in that reforming bureaucracy. He consumed and exploited the duplicate and triplicate correspondence. But he also participated in its ethic vis-à-vis the migratory laborer. Collins's and Steinbeck's concern for the Okies was authentic, as was their desire to see the wandering Oklahomans reattached to the American body economic. With this in mind, one could argue that Collins and Steinbeck feared that Reverend Georgie's claims to authority would work against the goal of resettlement, reintegration, and rebirth into modern America. And because her faith was neither obviously helpful in this process nor a cozy fit for the office files, Georgie was rendered "beneficially" grotesque. This is how "you" look to "modern America," the book tells spirit-filled Christians. Become more like us if you want to progress into the future.

Steinbeck and Collins cared for the Okie migrants, but not for their religious expressions. They acted and wrote accordingly. Do we understand their words and actions best if we treat them as slanders on Okie Protestantism? Are they more properly understood as critiques of the counter-modern religious practices that Steinbeck and Collins feared would hold the migrants back? Can the reforming, the altruistic, the compassionate be disentangled from the categorizing, the compromising, the marginalizing?

Or were these approaches as tightly intertwined in the camp office as are the stories of a destitute woman evangelist turned bad housekeeper, a globally itinerant former seminarian turned New Deal reformer, and the novelist who needed them both?

3

The Tent Platform

After a migrant or a migrant family came through the gate and registered with the camp office, their next stop was a wooden tent platform on a small, numbered lot, assigned by the camp manager. The platform measured twelve by fourteen feet. For the first three years of the program, the tent was not included. The tent platform was the place where newcomers would create a home and live for a few days, a few months, or occasionally more than a year.[1] As the camp program developed, new types of shelter were added to the camps: metal cabins, simple apartments, even three-room adobe homes. But rudimentary, temporary dwellings remained a constant feature of government camps.

The tent platform had a practical and a religious significance to both camp officials and migrant families. Along with being a structure that literally elevated migrant living spaces and migrant families above the dirt, the tent platform was a stage on which migrant families were expected to demonstrate their commitment to elevating themselves out of a dirty, disordered existence. Having come through the gate and registered with the camp office, migrants were asked to prove that they truly wanted to reform themselves, to rebuild homes, and to be redeemed.

The standards by which their redemption was measured and the means used by camp managers and staff to articulate and enforce those standards are clear evidence of how the government camp program was enmeshed in the fabric of American religious history. Like many populations before and since, migratory farm workers were seen by an educated, privileged, and empowered class as lost, deviant, even savage. The price of harmonious existence within a program conceived for their social and economic salvation was a willingness to perform the reformers' visions of domestic virtue.[2]

Given the shock with which observers reported on the living conditions of migrants, and given the connection that so many drew between unsanitary, exposed living and agricultural labor unrest, it was hardly surprising that sheltering migrants was an important aspect of the camp program. Program officials wanted those living in the camp to have roofs over their heads, even if those roofs were made of canvas. The chaos of mixed materials, the impermanence of cardboard and twigs, the social nakedness of living on the banks of a drainage ditch—all were to be relics of the world "out there." But tent platforms mattered for reasons that went well beyond shelter.

Tent platforms spoke of some degree of stability. Many migrants came west from domestic wreckage, landed in dirt and uncertainty, and were forced to remain uprooted and in motion in order to earn, to eat, and to survive. Movement around California's interior, while life-giving, took bad domestic situations and made them worse.

A key function of the tent platform then, was to slow and redirect movement. Migrants appreciated the fact that platforms gave them a fixed place from which they could depart and to which they could return. Camp managers thought of the platform as a way to limit migrants' movements and to fill those movements with purpose. They hoped to focus migrants' attentions on the mobility that was upward, economic, and metaphorical and, as soon as possible, to have them abandon the mobility that was lateral, physical, and actual.

Focusing on the tent platform helps us see more clearly connections between the camp program and broader concerns about the degeneration of white homes in Depression-era America. But the migrant camp program was also part of a longer North American history of reform movements directed at homes and home life. This history extends back to early European contact with indigenous people in the so-called New World, where Spanish, French, and English colonizers sought, relentlessly, and often violently, to reconfigure the ways that Native peoples lived and related to each other. Their explicit goal was to "civilize" indigenous peoples, to bring family structures, community geography, and domestic appearances into line with European norms.

Colonizing powers used residential arrangements (Puritan praying towns, Catholic missions, agricultural incentives, government boarding schools for Native American children) and combinations of evangelization and coercion to shape individuals and households toward European standards. With few exceptions, missionaries linked transformations of faith and transformations of ways of living; with good religion came good domesticity. Homes could be less than truly Christian, but the truly Christian could not be without a recognizable home.

The nineteenth century was replete with efforts to reconfigure the domestic situations of a wide array of groups—recently-freed slaves, immigrants from Europe and Asia, Native Americans, destitute old stock Euro-Americans—using techniques that were frequently evangelical in form and Christian in content. Writing of the social crisis that he knew most intimately from his tenure as a pastor in New York's Hell's Kitchen neighborhood, Walter Rauschenbusch observed, "One family to one house is the only normal condition. When twenty live in one tenement, twenty souls inhabit one body. That was the condition of the demoniac Gadara, in whom dwelt legion. He was crazy." Rauschenbusch was far from exceptional among American progressives, many of whom took for granted the degraded nature of the homes and home lives of the poor, the immigrant, and people of color, and who lamented, "The shiftless, and all those with whom natural passion is least restrained, will breed most freely."[3]

The American history of reading homes as indicative of moral fitness and of treating a person's progress toward a domestic norm as a sign of growing righteousness is historically and geographically sprawling. But in the decades prior to the Great Depression, public officials and home missionaries—those missionaries who directed their efforts toward populations in the United States—working in San Francisco wrote a chapter of this history rife with Progressive-era condescensions, and with the evangelistic dynamics that presaged the migrant camps' culture of domestic improvement.[4]

The historian Nayan Shah writes eloquently of efforts to convince Chinese immigrants to abandon their foreign-seeming, threatening domestic practices. Anglo-American reformers were particularly troubled by the bachelor houses into which Chinese workers crowded, and the dwellings of Chinese sex workers, imagined as syphilitic traps for vulnerable white men. Nativists directed their demonizing, marginalizing words at Chinese residents and their "Chinatown" neighborhoods. These attacks mobilized reformers eager to clean up Chinese homes and to remake Chinese residents in their white, middle-class, Protestant image.

The resulting reform efforts involved public health officials and other representatives of state and city government. But some of the most effective work was carried out by women serving as home missionaries, who saw an intimate connection between a clean, light-filled, orderly house and the development of morally upright, responsible citizens. As Shah writes, "At the edge of American empire in San Francisco, white women's projects of domestic reform in Chinatown mobilized the cultural practices of 'imperial domesticity' to manage and reform the 'foreign' within the nation."[5] He continues:

> Through the example of their domestic management and housekeeping advice, San Francisco Presbyterian missionaries . . . sought to tutor both Chinese and white women in the cultural practices of healthy American home life, that stood in sharp contrast to the lifestyles, standards, and norms of the Chinese race.[6]

This was an exercise of "soft power" carried out through visits, guidance, and example. But the absence of physical coercion and forced removal should not obscure the high stakes involved or the seriousness with which the Presbyterian women pursued these efforts. "Missionaries," Shah writes, "were insistent on teaching Chinese women to be 'practical housewives' and encouraging them in 'neatness of person and homes.' Ideas of cleanliness, sanitation, and middle-class white material culture were conflated as the indicators of Christian belief and 'civilized behavior.'" And if the Chinese community had hopes of joining the American cultural mainstream, or of developing a story that rebutted widespread racist tales of an Asian infestation, showing evidence of "Christian belief" and "civilized behavior" was required.

At the same moment that Presbyterian women were extending the gloved hand of fellowship and domestic guidance to Chinese women in San Francisco, the parents and grandparents of those who would find themselves on twelve-by-fourteen-foot platforms in federal camps throughout rural California were staking out homesteads on lands taken from native peoples; some were entering tenancy or share-cropping arrangements with those more fortunate than they. By the time Dust Bowl migrants reached California, homeless and starving, the explicit connections linking Christianity, middle-class domesticity, and whiteness had been partially obscured by more generalized discourses of domesticity, virtue, and good citizenship. Domestic ideals had not, however, lost their religiousness. Advancing commercialization, scientific rationales for cleanliness, and a growing awareness of families as economic units could barely dent, let alone dislodge, America's theology of the home.

Rather than describing a relationship in which the secular overtook the sacred, in which social workers, home economists, and federally-employed family selectionists elbowed Protestant reform agencies and home missionaries out of the picture, this history shows that their work and their ideas were fed from a spring in which religion and dwelling practices were always already combined. Just as denominational efforts to save souls and redeem families always concerned themselves with home life, so were governmental efforts to restore domestic order sustained by religious substructures: visions of divinity, promises of salvation, and a clear sense of how sin looked and acted.

Dwelling after Crossing

Migrant families arrived at their tent platforms at a moment, it is safe to say, that was not the pinnacle of their personal, familial, or vocational aspirations. Some had fallen just far enough to lose their hold on a settled life. Some had nothing left of former lives than scraps of old clothes and mouths to feed. In making sense of their Job-like fates and their many needs, migrants asked themselves and their God questions regarding location, identity, and meaning.

Living in Arkansas, Texas, Missouri, or Oklahoma established a certain geographical and historical awareness, what religious studies scholar Thomas Tweed has called a "watch and compass."[7] While migrants confronted a collapsing present and moved toward an invisible future, their home state, county, or town could locate them in a network of regional cultures and identities, and also in the arc of American myth-history: *Texas sharecroppers for three generations, family moved west after the war, pioneer stock; Oklahoma homesteaders, built the old place myself, hung on until the bitter end*. To a large extent, this sense of geographic home was, like a watch and a compass, portable. It could be pocketed, carried West, and held tightly even as hostile Californians cast aspersions.

Losing the structure and the contents of home was different. To abandon the buildings that sheltered and the land that nourished a family—the things that defined its most intimate sense of place and belonging—meant facing deeper poverty and greater instability. It also meant losing a world. John Steinbeck depicts the connection, loss, and disorientation early in *The Grapes of Wrath*, in the voices of anonymous tenant farmers arguing for a deeper kind of ownership of land than merely holding title to it:

> And now the squatting men stood up angrily . . . Grampa took up the land, and he had to kill the Indians and drive them away. And Pa was born here, and he killed weeds and snakes. Then a bad year came and he had to borrow a little money. An we was born here. There in the door—our children born here.

An unnamed tenant continues this plea when a tractor driven by "Joe Davis's boy" arrives to "bump" his house down. "I built it with my hands. Straightened old nails to put the sheathing on. Rafters are wired to the stringers with bailing wire. It's mine. I built it."[8] Muley Graves, the "ol' graveyard ghos'" whom Tom Joad and Jim Casy find among the abandoned farms and houses outside Sallisaw, Oklahoma, argues further that destroying homes and histories, letting legal ownership erase ownership derived from violence and work and memory, was, in actuality, murder. "Place where folks live is them folks," Muley says, "They ain't whole, out lonely on the road in a piled-up car. They ain't alive no more. Them sons-a-bitches killed 'em."[9]

Whether Muley is speaking only of his own killing or the killing of all displaced people, Steinbeck was convinced that the loss of home created existential crises. Familiar, self-made shelter was gone. So was the evidence of a person's past, left behind to be "bumped down" and to decay.

> The women sat among the doomed things, turning them over and looking past them and back. This book. My father had it. He like a book. Pilgrim's Progress. Used to read it. Got his name in it. And his pipe—still smells rank. And this picture—an angel. I looked at that before the fust three come—didn't seem to do much good. . . . Here's a letter my brother wrote the day before he died. Here's an old time hat. . . . No, there isn't room. How can we live without our lives? How will we know it's us without our past? No. Leave it. Burn it.[10]

Objects bearing the past, bearing memories and identities were left behind. These new pilgrims were cast adrift, abandoned to progress without the visual, tactile, and olfactory reminders that made homes and that oriented them in the world. They were forced to live on without their lives.

Steinbeck's reading of displacement need not be true for every migrant to have a great deal of truth in it, and a home need not have held Pilgrim's Progress and pictures of angels to be a site of deep religious significance. Tweed argues for the centrality of "dwelling" to religion. "Human collectivity originates with the home," he writes. "As the first and smallest inhabited space, its boundaries open and close to wider activity." Across a range of times and places and religious traditions, these intimate spaces have oriented people on the land and in time. They are the spaces of coming and going. They hold mementos, invitations to ponder irretrievable worlds, markers of the growth and contraction of a network of kin. "The religious . . . orient themselves by constructing, adorning, and inhabiting domestic space," Tweed writes, "Religion, in this sense, is housework. It is homemaking. . . . In other words, as clusters of dwelling practices, religions orient individuals and groups in time and space, transform the natural environment, and allow devotees to inhabit the worlds they construct."[11] Acts of dwelling, what Tweed calls "the kinetics of homemaking," occur both in recognizably sacred spaces and in domestic space—the "intimate controlled space, whether cleared or constructed, that provides for bodily needs . . . and usually, though not always, is inhabited by some members of the family."[12]

These insights matter on both ends of the crossings undertaken by the migrants. They help us to fathom the religious depths of the unmaking of migrants' worlds and to measure the religious stakes of remaking those worlds. What constituted a national domestic crisis to members of the camp program hierarchy was made up of thousands upon thousands of personal crises.

For some, the first rung on a ladder that might lead up and out of that crisis was a tent platform in a government camp. And for them, the act of setting up a tent on that platform was an act of world creation. Just as the camp gate separated a hostile outside from a civil inside and called those who passed through to live reformed lives, the tent created a domestic inside, in and around which migrants could perform Tweed's "kinetics of homemaking." This "inside" demarcated and contained domestic activity, privatizing and obscuring it properly, providing hints but not a full view of domestic performances. The tent's surroundings, the exposed parts of the platform and the small lot around it, were to be tended as well, and testified to the domestic righteousness of those within.

Further, the tent joined the family living inside to an ordered community of neighbors outside, creating a social and political world in and to which camp residents could belong. When a migrant family set up their tent, they claimed a new "watch and compass," relocating themselves in space and in time, and making a clear step toward dwelling in a civilized way and in community.

The domestic norms encouraged and enforced by camp program personnel were themselves religious. Reformers imagined these norms as foundational to a good (white, Christian) life, preached accordingly, and assessed a family's righteousness and fitness for reintegration into modern American community life based on their domestic skills.

And though surely unintentionally, Thomas Tweed helps illustrate the connection in the American consciousness, then and now, between civilizational advancement and domestic environments when he writes of homes around the world, "For some hunter-gatherers [home] might mean no more than a clearing in the brush."[13] True enough. For hundreds of thousands of Americans displaced and California-bound during the Great Depression, home meant roughly the same thing—a clearing in the brush. And that, in a nutshell, was the problem.

Settling and Domesticating

"When a farmer is continually on the move," a Farm Security Administration pamphlet published in 1941 offered, "he has little chance to put down roots in any community. He cannot become the best kind of citizen, because he is seldom in one place long enough to take part in community affairs, or even to join the neighborhood church."[14] For FSA personnel, the task across much of America's agricultural heartland was to "help needy farm people keep their foothold on the land," to encourage the small, self-sufficient farmer and his family to practice "a healthier relationship with their cultivated and domestic spaces."[15]

This project was not viable everywhere. As the same pamphlet continued, "there are many thousands of families which FSA was not able to help in time." These thousands had moved off of the land in search of some other living, some other place. The Resettlement Administration and the Farm Security Administration were especially concerned about those who had "taken to the highways in a desperate effort to make some kind of living as migrant farm laborers." Gone were their farms and homes. "Their only homes are temporary roadside camps, which seldom have any kind of sanitary facilities or even a decent water supply." Going, and nearly gone, was a great deal more. "The children have little chance for education, adequate medical care, or normal community life."[16]

Reformers in California and throughout the United States saw the national agricultural crisis in domestic terms. They were concerned about its negative effects on the domestic sphere. Further, they often connected problems in the home to problems for the home*land*. That is to say, echoing the late literary scholar Amy Kaplan, that many New Deal personnel treated the structure of the family, the maintenance of the home, and the division of domestic labor as both contributing to and indicative of the health and viability of the United States. Domestic deterioration would necessarily spread within the borders of the nation and weaken it.

This concern, articulated in the Farm Security Administration pamphlet cited above, was central to a speech that landed on Jonathan Garst's desk sometime in the spring of 1938. The speech had been given by Sue Taylor, associate director in charge of home management for the state of Tennessee, to the "annual meeting of the Southern Agricultural workers" in Atlanta, Georgia. Taylor's talk, titled "Home Management Plans with Rehabilitation Families," was important enough to Clara Thompson, chief of the home management section of the FSA's Rural Rehabilitation Division, that she decided to pass it along to Director Garst and to two home management specialists on Garst's staff. Ms. Taylor's words expressed RA/FSA thinking on the problems plaguing impoverished rural families and laid out the official vision for their rehabilitation and redemption.[17]

At the center of Taylor's talk was an analogy comparing the rural family to a wagon wheel, "with the farm family as the hub with tight-fitting spokes and a well adjusted [tire]. Any agricultural program that rolls along as it should will have the family as the hub. . . ." She presented an illustration of a sound, tight, strong wheel, with the elements labeled to clarify the comparison. She then described the harsh reality that New Deal workers found in the field and its dramatic divergence from the ideal. To go along with her description, she presented an image of a broken wheel that "many people" would want to "cast aside feel[ing] that it was too far gone ever to be mended."

Taylor urged her audience not to cast aside those deteriorating wheels, but to work diligently to restore them to fullness. Those "human resources" that the nation had "allowed to become impoverished physically, economically, educationally, and socially," deserved every bit as much attention as the "impoverished soil" that the nation was paying to restore.

The project of human rehabilitation and restoration would not be easy, Taylor warned. Strengthening the hub, tightening the spokes, and refitting the "felloe" (the rim of a wheel) would require "patience, tact, kindness, sympathy, and human understanding," but home management workers needed to keep two things in mind as they toiled away. First, they were working with materials characterized by "dauntless courage and will power." Though they looked a shambles now, it was only because these families had been through enough hardship to crush most people. Second, the stakes were high. It was a mistake to "think of our work only in terms of gardening, canning, screens, livestock, more cash income"—routine recommendations to improve the lives of poor rural folk—"and not in terms of a means of developing good citizens and leaders who can take their rightful place in their community."[18]

It was important to grow vegetables for canning and to keep bugs off of the kids. But the overarching purpose of domestic rehabilitation was to reengage these worn-out people in civic life and thus to enable the nation to roll confidently into the future.

Three thousand miles away in California, Frederick Soule, information adviser for the Farm Security Administration's Region IX, recorded similar thoughts. Soule agreed that the crisis of poverty, homelessness, and wandering in California, if ignored, would have consequences well beyond the state's agricultural interior. In a letter written on April 15, 1938 to Mrs. Blanche Premo of the American Association of University

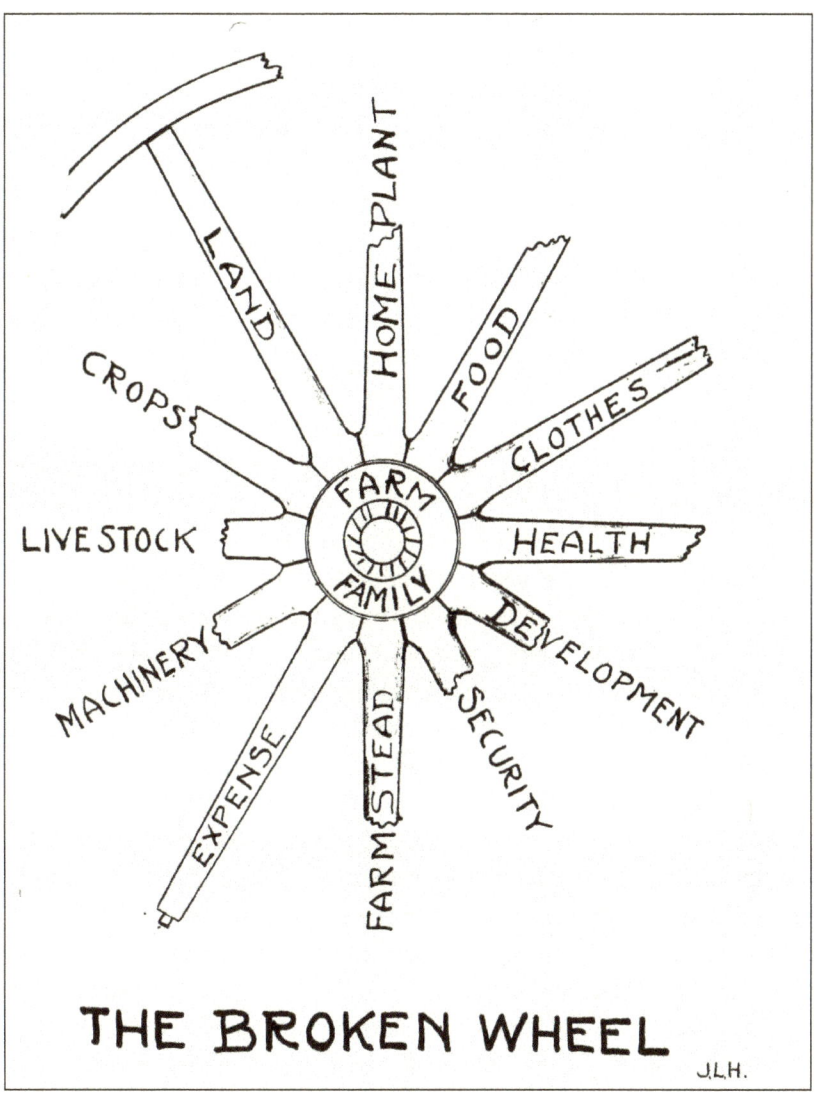

"The Broken Wheel." Illustration from Sue Taylor, "Home Management Plans with Rehabilitation Families" enclosure in Clara Thompson to Garst, May 6, 1938; 161-Speeches, March 1938—January 1939; General Correspondence, Box 30.

Women, Soule wrote, "It seems to me that one outstanding social problem with which women's groups must be concerned is the appalling hardships inflicted upon the women and children by the whole process of farm dispossession and migration. It seems beyond question that if this process is permitted to go on unchecked it cannot help but drag down civilization, culture and democracy in all stratas."[19]

The crises faced by individual families were crises for the nation, for democracy, and for civilization. Settling the wandering, and "educating up" the uncivilized were necessary strides toward redemption for migrants and for the society to which they might still contribute. This was nation-saving work, and Soule placed the responsibility for it squarely on the shoulders of women.

What, though, were the contours of this domestic crisis? Other than a broken wagon wheel, what did people see when they looked at this degraded domestic situation? Officials within the migrant camp system saw problems in both domestic relations and domestic environments. They saw marriages that probably should not have taken place, babies whose needs were not being met, and harmful family behaviors. They saw dirt, disorder, and utter disregard for the fact that weeds and trash and cigarette butts around a home spoke to observers about the quality of those within. In short, they saw multiple domestic messes in need of cleaning up.

In his reports to the camp program hierarchy, camp manager Tom Collins devoted a great deal of attention to the young migrant and pentecostal evangelist Georgie Nunn. He wrote often of her inability to fulfill basic household tasks. Domestic skills that one might have expected the young pentecostal evangelist to develop in her first twenty years were, Collins wrote, far, far beyond her. But Georgie came in handy in a different stereotypically female role: that of a shoulder to cry on. The tears were shed by Tissie, a seventeen-year-old Arkansan who traveled to the Arvin camp in the summer of 1936 to join the man she had married. Their relationship might have been solid back home, but it cracked clear through under the pressure of a new life.

In a late-summer report, Collins used Tissie's story as an example of migrant domestic malpractice. Tissie was seventeen. Her husband was "about 35." He came to the Arvin camp with his sister a few weeks ahead of Tissie and saved some money before sending for her. When the sister learned that Tissie was on her way, she let Collins know that Tissie "could neither read nor write" and thus might struggle to reach the camp on her own.

Collins alerted the bus station in Bakersfield and Tissie arrived without incident. The victory was fleeting. "When the child wife arrived at the camp . . . she made a tour. . . . She was like Alice in Wonderland. Children were playing croquet, some were bowling, others were making toys and many of the women were making dresses." Having come all that way, it was only after arriving in the Arvin camp that "[s]he was truly lost."

Collins was surely correct that Tissie did not know exactly what to make of her new social situation. She was as far as she had ever been from the home she knew. Games like croquet and bowling were probably unfamiliar. Alice in Wonderland, a seven-year-old character, was, however, a less-than-apt comparison for a seventeen-year-old facing the transition to married life in the close quarters of a government camp sixteen hundred miles from home. Confronted with croquet-playing children and quilt-making women, Tissie can be forgiven for not being able to see immediately where she belonged and for giving vent to her emotions. Collins wrote further, "Without asking permission or approval of another girl who was playing croquet, [Tissie] 'snatched' the croquet mallet from the girl's hand and gave the ball a hefty wallop. Then a good hair pulling contest took place. The new arrival got the better of the fight for she was an expert at kicking with her feet and her knees." On Collins's reading of the incident, the child-wife showed herself to be far more child than wife, disrupting an otherwise peaceful, civilized scene with unrefined backwoods behavior.

Two weeks after her arrival and assault on the croquet player (a scene John Steinbeck wrote into *The Grapes of Wrath*, with Ruthie Joad behaving like Tissie) Tissie's husband came to Collins to discuss his feelings about his wife.[20] As far as he was concerned, the differences between them were vast and irreconcilable. As Collins recalled the conversation.

> I kums ter tell yer I aint gonna haf that woman bout me fer no more time. . . . I plans leafing camp in the marning. I think I tak her 'long till we gits sum far plase and then I dumps her frum the car. . . . She ain't no decent womin and when a womin aint decent it aint no other thing ter do but dump her and ditch her sum plas.

Collins reported that he told the disgruntled husband that people sometimes left dogs and cats by the side of the road, but that doing such a thing to any woman, let alone one's wife, was unacceptable. He then pressed the man for his account of what made Tissie indecent. The husband responded with a list of grievances. She played with boys. She enjoyed playing ball and croquet. She had worn a bathing suit around camp. She had convinced another "bad womin" in camp to put curls in her hair. She fought with other women and entered tents "where men be sick abed." And while she was doing these things, her domestic duties were imperfectly fulfilled. She was late with meals. She refused to sleep in bed with him on hot nights. She refused to have sex with him at all. "Efry budy in camp noes it," he concluded, "and they all says she aint be desent."

Collins learned not long after that the husband and his sister had spread stories about Tissie around camp; that "the poor girl was certainly in the bad graces of all." It was then that he asked "Reverend Georgie" to help. Georgie, too, was young and "a recent bride." Perhaps she could help repair a marriage that was coming apart at the seams.

"Georgie kept the girl around the house and had her assist with the household duties," Collins wrote. "All the time Reverend Georgie was preaching the 'wiles of the devil' and the duties of a wife to a husband. She gave the girl many suggestions for winning back the husband['s] regard." According to Collins, Tissie eagerly followed Georgie's advice, but to no avail. "The husband ignored all the efforts of the girl, going so far as to refuse to eat whatever she cooked or permit her in the tent at night." When he threatened again to ditch her on a remote highway, Collins set the wheels in motion to get Tissie back to Arkansas. He provided her with a postcard to send to her husband when the journey was complete. It read "Arrived home OK, Tissie."

After she had gone, a neighbor in camp shared her thoughts with Collins as to what Tissie ought to have done to save the marriage. "[She] should a had a babee by him fer he lef Arkansas. At would a ben salvation fer bof." Not surprisingly, Collins disagreed that salvation could have been found in a marriage like Tissie's. The child-wife had enough to worry about without becoming a child-wife-mother. And her husband, chauvinistic and self-righteous, was unlikely to change his view of himself, of women, or of right and wrong.

So anxious to shoot others for playing croquet with his wife, and so willing to ditch her along the highway, his pure soul must be at rest with the thought he has done his duty before Gawd and man and rid himself of a deadly sin—Tissie. Tissie, but 17 years of age—who had her first bit of childish heaven at Arvin Camp, with the toys, the games, the dances etc. The way of the migrant women is so hard—and that hardness of life begins at a very young age.[21]

Bad religion was a plank in the platform on which this ill-matched couple sought to build their life. Bad religion obscured hypocrisy, justified oppression, and cast as sinful that which was natural (childhood) and joyful (recreation). Bad religion took hard lives and made them harder. Bad religion and bad domesticity went hand in hand.

As told by Tom Collins, this story portrays the domestic crisis among migrants as more than simply a crisis of shelter and differentiated space. One could protect migrants from the elements and from the prying eyes of neighbors, but this did little to improve their performance of domesticity.

Tissie and her husband were a problem for Collins and pointed toward a more general problem for the camp program. She was seventeen. He was thirty-five. She was a "child-wife": simple, immature, illiterate. He saw nothing wrong, in principle, with marrying a teenaged woman. Worse than that, he thought it not just acceptable but righteous to throw her overboard when the seas got choppy. Having been deprived of what Collins deemed a normal childhood, including the pleasures of play and the shaping influences of civilization, Tissie did not know that in social life, as in croquet, there was an order to things, wickets that one had to go through. And she seems not to have known that with her decision to marry, she was expected to inhabit new roles and follow new rules.

These qualities made the newlywed Tissie and her husband an especially apt example of domestic dysfunction. Their domestic performances departed dramatically from the norm, and they seemed to have little interest and less ability to learn their roles and their lines anew. Their lack of domestic talent was another indication that the "wagon wheel" of migrant domesticity was broken. The tire was flat. The spokes that were the family members were loose and degenerating. Wives and mothers were too young and too unable to keep house. Husbands did not value their wives as partners. Babies were agents of cohesion, valuable as the glue that held marriages together rather than valuable as themselves. And there were many too many babies for the too little attention and too few dollars the migrants had. Rather than solve problems through discussion or some form of mediation, migrant women would fight and cuss; migrant men would either turn and run from their wives, or ditch them. How could a nation regain its footing and grow strong again with such a problematic domestic ethic operating among its people? How could civic life flourish when domestic life was so flawed?

In April of 1937, Collins reflected on a different aspect of the domestic crisis: the state of domestic space and aesthetics. In the preceding month, he had repeatedly confronted the collapse of domestic life among white migrants outside the gate of the Shafter camp. Collins's weary typewriter unfurled page after page describing migrant living spaces that were barely recognizable as shelter, much less as homes. In a report to Eric Thomsen, written on April 2, 1937, he told of a grower whose private camp had been condemned, but who relocated the cabins and kept them available for squatters. "I found approximately 40 families there," Collins reported, "Nearest water supply—five miles!"[22]

A second camp belonging to the same grower, this one in the vicinity of Buttonwillow, had also been "ordered abandoned." In defiance of that order, ten families remained, resigning themselves to the primitive circumstances. "There are no sanitary facilities. Water is carried a mile."[23] Whether or not the domestic relations in these cabins were functional by comparison to Tissie and her husband, the domestic spaces themselves were a wreck.

A citizen of Kern County reflected on the meaning of all this in a letter to the *Bakersfield Californian* in March of 1937. She wrote to express her worry and her sympathy. "I too feel deeply concerned over the families living in the jungles. I cannot close my eyes and think that these people are there because they like to be there." And even if the exposed and dirty living reflected negatively on the "jungle families," the situation was just as damning for more settled, more respectable residents. "There can be no doubt," she wrote, "that it is a public shame to tolerate a condition such as this jungle camp represents."[24] White American children could read of jungles and might dream of traveling across oceans to

"Irish Americans, Kern County, Feb. 24, 1935."
Photograph by Dorothea Lange. Courtesy of Library of Congress. Image LC-DIG-ppmsca-19156, https://www.loc.gov/pictures/item/2004678009/.

tame them or evangelize in them, but it was shameful that they should be forced to scratch out a dirty existence living in the local equivalent.

This shame may have been amplified by the close proximity of a Mexican encampment that, according to Collins, was an example of domestic stability, discipline, and self-governance. This "Mexican village"

"White American. Squatters camp near Bakersfield. Lived in 3 years. February 23, 1935." Photograph by Dorothea Lange. Courtesy of Library of Congress. Image LC-DIG-ppmsca-19156, https://www.loc.gov/pictures/item/2004678009/.

had been serving Mexican migrants for decades. "Starting as a squatter camp years ago," he explained, "the Mexican colony now has its own town of adobe dwellings and board shacks. The Mexicans run their own settlement and it is seldom the sheriff is called." This relative stability allowed "two generations of Mexicans [to work] for the same farmers." And with stability came the chance to grow and develop. "Mexicans," Collins wrote, "remain in community and establish a home."

This critical mass of homes and people and history in the Mexican village made Mexican migrants in Kern County look more advanced, more civilized. "Migrant Mexican families do not camp on ditch banks nor on the desert edge," Collins observed, "They take up residence in the Mexican village," which had a Catholic church, a Baptist church, and a public school housed in the Catholic Church but operated by the school district.

By contrast, white Dust Bowl migrants lagged behind, living in squatter camps and filthy grower camps, leaving themselves open to exploitation.

Perhaps they dreamt of adobe dwellings, but they were not building them. In short, the project of domestic reform and rehabilitation undertaken by the RA and the FSA among white migrants was not as necessary in this community of Mexican migrants. They knew how to live. They knew how to build community. They made homes and raised children properly.

A widespread assumption among camp program workers was that white migrants were too quick to settle into bad domesticity and, left to their own habits and tastes, would never progress to good domesticity. They judged government intervention, education, and incentives to be necessary if the white citizens were ever to establish themselves as legitimate Americans alongside the civilized "foreigners" whose dwellings were much closer to the white American ideal.

I do not describe these critiques and comparisons to suggest that New Deal reformers in California were not humanitarians. They were. On an industrial agricultural landscape where violence and dehumanizing practices stalked the vulnerable and the needy, they were on the right side of history. It is important to recognize, however, that humanitarian efforts are always carried out by people who have ideas about who counts as human, who deserves help, what sort of help is appropriate, and how the righteous disadvantaged ought to respond to the grace of aid. These ideas are never universally agreed upon and are always changing.[25]

The shape of the government camp program and its implementation from 1935 through 1943 make these truths about humanitarian action clear. To begin, though the camp program officially forbade exclusion based on race, in fact, the federal camps were overwhelmingly white. Indeed, a major reason for launching the program had been the whiteness of the destitute. There was nothing new about migration in agricultural California, nothing new about homelessness and ad hoc shelters. What was new, was that white families were conspicuous among the migrants and were living uncivilized, pre-modern lives. Whiteness mattered both because the norms of American domestic life were supposed to be established and maintained by white families, and because the tragic collapse of life and home across the Great Plains had displaced a white population and thrust it into close proximity with racial groups to whom they were supposed to be superior.

As historians Nathaniel Deutsch and Thomas Leonard have shown, American understandings of race have long been malleable enough to

Migrant father with child, sitting on family's tent platform, Brawley Camp, 1939. Photograph by Dorothea Lange. *FSA migratory labor camp. Brawley, California. Father is home after a day in the pea fields. Note tent platform, standard equipment in Farm Security Administration camps.* February 1939. Courtesy of Library of Congress. https://www.loc.gov/item/2017771713/.

account for radically different capacities and classes within the category "white" and to allow that some white families were undeserving poor.[26] Yet, in a destitute and racially diverse environment, the incentive for assisting and elevating white families increased. Camp officials' efforts to help "true Americans," along with the regular trumpeting of white migrants' virtues, were part of an effort to rehabilitate, reassert, and defend a white domestic norm. On tent platforms in federal camps, migrants could begin to rebuild their worlds, reestablish homes, and demonstrate to themselves, their neighbors, and camp management that they were not as far gone as they looked. They could perform domestic life as an argument against those who thought they were savage, while camp management evaluated their domestic performances.

Indeed, evaluation was part of both the culture of the camps and the ideology of the camp system more broadly. Agricultural economist Paul Taylor made this explicit in a November 1937 letter to Regional Director Jonathan Garst. In writing of federal efforts toward rehabilitation of the migrants, Taylor, partner of the legendary photographer Dorothea Lange, described "a series of project types, related but varied" through which worthy migrants could move according to their ability to grow and persevere in redemption.

> In this way, persons capable of progressive rehabilitation can be selected advantageously from the simpler projects [migratory labor camps] and filtered upward to the more complex. . . . Since camps afford excellent opportunities for observing and selecting applicants for rehabilitation,

Migrant family from Mangrum, Oklahoma, consisting of mother, father, and ten children.
Photograph by Dorothea Lange. *Brawley, Imperial Valley. In FSA migratory labor camp. Family father, mother and eleven children originally from Mangrum, Oklahoma.* February 1939. Courtesy of Library of Congress. https://www.loc.gov/item/2017771601/.

prompt expansion of camp projects . . . may be of critical importance to the success of the other Farm Security projects for the rehabilitation of laborers and dispossessed farmers.[27]

These words of Taylor's paint the expansion of the camp program as vital not because it would give more destitute families shelter and water and medical attention, but because it would allow camp personnel to observe more migrants, evaluate more migrants, and filter more migrants.

It is interesting that Taylor used the concept of filtration in this context, the process by which solids are removed from a liquid or a gas by forcing the mixed substances through a medium through which only the fluid can pass. The camp program was not removing particulate matter from drinking water or dust from the air, it was filtering people, separating the worthy from the unworthy, those capable of "progressive rehabilitation" from those incapable. To do this, government camp personnel needed a vision of who should pass through and who should get snagged, who could be reshaped and reformed, and who could not. The tent platform was an essential element in that filter.

The Gospel of Mork: Managing Domestic Sin and Righteousness

The domestic values of the government camp found expression in a set of rules designed to make camp life clean, orderly, and outwardly virtuous. The rules were provided to each family when they arrived and were also posted throughout the camp. Camp rules sought changes in migrants' actions and appetites, a reformation of their vision and of their culture. Rules prohibited sins that progressives often targeted, such as drinking and gambling, as well as potentially disruptive social behaviors such as swearing inside camp grounds and noisy revelry after nine p.m.[28] Ordinances from the Arvin camp prohibited "disturbance of the peace, i.e. fighting, vulgar or profane language in a public place, especially in the presence of women and children," as well as:

Committing petty misdemeanors such as:

a. Fights involving children,
b. Profanity or vulgarity involving children,

c. Attempted curtailment of Civil rights or liberties,
d. Malicious, groundless gossiping, libel, or license, . . .
f. Appearing in Camp in possession or under the influence of liquor,
g. Loafing in or around Utility buildings,
h. Leaving radios on, or making loud noise after 10:00 P.M. on week nights, 12 Midnight on Sunday.[29]

Good people did not engage in verbal or physical assaults, defile their bodies, or waste precious time.

Camp rules also sought to shape the relationship between camp residents and their surroundings. Rules required two hours of work per family per week toward "the upkeep of the camp." They required "living quarters and lots adjoining . . . [to] be kept clean at all times," clothes to be laundered in the proper facilities, and "parents . . . [to] be responsible for the conduct of their children at all times."

Rules promulgated "for the benefit of our new campers" stipulated that those living in the Indio Camp "should have a small garbage can with a lid on it so the garbage will not draw flies" and asked residents to "use canvas to fix up your platform. But . . . not . . . any cardboard or paper." Paper was a fire hazard. Moreover, living under a paper roof or behind paper walls evoked the domestic deterioration outside the gate. Good people, the rules state, keep their domestic environment clean, use facilities properly, manage their garbage, tend to their children, and give some thought to the aesthetics, durability, and safety of their home.

The filtering power of these rules is evident in myriad stories, some long, some brief, of those who broke them, such as three families Manager Frank Iusi mentioned in his report for November 1940 report, whom "[i]t was necessary to evict . . . for being drunk and disorderly," and another that was thrown out of camp "for failing to assume their obligations to clean the utility building."[30] This basic, rule-based filtration caught more than a few families over the life of the camp program. But the hope of those working in the camp system was to redeem and settle the wandering, and to those ends they used their voices to urge migrants to refine themselves that they might be able to pass through the filter.

Ray Mork, manager of the Indio camp from 1937 to 1939 and the Shafter camp from 1939 to 1941, stands out from the fellowship of camp managers and officials for his colorful and prolific attempts to sculpt and evaluate migrant domestic behavior. Mork wrote an exceptional amount on the topic. His ideas about domestic standards and migrants' shortcomings were, however, typical. Mork's approach to reforming migrant dwelling practices involved two prongs, the first of which was environmental persuasion. From the beginning of his days at Indio, Mork argued that clean and orderly surroundings would encourage migrants to be clean and orderly. He wrote in 1937, "To inspire these families who have been living in filth, to keep clean we need to surround them with cleanliness, with order, which means in this case, lawns, flowers, trees, shrubs, contrasting colors, and all laid out neatly and uniform." Refined surroundings would elevate the migrants' aspirations beyond mere survival and cultivate in them a desire to be in harmony with the neatly-trimmed hedges and the well-mowed lawns. "It is my opinion," he continued, "that the psychological effect of a clean, attractive, well ordered camp cannot be overestimated."[31]

Mork also believed that the work of ordering and beautification needed to focus on the spaces where migrants made their homes. "The first work," he wrote, "will be done around the platforms as I think them the most important."[32] The closer the cleanliness and order came to the tents of a disordered, dirt-caked people, the greater the chance that it would reach inside, catch them unaware, and whisper to them of the virtue of living cleanly. Ray Mork was not one to apply a double-standard. He insisted that the lot in front of his home be well-manicured, both as an example for others and as an indication that his dwelling housed an orderly domestic environment.

The second prong of Mork's approach was sharper. Mork spoke regularly to the residents of his camps, encouraging them to put cleanliness and order first, to learn that goodness was clean and that cleanliness was good. Whereas his moral landscapes relied on grass, vines, and hedges to do the talking, his writings were frequent, strident, and attributed. Mork's brief treatise on changing migrants' lifeways and desires provides an introduction to his writings in the newspapers of the Indio and Shafter camps. The words of fellow camp managers Fred Ross, Frank Iusi, and Joseph McClain demonstrate the system-wide reach of this domestic catechism.

Though Ray Mork could wax poetic about the virtues of his camp residents, he most often proceeded on the assumption that they were broken down and in need of repair. He wrote to the FSA hierarchy in 1940, "Please never lose sight of the fact that these families . . . lived at a standard far below that which we must keep in our camps. Bringing them quite abruptly into a higher civilization is a problem that one must experience to realize."[33]

By the time he wrote those words, Mork had been managing federal migrant camps in California for nearly three years. He had witnessed and facilitated the transition of migrant families to what he called "higher civilization," and he had given some thought to maximizing chances of success. At one level, he noted, encouraging attentiveness to domestic environments was about keeping up with the Joneses. "Camp cleanliness, that is around the different platforms, is brought about by fostering a spirit of competition." And what better way to foster a spirit of competition than to pit groups of migrants against each other? He continued, "Each Saturday the camp manager inspects camp and awards first, second, etc. prizes to the different units," he continued. "To be last in this inspection isent [sic] a very happy feeling for the ladies, and being first of course means a lot to their pride."[34]

The competition involved comparison and evaluation, judgment and ranking of attempts at cleanliness and order. Who was doing it right? Who was falling short? It was also an exercise in value formation. Mork hoped that migrants would internalize this process of comparison and evaluation, that they would make the values undergirding the system their own. In explaining how his writings addressed the problem of domestic cleanliness, he wrote:

> Besides [the competition] the manager writes articles for the paper continually pounding away at the cleanliness angle, for instance trying to connect in their minds a connection between good families, good citizens, and cleanliness, that is that perhaps a dirty family is a low family, a lazy one, or one not up to the standard of others. Then occasionally I write for the camp paper a dialogue, wherein two familiar characters discuss in vernacular camp problems, usually one character is a dignified one, representing the correct views of the better camp citizen and then the other representing the undesirable citizen, the undesirable character doing things and disgustingly, that the right kind of camper should not do.

This combination of persuasive tools wasn't perfect, Mork conceded, but it did often "bring results." The results Mork sought included both aesthetics and behaviors. He wanted camp residents to change the way that they acted and to direct their energies toward cleaning and maintaining the spaces in which they lived. But his goal was also to reform the ways that camp residents saw and evaluated the world. He wanted to "connect in their minds a connection" between the clean and orderly, and the good. He often proceeded as if connecting this connection was without precedent in the lives of the migrants—as if they stood before him as a people dirty, lazy, and lost.

In late 1938, Ray Mork reported multiple times on the weekly cleanliness competition that he instituted at the Indio camp. The competition pitted camp "units"—groupings of tent platforms that shared a utility building—against one another. To involve migrant children in the process of cleaning, ordering, and evaluating and to get them to live his values, Mork started a "scout" program. The scouts, young boys and girls from each unit, monitored unit cleanliness and received a monetary reward when their unit won. This was a team competition, but it fell to individual families to maintain cleanliness and order around their platforms. In "Unit Four Wins Again," a December 10 article in the camp paper, Mork commented on the competition.

> What do you all suppose we can do about this thing of one unit winning so often? Yes, unit four won the prize again. One wouldn't think a unit could be as clean as four was. There wasn't any papers [sic] piled under any of the platforms, there wasn't any things strewed around on the ground. Three families moved out one evening, and did they leave a mess, and you know those scouts got . . . every bit of that cleared up the next morning.

Individual families had done their part and, when some lapsed—like the three who left a trail of garbage as they moved out—eager members of the community were on the job. The reward for scouts, "Alva Joe Perkins, Jack Rainier, Antha Lula Perkins, and Monica," was a twenty-five-cent piece. "Second place went to Unit One," Mork continued, "which also was very clean and orderly." Unit Five placed third. It was clean—a significant improvement over previous weeks—but Mork held against them the fact that someone "last week tore down the ladder on one of the entrances to the utility [lavatory] building."[35]

The sin of the broken ladder was forgiven the following week, as Unit Five vaulted over Unit One and finished in a dead heat with Unit Four. Mork expressed shock at the unexpected outcome, but explained how it happened. "The inside of the utility building in four was the cleanest but the tent spaces in five was the cleanest, so we declared it a tie and each of the scouts won twenty cent each." Mork continued the narrative, enumerating the problems that hindered Unit One and tripped up Unit Four on its march to a fifth consecutive victory.

> Unit One, the scouts worked hard but a few of the families there didn't keep their plots cleaned up, some of the shelves in the kitchens were very dirty, chips and trash was laying around and the garbage standing for days. Same in Unit Four. About three tents had paper and junk around the tents, garbage standing for days without being emptied.[36]

There were, in other words, weak links in the community. A few families who failed to pay adequate attention to their platform and its surroundings brought the whole unit down.

This contest was not just fun and games. It had a sharp catechetical edge regarding cleanliness and proper domesticity. Moreover, the fact of the contest and its monetary prizes held valuable lessons about cleanliness, virtue, and money. Those judged the cleanest were the winners, and winners were clean. Those judged unclean by comparison were not just tolerant of dirt, they were losers. Money went to the children of the clean and to children who worked toward cleanliness. The dirty received nothing.

Mork strove for cleanliness and order in the physical environs of the camp. He also sought to infuse social relations and the social order with concerns about and for cleanliness. As the contest also makes clear, he hoped to establish a strong association between proper domestic practice and social hierarchy, to clearly, cleanly ground claims of worth, worthiness, and moral strength in tidy domestic spaces and clean, orderly communities. Mork could be subtle, even playful, as he pressed camp residents to order their lives according to his gospel. But sometimes subtlety went out the window.

On March 25, 1939, Mork published an article titled "Filthy Human Beings" in the Indio camp paper, the *Covered Wagon News*. Far from the mild, overbearing summaries of cleanliness competitions, "Filthy Human Beings" featured the voice of an accuser confronting someone whose actions were an affront to the community. "This morning I found a tent platform so filthy, I had to tell the people there that either they cleaned the place up or they had to move out of camp." Their domestic environment was so offensive as to be intolerable. "I don't see how some people can be as filthy as they are," Mork continued, "[Their] platform was covered with matches and cigarette stubs, probably hadn't been swept in a week. Don't suppose it had been mopped since the family moved in." The litter and the lack of attention were significant in themselves. The mess also pointed to deep moral flaws inside the tent.

> I can't understand a family that don't have self-respect enough to keep a small platform clean. There is no mincing words with people so darn lazy. In the navy, if one of the sailors wouldn't keep clean, we would put him under the shower and scrub him with sand and a scrub brush. Rather harsh treatment, but it was effective. Only thing I can do here is speak to them, which I really hate to do in such a personal thing, but we really cannot tolerate filth with all the hot water there is available.[37]

Having traced the family's filth to its laziness and lack of self-respect (what else could explain it given the abundance of hot water?), Mork suggested once more that they could be cast out. "If speaking don't help," he wrote, "then we will just move them out."

Mork was going well beyond "speaking" in his attempt to reshape the family's behaviors. He was using the camp newspaper to publicize their domestic sins, interpreting those sins for the camp community, and arguing to the readership that domestic filth and the personality flaws that he associated with it were unacceptable in the camp community. Mork was addressing a particular family, but the sharp edges of his message were meant for all. Those who were clean and therefore virtuous were called to recognize and reject the filthy among them. Those who were dirty and therefore fallen had now been warned. To persist in the lazy acceptance of filth—in oneself or in others—was to be inferior and unfit for the camp.

There is much to analyze in Mork's words: the genealogy of his devotion to cleanliness, his anticipation of suburban values and neighborhood associations, his desire to evict, to ban, to purge the unclean. What I want to underscore, though, is the seamlessness and certainty of his move from exterior knowledge to interior knowledge, his confidence that a book could be known by its cover. What he said to the human beings in his camp, clean and filthy alike, was that no explanation beyond laziness and lack of self-respect could account for domestic mess. The exhausted, the ill, the depressed, and the otherwise over-burdened needed to prioritize sweeping and mopping and removal of papers and garbage over all other demands. To do otherwise was to court the wrath of both the camp manager and of the community.

Joseph McClain, who became manager of the Indio camp after Mork's departure, shared his predecessor's views and his penchant for harsh rhetoric. McClain wrote in the camp paper on August 26, 1939 enjoining readers, "Let's All Work for a Better Camp." The problem that he highlighted was a camp-wide disregard for cleanliness and willful ignorance as to the use of modern conveniences. "Unfortunately, this camp, in common with all others, has a few campers who are extremely careless about what might be considered little things, but which are more important than they may seem," he began. People were misusing toilets and "overloading the washing machines," leading to clogs, breakage, and "inconvenience for the campers." He gathered momentum as he wrote.

> Disorderliness and filth resulting from carelessness will not make this camp a beautiful and desirable place in which to live. It should not be necessary to have to bring this to your attention. Grown-up people with ordinary common sense and self-respect should know better than to do these things and they should be able to prevent their children from doing them. The Management is convinced that it is only a few of the campers who are responsible for this situation. We are asking any camper who sees others doing these things to report the matter to the office.[38]

In McClain's eyes, the domestic sins of the camp residents were signs of childishness and of deficits of both self-respect and common sense.

McClain acknowledged that the easy way out, the way least likely to make "enemies" would be to look the other way, "to shrug our shoulders and say . . . 'if they want to live that way, it's up to them.'" This would, however, cut directly against the mission of the camps. "We are here," he declared, "to do all we can to make this camp beautiful and healthful, as well as a pleasant place in which to live." And so he asked each camper to think of the whole camp but to act at the level of the tent platform. "Let each one of you consider him or her self a committee of one to see that your own behavior is what it should be."

Just one week later he wrote mostly encouraging words, praising the "fine spirit of cooperation displayed by most campers in all matters pertaining to camp welfare," while repeating his call to arms against dirt and disorder. "All campers are urged to keep their platforms and utility buildings clean and orderly and pay their rent promptly. This is our home—let's keep it clean and healthful."[39]

While serving as manager of the Arvin camp, Fred Ross worked with similar tools and toward similar goals, combining cleanliness competitions and harsh rhetoric to shape his camp residents' actions. He reported in the camp paper, the *Tow Sack Tattler*, that the "Saturday afternoon clean up inspection" had revealed that Units 1 and 4 were in "very good" shape, that Units 3 and 5 were "only fair," and that Unit 2 was somewhere in between. Unit 3 and Unit 5 had fallen down in the "Best Looking Unit" competition because there was "too much surplus junk scattered around." He encouraged residents to "pile your wood up in a neat pile on the right side of your cabins or tents" and to care for lawns and trees.[40]

One month later, in the October 25 edition, Ross described the results of the inspection under the headline "Who's Messy This Week?" He didn't name names, as readers might have hoped (or feared), but he gave the camp something to talk about, "I guess a lot of you clean folks living in dirty units have often wondered just who it was that was causing your Unit to lose so often in the clean-up contest." The clean folks didn't need to wonder any longer. "Some of you may have noticed me leaving slips of paper at various houses as I make my rounds. You can depend on it that whoever gets one of those slips has been one of the campers who caused your Unit to be found wanting in the weekly reckoning." To be found wanting one more time, Ross warned, would bring a summons to appear before the camp council and, perhaps, face eviction. When clearly articulated rules, an orderly environment, and the spirit of competition failed to inspire commitment to cleanliness, Ross too turned to ire, shame, and the threat of being cast out.

To camp managers, this was not only an exercise in encouraging housekeeping and gardening. It was also an exercise in the formation of citizens. Indeed, Ray Mork justified his program of rules and contests and praise and chastisement with reference to federal government investment and the expectation of a return. In a line of reasoning that has become all too familiar, Mork argued that those benefitting from government largesse owed the government improvement and should expect that proof would be required of them. "This may shock some," he wrote in December of 1940, "but I believe we should exercise much more control over the families that our administration is furnishing food and housing to." Improving exteriors was important, but outward signs were becoming less convincing. He wanted more reliable evidence of camper commitment to good domesticity. He wanted hearths and hearts to be cleansed and transformed.

> We demand cleanliness outside the tents, we have not gone inside the tents.... We do get into the tents as much as possible without seeming to do so, that is my staff and the camp nurse, we have no home management supervisor. I know we keep cleanliness outside the tent at a high standard. This is done by several methods.... It is not natural for the majority of the families that we get to keep their places clean, in fact it is the opposite, only a small minority will keep clean without supervision, even though facilities are available.[41]

In this late 1940 report, Mork sounded a negative note. His gospel, it seems, was not being carried over the threshold. "In many cases children are not bathed, the clothing is not kept clean, the inside of the tent is in bad shape. The standards of many of the families are on par or below that of families living in our worst slums." These problems were domestic in that they related to dwellings. They were also domestic in that they held consequences for the nation. "The food they eat, the way it is prepared, the homes they live in, the use they make of them, the clothing they wear, the training their children get, all on the funds that our administration furnishes them. In return our government should get better citizens." Better citizens would, without prompting or coercion, maintain cleanliness and order around tent platforms and on them as well.

Home Management as Home Mission

Public discourse in California's federal migrant camps overflowed with messages for migrant residents. Camp spaces must be cleaner. Tent platforms must be more orderly. Families must work to bring about this state of environmental, communal, and domestic harmony. Managers generated and broadcast these messages which, consciously or not, burdened migrant women with the labor needed to achieve this vision of home and with responsibility for most shortcomings.

As Ray Mork noted, managers seldom reached inside the tent to see how far their converts carried their faith. That work of monitoring and reporting also belonged to women: home management supervisors, who worked for domestic reform not in weekly diatribes and camp-wide proclamations, but in daily classes and personal consultations. Farm Security Administration literature described the home management supervisor as "a trained home economist who has several years of experience either in teaching home economics, home demonstration work, or in related fields." In the camps, she crossed the threshold into migrant dwellings in an attempt to lead migrant women to more modern ways of home-making.[42]

In this effort, home management supervisors continued the work of generations of home missionaries, working from the inside out and, implicitly, from women to men, to build households of faith. An anonymous voice from the FSA explains, "The home supervisor is interested in strengthening the family into a social unit to help them to achieve for themselves a condition of reasonable economic security, of good health through prevention and cure, of adequate diet for health protection, of clothing adequate for comfort and self respect." It also fell to her to help families achieve "a reasonably comfortable house, simple beauty in house and grounds, satisfactory home life, and gradually the family's participation in neighborhood or community affairs." The description continues in a clearly gendered, missionary vein.

> She arouses in the family a desire for better living conditions and, by consistent guidance, supervision, patience and understanding, teaches the

family to maintain this level. The home management supervisor helps the home maker to realize her full share of responsibility for the economic security of her family. She aids her in wise use of materials for the home, in production of a garden at home, and in the conservation of food products to be used during the winter months.

And because the home management supervisor was part of a federal agency and working in conjunction with the camp office, she also preached the righteousness of the paper trail. "One major duty of the home management supervisor is to help the farm family keep and use simple records of farm business and family living."[43]

This description of the home management supervisor and her work opens with a picture of a desired end state for the family: healthy, well-fed, strong socially, secure economically, and reasonably well-dressed; and for their home: comfortable, simple, a springboard to broader community engagement. The path to these goals, as described by the author, involves a plan that fits a family's "ability." More importantly, that path involves the home management supervisor in evangelization, conversion, and spiritual guidance.

Left to their own devices, these families would not want a better life or better living conditions, much less know how to reach and to persevere in such an elevated state. As she helped with this reorientation toward good domesticity, the home management supervisor had to be patient, she had to be a consistent guide lest the family stumble and fall. And the focus of her evangelistic work, the linchpin in the redeeming of a migrant family, was the "home maker," the wife and mother, the woman who needed to be drawn out of darkness and into the light of mindful moderation, resource conservation, and record-keeping. On the home maker's openness to the good news of modern domestic practice hung the family's chances for stability and respectability.

The precise contents of conversations between home management supervisors and migrant wives, mothers, and families—the tensions, the compromises, the misunderstandings that inevitably attend attempts at missionary reform—are absent from the federal archive. There is, however, a robust record of the programs offered to camp residents by home management supervisors and a reliable record of campers' participation in those programs. Migrant women (I have found no evidence of migrant men taking part) joined in programs such as quilt making, mattress making, and sewing. They showed up for classes on canning, healthy diet, and cooking.

As manager C. W. Kirkpatrick wrote from the Winters camp in October of 1940, "Under the direction of Miss Bingham, Home Management Supervisor, girl's and women's sewing groups were organized for the purpose of learning how to sew, crochet, etc., and to make over old clothes so that they might be usable. . . . [B]oth attendance and accomplishments are encouraging." Tom Collins reported two months later that the programs at Winters remained robust, "sewing for adults, averaging 150 garments made or altered per week; toy making . . . hobby shop . . . two cooking demonstrations—whole wheat flour uses—by Home Management Supervisor." Home management supervisors could also intervene in more dire circumstances such as when a "shockingly malnourished family" arrived at the Yuba City camp in the late summer of 1941. Manager Frank Iusi wrote, that the "HMS plans to visit her daily for a week armed with recipes."[44] Her roles were many, and in each of them the "HMS" was both missionary and model. Camp records indicate that most, if not all, migrant women appreciated the home management programs and took part in them.

On the front page of its September 22, 1939 issue, Arvin's *Tow Sack Tattler* announced the establishment of a "Home Management Club," in consultation and cooperation with "Home Management Supervisor Mrs. Hayes." Hayes seems to have come up with the idea for the club, and the article notes that she "called the meeting to order," but a migrant woman wrote the article and vouched for her—"We have a very very nice supervisor she is just another lady from the south" and described the agenda for the club.

> We are to study different branches of sewing and cooking and a number of things pertaining to Home Management. There are to be two classes each week and since a majority of the ladies plan to work in the cotton it [was] decided to have these in the evening instead of the afternoon. . . . So all you ladies come on out lets work together exchange ideas and get acquainted with our neighbors.[45]

Mrs. Hayes was willing to schedule club meetings to accommodate women's multiple roles, no one of which could be neglected without significant hardship for the family. And for those women able to pivot from twelve hours in the cotton to a class on sewing, the Home Management Club and its domestic curriculum would be there.

A report from Elizabeth Davisson, home management supervisor of the Brawley camp in December of 1941, described a striking series of missionary successes. It had been just two weeks since Japan attacked Pearl Harbor. Nazi Germany was tightening its grip on Europe. But there were signs of hope in Brawley, California. The Children's Welfare Committee, an outgrowth of the home management program, had launched a "milk program" for children ages two to six. Thirty children enrolled. Davisson wrote:

> The children assembled at noon, were served one hot dish, bread and peanut butter, applesauce and plenty of milk. They responded to the nursery school procedures of washing hands, preparing for nap and napping for two hours. At four o'clock a second glass of milk was served with a cookie. Of their own accord the women wore hairbands and aprons and assumed the responsibilities of the Program. It was their wish to prepare a 'Minute Report' of the Children's Welfare Committee for Council Meeting this approaching Tuesday, a copy of which I enclose.

These events played out in a public context, not within the sheltering walls of a tent, but they were encouraging nonetheless. The women came properly dressed, provided proper nourishment, encouraged the children to follow rules, and prepared a report on the program. They did all of this not because they were forced but because they wanted to. "It is, as I would like to stress again, their own initiative," Davisson continued, "I merely offered my complete attention to their initiative and fostered each individual's enterprise wishing deeply within my heart that we might see a coordinated expression from them." And because the milk program and all of the good that surrounded it had come about through the migrant women's initiative, it was the truest indication that the home management supervisor was succeeding in her mission.

Meanwhile, Davisson wrote, domestic instruction continued. While the Children's Welfare Committee was attending to the milk program,

Davisson was giving her attention to the women serving as "hostess" for a day at the Brawley camp's "Home Center." The Home Center included a demonstration kitchen, dining area, sewing equipment, and, on Davisson's initiative, a play pen to allow the hostess to have her baby near. Hostesses spent the entire day at the Home Center passing on domestic knowledge to fellow migrants and often using the kitchen to prepare their own family's meals. Davisson saw a teaching moment.

> It has been suggested that [the hostess] serve her family at [the] home center, setting up one of our tables with our dishes and silver. Wherever possible HMS plans her food buying for that meal... or offers her special information as to food values and preparing foods to retain the nutritional contents at the maximum.

Without even stepping onto the tent platform, Davisson could advise and oversee food selection and purchase, preparation and presentation, and even guide the migrant mother and wife in the proper setting of a table. Whether the family stayed in camp for another six months or moved on later that week, they would have the memory of this domestic ritual and might, when opportunity presented itself, recreate it.

Lest we imagine that the home management specialist's record was one of uninterrupted progress, the words of Davisson's immediate successor at Brawley provide an important corrective. A mere six months later, focus had shifted from milk program triumphs to tales of "terrific struggle with one crisis following close on the heels of another." The new home management supervisor, Miss Gene Nicholson, had run aground trying to unify nursery school volunteers in their approach to the children. She concluded, among other things, that "in a community where practically no one has had a significant experience in group participation, one should not expect very expert or even cooperative group behavior." Nicholson chronicled the divergent approaches and attitudes that had damaged the "Nursery School atmosphere":

> One woman, during a half hour absence of the [Home Management Supervisor] swept the nursery school, sorted out all the playthings and put them in boxes which she hid from the children who were huddled in one corner of the room when the H. M. S. came back. Another woman

scolded all the children individually in an attempt to manage the milk drinking before the H. M. S. could stop her, and another woman placidly watch[ed] all the children climb over the fence and go down the road.

Nicholson's response was to develop a list of rules for the volunteers, an "outline for . . . behavior" around the children. The first item on the list was "Speak very quietly." Item four was "Let the children govern themselves as much as possible" and was followed by a suggestion for filtration, "Remove the angry child from the group if he is in the wrong."[46]

Passing through Domestic Filters

Whether across a space of six months or six years, the domestic missionary work of the federal migrant camps ebbed and flowed. Setbacks followed close on the heels of progress in the struggle to cultivate proper dynamics on and around the tent platform. The supply of the unconverted, the divergent, and the recalcitrant seemed never-ending. The need to filter persisted.

This is not to suggest that the rules established by the hierarchy, the rhetoric of the camp manager, and the pastoral work of the home management specialist led nowhere. Indeed, Paul Taylor's vision of filtration became reality in most camps in the garden homes program. This program offered some "deserving low income families" the opportunity to move off of tent platforms and into a modest, newly-built adobe home in a community of similar homes directly adjacent to the main camp. As with tent platforms, the types of housing diversified over the life of the program, but the purpose remained the same. To quote Taylor, "The aim . . . is to lift the migrant one step above the camp, to provide a better base of operations for those who can find work in the vicinity several months out of the year." In garden homes in Arvin, Indio, Shafter, Brawley, Winters, Firebaugh, Yuba City and elsewhere, some families and not others were rewarded with solid walls, a firm roof, a taste of what had been and what might still be.[47]

To be considered for residency in a garden home, applicants had to meet certain criteria established by the camp program hierarchy and subsequently verified by camp management and a government family selectionist. The head of the family had to be between twenty-one and

Migrant family in front of their garden home in the Shafter Camp, 1938. Photograph by Dorothea Lange. *Type of house in Shafter camp for migratory workers, California. These homes represent a first step in stabilization of this group. This is the first family to be selected by Farm Security Administration for housing.* November 1938. Courtesy of Library of Congress. https://www.loc.gov/item/2017770777/.

fifty-five years old and employed in agricultural labor. The family could have no more than six members and had to "give evidence of internal harmony and ability to cooperate with the community."[48] Families that fit this description could apply for residency in the garden homes by filling out an application, undergoing a physical exam, and sitting for two interviews—one in the office and one in their tent. For most of the program, a committee of three camp staff conducted the initial screening and made a recommendation, but the final adjudicating authority was in the central office in San Francisco.[49]

Those chosen to live in the garden homes followed rules that were more exacting. The rules for living in the Indio camp garden homes are a hybrid of philosophy, expectation, and guidance. The list opens with a preamble:

> The family residing in this house has been chosen for rental privileges by your government representatives because of certain high qualifications and standards. We have faith in your integrity and your intention to be a good neighbor. We have sympathy for your desire to have a better, cleaner, and more homey home. To that end, please feel free to consult the project manager. At no time will the management ever attempt to interfere in any phase of your lives.

In spite of qualifications and standards and faith in integrity, the manager felt it important to explain the connection between domestic exteriors and domestic interiors.

Rule four reads, "Nothing shows more clearly the superior quality of a family than a home and yard well kept, neat, trim, and orderly; with trees well watered and healthy lawns cut and trimmed, gardens free from weeds and everywhere the appearance of care and preciseness." Put differently, if you want to answer all questions about the quality of your domestic life, weed your garden and cut your lawn. Rule seven focuses on expectations around domestic food production: "As we have furnished each family with a garden spot, we are anxious to see what wonderful gardens can be grown here." And while rule nine mentions again that families bear the burden "of watering and caring for fruit trees, shrubs and lawns," rule 5, back up the page, seems to lift the burden of close observation, "We are sure that families in these splindid [sic] homes will not need supervision as to the above, nor hints, nor advice."[50]

In 1940 and 1941, the FSA undertook what they called "Progress Surveys" of families living in garden homes. The reports, filed in the summer of 1941, provide a sketch of the families who were living in the homes and how the program was working. They help answer questions about who flowed through the filter at the camps in Yuba City, Indio, and Shafter.

Twenty families in the Yuba City labor homes, twenty-four from Indio, and thirty-three from Shafter completed the survey schedules.

The heads of families in the Yuba City homes were overwhelmingly from Midwestern and Pacific states, though one each came from India and Sweden. The average family size was four members. Husbands averaged thirty-six years old, wives averaged thirty, and the children were between eight and nine years old. The financial picture for the families that responded, while not exactly rosy, was also not bleak. Income was greater than expenses by roughly $160, and the average family's net worth was $352. Life in the labor homes also correlated to a dramatic increase in canning. The report summary states, "An average of 148 quarts of fruits and vegetables were canned per family during 1940 compared to an average of 99 quarts the year before they moved into the labor homes."[51]

The story of the Indio labor homes was similar. Twenty-two of the twenty-four heads of family were US born; six came from Arkansas. Of the two non-US families, one came from Mexico and one was from Canada. The average family consisted of 3.5 people with husbands and wives averaging thirty years of age. Indio labor home families were slightly better off than those in Yuba City, having earned roughly $275 more than they spent, and claiming an average net worth of $376. Canning was less popular in Indio, though labor home life still led to increased food storage and preservation. During 1940, labor home families canned "39 quarts of fruits and vegetable," after averaging only twenty-five quarts while living on a tent platform.[52] This was, as a percentage, a greater increase in canning than at Yuba City, though the practice seems not to have been as widespread to begin with.

The Shafter labor homes provide a third set of data points to consider. The heads of thirty-two of the thirty-three families were US-born. Twelve of these had been born in Oklahoma, seven in Texas, and "the remainder... in various midwestern and southern states." One had been born in Russia. Shafter families were a bit larger on average, 4.4 people, and somewhat older with husbands averaging thirty-eight, wives averaging thirty-five, and children between ten and eleven years old.

These families were not new to the San Joaquin Valley. They had been in Kern County, on average, four years and eight months before being accepted into the labor homes and had been in the homes nearly two years prior to the survey. In other words, they had arrived in the vicinity in the late summer of 1934 and had, quite possibly, spent five years in and out of camps before settling into Shafter's labor homes. But things were looking up for them financially. They were earning an average of $291 more than they were spending and had $138 left in their pockets each year after paying old debts. The average net worth of a Shafter labor home family was $438. In 1940, these families canned, on average, "154 quarts of fruits and vegetables . . . compared to an average of 122 quarts the year before they moved into the labor homes."[53]

These snapshots of domestic progress testify at least to the fact that certain types of domestic appearance and domestic performance earned families greater support from the camp program, an elevated status in the eyes of camp officials, and the responsibility of continued refinement, continued performance. They also testify to the fact that migrants could be energetic participants in the program of domestic reconstruction and filtration.

Voices of the Managed and Missionized

Migrant voices confirm further what the progress reports document. A moment described by Tom Collins in an early report from Arvin captures sentiments common among those who were able to create domestic space on something other than hard soil. It was February of 1936 and the newly-opened Arvin camp was still receiving materials to build its tent platforms. Camp residents were sometimes asked to help with the construction. Collins reported, "One of the women who had just installed one of the new tent platforms for herself and family must have gone into ecstasy over her good fortune." He did not witness the ecstasy firsthand, but relied on her husband for an account. "Yer shuld haf seed the ole lady when she got the new deck. She did a jig on it. Fust time I seed her danse sins wees be marred. Yes sir she was sur tickld. Did her mo good than two doses medcin."[54]

There are no other accounts of migrants dancing on newly-constructed tent platforms, but the archive is full of other stories of eager participation in home management activities, of efforts to keep the camp clean, and of a general embrace of the domestic norms that government camp staff preached.

Camp newspapers often conveyed migrants' support of camp domestic programs and carried accounts of them acting in accordance with standards of order and cleanliness. In the November 24, 1939 issue of the *Tow Sack Tattler*, an anonymous resident of the Arvin camp reminded readers of what living conditions had been like outside the gate. The author quoted from a 1936 survey conducted by the "State Relief Administration" in the Imperial Valley.

> Old tents, gunny sacks, dry goods boxes and scrap tin, these are the material from which the dwellings are constructed. All the shacks visited were... very dirty and swarming with clouds of flies, there were no sanitary facilities in evidence and the back yards were being used for a toilet and irrigation ditch half-filled with muddy water had been used for all purposes.

It was a disquieting picture of domestic apocalypse and, as the migrant author pointed out, it was not their domestic present. "Are you living under such conditions today? You would be if the Farm Security had not stepped in and done something about it."[55] As we saw earlier, another camp resident, Rosetta Spoehward, composed the poem "The Government Camp" for the *Tattler*, expressing appreciation for the chance the camp gave her and others to rebuild their domestic and civic worlds having "come here flat broke and lank." Transformation, Ms. Spouehward testified, began upon arrival. "Mr. Ross takes us in and gives us a tent / And all he requires is three Dollars rent." People would complain, she acknowledged, but they were the sort you would find anywhere, those who want something for nothing. For them and for the better type of folks, she had words of advice.

> If we would only think it over rite
> To live in this world is a pretty hard fight
> But we ought to be thankful for this place to stay
> And put all those foolish ideas away
> We could make the camp a beautiful town
> If we'd only give a smile instead of a frown
> And there's only one way this thing to do
> Do unto others as you'd have them do to you

For Rosetta and for the anonymous author above, dwelling in camp was a blessing to which residents ought to respond with gratitude, cooperation, and a cheerful neighborliness rooted in the Golden Rule. The beauty of the camp grew from individuals acting to brighten their twelve-by-fourteen-foot corner of it. They appreciated the stability of the camp, the restoration of order that camp environs brought. If they resented being told to clean and to be clean, they kept those feelings to themselves.

Another anonymous submission from "A Camper" framed the program of observation, inspection, and evaluation as helpful and good for all. The author let readers know that guards were going to begin inspecting lots and platforms throughout the camp to aid in beautification, "to look for cleanness around your lot, to instruct you as what to do to have it come up to standard after he has told you what to do." The author continued, "he is going to follow up and see that you have did that thing he has warned you to do." Some might be slow or forgetful in tending to domestic spaces. This inspection regimen, the author averred, was a migrant-approved program to address such shortcomings.

Eighteen months later, the Indio camp's paper, the *Happy Valley People's Word*, reported that camp residents had officially approved close observation of their house cleaning practices. In a brief item titled "Clean Up," readers learned that the camp council had voted to institute a "clean-up day" on Saturdays to ensure that "utility buildings and platforms are made clean and kept clean." Public discourse in the camps regularly included camp residents' endorsements of the camp program's particular "kinetics of homemaking." In this sense, the religion of clean and orderly dwelling was common among migrants and shared between migrants and camp officials.

For some migrants there was a clear intersection between Protestant faith and domestic norms. A glimpse of this intersection is visible through the dust of Tissie's collapsing marriage. Though obscured by Collins's clumsy reconstruction of the Arkansan's dialect, we can see that her husband's understanding of domestic behaviors and standards was grounded in his sense of "desent" and righteous behavior. John Auguston, a resident of the Indio camp and chairman of the camp council, provides a vastly more expansive treatment.

Auguston wrote regularly for the Indio camp's paper, and opened his December 9, 1939 column with the question: "How many of you folks would like to have a prayer meeting?" This was not a rhetorical question. "All that would like to meet one night and hold a prayer meeting, please come out to the council meeting Monday night at 7 o'clock at the social center." He followed this invitation with calls to mothers to watch that their children were not misusing toilets, washtubs, and other "conveniences." He also asked "everyone to cooperate with me in keeping their platforms and surroundings clean and sanitary."

> The flies are bad and unpleasant odors from garbage pails and dirty clothes are not only unpleasant to our neighbors, but unhealthy for us. Let us not have any family in our unit have to be moved to one of the other units from any such cause as being unsanitary.

As Ray Mork often did, Auguston held out the possibility of the ban for those who did not agree to live in a clean and orderly way. Elsewhere in the paper was an announcement that Miss Evelyn Jacobs, Home Management Supervisor, would be in camp holding "various interesting meetings, and . . . discuss[ing] general and individual problems of homemaking with campers and tenants of garden homes."[56]

Auguston opened the New Year by delving further into the connection between divine and domestic orders. He greeted readers with news that the camp was "in the best and cleanest condition I have ever seen it" and by encouraging residents to "keep our home clean and looking good, and we will not be ashamed for visitors to come in and visit through our home." Auguston continued, "Let's keep all trash and garbage cleaned up around our platforms and keep the water hose in place and then everything will be swell."

He also reminded parents to teach their children "that the utility building (the lavatory) isn't a playhouse." It was hard to keep the bathrooms clean—not to mention the children—if they were playing in and around the toilets. Auguston then transitioned to what he described as "a few lines of Scripture."

> There were animals feeding on the luxurious meadows or basking in the sunshine or gamboling in the valley, contented and restful in their

peaceful lair. These were a part of God's creation, but among them all there was not one to give glory or praise to the Creator, so man was made. In the image of his Maker, male and female created He them. (Gen. 1–27)

This is not the text of Genesis 1:27. It is not the text of the preceding verses in Genesis 1, which describe the creation of "living creatures according to their kinds," but leave feeding and basking and gamboling for others to imagine. But the point of Auguston's scriptural inventions lay beyond the words of Genesis. His interpretation of the text followed.

> The woman was made to be the helpmeet to man, a companion to share in his joy, to stand by his side as an equal who could be one with him in love and companionship. God himself celebrated that first marriage, and that sacred institution has come down to us from Eden days. Why anyone should question the authenticity of creation by the One Who is All-Wise and All-Powerful, when there are so many evidences of his supernatural power is beyond comprehension.[57]

The four parts of Auguston's January 6 musings, intriguing enough on their own, are especially so when taken together: 1) an entreaty to keep home (the camp, one's platform) clean and orderly; 2) a description of the created order (restful, peaceful) and humanity's role in it (give glory to God), 3) an assertion of proper human ordering (woman as helpmeet, companion, equal, one in love and companionship) and 4) a justification for that order (God himself celebrated it in "Eden days"). One through-line in Auguston's thought is personal and divine love of order and harmony. While he does not say that God created the world without balled-up paper and cigarette butts and requires the righteous to "keep all trash and garbage cleaned up around our platforms and keep the water hose in place," he seems to have wanted his readers to view ordered domestic spaces and matrimonial order as reflecting the proper ordering of creation and, therefore, as pleasing to the divine, the wise, and the powerful.

Auguston had his hand in two brief articles written for the February 10, 1940 edition of the *Migratory Clipper*, each focused on reforming the community and bringing exterior and interior states into harmony. The first was a description of the camp council's weekly meeting, during which the council members set the camp speed limit at "8 miles per hour not exceeding ten," and also decided to declare publicly that it "no longer approves of any disorder in camp, such as drinking, gambling, and using profane language." Cleaning up the camp's moral environment was, however, only part of the challenge, as Auguston spelled out "to the Clipper and its Readers" one page later.

> The camp is in very nice condition and I have to say that the camp council sure does appreciate that very much and [hopes] you will continue to keep every place cleaned up and help keep peace among the residents of the camp and by doing so you will do a Christian act and that is the right thing to do, so let's try to help each other and be good neighbors and we can kill a multitude of envy and strife and lets do good to those who do evil to us as evil for evil is sin.[58]

In one lengthy sentence, Chairman Auguston connected most of the principles of the camp system's domestic reform program and presented them for consumption by camp residents. The camp looked clean and good; orderly residents would keep it that way. Good residents would also work to maintain good relations with each other. This was the Christian approach to social living. An ordered environment and ordered relationships went hand in hand. Eradicating garbage and eradicating strife, envy, and evil were conjoined tasks. Auguston hoped for a movement toward Christian practice (prayer meetings), Christian homes (woman as helpmeet), and a Christian society. He called readers to eradicate social sins such as drinking and gambling, and to work toward peace among good, clean neighbors.

These moments of public discourse show camp residents making peace with and even embracing the camp program's vision of domestic righteousness. We see migrants telling other migrants to set their houses in order, to clean up their lives and their communities, and to dwell righteously. And while this was the majority position, there were also dissenters. Camp-wide cleanliness competitions with winners and losers underscore the need for evaluation and the fact that some did worse than others. The poetry of Rosetta Spoehward and the musings of John Auguston point to the failings of neighbors. Migrants whose practices set negative examples dot the records of the camp office, but rarely do they speak for themselves about their experiences of the camp program. George Burns, a resident of the Indio camp, is an exception. He penned a lengthy poem, "The Arkies Welcome," and submitted it to the *Happy Valley People's Word*.

> From Arkansas here in a Buick eight.
> The casings blow out as I enter the gate.
> I parked in front of the office door.
> To register and [wait] 'till I could buy some more.
>
> I registered in the office got a platform and tent.
> That was my new home with no worry about rent.
> At the FSA office I told of being in a rut.
> Asked for some sardines to fill my gut.[59]

In less than two stanzas, Burns has moved his reader through the gate, into the camp office, and onto the tent platform, and then back to the office to ask about a grant for food. His efficiency as a poet, perhaps intentionally, ends here. For the remainder of the poem, he focuses on the inefficiency and intrusiveness of camp life.

> They asked a thousand questions about my grandfather's life,
> The names of my children and the age of my wife.
> They told me they would have to investigate,
> I told them I'd survive if they wouldn't be too late.
>
> In a few days the investigator came around
> I handed him my [illegible] and he wrote it down.
> They gave me some sardines, rice and graham flour too,
> And said that was all that they could do.
> I asked him for a grant to buy fuel and clothes,
> And interrupted him when he tried to oppose.
>
> He finally put me down for a mighty welcome grant,
> But told me I could get work when the rancher began to plant
> My application went in, and my grant came back,
> But I had to work it out with a stick and a sack.

Burns had straightforward, common needs: food, shelter, clothing, transportation. Camp officials and the camp program hierarchy controlled access to these items and set the terms for their distribution. As we have seen, those terms included exerting oneself toward domestic cleanliness and order as proof of one's personal worth and the worthiness of one's family and home. Burns recorded this reality and his response to it.

> They told me to pick up papers, and clean up the ground.
> Grants are worked out at 40 cents per hour, just walking around.
> Some come here and write for paw and maw,
> But I had rather be on the farm back in Arkansas

"The Arkies Welcome" places a framework of immediate need around migrants' interactions with federal camps and their culture. Burns tells the story of his family's hunger being subordinated to the requirements of a system, of being subjected to the teachings of the Gospel of Mork, when all they needed was a place to live until they could get the Buick repaired.

In April of 1942, fully seven years after Tom Collins began implementing a plan to clean up the Hooverville outside the town of Marysville, Ruth Coe, an assistant supervisor in the FSA's Department of Community and Family Services, took a tour of the camp at Yuba City—just down the road from the Marysville camp. This was not just any tour. She joined the camp manager (Frank Iusi), the Home Management Supervisor, and the camp nurse "for the purposes of [a] sanitary inspection." Her report of the experience was short. With the exception of one cabin "occupied by two bachelors," living spaces were impressively clean. "The cabins themselves," she wrote, "were immaculate—floors had been freshly mopped—beds made and clean bedding was noticed throughout—dishes washed and cupboard in order—food covered with clean towels—clothes hung up."

There was near perfect correspondence between internal and external states. The work that had gone into cleaning and maintaining living spaces was in evidence on the plots of land around them. "Outside of the cabins the people were busy cutting the weeds and tall grass. Many small flower gardens had been started, and a small vegetable garden in back of the cabins."⁶⁰ As important to Coe was the fact that the camp residents seemed happy to be inspected. She reported that they were "eager and ready for us to call, and most of them invited us into the cabin and it was evident that they wanted us to 'set a spell.'" She wrote by way of conclusion that "each family was trying to outdo the other on maintaining a clean home."

Coe was in Yuba City to have a closer look at the practice of "inspecting the interior of all cabins each and every Saturday in addition to the exterior surroundings," which Manager Iusi had announced "with great pleasure and pride" in his monthly narrative report for February 1942. Iusi was so sanguine about the inspection regimen that he was also preparing residents of the Yuba City camp's apartment units for monthly inspections. He had heard that the apartments were in awful shape inside and, he opined in a voice that could have come from any camp manager at any point in the program, "there isn't much value in rehabilitation if we don't start out with a reasonable degree of living sanitation."⁶¹

Reports from Iusi and Coe prompted further discussion in San Francisco. Iusi began the weekly interior / exterior inspections during an outbreak of measles "as a means to discover all cases of disease" and out of the conviction that "filth and dirt and unsanitary conditions [are] a breeder for germs."⁶² These exceptional inspections quickly became the norm. Iusi and his team were verifying interior states camp-wide, just as Collins, Mork, Ross, and Iusi himself had dreamed of years ago.

Frank Iusi and the Yuba City camp were the focus of attention because they provided an exception to the "dirt and filth and unsanitary conditions" that remained a problem in the camps. To borrow from Ruth Coe, "FSA [has] been working with the migrant group for several years now and there are still too many families living in deplorable filth in the camps." As FSA officials mulled over the situation, a number of points became clear. Milen Dempster, Acting Chief of Community and Family Services, listed them.

1. That Mrs. Coe is correct in reporting that there are many families living in deplorable filth in the camps.
2. That Yuba City is perhaps the only camp really clean inside and out.
3. That their weekly inspection of cabins is succeeding both as a demonstration and as a habit forming process.

> 4. That it was not achieved by stimulating the residents to express their desire for it through the democratic process, but was imposed from above.[63]

Yuba City's cleanliness, though promising, was less than it appeared. The inspections were coerced. Writing to Myer Cohen, acting assistant regional director, Dempster, a former camp manager himself, wondered, "Could residents be stimulated to desire this weekly inspection and request it?" He promptly answered his own question.

> I believe that, with a careful approach, our able managers could succeed in stimulating the campers not only to want it, but to vote for it and support it. If the inspection can be kept in the mood of a friendly visit for the protection of health and the discovering of contagious diseases, and not be mandatory, the feeling that privacy was intruded upon could be kept at a minimum.[64]

It was all in the presentation, Dempster concluded. Arrive with a smile and a mission to snuff out harmful bacteria, and the migrants would embrace the inspection team. Not only would they welcome FSA officials onto their platforms, they would want them there badly enough to vote for the opportunity to welcome them.

As noted, seven years had passed since Tom Collins launched his work among the disordered, destitute residents of the Marysville squatters' camp. And still, those continuing his work in the camp system were working out the basics of their missionary approaches. Every camp manager worth his salt worried about keeping camp environs and tent platforms clean. Every camp manager implemented some sort of plan. And still the problem persisted. Conversions were not complete, or not verifiably so. Camp officials could often get migrants to clean their tent platforms and the surrounding areas. They could even get them to keep the interiors of twelve-by-fourteen tents and similarly-sized cabins neat and tidy. But could they get them to *want* it, to *desire* it, and to *vote* for it? That was a taller order, which points to a persistent problem in mission work and a conundrum in the progressive view of humanity.

Camp program personnel, from Collins to Coe and everyone in between, valued the migrants' freedom and would have defended the migrants' right to choose their own paths. Indeed, migrants chose their own paths every day. They chose to enter and to leave camps, to accept and to turn down work, to attend the camp council meeting or to smoke cigarettes and leave the butts around their platform.

At the same time, camp officials were exerting themselves mightily to improve the wants behind those choices. They found migrants at some version of point A (dirty, disordered) and tried to move them to a rather specific and clearly superior point B (clean, orderly). But what they wanted most was for migrants to want to make that move and to do so uncoerced. Camp program workers and officials acted every day on the belief that all people have intrinsic value. They also believed that this intrinsic value would not be fully realized in the "broken wagon wheel" place that most migrants occupied.

This is a good moment to recall an insight, however obvious, conveyed by Tom Collins in 1935 and echoed throughout the files and papers of the camp program: migrant families were not domestic cretins. They were not universally blind to the collapsed domestic spaces and deteriorated domestic standards. Many of them worked on their own to restore dwelling spaces and dwelling practices as quickly as they could. One way to read migrants' uses of cardboard, sticks, pieces of canvas, and scraps of corrugated tin to build shelters is as an expression of a profound religious longing for demarcated space that could serve, however provisionally, as home.

Indeed, migrants were alert to this crisis in the lives of those around them. There is abundant evidence of migrants helping other migrants settle and dwell in more civilized-seeming ways. Weekly and monthly narrative reports from the camps capture stories of welcome committees formed by migrant women, working to help new arrivals orient themselves and establish homes. Collins reported on such a committee in the Arvin camp in the summer of 1936. "Good neighbors" sprang into action when "families arrived in destitute circumstances."

> In such cases the destitute groups were referred to the good neighbors in the districts where they were assigned. The neighbors collected food and supplies from their own stocks to carry the groups over to the morrow. There groups were then given "guarantees" to the amount of $5.00 on a grocer and an oil station. . . . In all cases the new arrivals were working

within three days after arrival, and all sums advanced or guaranteed, were repaid. We believe this shows ... that the genius spirit of the Good Neighbor does continue to prevail at Arvin Camp.[65]

This spirit prevailed at the Indio camp as well, as Ray Mork reported in May of 1938. Two years later, Yuba City camp manager Frank Iusi proudly announced that residents of the Yuba City camp had organized a welfare committee, the function of which was to familiarize newly-arrived migrants with the domestic landscape of the camp and the programs to improve domestic lives. "The help generally consists of a credit authorization at the local coop and bedding or beds and clothes if any of these items are on hand." With materials for a rudimentary domestic space provided, the welfare committee could point the family toward the activities that would enrich life on the tent platform or in any home.[66]

Migrants could be effective domestic missionaries on their own, helping fellow migrants to eat well, sleep properly, secure income, establish credit, shelter themselves, and become aware of opportunities for betterment. The records of the camp office testify to this truth across the life of the program. Migrants' lives and their tents were often altars of improvement and domestic success.

Why, then, did the lambasting and the paternalism and the condescension continue? Collins praised the good neighbors but infantilized and shamed a bad housekeeper and an ill-matched couple. Mork praised migrant generosity and the diligence of his scouts, and then scalded the community with accusations of filth, ignorance, and lack of self-respect. Frank Iusi and Fred Ross joined in this ritual chorus of praise and condemnation. And in the face of successful inspections of exterior and interior domestic spaces, the camp hierarchy worried that migrants hadn't wanted those inspections badly enough.

One can explain these reactions with reference to the mixed and shifting body of migrants moving into and out of the camps. Members of this group practiced domesticity differently and reacted in a wide range of ways to the social and governmental pressures of the camp environment. From 1935 to 1943 there were both exemplary camp residents and really, really bad seeds. But this is only part of an explanation.

Missionary terrain is contested terrain. The doctrines and lifeways that missionaries seek to impart or impose are unstable. And the status of these beliefs and practices as necessary to human happiness, communal flourishing, or individual salvation requires assertion, reassertion, and defense. In this pattern of recognizing virtue and amplifying vice, we see the assertion of perspective and of power. The hallelujahs and the curses emerge from a passionate group possessing expertise, and eager, sometimes desperate, to convince both the non-expert faithful and the unconverted that *their* standards of domestic cleanliness and order were *the* standards of cleanliness and order.

The managers, the specialists, and the family selectionists also seem convinced that though migrants pursued those standards, they would never fully embody them. They would always, in some small way, be wanting. They might no longer be "filthy human beings," but dirt would still be apparent to the properly trained eye.

4

The Sanitary Unit

At least a few migrants encountered a camp sanitary unit before laying eyes on their tent platform or interacting meaningfully with the camp manager in his office. Sanitary units, sometimes called utility buildings, housed a camp's toilets, sinks, wash tubs, and showers. Reaching a toilet was likely an urgent goal for at least some arriving migrants. And as we shall see, proper use of the sanitary units was an urgent missionary goal of the government camp program.

As migrant families settled into life in a federal camp, they grew increasingly familiar with the sanitary unit. Even if they were reluctant to interact with its "conveniences," they could not have missed the structure itself. In describing the Arvin camp layout as part of his 1936 inspection, Special Agent Herbert Mensing noted that the camp's forty-acre grounds were divided into three plots measuring roughly 250 feet on each side "in the middle of which stands a utility building or sanitary unit." Each of the three sanitary units, he continued, served thirty-two tent platforms.

> The utility buildings are of frame panel construction with cement floors and are divided into two sections, one for women and the other for men. The women's section contains four cement laundry trays, six showers with hot and cold water and dressing rooms, six toilets, and a galvanized iron wash sink. The men's section contains only two laundry trays, four toilets, and a six feet (6') urinal trough. Water for baths and laundry purposes is supplied by a welded steel tubular water heater of three hundred (300) to four hundred fifty gallons, which burns Diesel oil.[1]

These structures and their technologies were central to camp life.

The sanitary unit, like the tent platform, was a space for instruction, performance, and evaluation. It was an obvious location for the practice of biopolitics, the exercise of power and the enforcement of norms on, through, and around the body. The sanitary unit was also an important location for the practice of electoral politics. Each migrant camp was divided into sub-communities based on the number of sanitary units it contained. Camp constitutions, like the one adopted by the camp council at Brawley, described the system and its structure. "Four (4) members shall be elected to the Community Council from each unit; a Unit shall be a political subdivision of the Community Council; the boundaries and/or extent of which shall be as follows THE UTILITY BUILDINGS SHALL BE NUMBERED FROM THE ONE ON THE S.W. AS NO 1, CLOCKWISE TO NO. 5 ON THE S.E. THOSE PLATFORMS AROUND EACH UTILITY SHALL BE CONSIDERED PART OF THAT UNIT."[2] Camp residents organized, petitioned, voted, and stood for election, based on where they showered, shaved, and (in theory, at least) peed.

Gathering migrants in a camp and housing them on tent platforms made the sanitary unit necessary. Without some communal space for

Shafter Camp, 1938. The sanitary units are the large white buildings in the center of the groups of tents.
Photograph by Dorothea Lange. *Farm Security Administration camp for migrant agricultural workers at Shafter, California.* June 1938. Courtesy of Library of Congress. https://www.loc.gov/item/2017770543/.

maintaining the body and disposing of its wastes, the camp program, with concentrations of people in rudimentary dwellings, would recreate or even intensify the messes its visionaries sought to clean up. The theology and the cosmology of the camp system also made the sanitary unit necessary. With such a strong connection between cleanliness and righteousness, and a pervasive insistence on the correspondence between exterior and interior states, federal camps had to provide technologies for the orderly management of bodily dirt.

In the world the camp program imagined, good people who inhabited clean homes could not have dirty bodies or be careless in the management of their waste. In an item submitted to the Arvin camp's weekly newspaper in November of 1939, "Miss Engeln" of the Kern County Health Department put it succinctly. "Each week there has been something in the paper about keeping our houses clean. I would like to say something today about keeping our bodies clean. Just as no one likes to be in or look at a dirty house, no one likes to be in the company of a person with a dirty body."[3]

The brief and sometimes troubled history of the migrant camp sanitary unit offers an opportunity to delve further into the functioning of federal migrant camps as missionary spaces, and to consider the discourses and practices surrounding dirt and cleanliness, contamination and purity, as they operated in agricultural California during the Great Depression. Camp managers and members of the communities surrounding the camps worried about migrants' bodies: the dirt that was on them and the waste that came from them. They worried because, as Miss Engeln's words indicate, they wanted migrants to be clean and to value cleanliness, and because they wanted to avoid contamination, both biological and moral. Always lurking about the edges of local and camp system concerns about the spread of biological contaminants were notions of social order, boundary, and belonging, which are every bit as important to understanding the sanitary unit as are ideas about how properly to dispose of waste.

In her classic work *Purity and Danger: An Analysis of the Concepts of Pollution and Taboo*, the anthropologist Mary Douglas described the need to approach dirt critically. "As we know it," she wrote, "dirt is essentially disorder. There is no such thing as absolute dirt: it exists in the eye of the beholder." California's agricultural society was especially prone to, and anxious about, the kinds of ambiguity that Douglas noticed. The state's agricultural economy was built on at least three ambiguous elements: soil, fertilizer, and migrant laborers. Remove these from their proper places, change the "eye of the beholder" by altering something as predictable as the harvest, and these essential elements become dirt, shit, and outsiders.[4]

A resident of the Indio camp wrote to the camp paper in 1938 describing this transformation. She called her piece "A Two Act Play With But Three Characters." In it, a local boy points out a "bum" to his mother. She corrects him, explaining that the man is not a bum, but a cotton picker. Two months later, with the cotton picked, the same boy points out the same man and calls him a cotton picker, "Mother answers, 'That isn't a cotton picker dear, that's a bum.'"[5]

Attempts to manage the ambiguity of these and other elements, to define and enforce a person's social place, were at the heart of exercises of government power inside and outside of the camp gate. At stake in

Sanitary Unit, Shafter Camp, 1940.
Photograph by Arthur Rothstein. *Utility house. Shafter migrant camp. Shafter, California*. March 1940. Courtesy of Library of Congress. https://www.loc.gov/item/2017774828/.

naming a person a cotton picker or a bum, in proclaiming the glories of the soil or demanding that dirt be removed from the body, were the ordered purity of California's agricultural communities and control over the migrant bodies that flowed through and around them. These attempts to manage dirt were central to the religious tasks of, to borrow from Douglas, "positively reordering our environment, making it conform to an idea." She writes further that "rituals of purity and impurity create unity in experience. So far from being aberrations from the central project of religion, they are positive contributions to atonement."[6]

Given the near constant attention that RA/FSA officials paid to issues of hygiene and sanitation, it is clear that camp rituals of purity and the spaces provided for their practice were central to the system's understanding of the world and to their modern religiosity. But these rituals were not as fully focused on the self as they might appear at first glance. They were also performed for the surrounding communities, all of which asked, albeit in different tones and at different volumes, for atonement from the migrants. The nature of the migrants' sins, like the nature of dirt, was in the eye of the beholder.

Sanitation, Submission, Salvation

The sanitary unit was fundamental to the migrant camp program. It was the space that most clearly differentiated a government camp from grower-owned and locally-managed camps with their barely running water and squalid, over-flowing privies. In a June 7, 1935 letter to the chief of California's construction bureau, Harry Drobish highlighted the centrality of the sanitary unit to the plan for the Marysville camp. "[The camp] will be located on a thirty-one acre tract on the outskirts of the city," he wrote. "The project submitted provides for the construction of 3 sanitary units of 32 families each and an administrative unit. No housing or shelter will be provided for campers."[7] Drobish's vision for the camps involved the trinity of demarcated space, bathrooms, and bureaucracy.

One year and one camp later, his vision remained stable. In his March 1936 appearance at the Commonwealth Club in San Francisco, Drobish described the Marysville and Arvin camps efficiently. "The camps provide minimum facilities," he began, "A good camp ground, proper

"Labor camp privy. Coachella Valley. March 2, 1935."
Photograph by Dorothea Lange. Courtesy of Library of Congress. Image LC-DIG-ppmsca-19156, https://www.loc.gov/pictures/item/2004678009/.

sanitary facilities, flush toilets with adequate sewage disposal through septic tanks, hot and cold water for showers, and facilities to wash their clothes." Those who imagined the camps as lavish governmental oases needed to revise their understandings. "This is about all we supply," he added, "besides supervision and an educational program."[8]

Sanitary units were, however, critical elements of each camp. Human waste was a daunting problem nearly everywhere the migrants went. A

"Sanitation near Bakersfield. Feb. 28, 1935."
Photograph by Dorothea Lange. Courtesy of Library of Congress. Image LC-DIG-ppmsca-19156, https://www.loc.gov/pictures/item/2004678009/.

"Report of Migratory Labor Conditions in Alameda County" submitted to the Resettlement Administration in 1936 by surveyor Richard Perrott, gives a sense of the potential for crisis. Alameda County includes the cities of Oakland and Berkeley as well as suburban, exurban, and rural communities extending about thirty-five miles inland. It is not as agriculturally focused as Kern or Imperial or Yolo counties but, Perrott reported, a major "influx of migratory labor" arrived every year with the pea crop. "In normal years the influx . . . is estimated at 5 to 6000 people [between April and June]."

The 1936 growing season was a difficult one. Nevertheless, the problem of "labor congestion" was serious, which meant that the waste problem was serious as well.[9] Even undernourished bodies expel waste, roughly one-half pound per day. To accommodate these bodies, the Alameda County Board of Supervisors began in 1935 to regulate and license "migrant camps" (they did not define the term further) and to inspect them as often as twice daily. "Every effort has been made," Perrott explained, "to improve sanitary conditions." Still, writing on March 28, 1936, he had troubling news. "At the present time there are only three camps established in the county with a small population, however, licenses have been issued for from 16 to 18 camps and last year there were a total of 24."

The first stage of the pea harvest was mere weeks away, and if every licensed camp opened, there might be accommodations for two thousand migrants: workers and family members. Put differently, the demand for housing and sanitation was going to outstrip the supply by as many as four thousand people. In Alameda County alone, un-housed workers might generate upwards of two thousand pounds of excrement per day during the fifty-six-day harvest.

Assuming that Harry Drobish had chosen his words for the Commonwealth Club carefully, the sanitary unit rose above most other elements of the camps in terms of importance. Drobish mentioned "supervision" in both descriptions of the camps and told the Commonwealth Club audience of Tom Collins's masterful work as manager. The sanitary units were a close and crucial second. There are showers and flush toilets, Drobish assured his audience, and the toilets provide "adequate sewage disposal through septic tanks." These are indeed "proper sanitary facilities."[10]

It is unlikely that his audience was interested in the details of sewage disposal beyond the reassurance offered by words such as "proper" and "adequate." Drobish's primary interest that evening was in presenting the sanitary unit as a symbol, a manifestation of his program's interlocking commitments to sanitary living, bodily discipline, and modernity. The sanitary unit was a profoundly important symbol in the life of the camp program; profoundly important but profoundly unstable.

The intended symbolism of the sanitary unit was at least twofold. To the migrants, it was meant to express the indissoluble connection between clean life in modern terms and respectability in American terms. The road to integration into American society led through a modern shower and a toilet stall and, importantly, away from a dirty body and the haphazard expulsion of waste. To the greater public, the sanitary unit was meant to symbolize both communal agreement as to the standards of modern cleanliness and the camp program's commitment to converting migrants to those standards. The buildings and their modern fixtures told visitors who saw them and audiences who heard about them that migrants had been living insufficiently hygienic lives and that the federal government's camp program was going to show them a cleaner and therefore better way.

These symbolic meanings help us understand the remarkable conclusion to the dedication ceremony for the Marysville camp in October of 1935. As we have seen, the event drew representatives of more than fifty local and statewide groups and featured patriotic music, a prayer of invocation, and an address by camp manager Tom Collins on the transformative effects of camp life. The ceremony was rife with symbolism. But surely the most memorable moment came when the music ended and the speeches were done and the privies that had served the Hooverville of more than one thousand residents were set ablaze.

What the program describes only as "Burning of the Privies" was as clear a statement as one could have asked for as to the symbolic significance of the sanitary unit. Life in a government camp would be committed to the incineration of old, unhygienic ways and to their replacement with the clean, the sanitary, the modern. Tom Collins, Harry Drobish, and Irving Wood surely had practical reasons for setting those pits of human waste ablaze: burning sanitizes. They just as surely wanted that fire to set the limits of community. Burning gives morality a spatial dimension. If you want to become a good neighbor, their actions said, move away from the flames. The fire also gave those who doubted the program's commitment to redeeming and reforming the migrants a rather unambiguous smoke signal to reassure them.[11]

The sanitary unit was, however, an unstable symbol, a fact made clear many times in the years of the camp program. This instability was connected to the fact that it was both a symbol and a piece of technology. In order to mean what it was designed to mean, the sanitary unit needed to work as it was designed to work. A loss of hot water in the showers or a dramatic back-up in the sewage line could quickly call into question the narrative of redemption through modernization.

Additionally, in order to teach and model what it was supposed to teach and model, the camp population had to be willing to use the sanitary unit as it was intended. The structures and substructures built to collect the dirt and the waste from migrant bodies and to move this material reasonably far away could only do their work if migrants agreed to commit themselves and their children to the observance of modern sanitary ritual. Camp staff worked mightily to stabilize the meaning of camp sanitary units by engineering them carefully and by policing their use and maintenance diligently. Seemingly simple sanitary and hygienic acts, instinctive to the twenty-first-century reader, forced migrants to acknowledge and participate in a world that saw them as what Mary Douglas might call "matter out of place" and that insisted that their worthiness could only be validated if they first accepted their unworthiness. In a classic rehearsal of missionary subjectivity, sanitary ritual became simultaneously a practical act and an act of submission.

Purity and Danger in Agricultural California

Officials in California did not set fire to privies every time they wanted to comment on the proper way to manage human waste or establish behavioral norms. They found other ways to argue for their understanding of physical and social purity and to shape the actions of those claiming membership in their communities. These attempts to define and enforce purity, and to marginalize and punish impurity, show the cultural complexity of perceptions of dirt and danger, and help illuminate the contours of the program of redemption that camp program workers developed in agricultural California.

In 1907, as Imperial County residents were laying the physical and ideological infrastructure of their industrial agricultural economy, local authorities enacted Ordinance Number 8, "An Ordinance to Protect and Preserve Public Health and Defining the Duties of the Health Officer and Other Persons and Providing Penalties for the Violation Hereof." The ordinance described some dos and don'ts of residential waste management. Section 12 states: "No privy vault, privy, cesspool or water closet shall be allowed by the owner or other persons in charge of the premises . . . to become foul or offensive." It also enumerated the powers of Imperial County to intervene in situations that threatened public health. Section 9 gave "the health officer or any public officer" the right to enter a home or other building "to discover or inspect any nuisance that may there exist." A law-abiding citizen, in other words, would manage her or his waste such that the receptacle and its surrounding area remained as clean as possible. An officer of the law had the right to investigate any circumstance inside or outside the home that he determined to be foul, offensive, or, presumably, both.[12]

County authorities wrote Ordinance Number 8 during the first year of county incorporation and in the aftermath of a catastrophe that was both manmade and absolutely biblical. Imperial Valley has two key ingredients for large-scale agriculture: mineral-rich soil and year-round sun. What it lacks is water. In the closing decades of the nineteenth century, state, local, and corporate interests worked together to create a series of canals to divert waters from the Colorado River to the previously sere landscape. From 1895 to 1905, the promise of irrigated farmland drew homesteaders to the region with dreams of making their mark and their fortune as growers.

But the waters of the Colorado River, the same waters that made the desert bloom, were inconsiderate of those dreams. In 1905, heavy rains in the mountains raised the Colorado to such a level that it breached the canal gates, blew out a newly created irrigation cut, and began to rip through the Imperial Valley with its full force. The rerouted Colorado River inundated the region, flooding two ancient riverbeds—today's Alamo and New Rivers—and creating California's largest inland body of water, the Salton Sea. After eighteen months and numerous failed attempts, engineers and builders were able to restore the river to its original course and the valley to a habitable state.[13] These events were barely a memory when Ordinance 8, with its concern for proper waste disposal, entered the books. With the flood waters gone and an opportunity to lay the foundations of local order, county leaders gave priority to the detection and management of foulness and offense, and the authority to manage them.

Two and a half decades after the valley was submerged by the technology that brought it life, Imperial County had become an agricultural powerhouse. A contemporary visitor wrote, "within its 4,000 square miles there is the largest irrigation project in the world, bringing year-round water supply to irrigate more than 600,000 acres. . . . Imperial County produces the world's most important lettuce and melon crop."[14]

In 1933, as Imperial County faced the early stages of a human flood and related acts of labor unrest, county authorities amended Ordinance Number 8 with Ordinance 101, using more graphic language and giving the law a sharper edge. Ordinance 101 is both an official attempt to defend communal purity and a testament to the place of the migrant in California agriculture. The ordinance imagines and regulates actions that pollute a community's resources. In the process it imagines the actors who pollute and, through its content and structure, reduces those people to a pollutant to be contained.

Tellingly, the focus of Ordinance 101 shifts back and forth between migrants and livestock, stipulating conditions for the housing of the former, laying out guidelines for the handling of the latter, betraying all along the ambiguous humanity of the migratory laborer in the local imagination. Section 1 mandates that a dead animal must be buried under at least three feet of soil and more than one hundred feet from a source of drinking water. Section 2 reads:

> It shall be unlawful for any privy or other receptacle for human excrement to be so constituted and maintained as to permit flies to gain access to the excremental matter therein; or to permit such excremental matter to flow over or upon the surface of the ground; or to permit or allow any privy vault, privy, cesspool, water closet, septic tank, or other receptacle for human excrement to be or remain within fifty (50) feet of any canal, stream, pond, lake or reservoir from which water is or may be drawn for the domestic use of any portion of the inhabitants of this County.

The very next section of the revised ordinance, Section 3, turns back to animals. It prohibits the keeping of livestock "within 50 feet of any canal, stream, pond, lake, or reservoir from which water is or may be drawn for the domestic use of any portion of the inhabitants of this County." Section 4 places a similar stricture on human subjects. "It shall be unlawful for any person or persons to camp or to establish and/or maintain a camp within a distance of Forty (40) feet of any canal, stream, pond, lake, or reservoir."[15]

Ordinance 101 seeks to maintain communal purity by managing two dangers. The first and most obvious is biological contamination, e.g., bacteria that might spread from the margins of the community, bovine or human, to its center. Decomposing cow flesh might make its way into the water and onto the lettuce crop. Flies might carry bacteria from an ad hoc privy up, out, and into the world of those who use porcelain toilets. Animal or human waste might reach domestically useable water. The force of law stands ready to punish those who are party to such violations.

The second danger that the ordinance addresses is that of the unmoored, wandering being, the person or animal whose free movement might pollute the community's resources or violate the community's boundaries. Herds of livestock and groups of migrants could not be just anywhere and be legal. They had to stay in place, and that place had to be fifty feet and forty feet, respectively, from the county's valuable water sources.

In both of these cases, invisible and fully human actors bear some legal responsibility for creating "properly sanitary" conditions. Livestock owners face fines and incarceration for the mishandling or mismanagement of animals (both living and dead) and animal waste. The same is true of the owners of private migrant camps, whose efforts to manage human waste were infamously half-hearted. In the eyes of the law, migrant camp owners had living beings moving about on their property and were responsible for managing their excrement.

In one sense, then, migrants were legally analogous to livestock, dumbly defecating without responsibility for the consequences. Yet Section 2 of Ordinance 101 also allows that migrants can act willfully. It threatens sanctions against those who deposit bodily waste in such a way as to attract flies. Section 4 addresses migrants directly, restricting those who camp from settling down (and, presumably, relieving themselves) within forty feet of the water supply. In these cases, migrants' circumstances are their own legal responsibility. They must dig a hole and go in it. They must know their place and stay in it.

The migrant's status before the law was thus somewhere between a Holstein and a respectable white citizen. The law understood that, unlike cows, migrants could develop some scruples regarding the when and where of defecation. But in contrast to the settled men and women of Imperial County, the law was, almost literally, in the migrants' shit. Migrants could defecate here but not there. If flies found a migrant's excrement, the migrant might find himself under arrest. Ordinance 101 acknowledged that landed residents exercised power over migrants. It then invoked migrants' humanity not as a reflection of the freedoms they possessed or the rights that were theirs, but as a prelude to punishment for willfully polluting the community.

The boundary most obviously present in Ordinance 101, the boundary that legitimates the boundaries drawn around irrigation ditches and the like, is the class boundary. The population targeted by Ordinance 101 consists of those too poor to live fully settled lives or to always dispose of their waste in ways seen as proper. But this boundary was thickened by another. The economic realities of Imperial County agriculture in the early 1930s—white and Japanese land owners, Mexican, African American, and Filipino workers—were such that class and race overlapped consistently, if not completely.

Laws such as Ordinance 101 affected the poor and the dark skinned more than the rich and the light. In 1930s Brawley, Mexican farm workers made up roughly half of the population.[16] They migrated locally and statewide as the crops dictated, but their settlements stood to the east of Brawley's railroad tracks. These dark-skinned agricultural workers were geographically contained and identifiable. When in their "proper" place, they were a threat to their own health and well-being but not to the purity of the wider community. Ordinance 101 gave local authorities a set of portable boundaries to use against farm workers no matter where they were. On a moment's notice, deputies could remind human contaminants of their place and make them pay for forgetting it.

When the federal migrant camp program began studying the Imperial County town of Brawley with an eye toward building a camp there, its representatives noticed this impoverished, dark-skinned population. The handwritten notes of T. T. Miller, an early surveyor of the "Brawley Migrant Camp Area," describe "several square blocks built up with an assortment of shacks, sometimes with three or four families living on one city lot." Miller had encountered a similar situation involving "mostly Mexicans" in the town of Westmoreland, but reported, "no attempt was made to count the number of families (several hundred) living under such arrangements."[17]

A second Resettlement Administration surveyor, Charles A. Clark, returned to Brawley in the fall of 1936 for a closer look at the town. Clark studied Brawley's demographics, its agricultural economy, its school system, and the structures of its society. Clarence Glacken used Clark's data and prepared an extensive narrative report for the directors of the camp program. Clark and Glacken described the agricultural, educational, economic, and social climate of the town in reasonable detail and concluded, "The presence of a camp here will undoubtedly be an immense step forward in social consciousness of a community in which relief and social standards are and have consistently been depressingly low."[18] A camp would create a sanitary environment for agricultural workers and give them an education in hygiene. It would also enlighten the more established residents of Brawley by modeling proper concern for and treatment of the least among them, something that had not come naturally.

Clark and Glacken also made space in their report for a description of Brawley's religious culture. Their treatment of religion in Brawley matters less as a directory of local congregations and more as a study in thoughts about religion, place, and belonging. The authors did not label religious identities as pure or polluting outright, but the religious world the authors described was infused with assumptions about place, belonging, and order.

In mapping the religious landscape of this corner of the desert they noted "the following churches have a small but active following—First Baptist, New Bethel Methodist, Roman Catholic, First Church of Christ, Scientist, Christian Church, Free Methodist, Japanese Methodist, Episcopal, The First Methodist, The First Methodist Episcopal, First Presbyterian, Mexican Presbyterian, and Seven Day [sic] Adventist."

It is a testament to the capaciousness of their worldview that Clark and Glacken noticed Brawley's Japanese and Mexican churches. Nonetheless, missing from their accounting is any mention of the Buddhist "church" located six blocks from the Japanese Methodist Church, and the local mosque and *gurdwara* that served Imperial County's sizable Punjabi community. Clark and Glacken's gaze was trained to notice the varieties of Protestantism practiced by the town's white minority, the Protestantisms practiced by Japanese and Mexican residents, and a Catholicism decoupled from racial identifiers.[19]

According to Clark and Glacken, race and Christian affiliation were coextensive: "the religious background of the population follows racial groupings into Protestant and Catholic faiths." Non-white, non-Protestant residents counted either as "Catholic" or not at all. Japanese and Mexican residents became religiously visible as they became religiously Protestant.

And at the same time that Protestantism made some non-whites visible, whiteness made Protestantism's myriad internal divisions invisible. There were denominational differences, of course, but in Glacken's account these were of little consequence in the searing heat and penetrating sunlight of the California desert. "This more or less isolated region, with its severe climate, is a little discouraging to the newer mushroom sects found so active in the Los Angeles area and only the tried and orthodox religions are actively concerned with [the] spiritual welfare of Brawley and its population."[20] "Tried and orthodox" Protestantism remained mostly white, mostly clean, mostly respectable. Religious fungi would wither and die in the Imperial Valley sun if their lack of concern for the "spiritual welfare of Brawley" didn't kill them first. In such a demanding climate, out-of-place theologies and out-of-place denominations, like out-of-place people, stood little chance.

Clark and Glacken described a religious world with important similarities to the sanitary and social worlds envisioned by Ordinance 101. This was a world of named and unnamed groups, visible and invisible boundaries. It was a world of places and of people assigned to those places. The affinities between these ordering documents and their depictions and assumptions about race, class, cleanliness, and religion deepened as the New Dealers reported more explicitly on questions of race. "The city reflects the racial lines indicated in the analysis of the population. It has a Mexican section; there the Mexican Indian and the Negro reveal the environment for which their social and racial origin has been responsible." This other-side-of-the-tracks "environment" was dirty, dilapidated, inferior to the environment for which white "social and racial origin" had been responsible. Glacken continued,

> The standards of resident workers of this region is [sic] low partly due to the predominance of foreign workers. Ninety percent of the stoop labor is supplied by Mexican Indians whose standard of living shows little improvement from year to year. Perhaps the most marked improvement is in dress and in their pitiful efforts at cleanliness, neither of which improves the bad living conditions in the homes.[21]

Mexican Presbyterians and Mexican Catholics confessed Christianity, but the homes they kept and the environments in which they were comfortable indicated that they remained, before all things, Mexican or "Mexican Indian" or "foreign."[22] They embraced a white religion. But they did not and could not embrace it white-ly. Moreover, Mexicans' low living standards were a pollutant, spreading like a contagion to the domestic lives of "resident workers" and depressing standards across the community.

These observations about non-white agricultural workers were not a prelude to action. They were not a racist antecedent leading to a program of reform. The poor living conditions that prevailed among "the Mexican Indian and the Negro" were, Glacken wrote, predetermined by race, which limited the extent to which rehabilitation made sense or was even thought possible. If the program aimed to encourage more sanitary, more hygienic living among camp residents, dark-skinned agricultural workers could not be a major presence.

"The proposed camp at Brawley," Glacken wrote, "is designed primarily for white itinerant agricultural workers and their families who are forced to face sharpest competition with large labor reserves of low-standard, and foreign, mostly Mexican, labor."[23] The former cried out for sanitation and salvation, even if those cries could be hard to hear. The latter could be left, indeed should be left, to the environments "for which their social and racial background has been responsible."[24]

Reading Imperial County Ordinance 101 and Clark and Glacken's report together brings us face-to-face with the possibility that concerns about sanitation and hygiene, both within and beyond the camp program, had as much to do with the pollution of whiteness as with the pollution of water supplies, and that efforts to shape the practice of hygiene drew energy from a crisis in the performance of whiteness. Depression-era California was awash in unsavory, racially-coded qualities: filth and domestic disorder, shiftlessness and persistent poverty, migration and marginality. These were not the kinds of conditions that white Americans were supposed to face or the social position they were supposed to occupy. Whites were not supposed to be unmoored. Whites were not supposed to attract flies with their dirt and excrement. Whites were not supposed to be limited by boundaries, they were supposed to draw them. But destitution and desperation and starvation gnawed away at these markers and the critical distinctions in which they were rooted.

Describing the situation in Brawley circa 1936, Glacken wrote of the inescapable nature of lived filth. "The health service of Imperial County has tried to improve the general health conditions of the itinerant farm laborer who moves into this valley during the winter months in large numbers, living along the highway and canal banks." Because of its warm weather, Imperial Valley was a popular winter destination for migrants. Glacken continued, "Many of these itinerant workers are forced to use the muddy water of the canal ditches for bathing and domestic uses. They are without the first rudiments of sanitation, a standard of living they have had for many years."

Similarly, while managing the Shafter camp, Ray Mork wrote that camp residents were "people of very low standards, with a history of shacks, dirt floors, extreme individualism, sloth, [and] extreme superstition."[25] The dirt, the laziness, and the irrationality of these offspring of pioneer-stock whites pointed to an erosion of distinctions that suffused not just agricultural California, but America as well. The path to solving "the migrant problem" required the cleaning and ordering of white bodies and the reassertion of old racial categories that had become uncomfortably blurry.

These words are hard to square with evidence of greater capaciousness and liberality on display at Brawley and the other camps. The minutes from a Brawley camp council meeting held December 13, 1938 note,

"The question of eligibility for residence in the camps was raised. It was explained that there is nothing in the regulations governing the Camp Program which in any way bars anyone from residence in Farm Security Administration Migratory Worker Camps because of race, color, nationality, or creed."

The letter of camp law, like the letter of Ordinance 101, was neutral. Non-white families did occasionally occupy tent platforms. But a regulation as written is not identical to a regulation as applied, and the spirit of the good neighbor, so central to the missionary message of the camp program, had always and everywhere to be applied by people, people whose ideas of the "neighbor" were informed by powerful racial, national, and denominational affinities, and by deep investments in racial, social, and economic hierarchy.

It is also true that well-intentioned people working to achieve a desirable goal can create entrapping, damaging circumstances for those they seek to help. Throughout California, New Deal administrators developed partnerships with local departments of public health to clear ditch bank camps and to condemn private camps that were egregiously unsanitary. Tom Collins described one manifestation of this partnership in an October 1937 letter to Edward Rowell. Collins noticed the presence of "bulletins on proper camp facilities" and their effect on officials in and around Brawley. "Dr. Fox, the county health officer, has taken a cue from them and has published notices, quite similar, for contractors and growers. He has also made it known he will enforce the camp regulations this year."[26]

This use of state power—county and federal officials working hand in glove—was for the public good. The diseases spawned in environments where excrement, water, and insects converge are truly dangerous, truly awful. A government serves its people well when it moves them away from such settings or, better yet, keeps the settings from developing in the first place. But there was also something profoundly entrapping in these efforts. "We believe, as a result, workers will find camping sites quite scarce in Calipatria," Collins continued, "so we earnestly hope FSA will have a mobile [housing] unit ready for that area." Local authorities and New Deal officials effectively criminalized behaviors that, given the shortage of proper sanitary facilities, were all but unavoidable in the context of Depression-era California. Often the alternative to foul privies was no privies at all.[27]

A Dispatch from the Coachella Valley, 1935

In late February of 1935, as part of an effort to determine the scope and severity of the crisis facing migrants and communities throughout agricultural California, Harry Drobish, then director of rural rehabilitation for the California State Emergency Relief Administration, sent a party of four researchers to the Coachella Valley east of Los Angeles. From February 27 through March 3, Paul Taylor, Dorothea Lange, Irving Wood, and Harvey Coverley traveled throughout the valley, visiting a mix of municipal, grower-owned, and makeshift migrant camps to evaluate living conditions up close. They gathered data, asked questions, and took notes and photographs. Their work provides a detailed picture of local attitudes regarding place, order, and concern about contamination that both produced and were reinforced by the legal, geographic, and racial boundaries that cross-hatched California's fertile interior.

The research team, or a subset of it, attended no fewer than fourteen meetings with individuals ranging from ranchers J. W. Newman and George Ames to Dr. T. P. B. Jones, county health officer, and Robert Edwards, chairman of the Riverside County Planning Commission. Their findings, reported by Harvey Coverley, were disturbing to say the least. The first of fifteen concluding points reads: "Housing accommodations of migratory and stable agricultural labor in Coachella Valley are, for the most part, inadequate for a minimum, decent standard of living, are unsanitary, a menace to community health and unfavorable to the moral and social improvement of the area."[28] Conditions among migrants threatened both public health and the moral future of the entire community.

Dorothea Lange and Coverley spent March 1 and 2 in the field taking pictures and interviewing agricultural workers. Almost without exception, they found "squalid and unsanitary conditions." The walls, roofs, windows, and framework of the "rural houses" they examined consisted of scrap material, burlap, sticks, leaves, and cardboard. The shelters were lit by candles. There was no plumbing. The "sanitary equipment" in evidence consisted of outhouses erected over open pits.

Much as the researchers might have wanted to attribute these conditions to the transitional state into which displacement had forced these people, further investigation indicated that what Lange and Coverley were seeing was actually a new normal. When Irving Wood joined them on a visit to "three camps in West Indio Heights" and a public camp south of Indio they found "conditions similar to those previously observed." "It became more obvious that a large number of agricultural laborers living under these circumstances were permanent residents," Coverley wrote. "Families who have dwelt in the same shack from two to four years were not uncommon." In short, the migrants were growing accustomed to this filthy life.

When Taylor, Wood, Lange, and Coverley weren't taking photographs and collecting data, they were surveying local officials, land owners, businessmen, and educators, hoping to ascertain their thoughts about the migrant situation and the extent to which community leaders would support efforts to improve it. These meetings do not appear to have been confrontational. Coverley's eleven-page report contains the names of those present at meetings and the opinions they shared. If the researchers had contradictory information or sensed that they were being told half-truths, Coverley whispered this parenthetically in the report, e.g., "(It will be noted that Dr. Gray's viewpoint on this matter is not shared by a majority of those contacted.)"[29]

Based on this report, many established residents of the Coachella Valley felt that the migrants were dirty. They had also noticed the troublesome filth that surrounded the migrants' makeshift communities. Ranchers George Ames and J. W. Newman remarked that "sanitary conveniences for . . . workers were sadly lacking and were needed most of all," and that "health conditions were very bad among these squatters."[30] Dr. R. M. Gray, health officer for the town of Indio, agreed. "Health conditions are very bad among squatters," he reported, adding that he would not "deliver any children in the homes of these farm laborers on account of unsanitary conditions."[31]

Migrants in the Coachella Valley clearly lived dirty lives. There were diverse opinions as to whether the migrants were themselves dirt— "matter out of place," in the words of Mary Douglas. There was also a range of reactions to the idea of federal programs to elevate and redeem them. The words of Elsie Patterson, attendance officer for the Riverside County schools, give an example of local ambivalence. During her February 27 meeting with Taylor, Wood, and Coverley, she shared school attendance records that correlated increases in student population with harvest cycles. She also offered words of warning. "Miss Patterson . . . expressed the opinion that there would be strong opposition in the Valley to any proposal to provide farm laborers with better housing, due to the fact that most of the growers in the Valley have had to struggle against nature to develop their farms and would resent any attempt of outside agencies to assist others to a better living standard who have not gone through the same difficult experience."[32] Coverley added that "information obtained from farmers in the Valley . . . does not confirm this opinion," but Miss Patterson's perspective was not only her own.

Dr. R. M. Gray echoed Patterson, reporting that "opposition to any plan to improve housing conditions" in and around the town of Thermal would be "great," even insurmountable. Moreover, Dr. Gray, who refused to deliver children in the migrants' "unsanitary" homes, told the researchers that he believed that any project to create better, more sanitary homes would "spoil the workers." Gray's overriding concern was not domestic filth, but rather the social and economic effects of giving agricultural workers something they had not earned. Jack Ross, county recorder and secretary of the county planning commission, spoke more generally when describing his concerns about a plan to improve the living conditions of agricultural workers. As Coverley reported, "He expressed a view that such a plan might have an adverse effect on the morals of the Community."

In these accounts we see both awareness of the presence of dirty migrants, and the belief that this population ought to be left alone in their dirt and distress. Their proper place was exactly where they were. Patterson, Gray, and Ross seem to agree that the unrelieved poverty of farm laborers reinforced the morals of Riverside County, morals that, Mary Douglas might say, made their environment conform to an idea and created unity in the experience of valley residents. Comfort and convenience, like wealth, were things earned. The structures of Riverside society, including social hierarchies and technologies for hygiene, testified to the rewards of struggling against nature. To the extent that migrants posed a threat to the community, it was as a contaminant of this idea. And this threat would only be realized if forces external to the community gave the migrants things—shelter, showers, toilets—that they did not deserve.

Another group of Coachella Valley residents voiced support for government efforts to assist the migrants and to create more sanitary living conditions for them, but in so doing also expressed a desire to see familiar social structures and categories upheld. Aid itself would not bring contamination to the Coachella Valley, but aid wrongly applied would.

Charles E. Johnson, manager of the Riverside Title Company and a member of both the county emergency relief agency and the Chamber of Commerce, supported efforts to house "migratory agricultural labor" but not "transient farm labor." The former were regulars who worked for long periods of time, performed reliably, and moved on when the job was done. They were familiar if not exactly respectable figures. The latter were unreliable "itinerants who come into the Valley irregularly for short periods . . . and then move on." Johnson did not label these itinerants "hoboes" or "agitators," but one can well imagine that he had such human contaminants in mind.

Among poor townsfolk, a group that stood to benefit directly from government efforts to bring cleanliness and order to the Coachella Valley, support for sanitary, low-cost housing was predictably strong. Yet some of these settled poor distinguished between the deserving poor (themselves) and the undeserving poor (squatters). Coverley reported that "a few expressed the opinion that it would be a big mistake to provide permanent quarters for those so-called 'Jungle Families.' One laborer expressed the opinion that he would prefer to have pigs in his house than such families."[33]

Rancher J. W. Newman seconded the anonymous commentator, but in a different register. While generally supportive of improved housing and thankful for the burden it would lift from his shoulders, he noted that the white migrants were a comparatively unsavory crowd. "Mexicans make better laborers than the so-called 'poor whites,'" he offered, "and are more interested in keeping a garden . . . and are more sanitary than white people of the same economic class." A concern shared among these residents was the possibility of contamination by people who don't know their place or refuse to stay in it.

Of course, some residents of Coachella Valley focused directly on the physical dirt associated with the migrants, the need to clean them up, and the importance of creating safe, sanitary shelter for them. Dr. T. P. B. Jones, health officer for Riverside County, described connections between the migrants' living conditions and the prevalence of disease among them. The "intolerable" conditions in which migrants were living, he said, led to "a greatly disproportionate percentage of the typhoid fever cases in the county" and "many other serious health problems." In his words, migrants were a "menace to the health of the community." Robert Edwards of the Riverside County Planning Commission was so eager to diminish this menace that he stated flatly, "he was in favor of any project to improve housing conditions for farm labor in the area."

Jones and Edwards saw dirt and filth, and wanted it cleaned up. They saw human matter out of place and believed that the out-of-placeness was a threat to their community. In the few words of theirs available to us, they justified support for migrant housing by arguing that if something were not done, sickness would spread.

The motives of those Coverley quoted are difficult to know in their entirety. But the words contained in his report from the late winter of 1935 indicate that local plans for assistance were not conceived primarily as plans for assistance, that efforts to improve cleanliness were not justified in terms of the benefits they would provide to the dirty. Assistance and improvement were justified or condemned based on the benefits or the costs to the comparatively comfortable.

Those who supported the concept of state or federal housing for the migrant poor were not always explicit about the moral threat presented by action, inaction, or by actions wrongly calibrated. Nevertheless, they were interested in protecting their community from social and economic contaminants. Transients were bad, irredeemable. Hard working, garden-keeping Mexicans were good. Poor whites "of the same economic class" were not. The settled poor were deserving poor. The poor living out on the ditch banks? Worse than pigs.

If we think of local attitudes toward migrants and of the government camp system's sanitation and hygiene program as driven only by bacteriology and concerns about infectious disease—a language that reformers and public health officials often spoke—we are hard pressed to account for a range of statements describing filthy conditions among migrants as "unfavorable to the moral and social improvement of the area."[34] Lives lived in dirt or as dirt—not to mention foul, open privies—could "overflow" into the community in more ways than one.

The Substructures of Purity

The things that maintain communal order and cleanliness, if not purity exactly, are sometimes visible: railroad tracks, fences, irrigation canals; and sometimes not: laws, attitudes, customs. The sanitary unit fell into the former category. The substructures that made it work fell mostly into the latter. The buried systems for managing human waste, without which the sanitary unit would have been a fiction, required more thought and planning than any other element of a camp's built environment. Each network of pipes and tanks and receptacles had to adapt to the possibilities of the land and serve the needs of seasonally waxing and waning populations. These systems reveal a great deal about the sanitary unit as a location for modeling and staging rituals of purity and impurity.

For the handling of human waste, the most obvious potential contaminant associated with the sanitary unit, many of the camps used a piece of technology called an Imhoff tank. Imhoff tanks are usually made of concrete and are housed mostly below ground with pools open to the air. They receive raw sewage and, according to H. M. Beaumont, writing in the *Sewage Works Journal* in 1929, "remove . . . settleable suspended particles present in the sewage, and by bacterial digestion . . . liquefy, gasify, and stabilize the organic matter present in the resulting sludge."

Imhoff tanks create three by-products, gas, effluent, and sludge, the latter two of which need to be managed further by tank operators. Effluent, consisting of waste water less the solids, can be drawn off, filtered, and discharged. The mostly decomposed excrement that constitutes "sludge" is generally pumped or released into drying beds, from which it can be disposed of in many different manners. Beaumont, assistant engineer in Philadelphia's Bureau of Engineering and Surveys, had this advice for the conscientious Imhoff tank operator:

> He should insist that the structures and grounds present a well-kept appearance and that cleanliness and neatness be maintained at all times. He should strive to create the interest of the public in the sewage works by having them visit it. A bushel of air-dried sludge donated to a tax payer for use in his home garden will at times awaken an interest which may be passed along to others.[35]

Imhoff tanks are not maintenance-free, and they are vulnerable to clogging from non-biodegradable materials, but in the eyes of camp program personnel, they became important as a technology for creating and refining order. Substructures that gathered and moved the waste of hundreds of migrant camp residents also moved those women, men, and children, from the category of ordinance violators to respectable, law-abiding citizens.[36]

The summer of 1937 was a season of expansion for the migratory farm labor camp program and was, therefore, a busy one for Burton Cairns, Regional Chief of Architecture and Engineering for the Resettlement Administration. It was one thing to tell audiences in San Francisco about the program's expansion and the promise of "adequate sewage disposal," as Harry Drobish had done the previous spring. It was another to make those expansions and adequacies real. Part of Cairns's work was to design sewage disposal systems for new camps at Brawley, Indio, Shafter, and Winters, and to adapt the system at Marysville to accommodate a planned doubling of its capacity.[37] Once the systems were designed, Cairns had to obtain approval for their construction from C. G. Gillespie, chief of the Bureau of Sanitary Engineering for California's Department of Public Health.

Correspondence between Cairns and Gillespie that summer was both frequent and rich in detail, owing to the fact that both men were working hard to reduce the possibility of biological contamination and to counter concerns about social contamination. The proposals that Cairns submitted to Gillespie are quite similar structurally. Cairns begins by informing Gillespie of the envelope's contents (plans, drawings, etc.) and describes how waste will be gathered and moved away from the camp. He then addresses the question of what should become of the waste. What, in other words, is its proper place? The plans and concerns and approvals that moved back and forth between Cairns and Gillespie demonstrate not only a faith in modern systems to manage impurities, but also a belief that involvement in the system created purity for those who deposited their wastes and cleaned their bodies properly, and for the soil and waste itself.

Cairns sent two sets of plans to Gillespie in June of 1937. One described the system for the Shafter camp in Kern County; the other addressed the Brawley camp in Imperial County. Of the Shafter camp plans and enclosed drawings he wrote, "It is proposed to construct a vitrified clay sewer pipe collecting system to carry the raw sewage from the camp buildings to a sump located approximately 500 feet west of the most westerly row of tent sites." Before anything could be done with the sewage, it had to be moved away from the camp and its residents. "A duplex pump will lift the raw sewage from the sump to an Imhoff Tank where the solids will be settled out. The Imhoff Tank sludge will be removed by gravity to two sludge drying beds located adjacent to the Imhoff Tank on the east." He concluded, "It is expected that the dried sludge will be disposed of by use as fertilizer." (Eschewing the advice of H. M Beaumont, he said nothing of bringing bundles of sludge to the taxpayers.) Cairns then reminded Gillespie that he had a tight deadline and would appreciate his "approval or criticism as soon as possible."[38]

Gillespie complied and responded in early July. He gave the project his conditional approval, but noted that he wanted to see some protective structure around the Imhoff tank and also larger sludge drying pits. With the pits so close to the camp and "very small," he noted, "we fear [sludge] will be piled so deep on them that it will cause a nuisance from odors and fly breeding."[39] It would be counterproductive to gather so many needy migrants only to subject them to the smell of their own drying waste.

The Brawley proposal had much in common with Shafter. Cairns wrote by way of introduction, "We are enclosing plans and specifications covering the proposed disposal of sewage at the Brawley Unit of the California Migratory Labor Camps, together with a sheet showing the figures used in designing the disposal layout." The solution to the problem of gathering waste in the camp and moving sewage out was basically the same at Brawley as it was at Shafter. "It is proposed, as shown in the plans and specifications, to construct a collecting system of vitrified clay sewer pipe to carry raw sewage from the camp buildings to an 8" clay pipe disposal main. This disposal main will carry the sewage via a 10-foot sewer easement along the west side of the [camp]."

But whereas the Shafter proposal included a sump, a duplex pump, plans for an Imhoff tank, and the treatment of sludge and effluent five hundred feet from the camp, the Brawley proposal did not. The extra effort and expense of sewage separation and treatment was not necessary. Cairns explained, "This disposal main will carry the sewage to an outfall

Imhoff settling tank with sludge beds in the background. Visalia Camp, 1938. *Interior view, California migratory labor camp. Visalia migrant camp sanitary plant. Secondary settling plant.* 1938. Courtesy of Library of Congress. https://www.loc.gov/item/2017765351/.

on the southeast bank of the New River. . . . The raw sewage will be disposed of by dilution in the New River, a proposal verbally approved by you several months ago."[40]

Though less common in 1937 than it had been in 1907, disposal of raw sewage by dilution, which amounted to dumping it straight into a body of water, was still an accepted practice in areas like Imperial County, where the population was comparatively small and rivers, however accidentally created, were easy to access. Correspondence between camp program officials and authorities in Brawley and Imperial County confirms that the town of Brawley disposed of its untreated waste in the same way.[41]

Not quite a month later, another proposal from Cairns hit Gillespie's desk. This one related to the Winters camp in Yolo County. Once again Cairns "proposed to construct a collecting system of vitrified clay sewer pipe to carry the raw sewage by gravity flow from the Camp buildings to an Imhoff tank to be located on the north bank of the Putah Creek about 500 feet southwest of the [camp] Isolation Unit." This situation presented additional complexities because Putah Creek "is subject to flooding to the 120 foot contour," requiring the construction of a levee to protect the Imhoff tank. The Winters design relied on gravity to move the "Imhoff tank sludge" through an "8-inch vitrified clay pipe line" to a drying bed built from the creek's "natural gravel deposits."

In spite of the levee, Cairns anticipated regular flood damage to the sludge beds. He wrote, "It is expected that the filter beds may be washed out each year at times of flood stage in Putah Creek," he wrote, "but the design is simple enough to be replaced inexpensively with Camp labor." Each year after flood season passed, he repeated, "labor will be provided by the camp to reconstruct the sludge beds and filter beds to the original condition." Putah Creek would damage this system, but the migrant workers were on hand to shore it up.[42]

To read these documents one after the other is to witness some consistency among RA/FSA personnel and California's Department of Public Health in the proper management of pollutants. What matters most and what Cairns describes most consistently is the creation of distance between camp residents and their waste. Systems of vitrified clay pipe gather waste from the sanitary units and carry the raw sewage underground to some other system at least five hundred feet distant. Those other systems, the ones designed to treat and finally dispose of the waste, show that geography and not biology or ideology determined the proper uses and proper places for waste.

Variations among the three plans demonstrate differing degrees of concern about controlling waste, perhaps differing levels of certainty as to where it belongs. The most controlled, most closed system was the one planned for Shafter in Kern County. From the sanitary unit to the sludge drying beds and beyond, the camp system hierarchy had plans for migrants' excrement and urine. That which the migrants deposited in a camp toilet would complete its journey as fertilizer, a perhaps unwitting contribution to the fertility of the Kern County cotton land. The system proposed for Winters exerted a similar level of control from sanitary unit to Imhoff tank and drying beds, but disruption, degradation, and diffusion by flood waters were part of the plan. The boundaries of acceptable handling were wide enough to include the washing out of the treatment beds and the seasonal release of human waste products into the creek, but structures and labor were on hand to restore order to the system. At Brawley, the camp hierarchy chose to exert control in the flushing, gathering, and movement of the waste, but none whatsoever past the end of the "outfall." The New River, born of the collapse of a modern engineering project, would carry the sewage away.

Each of these systems expressed a different modern view of how and when waste became a contaminant. They agreed that a breach or breakdown within the system would create contamination. But the systems were of different lengths and purposes. One was not complete until it had created usable fertilizer from human waste. Another was built for the sole purpose of transporting sewage to the nearest river. Matter became an impurity when it departed prematurely from the system engineered to handle it. Put differently, shit was shit until the system said it wasn't shit anymore. Its proper place was in the system until the system was done with it.

The plans created by Burton Cairns were well enough conceived to satisfy the demands of modern sanitary ritual being preached in the camps, not to mention the well-documented sensitivities that shaped the sanitary practices and attitudes of local residents. It was not long, however, before the Shafter system, ostensibly the most controlled, created the very problem that C. G. Gillespie predicted. His concern about under-sized sludge drying pits creating an odor nuisance was realized in the heat of the summer of 1938, but not by camp residents. "The main complaint," C. F. Baughman, Kern County's "Chief Sanitarian" wrote, "comes from the Bender brothers of whom there are four, each having ranches in this immediate vicinity south and east of the [Shafter] migratory camp." The Benders had lodged numerous "bitter complaints."

> Owing to the fact that the prevailing winds are from the northwest, all of these people have their sleeping quarters on that side of their dwellings

and in the summer time when the temperature ranges about 100 degrees until after midnight, it requires no stretch of imagination to picture the annoyance that this odor nuisance is creating.[43]

Baughman expressed his thanks in advance for "anything you may be able to do with regards to this odor nuisance" and his gratitude for "past cooperation."

The files are silent as to whether and when the Bender brothers were able to sleep more peacefully, though a hand-written note on Baughman's letter indicates that camp program officials did not see their complaints as urgent. Plans to expand the Shafter camp were in the works, meaning "[the] sewage plant will have to be completely restudied." The author of the note concluded, "Could put this off until then, it would be better for us." It would be surprising if Jonathan Garst and the other RA/FSA officials involved in this correspondence couldn't sympathize with the plight of those experiencing the "odor nuisance." But their inaction is not surprising, and not because of the poetry of the situation. In terms of the system that they had designed and operated to manage impurity and to catechize purity, the odor was no contaminant. It was planned and very much in place.

Confronting and Converting Contaminants

C. G. Gillespie waited until December of 1937 to visit the new Brawley camp, plans for which he had approved the previous June. The Imperial Valley is famously hot in the summer. Many who can leave the area do so. Moreover, work was progressing on the camp, and it made sense to wait for the site to be all or mostly finished. When the weather cooled and the camp gate opened, Gillespie journeyed south and was welcomed to the Brawley camp by its manager Charles Barry and, most likely, by Tom Collins. Collins, serving as manager at-large for the camp program, had traveled to Brawley to help Barry with the camp's opening rush.[44]

As predicted, some local residents had opposed the camp strenuously, writing "the establishment of such a camp would tend to draw thereto, migratory and itinerant persons who are not actually seeking employment . . . and who would be a disturbing element within our county."[45] Collins described an encounter with one Mr. Jacobsen,

"Assistant Manager, Bank of America, Brawley," who protested that the camp "would bring undesirables . . . would cause a wave of thievery and lawlessness . . . [and] would be a nest of communistic activities." He had also heard "that the people were not clean and that they did not make use of the sanitary facilities."[46] But a mixture of charm, economic logic, and governmental power cleared most obstacles. The need for housing in Imperial County was acute, particularly in areas north of Brawley where larger industrial farms relied on small armies of pickers to get fruits and vegetables out of the fields. By December of 1937, the federal camp was not just open, it was filled to capacity.

Whatever sense of accomplishment Gillespie may have felt upon arrival did not last long. He wrote to Jonathan Garst having learned of a "disturbing condition at the Brawley Camp."

> I visited the camp last week and learned that one of the very first problems Mr. Barry had was the defecation of the occupants in an irrigation ditch that supplies several farmers with water. Unfortunately, the camp was laid out so close to this ditch that there is only a roadway and then a narrow space of a few feet between the road and the ditch. As a result, evidently scores of the occupants go over into this ditch to defecate. Mr. Barry has had quite a time burying the material. But I asked him to shovel it out of the ditch and bury it on the banks and he agreed to keep a guard along the ditch or else to move the occupants to the opposite side of the grounds.[47]

Garst acknowledged receipt of Gillespie's letter and advised him that one of his best employees, Omer Mills, an economist by training, was willing to give "his personal attention" to "the nuisances committed by campers along the irrigation ditch."[48] According to Gillespie, this was not a small-scale problem. "Scores" of camp residents were committing such "nuisances." And while Charles Barry, the man with the shovel, was surely bothered by the addition to his job description, the situation must have been especially frustrating to Gillespie and to his frequent correspondent, Burton Cairns. They could bury as much clay pipe and construct as many Imhoff tanks as they wanted. None of it mattered if the appeal of a modern toilet couldn't overcome the familiarity and convenience of an easily accessible ditch.

As much as camp officials might have prayed that this was an isolated situation, one that a guard and a fence and a well-placed sign could remedy, it was not. For much of the life of the camp system, camp managers had to reckon with the problem of defecation "out of place," and the more general challenge of teaching camp residents the rules of modern hygiene and sanitation.

In early reports from Marysville and Arvin, Tom Collins told stories of migrants being flummoxed by the flush toilets. In March of 1936 at the Arvin camp, Collins was inspecting a sanitary unit on a Friday night when he found a little girl, "sitting right in the toilet bowl, splashing water with her hands and feet and giggling and laughing."[49] Later in the year he discovered an adult woman "our new neighbor from Arkansas sitting on the concrete floor, legs stretched on both sides of the toilet bowl. Beside her was a pile of 'freshly laundered' clothing. In the bowl was more clothing." Unaware that her actions were disorderly, she observed, "The fella who dun built this air wash tubs must a thot al wimin be plenty short."[50] Another woman simply relieved herself on the floor. The latter case, whom Collins referred to as "Mrs. Pawnee," explained her approach by saying, "I aint dumb—I jest kain get usto them ther things." Writing further of Mrs. Pawnee, Collins noted, "This woman was only one of many, many women and men who went through the same ordeal before our problem of public sanitation had been solved."[51]

With new arrivals came the need for further education. Collins reported in January of 1936, that "eternal vigilance is necessary to keep the campers interested in this important part of the camp program."[52] In his monthly narrative report for May 1940, Frank Iusi wrote rather vaguely from the Yuba City camp, "The use of utility buildings is our next source of trouble. Many still do not take pains to use common sense and consequently they are reported for their negligence."[53]

Regulations and reports penned by migrants themselves indicate that the problem of misuse was pervasive and persistent. S. E. Eastton, who represented Sanitary Unit 3 in the Arvin camp council, wrote to his constituents sometime in 1936 to "please instruct your children not to stand on the toilet bowls or seats and not to hang on the showers." He also asked that "when toilet paper is exhausted [campers] please call at the office for another supply. Do not use newspaper or wrapping paper in the toilets." One ordinance passed by the camp council of the

Indio camp in January of 1941 forbid "standing on toilet seats." Another banned children under the age of six from the building unless accompanied by a parent. Nobody could take for granted that camp residents would see the sanitary units as useful, much less desirable.[54]

The use of other fixtures in the sanitary unit also posed problems. An early report from Arvin described a teen-aged boy so fascinated by the hot water showers that he bathed three times in one morning but did not use soap.[55] In November of 1939, an item titled "Body Cleanliness" appeared in Arvin's *Tow Sack Tattler*. The author stated that "Cleanliness has a great deal to do with health," and then offered detailed guidance:

> A quick bath every morning, ending with a brisk rub down, helps to keep the skin healthy. In this cool weather it is better to take a warm shower but end it with a dash of cool water. Try this kind of bathing and you may have fewer colds. . . . Twice a week take a longer bath with warm water and plenty of soap. We know that the skin as well as the bowels and kidneys throw off poisons and waste. The warm scrub is needed to keep the pores open and active. After [your bath] put on fresh clothes, at least clean underclothes.

The author, a representative of the Kern County Health Department, also had special concerns about children's bodies. "I am finding quite a few children not as clean as they should be. Mothers, teach your children to look at themselves in the mirror before going to school. If you do not have a mirror look them over yourself, and once a week help them to shampoo their heads." The instructions concluded with a poem aimed at transforming hygienic practices.

> B is for bathing
> G is for grime
> Use plenty of soap
> Keep clean all the time
>
> C is for cough
> And its Cousin the sneeze
> Cover them both
> With your handkerchief, please.

216 | THE SANITARY UNIT

Boys Washing Hands, Visalia Camp, 1938.
Men's lavatory. Visalia migratory labor camp, California. 1938. Courtesy of Library of Congress. https://www.loc.gov/item/2017765354/.

Within the camp, dirty bodies and human waste were daily realities. The missionary task was to convince all residents that something vital was at stake in following the proper, modern script for rituals of purity and impurity and in treating the space for those rituals properly.

The struggle over proper uses of the sanitary unit was especially public and therefore especially noticeable at the Arvin camp under the management of Fred Ross. His accounts of the situation, his guidance, and his frustration frequently appeared in the *Tow Sack Tattler*, the camp's weekly paper. Manager Ross took many pages from Ray Mork's playbook for shaping migrant behavior. Like Mork, he wrote both gently and forcefully, and sometimes created characters and dialogues intended to reflect the perspectives of camp residents. His evangelistic approach, like Mork's, was multi-pronged but unified in its underlying message: belonging in the camp community depended upon accepting the official view of sanitation and adopting the attitudes and practices the manager prescribed.

In October of 1939, Fred Ross wrote an open letter to the residents of the Arvin camp titled "New Clean Up Schedule." All was not well around the sanitary units. "Well folks," he began, "I didn't think it would ever come down to this. I sort of hoped that you could reason with people

"Men's showers, Visalia utility building. California." Visalia Camp, 1938. Courtesy of Library of Congress. https://www.loc.gov/item/2017765350/.

and show them that certain things just had to be done around Camp for the benefit of every one living in Camp—and that everyone would go ahead and do those things, sort of natural like." Ross was referring to residents' refusal to clean the sanitary unit "when their turn [came] around." He reminded residents that they were living in a "Government camp . . . and while we're living on Government property, we're subject to Government laws." (Camp residents might have pointed out to Manager Ross that they were subject to government laws no matter where they lived.) Those who didn't like the system, he continued, could "just move off the property." Those who stayed could expect to see stricter enforcement of the cleaning schedule and the eviction of scofflaws.

As vexing as the failure to clean sanitary units was to Ross, the nature of the mess was more troubling still. Slipping into a less censorious voice, Ross raised the topic of the misuse of toilets. The offenders, he was sure, were children. "A kid can get into a heap more trouble accidental-like than a grown-up can a' purpose. But when a kid sets about doin' something a' purpose, look out; there's no knowing where it will end." Ross sensed that the violators of sanitary unit ritual were willful and promised to punish them if they continued:

> They's some little girls in Unit 1 and Unit 2 who had better learn pretty pronto that the Utility Building floor is to be walked on, not jobbed on. And just last night some little girl did a nasty trick on the wall and all over the toilet box in No. 2 Utility Building. That's the sort a' thing dogs do that ain't house-broke.

Ross wrote further that he and the camp guard, Sam Trask, would be watching for "little girls up to any more of these jobs" and would treat them the same way one treats "little dogs when they do anything like that around the house." Though the euphemism "jobs" and "jobbing" is non-specific (and odd), the context makes it clear that what it referred to belonged in the toilet.

Ross's threats of corporal punishment, however serious, were ineffective. Two weeks later he used his weekly letter in the paper to excoriate the offenders and their irresponsible parents. "Well folks, we've joked and explained, and cleaned up—cleaned up, warned and explained, but we still haven't gotten the job done; some children are still getting their jobs done all over the floor in the Utilitie [sic] Buildings." From Ross's perspective, there were a number of different explanations that could account for the persistent trouble. "Either the children are too short to reach the toilet seats, or [too] narrow to sit on them once they reached them, or they are big enough both ways but just don't care, or don't know any better." The fault, irrespective of the explanation for "the job" ending up on the floor, rested with the parents. The solution was their responsibility as well.

> If your children are too small to do the job where it is supposed to be done, [then] it's to you mothers and fathers to take them over to the Utility Buildings and see to it that everything comes out alright. If you children don't know any better, or just don't care, you mothers and fathers will be expected to explain to them about all whys and wherefores of clean toilets and see to it that they do know and care about it.

If the voice of the camp manager wasn't enough to reform migrant behavior, perhaps the power of the state would be. Ross made clear that if children could not place their waste properly, the consequences could be dire. "The Kern County Health Department has requested names of every family whose children are messing up the toilet floors. The parents will be held responsible for the acts of their children and will be booked as a menace to the health of the entire community. They may also be booked on a Public Nuisance charge and a willful Defacement of Federal property charge."

Though Manager Ross warned that the "parents" would be held legally responsible, the moral responsibility rested with women. "So in order to prevent any trouble or court action, will all of you ladies in camp please have a long, serious talk with your children, take the children to the Utilities and teach the children the right way to do this thing." Women were to train children in proper sanitary rituals and thereby to protect the health "of the entire community."

Ross framed the issue somewhat differently the following week in a regular feature that he called "As the Feller Sez." Written in a voice styled after migrants' accents and speech patterns as he heard them, "As the Feller Sez" was Ross's attempt to seem less officious in shaping migrant behavior while still being quite officious. Ross's effort for October 28,

1939 centered—superficially—on the importance of cooperation. "As the feller sez, there's one word ought to be heard a heap more around these camps than it is heard. Yep, they's one word ought to take its place beside all them Camp Conversation gems like 'lard' and 'Relief' an' 'Commodities.' That word," he wrote, "is Cooperation."

The "feller" acknowledged that cooperation is a hard thing to envision when everyone is hungry and poor and just trying to survive, but he argued that it was the only way out of living in "Rag-town" and eating "beans and sardines." Pressed by an imaginary conversation partner to define cooperation, the feller pivoted. "I can tell you what it isn't easier'n I can tell you what it is," adding:

> Now COOPERATION sure isn't throwin' dishwater on the lawn, or dumping garbage in the washtubs, or jobbing behind the house or on the Utility floor. Only ones you're cooperating with when you do that are the flies and the germs, and they don't need anybody else cooperating with them: they're too well organized as it is. Same thing goes for a man who'll work for less wages than all of his neighbors. He's cooperating with someone who'll probably manage to make out without his help.

Couched within a discussion of aspiration and unity in the face of exploitative labor practices, the issue of approaching and hitting a toilet became less a matter of personal preference or custom and more a matter of community health in the broadest sense. The person squatting behind his tent platform or using the sanitary unit for its privacy and not for its receptacles—or allowing children to do the same—was betraying his fellow camp residents just as egregiously as the man who undercut his neighbors' wages. Misplaced waste, like misplaced loyalties, endangered the entire community's prospects for upward mobility.

"The Feller" was back on the topic six months later when a different problem of waste management and disposal caught his attention. This time Ross was concerned with the use of chamber pots in residents' tents and cabins, and what became of their contents in the morning. The Feller was engaged in a conversation about ongoing misuse of the sanitary units' various technologies. "I used to kinley figger I knowed what wash-tubs was used fer 'lowed as how I knowed what garbage cans an toilets was fer." His conversation partner knew the correct uses too, but predictably, some around camp did not. "Tryin to wash clothes in a washtub full of garbage an human leavins is 'bout the hardest job I ever come up again."

The two "fellers" then went back and forth expressing their frustration and confusion over campers dumping their "night chambers" in the wash tubs and garbage cans. These pseudo-insider voices proclaimed the marginality of those who handled their waste in violation of clearly articulated but still contested norms. They called others to recognize the right and to align their behaviors with it. This front-page item was given extra force by a "notice" from Manager Ross on page four of the same paper. "Any one caught dumping slop jars, night chambers, or garbage in the wash tubs or allowing children to do their jobs any place but in the toilets will be summoned before the camp council for eviction and turned over to the public health authorities for prosecution on a public nuisance charge."

The Feller had confessed that he was "bumfuzzled" that his fellow migrants could so egregiously misuse waste receptacles. Manager Ross was more direct. Adhere to the rules for proper placement of waste and teach your children to do the same, he announced, or you will face punishment. Like so many authority figures interacting with migrants in California, he promised legal consequences for those who refused to embrace the practice of modern sanitation.

To understand why, in 1937, Charles Barry had to busy himself burying poop that he fished out of an irrigation ditch in the California desert and, in 1939 and 1940, Fred Ross had to clean errant "jobs" off of the floor and walls of a sanitary unit in the San Joaquin Valley, we need to consider the sanitary aspect of the camp program from above and below, as it were. How did camp program workers want migrants to dispose of their excrement and why? What sorts of ritual prescriptions governed migrants' approaches to defecation?

As Tom Collins's performance at the October 1935 dedication ceremony in Marysville and Burton Cairns's detailed sewage management plans indicated, New Dealers wanted migrants, first, to view human waste as a contaminant and, second, to use modern technologies to dispose of it. Excrement was something to be deposited indoors, individually, privately, and then, as quickly as possible, flushed away. The communal use of a pit privy, whether topped by an outhouse or a few simple boards was, in the eyes of camp officials and administrators, disordered and dangerous behavior. Defecating in ways other than the camp program's modern approach was both retrograde and reckless.

The New Dealers were confident that with the symbolism of a ritual burning, the availability of modern facilities, and some guidance in the use of flush toilets, they could create new awareness and new practices in the migrants. When this confidence proved misplaced, as it often did, someone had to grab a shovel or a mop to address the problem of dirt. Someone also had to stand guard to put an end to the improper practice. And someone needed to remind the population of the boundary they had crossed.

For the migrants' part, the draw of the irrigation ditch over the modern toilet indicates that at least some thought differently about order and contamination than did the women and men working to redeem them in the government camps. Some of the migrants likely did not see human excrement as much of a contaminant at all and were simply continuing the time-honored practice of leaving it where it was easiest. It is also likely that some migrants saw excrement as a contaminant but thought that depositing it in the open air and leaving it undisturbed were ritually proper ways to handle it. One can well imagine that someone who works in the fields all day, miles removed from an outhouse, has baseline sensitivities about bodily functions that are different from those of a banker. According to a (notorious) Kern County grower, ten migrant families living on his property refused to enter the federal camp because they "didn't want to walk fifty yards to go to the toilet or empty garbage or dishwater."[56]

It was surely also the case that some migrants saw human excrement as a contaminant but, as a result of years of living on the edges of ditch banks, roads, and deserts, had stopped caring about how and where they placed it. California agricultural life all but required those on its lowest strata to live lives of dirt and filth. Even if a migrant had only been comfortable defecating in a modern toilet or a well-maintained outhouse at first, circumstances forced them to forget discomfort. To this group, the irrigation ditch might have seemed as good a place as any and a better place than most.

The systems of clay pipe and the modern flush toilets that fed them demanded very little of the matter that flowed through them, only that it continue to flow and, as comes naturally to organic matter, decompose. The systems of reform and redemption established by the RA and the FSA operated on a similar set of assumptions as far as movement through the system and doing what came naturally were concerned. Those who were poor and white ought to aspire to move out of poverty and to live white lives. The purity that they saw as important to whiteness was a purity born of modern technology and proper interaction with it.

White bodies ought to be clean. White waste ought to be managed. Entering into the sanitary unit and using it properly was a sign of acceptance of these norms and, circularly, of dependence on the sanitary unit to maintain them. To defecate or urinate out of place, to ignore pleas for regular showers was to perform rejection of those norms and, bodily, to declare a kind of independence from the systems that preached and enforced and adjudicated them. Throughout the valleys that they worked, the hand of the law was ready to punish migrants if they didn't place their waste properly, or if they didn't have access to the proper space at the necessary time. Is it so improbable that some campers in the new Brawley camp were using the irrigation ditch to offer commentary on a system that was suffocating to them?

Religion, Sanitation, and the Ironies of Modernity

The scholar and critic Talal Asad has written incisively of the puzzle that is religion, secularism, and modernity. Always careful to measure his judgments when describing the inconsistencies and hypocrisies of modernity, Asad nevertheless has made western readers painfully aware that certain, seemingly immovable conditions of our age: "modernity," "civilization," "religion," and "secularism" are defined and worked out by men and women in history. Being historically situated subjects, their vision, like ours, is limited. We should not be surprised to find that the concepts they deployed as neutral or even universal bear the marks of particular and contested cultures and values.

Asad's conclusions about modernity apply well to the interplay between migrants and New Deal agents in Depression-era California. There and then, a multi-level program informed by science, medicine, and legitimate public health concerns, and also by racial hierarchies and persistent concerns about the appearance and performance of whiteness, shaped the worlds of migrants from the Great Plains. It encouraged and at times coerced them to be more modern (less disordered) and more white (less filthy, less Black, less Mexican) in their behaviors.

One focus of this program was the proper use of modern plumbing to cleanse the body and to purge and manage its wastes. Sanitary units and utility buildings were central features of each migratory farm labor camp in terms of its geography, ideology, and civic structure. This centrality allowed program officials, camp managers, and residents to see and experience the redemptive power of physical and communal cleanliness as part of the project that is modernity. There is much that was and remains right and defensible about this vision.

As Asad and Mary Douglas before him note, however, we do well to approach concepts like pollution and cleansing with caution wherever we find them. New Deal practices of sanitation and hygiene, and the understanding of pollution that undergirded them, were a hybrid of science (microbiology, communicable diseases, public health) and of socially constructed, religiously-informed norms. The excrement of five homeless migrants, left within forty feet of an irrigation ditch, was a crime, a problem, pollution. The excrement of five thousand people, flushed from modern toilets and piped directly to a nearby river, was a norm, a solution, sanitation.

County, state, and federal agencies directed the policies and practices informed by this hybrid knowledge at a type of human pollution that, if not cleaned up and properly assimilated, would cloud the distinctions that ordered the moral and religious world of agricultural California and of the nation it supplied with produce, cotton, and grain.

Modernity as confessed and practiced in California's agricultural valleys had many blind spots. It also had more than its share of ironies. Efforts to contain pollution led to the spread of pollution. Efforts to move pollution away from bodies brought pollution back to these bodies. Efforts to demonstrate government concern instead revealed government struggles.

Irony was likely not on the mind of either Elizabeth Davisson or Frank Iusi when the limitations of the government camps' modern sanitation systems became all too apparent to them. Exactly one week before the Japanese Imperial Navy struck Pearl Harbor, Frank Iusi, longtime manager of the Yuba City camp, woke to a different kind of surprise. He and his family learned the hard way that when the camp's main sewage line backed up, the modern toilet in the manager's home was the primary outlet point. Iusi wrote to Harvey Coverley. "Yesterday morning (Sunday, November 30th) I had the unpleasant experience upon getting up from bed of stepping into 1 1/2 [feet] of stinking sewage water which had backed through the base of the toilet stool from the project's main sewer line. . . . Needless to say the inconveniences and damages to my family's health must be corrected immediately."

Iusi was under no illusions that he could remedy this problem on his own. He was sure that the "fall" of the entire system was inadequate to move waste reliably from the utility buildings to the Imhoff tank. The line from his house to the main line was, to paraphrase his letter, especially deficient. Before cataloging the damage done to his family's possessions, Iusi suggested that "an overflow pipe, separate cesspool, or septic tank . . . be installed immediately."[57] Within two weeks, a work order had been issued and the engineering division was moving toward addressing "this emergency situation."[58] Iusi emphasized that the "health dangers . . . can not be experienced in the future with any degree of pleasant expectation," which was no doubt true.

Faced with a similar crisis, Elizabeth Davisson, a home management supervisor in the Brawley camp, put pen to paper on February 28, 1942, hoping to obtain a copy of the USDA pamphlet "Simple Plumbing Repairs." She explained to her supervisor Addie L. Swapp:

> We are in a period of stress on the Brawley Project regarding our sanitation. Upon my return to Brawley . . . my inspection of the utility buildings revealed that in four of the five utility buildings immediate repairs are needed to safeguard public health. It is, rather, a matter of simple repairs needed than carelessness in the use of toilet facilities by camp residents. The women I talked with had done all each one of them could to keep as sanitary a utility building as possible under the existing conditions, of long duration.[59]

Davisson was likely correct that camp residents were not careless. Given the history of threats related to misuse of the sanitary unit, they seem to have taken great pains to convince her that nobody was "jobbing" on the floor. Davisson's willingness to work on the problem herself is admirable. Unfortunately, the problem was never going to yield to the wisdom of "Simple Plumbing Repairs" or any other USDA pamphlet. Eighty percent of the camp's toilets had been refusing to flush or were otherwise backing up due to "excessive overload" and, predictably enough in the middle of a desert, insufficient water.

The year 1942 saw pressing problems in Europe and Asia become America's problems as well, but the men and women who had been "the migrant problem" were still on hand, more integral than ever to the success of California agriculture. Demand for space in the Brawley camp remained high four years after its opening. Toilets were as popular with the migrants as C. G. Gillespie and Burton Cairns could ever have hoped.

The water that keeps the Imperial Valley's farms productive, local landscapes green, and residents' bathtubs full does not, however, fall directly from the sky. It flows from the Colorado River. Until a water use contract could be worked out with the city of Brawley, one that directed a great deal more of the town's precious water toward the migratory labor camp, the local outpost of New Deal modernity would remain almost intolerably, almost uninhabitably filthy. Chronically backed-up toilets in these missions of modern sanitation revealed that sanitation and modernity were unstable, unfinished projects and that the US government, try as it might, could not guarantee the final success of either.

5

The Community Center

Precisely when a camp resident first darkened the door of the community center in a federal camp depended on what was going on there, how appealing the activity was, and, more generally, how that person felt about socializing. It was, however, a matter not of if, but rather of when, residents would make their way toward this hub of camp community life.

By all accounts, camp residents used the community center and related public spaces regularly. They attended educational events and political discussions there. They turned up for evening entertainment and demonstrations of domestic skills. They gathered to learn, to argue, to organize, to relax, to worship, and, sometimes, simply to gather. Camp officials were pleased to see these displays of social energy. The camps were built around the assumption that community life, with its elements of cooperation, conflict, and compromise, helped to restore something that had been damaged in the migrant. To see camp residents come together in their leisure time was to have an important aspect of the program validated.

The community center was the space to which migrants were called for the work of social repair. It was the space in and around which the community became visible and observable to itself and, therefore, to others as well. As Tom Collins wrote to Irving Wood from the Arvin camp in January of 1936, "The community center has been of great value in many ways. Campers now go to the center, evenings, bathed and shaved and cleanly dressed. The center has allowed them to become better acquainted one with the other."[1]

Through the community center, Collins reported, the migrants were coming to know one another and were feeling and responding to community expectations with respect to appearance and behavior. One month later, Collins noted that, despite the significant hindrance created by "the lack of tables and benches" and fewer games than camp residents desired, "the community center grows in popularity daily."[2]

The community center was not, however, the Arvin camp's only official gathering space. While the camp was being built in late 1935, Wood and Collins agreed that "a camp platform for entertainment and recreation is an immediate necessity to the success of the camp." Wood thought immediately of dimensions, layout, and possibilities. "My idea is that we should have a platform at least 50 ft. square with a stage at one end standing not less than 4 feet above the level of the platform, with back or sounding board, and perhaps a roof."[3] Whatever else it might be used for, this space could accommodate audiences and performers. It would also be a place for the migrants to come together. The stage and platform were built and in use by the second week of January, 1936.

Community centers existed in one form or another in every government camp, but the functions served by those specific buildings were met in other camp spaces as well. And so, while considering the role and function of the community center in camp life, it also makes sense to include not just the outdoor platforms that most camps used for dances and concerts, but the fields where camp managers and recreation directors organized baseball and volleyball games, and even croquet.

When prompted to think about community activity and recreation, Irving Wood, the first director of the camp program, thought of both the community center and the outdoor platform. When thinking about the possibility that migrant workers might misuse leisure time, Tom Collins saw the community center, the platform, and athletic fields as solutions. Most important, when camp residents gathered for leisure activities, they did so at the community center, on the platform, and in the camp's fields.

By considering the plans for activity in these recreational spaces, we can see both their unspoken religiousness and the particular way in which those spaces shaped migrants' Protestant practices. The films shown and the radio programs broadcast, the boxing matches staged and the mattress-making projects undertaken, were all part of an effort to encourage and improve social interaction and to model and impart a restrained, mature approach to leisure. The activities staged in the

Tulare Camp Community Building, 1938.
Visalia, California. Community building at the Farm Security Administration Tulare camp for migratory workers. 1938. Courtesy of Library of Congress. https://www.loc.gov/item/2017765319/.

community center and related public spaces were intended to sculpt the community around the camp program's goals for the civilization and modernization of California's migratory farm workers.[4]

In thinking about the community center and its role in migrant camp life, there are three subjects to explore. The first, the rationale for its construction and its early uses, illuminates both the goals of recreation in the eyes of camp program officials, and the affinities of these goals with those articulated by reform-minded Protestants of the nineteenth and twentieth centuries. The second is the way that Protestant discourse and practice were present in the community center and related spaces, which shows the program's bias toward Protestant worship that was scheduled, ecumenical, and professional. An important aspect of the camp's modernization program for migrants was directing them toward what Bruce Lincoln has termed a "minimalist" model, demonstrated in limits placed around the practice and the influence of a religious tradition, in this case Protestantism.[5] Camp residents took part in official religious activities in the community center and on the outdoor platform, but they did not always accept the camp program's vision for the place of Protestantism in their lives. Thus, the third subject is camp residents' resistance to or subversion of the official approach to Protestant practice, which shows the migrants' tendency to let their Protestantism spill out from the containers in which camp officials hoped to hold them, and flow into other parts of their lives.

The practice of Protestantism in the community center and related spaces was governed by the reality of shared space and scheduling. In this structured social environment, religious practice was just another activity, a choice that migrants could make or not, like joining the baseball team, making a quilt, or sending the young ones out for a hike. And in the eyes of camp officials, no one choice of sanctioned activity was better than another. Boxing and volleyball, hymn singing and crafts, all contributed positively and in more-or-less equal measure to the well-being of the participant and the community.[6]

Activities that appear devoid of theological content or without connection to the traditions and practices of Protestant Christianity became part of camp life for reasons and in ways that would have been immediately familiar to earlier, more explicit religionists. Camp officials encouraged migrants to participate in secular-looking games, concerts, and pie-suppers with particular missionary ends in mind. They hoped to reform the migrants' approach to recreation, to acclimate them to a more modern view of religion, and to domesticate their remaining religious energies so that they would set their moral compasses by the true north of modern community life. As has often been the case in missionary environments, some of the simplest activities and most innocuous objects of migrant camp life—published schedules, story hour, a game of checkers, a square dance—were part of an environment expected to bring redemption to the unconverted.

Protestantism and Recreation

In February of 1936, after two months of sizing up residents of the Arvin camp, Tom Collins felt attuned enough to migrants' attitudes toward recreation, entertainment, and religion to try to regularize all three. And so, he wrote, he was, "following our procedure and plans for the proper use of leisure," by which he meant encouraging camp residents to gather regularly for activities.[7]

Collins was aware, however, of the existence of a competitor vying with equal fervor for the attention of camp residents. Money was tight. Work was hard to come by. When faced with privation, Collins observed, migrants focused on physical and spiritual sustenance. "So we see that as the unemployment situation grows more acute," he wrote, "the minds of the migrants turn to religion and fear of hunger." Religion and fear of hunger, but mostly religion. "To them, religion is their only source of emotional outlet," he continued. "Without it they would be a miserable lot. It is their duty in times of work and plenty. It is their joy in times of distress and want."[8]

The most important word in these five sentences is "only." Turning to religion as "duty" or "joy" was acceptable provided it was not the "only" source of joy, and that other connections kindled feelings of duty. The "proper use of leisure" required multiple emotional outlets. When Protestant belief kept migrants from participating in recreational activities, Collins felt the need to counter and circumscribe it.

It is not surprising that the "proper use of leisure" concerned Collins and his colleagues, and that they saw religion as a potential obstacle to this. Progressives and reformers like those who imagined, built, and ran the government camps were no strangers to debates over proper leisure. They knew well the work of fixing broken, out-of-date religion.

They had also been vocal proponents of the power of communal life and recreation to rescue lost souls. The first two Resettlement Administration camps in California opened in 1935, less than two years after the repeal of Prohibition, a lifestyle control movement championed by Progressive activists to whom moderation was little more than a filthy lie. The century-long movement that made Prohibition the law of the land was animated, in no small part, by a dim view of the choices Americans made in their leisure time and, more generally, a desire to lead Americans toward a particular, abstemious, Protestant vision of virtue.

Progressives were also architects, advocates, and practitioners of the Social Gospel, which lifted the blame for sinful lives from the shoulders of the individual and placed it on society. Their belief that sin was a social rather than an individual problem meant that their solutions to sin were also, of necessity, communal. As progressive theologian and pastor Walter Rauschenbusch wrote in the final paragraphs of his classic *Christianity and the Social Crisis*,

> Perhaps these nineteen centuries of Christian influence have been a long preliminary stage of growth, and now the flower and fruit are almost here. If at this juncture we can rally sufficient religious faith and moral strength to snap the bonds of evil and turn the present unparalleled economic and intellectual resources of humanity to the harmonious development of a true social life, the generations yet unborn will mark this as that great day of the Lord for which the ages waited, and count us blessed for sharing in the apostolate that proclaimed it.[9]

Prohibition and other attempts to reform social lives reflected the political theology of the Social Gospel in the work they did to remove sin-producing attitudes and institutions from society and to move the collective closer to the "great day of the Lord."

Progressive Protestants were also prominent theorists of the intersection of religious practice and physical exercise. They were among the most vocal promoters of muscular Christianity, a movement that portrayed Jesus as active, rugged, and occasionally combative, and that emphasized the spiritual benefits of athleticism and physical endeavor. Advocates of muscular Christianity encouraged the faithful to pursue activities—boxing, football, hiking, camping—that built physical strength. They encouraged young men to seek mastery of themselves and leadership in church and society.

As historians Gail Bederman and Clifford Putney have shown, the muscular Christianity movement grew out of white Protestant anxieties about the feminization of churches, the ascent of non-white, non-Protestant communities in the US, and the enervating effects of urban environments and office jobs on white men. Athletics and rugged, outdoor recreation could not solve every problem dogging early-twentieth-century America, but they could energize white men for the struggles of life in a rapidly changing society.

This belief in the power of recreation to mend runs through an announcement penned by Ernest Comer, WPA recreation director for the Arvin camp, and published in the *Weed Patch Cultivator* in October of 1938:

> All those wishing to take part in some form of recreation please report to the dance floor every day from 1:30 to 5:00 O'clock except Saturday and Sunday. At the present time, we have boxing, heavy punching, Soft ball, Horse shoes, etc. However, if there is some other game that you wish to take part in, just let us know and we will do our best to get it started.... We urge everyone [sic] of you to take part in this recreation, as it will take quite a load off of some of the minds that are troubled by the strike. Recreation is something that everyone needs, to make you healthy and full of pep. If everyone would take part in some kind of recreation, it would make life much happier.[10]

Sport was important for the sport of it. Play was meaningful for the play. But as Comer wrote, the reasons to engage in recreation and in entertainment also included distraction from stress, improvements to physical health, and greater overall happiness.[11]

Tom Collins and Irving Wood felt that the proper use of leisure time was "of great value" and was "an immediate necessity" from the first days of the camp program. Camp-sanctioned recreation would keep the migrants engaged in healthy pursuits and would draw them out of their tents and into community. But Collins, reflecting on the origins of camp community-based entertainment in the camps, revealed also the complexity of his own motives regarding recreation. "We realized," Collins told those gathered for the dedication of the Marysville camp in October of 1935, "that the hours of leisure after the days' toil and Sundays, were danger points if left to themselves." The idle hands of migrants, no matter how calloused, were the devil's playground. And so those hours of leisure, and those Sundays, needed to be filled.

The beginning of an answer, Collins recounted, was close at hand. "Many of the campers had their own musical instruments. With these we developed a camp orchestra of eleven stringed instruments." The wisdom and the value of this plan showed immediately. Not only were the hands and bodies of eleven migrants kept busy making music, but the entire camp suddenly had a source of wholesome community entertainment. "This made possible evening concerts, bi-weekly dances and community sings," Collins continued, "There was something interesting every evening and every Sunday." The sorts of mischief that might surface in the isolation of a tent or a garden home could be countered, even chased away, when the community gathered.[12]

Communal events and entertainment presented wholesome opportunities for the camp residents. They also presented important opportunities for the camp managers to observe the migrants as a people, to place them under the anthropological gaze and to study them as a somewhat coherent cultural unit. Put another way, the "something interesting every evening and every Sunday" was interesting both to the migrants and to camp staff, albeit for different reasons. In and around the community center, camp managers and staff could take the measure of the migrants as social beings and adapt the camp's missionary environment to suit them.

An oft-noted problem was the migrants' tendency to lose themselves and to slip backwards, whether in age or level of civilization. Tom Collins observed this in two encounters at the Arvin camp community center in the spring and summer of 1936. When the camp received "several boxes of clothing from Berkeley" in July of 1936, Collins had them "catalogued" and "hung on racks in the community center" before inviting the migrant women to look them over. He reported, "from 65 feminine throats came 'AHS'—'OHS'—'GEES'—'AINT EM PUTTY'—'KAIN YER BEET IT!'" After the vocalizations came "much handling and 'feeling'" of the clothing. According to Collins, physical contact with the items pushed the gathered women over the edge.

> [T]he temptation was too great for all the women and for half an hour pandemonium broke loose. There was shouting, tugs of war, hair pulling, hefty fists flew, shoes went through the air—foot ball tactics were used to tackle women and girls as they went out the community center doors with the precious 'purty things.' When the dust cleared away nothing was left.[13]

Saturday dance at the Tulare Camp, 1940.
Photograph by Arthur Rothstein. *Saturday night dance. Tulare migrant camp. Visalia, California.* March 1940. Courtesy of Library of Congress. https://www.loc.gov/item/2017774858/.

Collins paints an unflattering picture of the migrant women as a group. Gathered in community they can be civil and civilized, but that veneer falls away upon first contact with "purty things." When migrant women encounter things that they desire, order breaks down, decorum vanishes, and the competition for possession devolves into a brawl.

A similar scene unfolded at the community center after residents had developed the habit of gathering but before they had sufficient activities to occupy them. The camp council tried to collect money from residents to buy board games and decks of cards, but the plan failed. Collins, sympathetic to the need and eager to keep the community center vibrant, intervened. "We entered the community center one evening this week, carrying two packs of playing cards and two sets of checkers. The center was packed to the walls with men, women, and children." When the crowd noticed Collins bearing treasures, the line separating adult from child vanished. "There was an immediate rush for the items mentioned, and for a little time there was a tug-of-war and much fussing too.... The grown ups were more like kids, so great was their pleasure and delight." Although no tackling and hair-pulling took place, order still broke down and adults regressed, driven by excitement over the scarce items. And in this case, a milder version of the chaos was recapitulated on a regular basis. "Since then there is a rush each evening to get the checkers or cards."[14]

Migrants had a tendency, described as child-like, toward enthusiasm in moments of encounter. Contemporary educators and psychologists would likely have noted that the hyper-emotionalism and rash behavior that the camp staff noted were a function of culture and of upbringing. Even in better, more settled times, sharecroppers and tenant farmers from the Great Plains and Appalachia were not known to outside observers as models of sophistication and Victorian reserve. And to the extent that observers could generalize about the migrants' childhood years, they would almost certainly have emphasized a lack of proper structure and guidance.

In contrast to the over-civilized, urbane, neurasthenic children of privilege about whom educational theorist G. Stanley Hall and his acolytes worried, these children spent too much time in the "savage" stage of development and too little in the civilized. This cultural and personal weakness emerged in many realms of life, but was especially evident in and around the community center. One remedy, also evident in the community center and camp recreation more broadly, was to structure time and, in so doing, to teach inhibition and restraint.

Mary K. Davies appreciated the value of structure as much as anyone. She served as the head of the Yuba City camp nursery school, which operated out of the camp community center / recreation hall and served between fifty and sixty children. In 1941 she wrote to the camp program hierarchy describing the children of the camp and the effects of her work.

She recorded her thoughts on older children first, those not in her direct care. "Our Yuba City Camp children of elementary school age are too accustomed to a free, unrestrained life to really enjoy school ways. In the short time they have been alive, they have not become aware of social living." Of the "younger adolescent" set, Davies wrote, "They lack the initiative necessary to make the break from camp life to a more exacting responsible adult life." The arc of an unscheduled, unstructured youth was short, and it bent towards sloth. To break this deleterious pattern, one had to intervene early, as Davies was doing. She wrote of her nursery school charges and the changes being wrought in them by living in and with structure.

> In the nursery school many children are for the first time learning to be wholesome individuals functioning happily in a larger social group. Little roamers, once lacking in self-restraint and grace, now have anchorage in activities such as clay modeling, crayoning, bead stringing, block construction, housekeeping, play and dramatic playing about boats and trains. Little destroyers are learning to enjoy construction with block, or with wood and nails, or clay. Little hoarders, grabbing and hanging grimly to armfuls of toys are fast disappearing.... As self control and self restraint develop, skills improve and as skills improve, self assurance and poise result.[15]

These words, significant enough for what they reveal about one teacher's views of the migrant children in her camp, take on added meaning in a camp environment where the infantilization of migrants was common, and in which reform and catechism were pervasive and multi-layered. Davies's words reflect not just her view of children, but the view of migrants; not just one nursery school's pedagogical aims, but the camp system's aims for its residents.

It was important to bend the arc away from roaming, destroying, hoarding, and other social pathologies, and toward activities, crayoning and bead stringing and vacation bible school for some; chess, checkers, amateur music night, and an hour of worship every Sunday or so for others. Leisure activities such as these were not "just" leisure. They were opportunities to evangelize restraint. They were moments to take stock of the migrants' progress toward modern communal living.

One obvious place to find this gospel of restraint is in camp vice rules, which designated some recreational activities—drinking and gambling, for example—as immoral and therefore forbidden. Camp staff did not always have sterling records of restraint and virtuous action themselves—Tom Collins was a heavy drinker and abandoned two families; camp manager Bob Hardie ran off with a camp nurse—but they could be adamant to the point of rage when it came to establishing norms around the migrants' leisure time. Camp manager Ray Mork provided an especially white-hot moment for readers of the Indio camp's weekly paper. In his "Weekly Letter from Your Manager on the State of the Camp," published on February 4, 1939, Mork responded to charges that he was an overbearing "so-and-so" with a sweeping attack on drinking in camp:

> I hate with all my power of hatred the practice of fathers spending money on intoxicating liquor when their children need better food and better clothing and the wives need shoes and dresses, and it is not because I think it is my job to interfere with people's morals. But in this camp where money is furnished by the government to a father to take care of his family and he gets intoxicated, that man will get no sympathy from me, then and there I will have him turned over to county authorities. A father who brings children into the world and hasent enough manhood in him to try to take care of them, specially when his government gives him money to do so with, dosent deserve the sympathy of any one.

Mork may have imagined that his logic was novel. It was, in fact, derivative of broader American progressivism down to the last jot and tittle. Fathers who drink are turning their backs on their children and wives. The parameters within which recipients of government assistance can spend and consume must be externally established and strictly enforced. Men who do not comply with these rules are no men at all. As far as the government is concerned, they can (and will) go to hell.[16] Mork concluded, "To the end of keeping the camp clean, protecting the children in it, giving to all the civil rights guaranteed under our constitution do I intend to run this camp, let the chips fall where they may."

At the Shafter camp in May of 1939, camp manager Charles Barry issued eviction notices to E. J. Snow, Fred Craig, Marvin Hood, and Filander Nichols for violating camp rules regarding "intoxicating liquors." "You have been charged with raising disturbance while drunk," their notices read, "The Camp Council voted May 16 to have you evicted from Camp."[17] How one unwound said a great deal about where one belonged.

Camp rules also banned gambling, though less adamantly. Minutes from a camp council meeting at the Arvin camp in April of 1938 showed that there was room for some distinctions. "The playing of dice is not to be allowed on the camp grounds, and if anyone is seen playing, they must be reported immediately. Playing cards was debated upon, and was decided that this would not influence children."[18] A more strident prohibition appeared on a camp permit in use at the Shafter camp in the summer of 1939. "NO GAMBLING OF ANY KIND PERMITTED IN CAMP OR ON CAMP GROUNDS."[19]

The specific logic of these bans—on dice, on all gambling—surely went hand in hand with the logic Mork applied to the practice of drinking. Anyone poor enough to be living in a government camp did not have money to waste. Anyone who chose to waste money on games of chance, possibly influencing those around him to do the same, showed himself to be unworthy of the benefits found within the camp gates.

Ray Mork and the camp program leadership meant well. They were concerned about the health and well-being of camp residents, and did not want to see husbands drink or gamble away money that could have been used to feed and clothe their children, furnish their living spaces, or build savings. They were also concerned about the place of the migrants in a future America, where and how they might fit. According to Mork and his fellow camp managers, the migrants were hardworking and individualistic. They were also immoderate and lacked restraint. Migration and homelessness had broken down the traditions and tendencies of communal life in a people who had never been well socialized in the first place. Camp officials believed it was important to convert migrants to a new way of being—scheduled, bounded, restrained—one activity at a time.

Some boundaries marked certain activities as beyond the pale. Other boundaries kept types of recreation, and therefore types of time, distinct. An early episode precipitated by the outdoor platform and stage at the Arvin camp demonstrates something of the reformers' efforts to limit and restrain the influence of Protestantism among the migrants.

As a manager committed to communal gatherings, Tom Collins was enthusiastic about the outdoor platform and the possibilities it opened up for dances, plays, and concerts. He noticed, however, that a group of women did not share his views. "Many of our campers are ultra religious," Collins reported, "so much so that they have given the stage and platform wide berth. They even keep a watchful eye out to prevent children WALKING on the platform." In Collins's eyes and surely those of his superiors, this was problematic. Leisure was meant to be relaxing, fun, and unifying, not an arena for the expression of sectarian attitudes.

In service of this vision of leisure, Collins reported that he was "gradually breaking this condition" of shunning the stage. This "breaking" of the "ultra religious" is perhaps better understood as Enlightenment-style restraining of religious excess. Migrants could believe what they wanted regarding the divine or, as Thomas Jefferson famously stated, whether there was one god or twenty. What Collins asked is that they reconsider beliefs and practices that, in his eyes, were beyond the realm of religion, especially those that threatened to douse communal fun.[20]

Predictably, Collins focused his missionary energies on the soft flank represented by children rather than the hardened front lines of their mothers. "Evening finds the camp manager in the center of the stage," he wrote of himself, "sometimes sitting within a circle of small children while he tells bedtime stories; sometimes supervising the children in folk plays hop step and jump games, etc. etc." The idea was to model wholesomeness not anchored to holiness, and to appeal to what he saw as a true universal—the right of children to play and be entertained. If the children of the ultra-religious families took part in recreation on the stage and returned to their tents happy (and not demon-possessed), their parents might be more open to "the proper use of leisure." It was too early to be certain, but Collins thought that he might soon "win a victory."

> We have two of the mothers who strongly object to the platform (account of dancing) coaching 12 girls in a short playlet that we shall produce very shortly. The mothers mentioned are keenly interested in the coaching. (In fact we have been quite concerned that they take it too seriously). A few moments ago one of the mothers told me they were coaching the kids to sing three songs on the day we present our first community play. That interests us immensely—SONGS—and not HYMNS.[21]

If Collins had reflected on this apparent victory further, he might have seen it as doubly significant. Not only had he restrained a Protestant impulse to shun a worldly space and thus made it possible for more residents to appreciate the entertainment that took place there. He had also set the posts for a fence that would, for at least two "ultra-religious" mothers, keep their Protestantism penned up and away from social realms in which it did not belong. The language used by an ultra-religious mother—"songs" not "hymns"—indicated to Collins that her world now included space for the wholesome secular.

By the time of the first inspection of the Arvin camp in the summer of 1936, Collins had created a decently balanced environment for group gatherings and entertainment. He had also made adequate space—at least to appearances—for the expression of Protestant preferences, without surrendering the center of the community or the interpretation of the community center to "ultra-religious" Protestant faithful.

When the inspector, Special Agent Mensing, arrived in the camp, he found an "18' x 38' two room building designed for a warehouse but being used at present as the camp office and community center" near the entrance to the camp. The "assembly platform" was located deeper into the camp, alongside the "pump and tank house." It measured "48' x 50' . . . with an 18' x 30' roofed stage and piano pit." When Mensing talked to Collins about the assembly platform, he learned "that on Wednesday evenings a camp meeting is held . . . with community singing, lectures, or other entertainment provided, most of which is done by the campers themselves." Special Agent Mensing continued:

> On Saturday evenings a square dance is held the music for which is furnished by an orchestra organized by the campers themselves. Mr. Collins explained that the popular style of straight dancing is not permitted because these people, being deeply religious, regard it as being immoral. Attendance at these square dances is limited to members of the camp families and friends from the surrounding community who have received written invitations.[22]

The assembly platform was a social hub for the camp, much as Irving Wood envisioned it. It was also a space for expressing the culture and the religious and moral orientation of the community. Religious attitudes were woven into the gatherings and performances in ways both obvious and not. Protestantism influenced the type of dancing and singing that took place on the platform but didn't keep the dances and community sings from happening.

Collins's relief at having a sanctified ally in this work is palpable in a report of March 14, 1936, that describes the campers' selection of "'a Full Gospelite' preacher for their Sunday school." Collins was aware that the preacher "represent[ed] a sect opposed to dancing," but found that he was "a good sport" when it came to keeping his beliefs in check. With a congregation gathered on the outdoor platform for Sunday school, the preacher selected "a chapter from Isaiah, in which dancing is approved." For Collins, and surely for many of those gathered, it was a welcome message.[23]

With Protestantism properly restrained, the Arvin camp's community center and outdoor platform could be used to maximum benefit. The realization of this blessed vision happened in September of 1936 with an evening sing for the whole camp. Collins was understandably moved.

> The community sing this week was a magnificent demonstration of community effort and cooperation. The whole population was out. It simply thrilled us to see how happy and joyful our workers are. The program was well arranged and was the finest we have had since the community was organized. Men, women, and children took part. There were musical numbers, solos, duets, quartets, dialogues, singing en masse, jigs and etc. The population warmed up to the occasion and as a result some old folk songs heretofore unheard in this section of the country came to the fore.[24]

The diversity of song types and genres mattered to Collins, as did the diversity of motives and orientations expressed in them. Camp residents used song to express frustration with the economics of large-scale agriculture, singing together "Eleven-cent Cotton and Forty-cent Meat." They used song to express cross-generational perplexity and judgment with "Why Do You Bob Your Hair Girls?" And, of course, some camp residents used song to express their faith more directly, singing a hymn titled "It's the Wrong Way to Whip the Devil."

Collins focused his description of the evening's entertainment first on the singing of "Eleven Cent Cotton," written in 1930 by Memphis-based songwriter Bob Miller. This well-known song, which Collins also referred to as "A Share Cropper's Lament," "brought the old folks to their toes and brought encore after encore." He believed that the community responded so emotionally to the song because it was "so packed with the life of the miserable share cropper." He submitted lyrics as part of his report.

> Eleven cent cotton and forty cent meat
> How in the world can a poor man eat?
> Flour up high, cotton down low,
> How in the world can you raise the dough?
> Clothes worn out, shoes run down,
> Old slouch hat with a hole in the crown,
> Back nearly broken, fingers all worn,
> Cotton going down to raise no more.
> Eleven cent cotton, eight bucks pants
> Who in the world can have a chance?
>
> Eleven cent cotton and forty cent meat
> How in the world can a poor man eat?
> Mules in the barn, no crop laid by,
> Grist mill empty and the cow going dry.
> Well water low, nearly out of sight,
> Can't take a bath on a Saturday night.
> No use talking, any man's weak,
> At eleven cent cotton and forty cent meat.[25]

This song of frustration captured what Collins thought ought to have been the central concern of the entire camp: an economic system that set them up not just to fail, but to fail, starve, live in filth, and die ashamed. The words captured "the miserable life of the share cropper" and, ideally, would lead those who gave their voices to the song to consider their misery and ways to address it.

"Why Do You Bob Your Hair Girls?" presented a picture of migrant concerns that diverged from the theme of economic justice and moved into the realm of Protestant values. In describing this song, Collins focused less on the maximalist Protestantism it expressed and more on the circumstances that led to its public performance. Toward the beginning of the summer, he wrote, a fifteen-year-old girl with blonde hair down to her knees had moved into the camp. She wanted to bob her hair as many other girls in camp had done, but her mother refused to allow it. According to Collins, the girl's hair was an attraction for the older women who would "comb and fondle" it.

The family moved away at the end of the summer, but the girl returned to visit friends in camp and, without her mother's permission, had her hair bobbed. The older women in the camp noticed immediately and were crestfallen. One of the women commented to Collins, "Aint it sinful how sum of this hear young uns jest wastens ther holy poss'sens." The singing of the anti-bobbing song by "three girls . . . ages 18, 16, 15 . . . all of them [with] their hair bobbed" was, he reported, directed at the girl. Two verses described the benefits of hewing to more traditional styles.

> Why do you bob your hair girls?
> It does not look so nice
> It's just to keep in fashion
> And it's not the Lord's advice
> And every time you bob it
> You're breaking God's command
> "You cannot bob your hair girls,
> And reach the promised land."
>
> Why do you bob your hair girls?
> It's not the thing to do,
> Just wear it, always wear it
> And to the Lord be true.
> And when before the Judgment
> You meet the Lord up there he'll say
> "Welcome fair wanderer for you never bobbed your hair."[26]

In the eyes of a group of older migrant women, choices of hair styles were not simple fashion statements, they were declarations of one's commitment "to the Lord." Moreover, the decision to bob or not to bob came with eternal consequences. Collins made no mention of how the song was received, though he likely would have let the camp program hierarchy know if it had met either widespread or exceptionally vocal disapproval.

The final number that Collins described, "That's the Wrong Way to Whip the Devil," was the most overtly theological. It had been written by a camp resident, "Sister Hale," and was sung to the tune of the Great-War-era song "It's a Long Way to Tipperary." Collins described it tersely as "a hymn now popular among the church going workers."

> When the saints they come together
> For to pray and worship God
> To sing and testify and preach his precious word,
> There are some who get offended
> And sit back and pout
> While others they get jealous
> When they see a sister shout
>
> That's the wrong way to whip the devil
> That's the wrong way to put him down
> The spirit of God is not present
> When division can be found
> Saying good bye to sin and satan
> Farewell old world adieu
> I have my eyes upon my savior
> With his help I'm going through.[27]

Subsequent verses warned against being discouraged by another's backsliding, being angry at the preacher, quarrelling, and gossiping, all of which were also "the wrong way to whip the devil." The theology expressed in this hymn was certainly not in line with Collins's views on the divine, but its presentation as evening entertainment served to smooth its rough edges and to align it more fully with the camp recreation program. Surrounded by other types of entertainment and presented to an audience that had gathered to be entertained, the hymn became entertainment itself. To use Collins's own distinction, the setting made the "hymn" into a "song."

In Collins's eyes, the community sing was magnificent. He was thrilled by the joy he saw among the camp residents and by their ability to organize the program. In his reporting to camp program headquarters, he favored the "songs" more than the "hymns," and preferred to see communal identity congeal around songs of economic woe and protest rather than songs focused on Protestant theology. Indeed, Collins devoted far more commentary to "Eleven Cent Cotton, Forty Cent Meat" than to "It's the Wrong Way to Whip the Devil" and gave the former (and the protest song tradition) pride of place in the history and culture of sharecroppers and tenant farmers.

All told, though, the evening was pleasing to Collins. Protestant influences had been present but were not the main story. "Religion" had appeared on stage but was not the "only emotional outlet" for the crowd. "Eleven Cent Cotton" and the forgivable loopy-ness of migrant women on the question of cutting hair made the moralistic and theological songs performed by camp residents far more palatable. The sing was a promising step toward more restrained Protestantism in recreational contexts. This expression of migrant community demonstrated progress toward social maturity.

Three years later, in the Indio camp, Ray Mork committed himself to theological and ethical readings of two community events, the sanctity of which might have escaped camp residents. In both instances, Mork urged camp residents to appreciate the religious significance of an activity that stretched the definition of Protestant practice. The first was a January 5, 1939 visit and lecture by birth control advocate Margaret Sanger. The medium of a public lecture was familiar enough to the camp residents. The message Sanger delivered seems to have been less so.

In the January 14 edition of the *Covered Wagon News*, Mork argued for the theological significance of Sanger's life and work. He noted first that "the camp was signally honored by a visit . . . of one of the finest as well as one of the best known women in America." He then wrote forcefully in defense of Sanger. Mork wanted her enemies to know that they were part of a centuries-long pattern of foolish resistance.

> Small smug minds, void of any freedom of imagination, condemn as they always have those whom they are incapable of understanding and appreciating. Since Christ it has been the lot of the great to have been persecuted by those whom their effort would have aided. . . . We here in this camp are of those whom this great woman has aided the most, because we needed her help most. We know that she has lived a useful life in our behalf and . . . we want to say that we appreciate it all.

Between the lines of Mork's editorial, one can see that some of the "small smug minds" "incapable of understanding and appreciating" her were readers of the *Covered Wagon News*. Mork hoped to persuade camp residents not to make the age-old mistake of persecuting Sanger because of her attempts to aid them.

In case readers could not see their stake in Sanger's program, Mork described the connection she made between families with too many children and persistent poverty, her authorship of the pamphlet "Family Limitation," and her heroic efforts to distribute it to "working mothers in America, telling them what to do to avoid large families." The entirety of the camp audience, Mork continued, should be thankful for this work and should follow Sanger's advice. To do otherwise would be to join the sad parade of those who were deaf to saving truths. Mork linked Sanger and Christ to argue that her program was not scandalous or obscene, as others had mistakenly concluded, but rather represented true and good religion, and was a blessing to souls desperately in need.[28]

In mid-February of 1939, Mork again used the pages of the camp paper to describe and interpret a public event. This time it was a showing of the French movie *Golgotha*, which had been released in the United States in 1937 as *Behold the Man*. Apparently the movie had not held every camper's attention the way lighter fare at the community center had.

Those who were too focused on entertainment value had left "after the comedy and western pictures were shown." Others with insufficient attention spans were bored by what Mork described as the "slow moving story of Christ." There were also those with faulty understandings of Protestantism. Mork described this group as "those to whom religion means only sad songs, sad faces, and restrictions of liberties of youth." If they were present at all, Mork opined, they would likely have found "the picture . . . tiresome." Then there were those whose views were well calibrated, the true audience for such a film, the properly devout, "those who . . . attempt to follow in what ever light they have, the teachings of the master," and those who "see in the persecution of Jesus the modern fight for liberty and salvation, the modern strong preying upon the modern weak, the modern idolaters worshipping in the temples of Mammon."

The inspiration that camp residents ought to have found in the film, Mork continued, was derived from the Christlike struggles being undertaken, as Sanger's work was, for their benefit. One did not have to pore over scripture to learn the story of Jesus of Nazareth. It was unfolding in California every day. If migrants paid close enough attention, they could see and feel the oppression against which Jesus struggled and the obstacles he met in the fight. As Mork wrote,

> How often in the struggle for those who work have we seen leaders sold to Mammon for pieces of silver, how often have we seen them carrying the cross of persecution, laden with those whom they would serve, false leaders masking under the banners of patriotism and ritual. The high priests of the day, living not among the poor but with the rich, called him a rabble rouser, a false prophet. A simple man fighting for simple folk from which he sprung and whom he loved.

The film, presented as entertainment in a space designed for entertainment, was also a key to a proper reading of the Protestant present. An awakened community could see in its depiction of the life of Jesus an inspiration for their earthly struggles and a clear indictment of the myriad oppressions they faced.

Having reflected on the meaning of the film for the migrants' lives in the fields, Mork turned his eyes to an apocalyptic future. He did not fix dates or connect his prophecy to the rise and fall of empires and the assassination of world leaders. Instead, he enjoined readers to avoid mistakes recorded in the gospels when an anointed leader came around again.

> Some where, some time another shall rise and put upon his back the cross of the centuries. But he shall not come in peace, he shall come giving an eye for an eye and a tooth for a tooth, he shall be a leader among men. When he comes, let us not like Peter deny him, nor like the followers of the priests of Mammon stone him, nor like Judas exchange him for pieces of silver.

The film that had "flashed upon the silver screen in the camp auditorium" had told the story of "the greatest martyr since the dawn of time."

Mork insisted that the proper reading of that "picture" was at once focused on the here and now, and on the Apocalypse. The life of Jesus as depicted in the film could help camp residents navigate the challenging terrain of agricultural California. It could also help them identify the next savior. *Golgotha* was not primarily a story of human sin, the divine in human form, suffering, resurrection, salvation. It was a story of the clarity that Jesus could bring to current situations—family situations, labor situations—facing the poor. According to Mork, the properly Christian camp community saw Jesus in many times and places, especially among the earthly liberators.[29]

The stances that camp officials took vis-à-vis family planning (pro) and organized labor (also pro, though tempered) are certainly worth noting. What is more important to this story, though, is the relationship that Mork described between the migrants' historical moment—his historical moment—and Christian sacred narrative, and the extent to which this historical relationship interacted with the community center as a missionary space. Just as migrants ought to pull their noses out of their Bibles to see the redeemers and the betrayers around them, so too should they move easily and faithfully between lectures, sewing classes, worship services, and community boxing championships. In his reading of Sanger's visit and of the movie *Golgotha*, Mork was both reacting against and trying to confront what he saw as a retrograde and self-defeating religion. A religion that placed its sources of truth and inspiration outside of history, that leaned heavily on individual sinfulness—chastising young people, judging behaviors that didn't need to be judged—would certainly miss the bigger picture, which was crucial for his migrant community.

In the struggle over public Protestantism, Mork saw, as Collins did before him, the need for a counter-narrative, a story that presented Protestantism in different packaging and to different ends. The widened ranges of Protestant moral exemplars (from ancient martyrs to the contemporary persecuted) and sources of divine inspiration (from scripture, to current events, to film) were reflected in the built and scheduled environment of the community center, with its multiple, co-located activities, each offering a form of social redemption and individual edification.

Moreover, in operating the community center as they did, Mork and others created an environment in which traditionalist and/or maximalist

Protestantism was marginalized not just rhetorically—e.g., "small, smug minds;" "sad songs, sad faces, and restrictions of liberties of youth"—but structurally as well. For the rules of engagement with the community center all but required acceptance of a Protestantism that rubbed elbows comfortably with radio dramas, checkers games, and messages from the Margaret Sanger Foundation.

Protestantism as Recreation

The range of activities offered in the community center and other shared spaces was impressive. It was not uncommon to find sewing classes, political discussions, movie screenings, union meetings, amateur music nights, camp dances, and special events for children all scheduled during the same week. Some form of Protestant practice—Sunday school, Sunday worship, Bible study, a hymn sing—was almost always included

Migrant residents of the Arvin Camp perform a play for residents of the Tulare Camp, 1940.
Photograph by Arthur Rothstein. *Play given by visiting Arvin camp. Tulare migrant camp. Visalia, California.* March 1940. Courtesy of Library of Congress. https://www.loc.gov/item/2017774841/.

Tulare Camp residents gathered for the play performed by Arvin Camp residents. Photograph by Arthur Rothstein. *Audience watching play given by Arvin camp. Tulare migrant camp. Visalia, California.* March 1940. Courtesy of Library of Congress. https://www.loc.gov/item/2017774798/.

among those events. Protestant practice was usually scheduled two to three times per week. It was deliberately and unabashedly ecumenical, and was usually outsourced to religious leaders from the surrounding community. Each of these qualities was the result of a deliberate choice, a policy decision.

The least noticeable choice and quite possibly the one that felt like no choice at all was the scheduling of worship and religious education: Sunday school and worship on Sundays, Bible study or a hymn sing on Tuesday or Wednesday evening. This rhythm surely felt familiar to many migrants. To some of the camp staff and hierarchy, multiple days for Protestant practice likely seemed excessive. But among a people accustomed to revivals and urgent evangelism, the schedule was a statement. Protestant worship, like amateur music night, happened on a day, at a time, in a place. It was regular and contained. It began and it ended.

Robert Brown, acting manager of the Brawley camp, described the situation vis-à-vis "recreation" in the camp in his monthly report for November of 1939:

> Boy's and Girl's Clubs have been started by the Management. These groups have elected their Chairmen, and have been turned over to the respective groups. Womens clubs were started. Dances are held every Saturday night. Church and Sunday School were started Sunday November 26.[30]

The categorization of church and Sunday school as "recreation," and their inclusion in a list with dances and the Boy's and Girl's Clubs, shows something of Brown's stance toward Protestant practice. He thought of it as most like the activities that brought migrants together to be entertained and to socialize.

Manager Guy Griset, himself a former migrant worker, saw Protestantism somewhat differently. Filing a monthly report from the Indio camp in March of 1940, Griset placed his account of Protestant worship under the sub-heading "Education," which he used to group the nursery school, the Home Management Supervisor's "splendid" work "helping the ladies in the camp," and the camp's need for more teachers. "The Ministerial Association of Coachella Valley . . . handles the religious activities, they being quite well attended," he wrote, and then continued "every Monday night we have an open Council meeting which is quite educational and well attended. Every Wednesday night the Worker's Alliance meets."[31]

For Griset, Protestant worship had the most in common with awareness-building, skill-imparting activities, especially those focused on children and the home. In the following month's report, Griset said nothing at all about Protestant worship. Instead, he reported happily that the WPA had sent a recreational director to the Indio camp, who was responsible for "supervising the campers' play activity." He concluded proudly, "There is something doing every night in our Social Center."[32]

Camp newspaper announcements from late 1939 and early 1940 give a more detailed portrait of the timing, structure, and leadership of Protestant worship, whether seen as recreation or education. In November of 1939, the Indio camp's *Migratory Clipper* reported that "Church Services" were going to take place on "Sunday evening from 7:30 to 9 o'clock." The author continued by noting, "the Reverend James A. Miller of the Church of God will conduct divine worship at the social center. The Reverend C. B. Sanderson of Oasis will assist." For those with evening plans or with different denominational tastes, the camp also offered a "2:30 in the afternoon church service . . . under the auspices of the Coachella Valley Ministerial Association."[33] The two services were not meant to compete with or to exclude each other. "All campers will be cordially welcome at both meetings," the announcement concluded. In the space reserved for announcements and commentary from the camp manager, Joseph McClain wrote:

> I wish to welcome the Coachella Valley Ministerial Association and Mr. James A. Miller. The ministerial association will have someone here every Sunday afternoon from 2:30 to 4:00 to lead us in religious services. Mr. [James A.] Miller will be with us from 7:30 to 9:00 o'clock Sunday evening. I know these men will plan splendid services for us, and I hope as many of you folks as possible will attend. They are giving their time and work for us. Let's support them.[34]

Reverend Miller became a fixture of camp worship and, as planned, the Coachella Valley ministers rotated through. Reverend Phillip Lascellos, president of the association, preached the week of November 11. The week following it was P. A. McGuire of the Church of the Nazarene. For worship the week of December 2, "Reverend Mr. McCartney" drove thirty miles from Palm Springs to Indio.[35] On the day that Reverend Lascellos preached, a brief notice from him appeared in the *Migratory Clipper*:

> The Coachella Valley Ministerial Association wishes to express its appreciation to the members of the camp council and the camp for the courtesy extended to it, in allowing it the use of the building on Sunday afternoon from the hours of 2:30 p.m. until 4:00 p.m. for the purpose of conducting Sunday School and services for the residents of the camp. They will be glad to see all who wish to attend these services at any time. It is hoped that these services will be supported by your attendance, so that you might profit by them.[36]

Sunday school at the Tulare Camp, 1940.
Photograph by Arthur Rothstein. *Sunday school. Tulare migrant camp. Visalia, California* March 1940. Courtesy of Library of Congress. https://www.loc.gov/item/2017774829/.

Sunday school hymns at the Tulare Camp, 1940.
Photograph by Arthur Rothstein. *Sunday school. Tulare migrant camp. Visalia, California*. March 1940. Courtesy of Library of Congress. https://www.loc.gov/item/2017774830/.

The calls for "support," included in both Manager McLain's and Reverend Lascellos's announcements, are worth pausing over. They seem to confirm, at least partially, a view of Protestant worship and ministry as performance or entertainment. Worship is presented as an opportunity to go see someone do something, to watch an event and to appreciate it. The notion that taking part in worship is an expression of support for the minister subtly frames Protestant practice as recreation. Put another way, the meaning of attending worship—support for the person at the front of the room—becomes the rough equivalent of the meaning of attending an amateur concert, a craft demonstration, or a play put on by the camp's children.

During October and November of 1939, the situation in the Arvin camp was roughly the same. In an item titled "Sunday School and Church News," an anonymous contributor reported, "We have Sunday [School] every Sunday at the dance hall starting at 2 o'clock. Church service every Sunday Evening at 7:15 under the leadership of Rev. Delbert Coble."[37] The paper presented an impressive list of "Sunday School officers and teachers" and encouraged all to come to "build up good attendance."

The paper's report from a few weeks later, November 17, read, "Sunday Night: Had Sunday school in the afternoon which was fairly well attended by the children, would like to see more children turn out also you grown folks. The Rev. Mr. Moore gave his sermon in the evening: 'War in which all Veterans were invited!' Help build up our Sunday school to where we will be proud of it."[38] The Arvin camp, too, offered Protestant worship in distinct, well-defined forms. After "game night" on Tuesday, the "pie supper" fundraiser and musical offerings on Wednesday, community singing on Thursday, boxing on Friday, and the camp dance on Saturday, one could, if one chose, "come and take part in our church and Sunday school"[39] An active, well-balanced social life included some or all of these events, and "good attendance" indicated a thriving camp society.

In Arvin as in other camps, a subcommittee of the camp council usually oversaw the scheduling of social events and worship services, and worked with the broader camp population and the camp staff to revise and enforce schedules as necessary. When, for instance, "church activities in tents at late hours were reported keeping some of the campers from sleeping," as happened at the Arvin camp in March of 1938, the camp council and the church committee, represented by camp resident C. H. Nichols, determined that "quietness should be obtained" (read: worship should stop) in the camp after 9:30.[40]

The official stance of the camp program toward Protestantism was ecumenical or, at least, multi-denominational. The idea behind this approach was twofold. First, camp managers believed that religious discord weakened communal bonds and should be avoided at all (or most) costs. Second, camp managers and camp program officials saw the varieties of Protestantism at work in their world as similar enough that clear-headed people could find satisfaction (and God) regardless of the flavor being offered on a particular Sunday. In the interest of avoiding and, in the long term, unwinding religious conflict, camp managers implemented a program that allowed for different Protestant denominations to have the outdoor platform or the run of the community center for a Sunday, before passing the baton to the next indistinguishable member of God's team. Good neighbors, solid community members, would embrace this program and its theology.

The inaugural issue of the Indio *Migratory Worker*, published on November 26, 1938, carried an announcement of "Sunday Services" that described government camp ecumenism perfectly:

> To those who like to go to church on Sunday or to send their children to Sunday school, don't forget that the ministers of the valley come in each Sunday afternoon at 3 O'clock. I think it's very Christian like that they volunteer their time for us each Sunday; maybe we ought to attend and work with them. Some time there are two or three at a time. You see there are six ministers in the valley and they arrange turns between themselves to hold services here. The six ministers probly [sic] represent every type of belief in camp.

Two months later, camp resident Ruby Nell Massey of platform 439 wrote to her fellow migrants, in the pages of the renamed *Indio Covered Wagon*, that "We have had some very good service at the Social Center every Sunday Afternoon at 3 o'clock." The previous week had seen "Paul Cook, from the Assembly of God at Indio" do the preaching. But, she reassured camp residents, "there are other preachers who take part in the services," and the experience was upbeat. "We sing songs and have a very good time. So please come out to Social Center every Sunday and take part. I am sure you will feel better and like coming back the next time."[41] The through-line in public communications about Protestant worship in the camps is an intentional ecumenism, a desire to welcome all "regardless of denomination."[42]

This predilection for scheduled, contained, non-divisive, out-sourced Protestantism permeates official correspondence about religious practice and emerges too in the camp papers' announcements, descriptions, and commentaries on worship and religious education. In the process of reporting camp religious life to the hierarchy and informing camp residents of the time and location of services, camp managers and newspapers were also clearly identifying legitimate religious practice to distinguish it from less legitimate expressions. Ray Mork reported that, as of September of 1940, the Shafter camp had seven "recreation workers" assigned by the WPA. The camp had a nursery school, a vibrant cooperative store, a "unique organization" for men called the "Spit and Argue Club," and church services.

> Permission to hold church services, controlled by camp committee, as with other meetings held in camp. Services are mixed, that is they are not controlled by any given denomination. Have no information as to the church membership or denominational choice of those attending religious services. Sunday school services are usually held Friday, Saturday, and Sunday of each week. These are conducted by local people, not campers.[43]

Weekly reports on camp activities show that "church services" of one form or another (worship, Sunday school, hymn sing) usually took place three to five times per week in Shafter, drew from 125 to 250 camp residents, and were, in Mork's words, either "undenominational" or run by "3-denominations." Amateur night, the weekly dance, a movie screening, and the boxing and wrestling matches had higher attendance per event, but in terms of the total weekly head-count, church services were second only to boxing and wrestling in popularity.[44]

Worship services and other sanctioned religious activities were part of the regular rhythm of camp life. These services presented

Protestantism as having a particular shape, duration, and sphere of influence. That shape came, in part, from the theological inclinations and the cultural and educational backgrounds of the RA/FSA camp staff. It came also from the other activities around it and the space in which it was practiced. And behind all of it was a normative position that a shaped, restrained Protestantism was the proper way to think about Protestantism. Extreme commitment in the realm of religion, the officials said quietly among themselves, is a sign of imbalance and immaturity.

Manager Frank Iusi's assessment of the proper shape and place of Protestantism is apparent in his monthly narrative report for July 1940, in which he extolled camp residents' efforts to preserve food. "Our greatest worthwhile activity," he wrote, "is the home canning that is being done at present. I can safely say this camp will can around 4000 to 5000 cans this season and next year will have a big year, for the apartment house renters will have been able to plant their gardens." He followed this description with news of another activity: "We also had a two week bible study group for children which was a huge success. Over 150 of approximately 196 children attended, and they constructed many worthy articles."[45]

The juxtaposition of the two activities and Iusi's tone in describing them show that both mattered to him and that he was happy that both took place. The domestic work of canning and preserving is the "greatest worthwhile activity." The children's Bible class was a "huge success." Both contributed positively to camp life. One helped a family lay in food for the winter or some other season of need. The other kept the young ones "well occupied" and taught the discipline of constructing "worthy articles." Canning was worthwhile for what it would do to sustain the family. Bible class was worthwhile because it kept the children engaged while other members of the family worked to help the family flourish. The class wasn't only instrumental, but one can imagine Iusi hoping that the Protestantism taught in the class would itself be canned and preserved, maybe stored in the pantry to be taken down and opened in times of need.

Manager Robert Allen's report from the Winters camp in the summer of 1941 reasserts the idea of Protestant practice as recreation. A good amount was going on in the camp, even though the community center was all but unusable. He wrote in his monthly narrative report, dated August 9, 1941, that "the current building program [had] seriously curtailed activities" during July and August, among other things, forcing the camp council to meet outside "under a street light." Allen also reported that "the weekly dance and amateur programs had been stopped by the construction" and that "people are missing this wholesome self-entertainment," which necessitated a work-around. "Last week a large part of the community population participated in an outdoor party with games and refreshments, devised as a temporary substitute for the amateur program."

The effect on worship in the camp had been similar. Reverend Zimmerman, longstanding minister to the Winters camp, had been forced to stop "Wednesday evening meetings," but was still holding his regular services on Sunday. Allen concluded by noting, "The Manager and Home Management Supervisor . . . have attended practically all activities with the exception of church."[46]

Classified as an activity, compared to activities, disrupted and skipped like an activity, the practice of Protestantism in the migrant camps was framed, systemically if not always intentionally, as an activity. What is remarkable is just how unremarkable a thing the camp officials took Protestant worship to be. When those within the hierarchy spoke and wrote of its official presence in their camps and in their program, they did so in a way that was legitimizing of religious practice in so far as it conformed to this model: Protestantism as canning, canning as Protestantism, Protestantism as unnecessary for camp personnel to engage, because life apart from it was itself so engaging. Should we be surprised to find that the Arvin camp baseball team had a game scheduled for two p.m. on Easter Sunday when Sunday School started at 1:45 and worship was scheduled for three? April was a busy month in the camp, and even though it was Easter, those struggling to choose between official worship and the ballgame could worship on Tuesday at seven p.m., with Marie Emerson preaching on a subject as yet "unknown." The happenings on the field and in the community center filled similar functions and would benefit participants roughly equally. What did it matter if one missed worship to cheer on the camp team?[47]

Baseball game at the Tulare Camp, 1940.
Photograph by Arthur Rothstein. *Baseball game. Tulare migrant camp. Visalia, California.* March 1940. Courtesy of Library of Congress. https://www.loc.gov/item/2017774655/.

The Limits of Recreation

The contents of regularly scheduled worship services in the camp community center and elsewhere are, for the most part, lost. What remains are imprints: chronologies, names, some ambient language: "come on out," "let's build it up," "support them," "all are welcome." We turn these archival fossils over in our hands, wondering what the living thing looked like as it moved and breathed and took in the world around it. How did the migrants look when they gathered for worship? How did they respond to the sermons? Did they arrive on time and stay until the end? Did the children behave?

It is fair to ask whether these fossils can tell us anything, and to wonder whether the process of interpreting them isn't, at the end of the day, little more than creating a mythical creature from vestigial parts. For my part, I believe there is much to learn from these remains. I believe, too, that we can learn from those things that New Deal reformers looked past and did not record. It tells us something, for instance, that little substantive material from regular worship services survives. Given the devotion of the camp office to record keeping, this absence indicates that camp managers and other officials thought the material was of little consequence. If it had mattered to them, they would have recorded it.

Also significant is the extent to which religious services and other recreational meetings were structurally similar. Similar chronological frames, locations, and publicity, as well as similar rhetoric around Protestant practice and amateur night, point to a camp missionary program designed to limit the influence of Protestantism, to deemphasize its significance, to blend it with other activities into one stream of communal events. Relatedly, though it is tempting to think of the camp's religious program as aimed exclusively toward disenchantment, an effort to convince a "superstitious" and "emotional" people that they were living in a material world, I think the reforming of religion undertaken in the camps was at least as much about routines and restraint as it was about the removal of the supernatural.

Finally, these efforts at restraint in the camp seem in many cases to have worked. With a few exceptions, neither the camp program archive nor the camp newspapers record much in the way of direct critique of the ministers or the messages of this official Protestantism. In a few letters submitted to the *Tow Sack Tattler*, Roy Carter, camp guard at Arvin, expressed concern about low attendance at worship services. This could indicate migrant ambivalence about worship services, but it could as easily indicate Carter's high expectations, as well as his deep desire to support the ministers. The official record is quite positive in its evaluation of official Protestantism.

To say that Protestantism was restrained in the camps is not, however, to say that the restrained version of Protestantism satisfied all. Indirect evidence of a desire for something more than, or different from, what the community center offered emerges in published announcements—some banal, some poignant—in the Indio camp paper in 1939. At the start of the year, the camp committee in the Indio camp rejected a request from "two outside church organizations . . . to use the auditorium." The camp secretary, J. H. McClain, wrote in the January 21 edition of the *Migratory Clipper*, "we have had to . . . say no, because there are about four churches in camp who wish separate services, that too is impossible."⁴⁸ The Coachella Valley Ministerial Association's services and the ecumenism they required were, apparently, unsatisfying to some.

Roughly one month later, "Our Calendar," a new feature in the paper, began offering a week's worth of sayings for readers. The daily meditations, suggestive of early prosperity gospel influences, carried Protestant theology out of worship services and into the wider world.

> MARCH 17:
> Talk happiness, and let its magic power
> Inspire kind words and deeds each passing hour.
> Talk happiness, make it a special theme.
> Start merry brooklets toward the larger stream.
>
> MARCH 19:
> "I, the Lord, am with thee, be thou not afraid.
> I will help and strengthen, be thou not dismayed.
> Yes, I will uphold thee with mine own right hand
> Thou art called and chosen in my sight to stand."
> Onward, then, and fear not children of the day;
> For his word will never, never pass away.
>
> MARCH 23:
> Know now thou art a child of God
> and all His treasures thine;
> Go forth and claim thy just award,
> And know thou art divine.

"Our Calendar" provided these prayers and bits of wisdom for readers to apply in their weekly life; they were thoughts that would give additional purpose to the migrants' days beyond Sunday. In contradistinction to Reverend Lascellos's characterization of worship services "profit[ing]" those in attendance in unspecified ways, these prayers and meditations offered readers daily "treasures," divinity, and the transformation of daily life.

Finally, tragically, toward the end of 1939, the *Migratory Clipper* recorded the deaths of three children from the Indio camp, the oldest of whom had just celebrated her second birthday. On October 29, Thomas David Collins (no relation to camp manager Thomas Collins) died of unnamed causes. The paper listed his home address as "Unit 1" and described him simply as "the infant son of Mr. and Mrs. T. B. Collins." He was three months old. Little more than a week later, Norma Jean Bramlett, "infant daughter of Mr. and Mrs. Eddie Bramlett of Unit 5" died in a local hospital, six weeks shy of her first birthday. Both of these little ones were interred in the Coachella Valley Cemetery. With the Christmas holiday fast approaching and talk in camp of a major celebration for the children, the pain of these losses was likely amplified for families that had already suffered so much.

Mary Alice Wells lived long enough to enjoy Christmas in the camp, but in its first issue of 1940, the *Migratory Clipper* bore the sad news of Mary Alice's death on December 29th. She had turned two in October. Mary Alice's parents, Mr. and Mrs. Elmo Wells, wrote to the paper to thank those "who donated to help us in our hour of darkness" and "all of you" who made "the beautiful floral offering possible." The Wells family's sorrows were deep, but the Indio community helped all of them, including Mary Alice's sister, brother, aunt, and uncle, with multiple acts of kindness. Mrs. Ralph Richardson, who made her home on platform 338, even wrote a poem, "There is a New Star in Heaven Tonight," in memory of the little girl. Her final stanza read,

> Then again we hope to meet thee
> When the storms of life have fled,
> Then in heaven we will greet thee
> Where no farewell tears are shed.

The attention given to the death of Mary Alice Wells extends well beyond the terse obituaries for the infants Collins and Bramlett, but still there is no mention of a cause of death.

These records of family tragedy, though brief, bring into focus a deficiency in community center worship that might otherwise pass unnoticed. In their "hour of darkness," the Collins and Bramlett families did not turn to the Coachella Valley Ministerial Association or any of its rotating representatives. They sought consolation in the rituals and the theology of Indio's Four Square Gospel Church. For their part, the

Wells family sought out James A. Miller of the Church of God, who worked regularly within the migrant camp, but was not in fellowship with the ministerial association. Were it not for references in the Collins and Bramlett obituaries, there would be no official record of the migrants' affections for Aimee McPherson's Four Square Gospel, not to mention its local representatives, Brother Demarest and Brother Fred DeMort, who held those two families up as they lay their youngest members to rest.[49]

In reading these terse obituaries against the Protestantism of the community center, we can make two assumptions. The first is that in times of trauma such as the loss of a child, people turn to the source of comfort that is most comforting. Put more locally, while the Coachella Valley Ministerial Association may well have satisfied a desire to worship in community on a Sunday afternoon, the death of Tommy or of Norma Jean called for someone capable of soothing acute pain.

The second is that even if the Collins, Bramlett, and Wells families were exceptional in seeking religious ministrations beyond the official camp offerings, there is something significant in their efforts. Protestant practice was, to them, at once larger and more specific than restrained camp Protestantism. Their Protestantism was not an undifferentiated mass of theologies and rituals and styles, with all beliefs negotiable, all parts interchangeable. The details mattered. Ecumenism was not as good for these migrants as it was for the manager. Though it worked as a civic approach, there were needs that community center Protestantism could not address.

These stories of loss and grief remind us that the official Protestantism of the camp community center was triangular, involving the camp manager, the migrants, and the person or people leading worship, whether clergy or laity. The archival record of community center Protestantism was created and maintained by camp managers. It features stories about migrants and sometimes records their voices. However, time has mostly reduced the clergy and lay leaders of official worship to names on paper.

Chris and Rheba Ummel are an important exception to this rule. They remain visible and somewhat knowable due to an unpublished memoir, the work of a University of Southern California graduate student, and Ray Mork's reports from the Shafter camp. The Ummels' perspective on Protestantism and ministry in and beyond the community center helps us to feel the limits of the official and to experience the freedom that they found, ironically, in restraint.

Chris and Rheba Ummel first appear in a document filed by Ray Mork in the summer of 1940. In response to a system-wide questionnaire regarding the social and recreational life of migrants in the camp, Mork offered a fairly detailed account of the camp's religious activities. He began by noting that "services are held . . . from 10:00 AM to Noon" on Sunday mornings. The faithful gathered for forty-five minutes of worship before dividing into Sunday school classes for another forty-five minutes. Men, women, and children then reconvened for thirty minutes of singing and a benediction.

At the time of his response, there were two groups holding worship services in the camp, but Mork did not say whether or not they both followed this schedule. He did note, however, that "Seventh Day Adventists from Bakersfield" led one group, and that the other was led by representatives of the Migrant Gospel Fellowship, based in Turlock, California. These representatives were the fellowship's founder, Reverend Paul Pietsch, and Chris and Rheba Ummel. The groups met separately— Adventists in the community center, the Migrant Gospel Fellowship in the smaller sewing room—Mork indicated that they were ecumenical enough to coordinate leadership of a Sunday evening service on a rotating basis. He wrote further of the Ummels, "[they] hold very successful community singing groups every Tuesday evening in the Center Building. Religious songs predominate. The group have made themselves very popular to the campers and in our opinion are rendering a very worthwhile service." Mork described the Migrant Gospel Fellowship as a "Non Denominational Church Group" committed to the "spiritual welfare of the campers," but did not describe their theology, their rhetoric, or their view of scripture. He saw that roughly 250 migrants per week were attending these events, and he was pleased.

Ray Mork was attuned to and grateful for the work that the Migrant Gospel Fellowship did to benefit migrants spiritually. Mork took his work seriously and appreciated all (or most) of the help that he could get. His attention to the hard work of rebuilding individuals, creating community, and keeping the camp in good shape likely account for his not recording or, perhaps, not knowing of another explanation for the Ummels' popularity among camp residents. Or perhaps Chris and

Rheba, whom Mork eventually described as "camp pastors," never told him that they came to California when the Depression made farming their piece of the Great Plains untenable. Like the men and women to whom they preached, the Ummels were migrants.

Prospects had been good for Chris and Rheba Ummel in 1925. Engaged but not yet married, they looked forward to a long and happy life on their west Kansas farm. Chris was handy and built not only the "five room bungalow" that would be their home, but all of the "farm buildings" that they needed to run a successful wheat and chicken operation. The going was not easy. It never is. But Chris and Rheba were fond of their corner of Kansas and were proud of what they had done with it. Looking back on that time in their lives, Rheba wrote, "we loved our farm—it was part of us—every building, animal, tree, post—everything—we had placed it there." The Ummels' world, already bright with love for each other and love of their land grew brighter still in 1926 with the birth of a daughter, Gwendolynne.[50]

Not long after the couple married and settled into their new home, the leadership of their church in Kansas changed. "A young couple that had just graduated from Biola" arrived and brought with them a different way of being Christian. The Ummels wrote nothing substantial about their religious lives before the Biola products came to town, but they noted that things changed with the arrival of the new pastor and his wife. "They were a real challenge to us and we really grew in the Lord." To grow in the Lord meant to be more active in church causes. Chris had been a churchgoing man, but soon he was teaching Sunday school as well. Eventually he became the Sunday school superintendent. Rheba also taught Sunday school and the two participated together in "Christian Endeavor activities." If the Ummels' faith life had been dull before, it was not any longer.

The couple from Biola reshaped the Ummels' Protestantism in another crucial way. They presented Chris and Rheba with a copy of the Scofield Reference Bible. Though not new to the United States in the late 1920s, the Scofield Bible was nevertheless a revelation to the young Kansans. They read their new Bible through "including the footnotes," and found their views of scripture and of God's relationship to the world utterly changed. "The Bible became a living book," Rheba noted, and

God's will for them became evident, at least potentially so, both in the biblical text and in the events unfolding around them.

The Ummels were among hundreds of thousands of American Christians who encountered the prophetic thought of Englishman John Nelson Darby in Charles Scofield's illustrated, footnoted, cross-referenced, best-selling edition of the Bible. Many who encountered the work became convinced, as Darby and Scofield were, that the end times were coming quickly and that developments in the world were, if seen properly, portents of the eschaton. The Bible Institute of Los Angeles was one important locus of Scofield-driven prophecy. So too was Charles Fuller's Old Time Gospel Radio Hour, which was just getting started in the early 1930s. These and other fundamentalist or quasi-fundamentalist groups and individuals devoted spectacular amounts of energy to discerning signs, anticipating the end, and reminding those who listened that if they were not saved, things were going to get very, very ugly.[51]

Looking back on the early 1930s in Kansas, Rheba Ummel wrote that her newly-alive Bible helped her see God's activity in their life. "The Lord began talking to us," she explained. A string of minor catastrophes hit the Ummel farm, but the Bible taught them that catastrophes were never just that. "A choice three year old colt died, the hatchery where we sold our eggs from our certified laying flock went out of business, a severe storm was brewing—it began to rain and then hail fell just mowing our wheat field that was ready for harvest and leaving other farmers' fields around us standing."

Neighbors likely saw these developments as tragic and unfair—*damn the luck, hard times all around*—but Rheba and Chris insisted that something else was going on, something miraculous. "Friends and loved ones sympathized with us over our loss, but the Lord became more precious. We knew he was talking to us."

The Ummels' dramatic response to God's voice may have surprised their friends and loved ones, but it surely delighted their new pastors. As Rheba recalled, "We began to prepare to study at Biola in the fall." They readied the Model A coupe, loaded Gwendolynne, their possessions, and two members of the extended family into the car, and began rolling toward California. Chris's mother and brother were going to try to save the farm. Chris and Rheba were off to save souls.

The Ford carried the would-be preachers from Kansas to Dalhart, Texas, through the mountains of New Mexico, and across the sere landscape of Arizona before finally, one week later, depositing them in Los Angeles. The Ummels hit the ground running in their new city. They attended services at the Church of the Open Door. They found a modest place to live. By their account they benefitted frequently from the Lord's generosity. Whenever they encountered an obstacle: a health problem, inadequate housing, a need for work, childcare, schooling for Gwendolynne, even an unscrupulous auto-repair shop, "the Lord provided" or, put differently, "our MIRACLE working God . . . provided again." The world around them was torn by the greatest economic crisis the nation had ever faced. Entire families were starving in Los Angeles and across the states they had just traversed. Their lives had been altered by disasters both natural and man-made. But still the Ummels walked an enchanted landscape.

Sometime in early 1940, roughly four years after arriving in California, Rheba and Chris happened to attend, separately and without telling each other, meetings led by Reverend Paul Pietsch, an energetic, peripatetic, multi-vocational Baptist. In 1939 Pietsch had founded the Migrant Gospel Fellowship with the support of the Christian Business Man's Association of Turlock, California. His goal was to build a ministry focused on migratory agricultural workers. When Chris and Rheba discovered that they had both heard and been moved by the same presentation, they wondered if this too might be a sign, if "the Lord might be able to use us in the camps."

In their eyes, the coincidence was evidence of a divine nudge, but it made sense for earthly reasons as well. "The people were from the farm as we were. We had survived the dust storms of the early thirties." So, in late summer of 1940, the Ummels decided to drive to the San Joaquin Valley to survey the situation. By the middle of September, they had relocated from Los Angeles to Shafter and were participating fully in the Migrant Gospel Fellowship.

Not long after beginning their work with Reverend Pietsch, the Ummels appeared in Ray Mork's report, which described their popularity and their work for the spiritual benefit of the migrants. For their part, Chris and Rheba also wrote about the camp Sunday School program that they helped Pietsch run in the camp sewing room. Their account of the religious culture of the Shafter camp lines up with Mork's in noting the presence of a second group, though the Ummels did not identify them as Adventists. They did, however, provide a little more detail than Mork as to attendance numbers and the relationship between the groups.

According to Chris and Rheba, thirty-seven worshippers attended their first session of Sunday School. Just one month later their group had grown to "over one hundred." That same weekend, the Adventists had just nine. In response to the growth of the Migrant Gospel Fellowship meeting and the atrophy of the Adventists, the Camp Council orchestrated a swap of meeting spaces, giving the larger community center to the Ummels and assigning the Adventists to the sewing room or, weather permitting, the shade of a nearby tree. Apparently, the Adventists decided that a camp mission was no longer worth the effort, or maybe they felt that the people had spoken. They stopped leading worship and returned only occasionally to distribute flyers.

For at least the next three years, Chris and Rheba Ummel ministered to migrants in and around the Shafter camp. They visited campers in their tents, organized and ran vacation Bible school in the summer, put together Christmas services, and published a page of religious news and commentary in the *Covered Wagon News*. Their ministry to the migrant community can certainly be described as a success. For three years they were the face of Protestantism in the Shafter camp. Other religious voices in the historical record are faint echoes by comparison.

The Ummels' ministry can also be described as a victory. For in the eyes of Reverend Pietsch and his fellow workers in the Migrant Gospel Fellowship, there was a battle raging to win migrants' hearts for Jesus. And not a generic, empty-vessel Jesus, not a Jesus brought to life in the community center through a French movie with subtitles, not an activist whose sufferings were Christ-*like*, but Jesus as known, interpreted, and taught at the Bible Institute of Los Angeles and defined by the Migrant Gospel Fellowship creed. There were Protestants who did not know *this* Jesus, who taught error, who would lead wandering farm workers astray.

The Migrant Gospel Fellowship wanted to clear the public square of these errors and to build migrant religiosity on a proper, fundamental, biblical foundation. Asked to describe that foundation, the Ummels and all other Migrant Gospel Fellowship workers would likely have responded in terms similar to those delineated by Pietsch and used as the group's confession of faith.

1. I believe in the scripture of the Old and New Testaments as verbally inspired by God, and inerrant in the original writings, and that they are of supreme and final authority in faith and life.
2. I believe in one God, eternally existing in three persons, Father, Son, and Holy Spirit.
3. I believe that Jesus Christ was begotten by the Holy Spirit, and born of the Virgin Mary and is true God and true Man.
4. I believe that man was created in the image of God; then he sinned, and thereby incurred not only physical death, but that spiritual death which is separation from God, and that all human beings are born with a sinful nature and, upon becoming morally responsible, are lost.
5. I believe that the Lord Jesus Christ died for our sins according to the Scriptures, as a representative and substitutionary sacrifice by the shedding of his blood, was buried and rose from the dead for our justification, and that all who believe in Him are born again of the Holy Spirit, thereby becoming the children of God.
6. I believe in the physical resurrection of our Lord Jesus, in His ascension into heaven, and in His present intercessory work as our High Priest and Advocate.
7. I believe in "that blessed hope," the personal, premillennial and imminent return of our Lord and Saviour, Jesus Christ.
8. I believe in the bodily resurrection of the just and unjust, the everlasting blessedness of the saved, and the everlasting conscious punishment of the lost.[52]

Migrant Gospel Fellowship workers were committed to spreading these fundamental truths among the migratory farm workers. They did not, however, think much of the community center as a venue for evangelism. The Ummels and the other Migrant Gospel Fellowship workers were absolutely willing, even happy, to lead public services, to gather migrants in song, and to organize and preside over Christmas and Easter celebrations. But in their eyes, the heart of evangelism was the home visit. It was in sitting down with a person or a family on their tent platform that a Migrant Gospel Fellowship missionary could have the kinds of conversations and pray the kinds of prayers that were actually transformative.

Migrant Gospel Fellowship representatives visited newly-arrived migrants in their tents, eager to pray with exhausted and lonely women and men at the end of long work days or longer journeys, eager to gather in spaces where social pressures were less acute. Chris and Rheba wanted converts who were properly restrained and fundamentally sound. The latter half of that project—teaching and reinforcing the fundamentals—could not happen in the community center. Yet the community center played a role in their ministry. As Chris confessed to a researcher in 1942, public worship was a strategic event.

> Our main objective is to reach the people through personal contacts in their homes. Our public meetings are more to prevent other people from having such meetings. It is very hard to reach these people though public meetings as they are so shifting. It would be unfair to judge the Migrant Gospel Fellowship by its public meetings, for our most lasting results are obtained in the homes.[53]

Elbow other competitors off of the community center stage and the triumph of true Christianity over false alternatives was more likely. Call this strategy underhanded or unfair, but in the Ummels' eyes the stakes were too high for ecumenical scruples.

Beginning in 1939, the Migrant Gospel Fellowship was a common presence in the religious life of the camp system. Arthur Bakker of the Migrant Gospel Fellowship worked in and around the Brawley Camp. Sarah Heinrichs, an MGF worker, helped develop religious programming at the Winters Camp. At Yuba City, Reverend Pietsch himself organized Sunday school classes and, according to camp manager Frank Iusi, a daily Bible class attended by upwards of eighty campers. By 1942, Pietsch's fellow MGF missionaries "Reverend and Mrs. Laverne Olsen" had taken over meeting the "religious needs" of the Yuba City camp with the full and explicit support of the camp council and the home management supervisor.

The Migrant Gospel Fellowship's own papers describe a ministry more widespread still. A 1942 brochure titled "Reaching Families with the Word of Life" lists twenty-five "workers" active in camps in Oregon, California, and Arizona. Though they came to the camp system four years after it began, Paul Pietsch and his ministry quickly became part of it.

The files from the Shafter camp show no awareness of Chris and Rheba Ummel's theology and reflect no suspicion of the uses to which they put the community center. In fact, in the monthly narrative reports and internal RA/FSA correspondence, there is not a single critical word about the Ummels, Reverend Pietsch, or the Migrant Gospel Fellowship. There is no mention of their fundamentalist theology, no concern about other-worldly apocalypticism, their inattention to the social gospel, or their spirit of divisiveness.

This is somewhat remarkable. The RA/FSA was a diverse organization. One might expect that someone would have let slip a negative word, maybe two, about the Migrant Gospel Fellowship. On questions of theology the MGF and the camp staff were quite far apart. The former had close connections to Biola which, in the 1930s, was a frequent source of anti-communist, anti-socialist, anti-New Deal theology.[54] Camp system workers came from more progressive religious backgrounds and, obviously, did not see the New Deal as a tool of Satan. But when it came to Paul Pietsch and Chris and Rheba Ummel, theological differences elicited no comment.

How are we to make sense of the Ummels' fundamentalist ministry succeeding and enduring under Ray Mork's nose, unremarked? Mork, who had leveled such harsh criticism at the type of Protestantism the Ummels' preached, must have struggled with their message. Or perhaps not. For their many departures from modernist theology and the social gospel, the Ummels played by minimalist rules and worked within established limits. They kept to a schedule. They led welcoming services. They did their hard, creed-centered evangelism out of sight.

The religion page of the *Covered Wagon News* for the week ending Saturday, January 10, 1942, captures their public face. "Rev. + Mrs. Chris Ummel (Camp Pastor and Wife)," as they signed themselves, used the page to announce the schedule for the coming week. Morning services were going to take place at 10 and 11:30 on Sunday, January 11. The "Community Sing" was scheduled for Thursday evening from 6 to 7. The Ummels reminded readers of the location of the services (the community center) and reported "there were a few over 80 in attendance last Sunday."

After urging readers to attend the "Sing," the Ummels switched to a devotional tone and wrote, "Now for a few minutes of meditation on the Bible, God's book, God's word. Will you open your Bible to the book of Philippians, the eleventh verse of Chapter four. We read 'I have learned in whatsoever state I am, therewith to be content.'" They continued, "Those who are God's without reserve, are in every state content; for they will only what he wills, and desire to do for him whatever he desires them to do; they strip themselves of every thing, and in this nakedness find all things restored as hundred fold."

The message is a far cry from Ray Mork's reading of Margaret Sanger's life and his interpretation of the movie *Golgotha*. Rather than calling followers to challenge the wealthy and to sanctify those who bring relief to the overburdened, this Protestantism equates unreserved belonging to God with being "in every state content." How Ray Mork made peace with this reading of scripture and history is impossible to know for sure. But at least a partial answer is found in the emphasis that official camp Protestantism placed on form and on the blurring it encouraged between Protestant practice and recreation.

At the end of the day, what the Ummels were doing fit perfectly into the delineated spaces and also drew a crowd, two key markers of good, successful Protestantism. And as long as the migrants were happy with the theological fare and the Ummels continued in their performance of ecumenism, there was no obvious reason to think twice about the word they preached when a migrant family welcomed them into their tent.

6

The Paper

The Indio Migratory Farm Workers' Camp had been open for almost a year when the camp council created a new space for migrant life. Unlike other spaces through which camp residents moved each day, this one could be folded up and stuck into a pants pocket, passed from one family member to another, even used to help start a cooking fire. It was a small but busy space, a venue for political organization, community imagination, theological reflection, and artistic expression.

In the waning days of 1938, the Indio camp council voted to create a camp newspaper. They called this new space the *Migratory Worker*. The first issue appeared on November 26, 1938. Though it looked more like a handbill than a more familiar broadsheet or tabloid, the first article of the first issue connected the Indio camp's newspaper to the highest traditions and the noblest principles of American journalism. The author of the lead article, "Voice of the People," wrote proudly,

> One of the greatest influences in our country today, both for good and for evil, is the newspaper. Surely as an American community with our own government, our own laws, being conscious of our identity as a workers group, we need a common voice. A voice with shackles as free as the air we Americans breathe. A paper in which truth is news and news is truth. A paper that not only tells of our community life, but also of the world surrounding us. A paper striving in our own little way to exchange thoughts and to aid in more closely knitting the families of camp life.[1]

It was an ambitious undertaking for the residents of a government camp populated by itinerating pickers and farm hands, but the men who launched the project, migrant brothers Roy and George Hildebrand, emphasized that all voices were welcome, no matter the accent. "There are people so narrow that they will look aghast if one says 'aint' or 'you all' but who will not flicker an eye if they see a hungry child." Those were not the kind of people in charge of the *Migratory Worker*. "If anybody has anything to say," they continued, "this paper has a place to say it for you all."²

Religion appeared in the inaugural issue of the *Migratory Worker* in an announcement of "Sunday Services" and a tongue-in-cheek astrology column attributed to "Yogi Dnarbedlih Yor," (Roy Hildebrand spelled backwards). The self-proclaimed yogi promised to "tell you what influences the stars have on your nature & temperament." Those born between November 26 and 28, he wrote, were freedom-loving and "not submissive to the will of others." A December 1 birthday meant a "mind well balanced at all times." Those born on December 2, Hildebrand concluded, "love deeply."

The next issue came out under a new name, the *Covered Wagon*, and was three times as long. Camp staff and migrants answered with gusto the Hildebrand brothers' call to exchange thoughts and to tell of life within and beyond the gates. They shared articles, poems, drawings, and gossip. Residents of the Indio Migratory Farm Labor camp wrote like a people unshackled.

Similar moments of genesis happened at different times in federal camps up and down California's agricultural interior. On September 2, 1938, the Arvin camp's *Weedpatch Cultivator* announced itself to the world with the headline, "Camp to Have a Weekly Paper." The article that followed explained that the editorial staff wanted to "serve the people of Camp in these ways—(1) to inform them of working conditions . . . (2) to make it possible for them to discuss ideas or events . . . [and] (3) to let the campers know what is going on in Camp." Most important of all was that camp residents feel attached to the paper, that they internalize the truth that the *Weedpatch Cultivator* belonged to them. Many migrants seem to have felt the intended sense of ownership. Their editorial and design work, their reporting and creative submissions, gave life to camp newspapers in Indio, Arvin, Shafter, and beyond.

Like tent platforms, sanitary units, and community centers, newspapers shaped life in the government camp. They also contained that life. They gave those living as migrant farm workers another structure in which to live, or from which to turn. The fact that the camp paper accepted poetry surely inspired some camp residents to record poems they had learned or to write their own. Extensive reporting on camp boxing matches and baseball games sparked dreams of athletic glory and

"50 feet from Highway US 99 near Bakersfield" a migrant man reads a newspaper outside of the tent set up over his car. February 23, 1935.
Photograph by Dorothea Lange. Courtesy of Library of Congress. Image LC-DIG-ppmsca-19156, https://www.loc.gov/pictures/item/2004678009/.

drew residents to participate in recreational activities. And the publication of camp inspection results with commentary about the connection between unsightly tent platforms and unsavory people prompted some families to clean up their act, just as it led some to leave camp in search of less oversight and less judgment.

The newspapers published in the camps also contained Protestantism. They did this in two senses. First, the pages of camp newspapers regularly brimmed with Protestant theologies, chronologies, and values. They gave itinerant ministries space to explain and promote themselves. They gave ministers who aspired to some level of permanence in the camp a public space in which to claim the status of "camp pastor,"

Migrants working on the camp newspaper, Tulare Camp, 1942. Photograph by Russell Lee. Courtesy of Library of Congress. LC-USF34-071733-D [P&P] LOT 358, https://lccn.loc.gov/2017817310.

or, occasionally, "camp pasture." Camp papers were an ideal discursive space for the presentation of sermons, both clerical and lay.

And in doing all of these things, the camp newspapers also *contained* the migrants' Protestantisms by placing them on a page, drawing lines around them, arranging them alongside "Nursery School News" and "Camp Council Minutes," and presenting the scheduled, the poetic, and the sermonic as the accepted avenues of higher Protestant experience. In *this* work of containment, the papers also did the work of domestication and modernization that characterized the camp program's approach to migrant Protestantism more generally.

This is not to say that Protestant identities as expressed in the camp newspapers were inconsequential. Indio's *Migratory Worker*, Shafter's *Agri-News*, and Arvin's *Weedpatch Cultivator* portrayed a migrant community in which Protestantism enjoyed a privileged status. As a communal and a personal religious identity, Protestantism quietly but demonstrably dominated the camp papers. There were only Protestant voices and Protestant theologies in the papers' pages. Protestantism defined both mainstream and margins. But what did this Protestant vibrancy mean on the printed page? How should we think about the coming together of Protestant content and the form of the camp newspapers?

The content, of course, matters. It matters especially because it reveals that at least some camp residents knew their scripture and their theology, and were willing to publish their views on Protestantism's demands of the faithful. The layout and the form of the news are also meaningful for the Protestantism of this particular space. The Protestantism of the papers was vibrant and occasionally diverse. It was also managed and situated within a medium that simultaneously gave space to migrant theologies and encouraged readers to think in particular ways about those theologies. This constructive project, expressed subtly in form, also had an explicit theological expression in the sermons of self-described camp pastors.

There are two significant factors to consider when reading the Protestantism of the camp newspapers and thinking about its relationship to life in the migrant camps. The first is the form of the camp papers—camp newspaper as spaces—and the ways that the papers' presentations of news mapped out a vision of migrant life characterized by the separation of social realms and differentiation of authority within those realms.³ Put another way, when reading the camp newspaper, migrants were also encountering a model for a modernizing community, a community where health care, child rearing, recreation, governance, gossip, entertainment, and Protestant practice were different, largely non-overlapping endeavors. Like the camps they served, the camp newspapers were dynamic entities and reflected the ideology and the theology of the camp system. Developments in the papers' layouts, structures, and self-presentations illuminate these ideologies and the work that they did to shape migrants' understandings of their world.

The second factor is the actual content of the papers and the way that camp staff, religious leaders, and the migrants themselves described and contributed to the Protestantisms of camp life. Protestant voices made themselves heard through the structures of the camp paper: announcing worship services, offering guidance, sharing devotional poetry, predicting apocalypse. Sometimes they contended with each other. But to the extent that the camp newspapers presented a picture of religious difference, they did so in ways that made crystal clear who occupied the center and who the periphery. And as much as they could, camp newspapers turned attention away from religious difference and toward shared communal identities.⁴

Though we are considering here newspapers from across the camp system, the primary focus is on the Shafter camp newspaper, which began its life in 1938 as the *Agri-News* and was renamed the *Covered Wagon News* in September of 1939. The archived issues of the *Agri-News* and the *Covered Wagon News* are especially abundant and continuous. Changes to its form and developments in its content demonstrate with particular clarity the dynamics of the newspaper and their relationship to life in and around the camp.⁵

Reading the Form of the News

In approaching newspapers as managed ideological spaces, I am drawing on the work of media historians who encourage us to think of news as "by definition . . . messy." The work of newspapers, they argue, is to clean up the mess, to tame the "weird, new, and dramatic . . . jumble" that comprises a day's events. Over time, newspaper editors' thoughts about what a cleaned-up mess ought to look like have changed. A common nineteenth-century approach was to present the jumble to the reader and to let him or her do the taming. "The 'primitive' or Victorian newspaper . . . subjected [readers] to a bombardment of undigested stuff . . . [and] design elements [that] were used inconsistently." The modern newspaper created an intentional and value-laden map that was "rational, functional, premeditated, [and that] tam[ed] the mess by artifice."[6] Modern newspapers were deliberately hierarchical in terms of the types of knowledge that mattered, and reasonably consistent in classifying information.

The 1920s and 30s were pivotal decades for newspapers in their move from a "Victorian" or "primitive" to a modernist aesthetic. This shift was about more than just a new look. "The design shift inaugurated around 1920 might best be thought of as the visual analog of professionalism. The modern newspaper replaced the 'primitive' (or Victorian) newspaper in the same fashion as the medical doctor replaced the itinerant snake-oil hawker."[7] In short, modern ways of thinking and knowing traveled in tandem with modernist style across the United States' newspaper industry. The 1920s and 30s saw the widespread division of newspapers into sections, the clear, orderly presentation of stories, and the emergence of journalism as a profession practiced by a group—journalists—who asserted authority in gathering, organizing, and reporting knowledge.

Attention to form is as important to a complete reading of the Shafter camp's *Agri-News*, or any of the government camp newspapers, as it is to mass circulation papers. From the claims made by the *very existence* of a newspaper—we are a legitimate community; we are aware of and engaged with the world; we make news—to those made by text and image on its front page, we can see the development of a community map, an effort that developed over time to create and recreate "framework[s] for understanding the social world."[8] Camp newspapers, though small, were self-aware publications. They sought to order in a relevant way the world in which the migrants moved. Residents of the migrant camps woke every morning to the immediate challenge of finding their way in a hostile world, and the longer-term work of making some sense of just what the hell had happened to them. They needed a map as much as anyone in America. As media scholars John Nerone and Kevin Barnhurst wrote, "In a social and cultural environment characterized by turbulent change, the newspaper's calm, rational face was an expression of the new professional authority of journalists and designers.... The modern newspaper told the reader, 'You feel the world is out of control, but don't worry, we'll explain everything.'"[9]

In attempting to read their newspapers fully, we do well to keep in mind also that camp papers, like larger publications, were maps and not mirrors. That is to say that they were interpretive presentations, rather than direct reflections, of camp life. These presentations were shaped by ideology, plotted and drawn with a strong, albeit multi-directional sense of how things ought to be. And as with all maps, details and dynamics of the landscape are missing. No matter how closely one studies them, one only gets a partial sense of the actual place, and they reveal very reluctantly the presence of an artist's hand.

It is tempting to think of the developments and dynamics of the quirky, 8 ½" x 11", mimeographed, intra-camp sheets considered here as unrelated to those affecting major newspapers across the United States. It is also tempting to think of the government camp as immune to the forces at work in the business of reporting news. Editorial staffs in the camps were not selling their papers, after all, and did not have to worry about being profitable. Their primary readership, one might argue, consisted of women and men whose lives were largely unaffected by modernization in media.

And while it is true that those writing, editing, and printing the camp papers were not professional journalists, neither were they oblivious to the outside world and its sources of news. Large- and small-market newspapers were a consistent presence in the camps.[10] Moreover, the migrant camp system run by the RA and the FSA was itself a modernizing project. At nearly every turn, camp managers and their staffs sought to chase "snake-oil hawkers" and revivalists from the lives of migrants and to replace them with "medical doctors" and camp pastors; to marginalize the primitive and to mainstream the modern. Camp newspapers, too, were involved in this missionary goal.

Yet the maps presented by camp papers were not straightforwardly ideological. They were drawn by many hands, the relationship among which is not entirely clear. While serving as manager of the Shafter camp, Ray Mork explained to readers that migrants controlled the paper, and insisted that inclusion and openness were the rules. He wrote in the

November 11, 1939 issue that "as far as the management is concerned, our only interest in the paper is that nothing is printed in it that would injure any citizen living in camp, or injure the camp." Squelching opposition or editing out dissent were un-American approaches and would reflect poorly on everyone. "The paper belongs to the camp," Mork continued. "The paper is bought by the camp fund, the paper is printed under the direction and with the authority of the camp committee. Everyone in camp has the right to contribute articles to the paper, if those articles do not injure anyone in the camp directly or indirectly. Citizens in a government camp have all rights given any other citizen by the great constitution, such as freedom of speech, of press, and of assemblage."[11] Mork closed this declaration with praise for the paper, calling it "one that the camp should be proud of."

There is ample evidence to support Mork's characterization of the *Covered Wagon News* and other camp papers as well. The editorial staff of each paper was made up entirely of residents of the camp. Migrants actually wrote and submitted a great deal of material to the paper. Moreover, migrants seem to have taken the papers seriously as an expression of the morals and commitments of the camp communities. In the first year of its life, the *Agri-News* included a regular pro-union column which the camp council voted to remove. Later, a controversy developed in camp around a series of stencils of half-naked women that ran in the paper apparently as a joke. They too were discontinued after numerous complaints and a ruling by the camp council.

The February 10, 1940 issue contained an anonymous poem written in the voice of the paper. In it, the *Covered Wagon News* addressed camp residents, explained itself, and asked for help.

> I'm just your Covered Wagon paper,
> But I hope you'll listen to me,
> For I do my very best
> Each one of you to see.
>
> Please folks, write me a letter,
> Give me all the help you can,
> And I will grow much faster
> If you will help me plan.

Please send me all news of interest,
Tell about your work and play,
And we will have a better camp,
At Shafter—F*S*A*.¹²

The poem captures well the camp newspapers' real reliance on camp residents for news, the truth that the camp paper had a "plan," and the belief, shared by editorial staff and the camp manager, in a connection between a vibrant, planned paper and "a better camp."

There is, however, another reality to be named and reckoned with. People other than the migrants created the majority of a newspaper's news. The camp staff—from the manager, the camp nurse, and the recreation director, to the librarian, the nursery school director, and, when there was one, the camp pastor—wrote regularly and voluminously in the paper.

Additionally, Mork's insistence that the paper was open to migrant-written articles and poems, memorials and jokes, did not broach the topic of layout and form. In the case of the Shafter camp's paper, there are strong indications that a camp manager could affect dramatic and consequential change. A paper could be made to model an ideal community; pages could be arranged to amplify particular voices. Though the papers were open to submissions and were edited, typeset, and printed—for better and for worse—by the migrants, the structures, forms, and sources of the news regularly amplified official voices and government priorities.

The Form of Camp News

The early days of the *Agri-News* in the Shafter Migratory Farm Labor Camp were days of jumbled news. From one week to the next, there was no telling what would appear on the paper's front page, or where stories placed on the front page might end. Stories that began on page one of the *Agri-News* wound their way through the newspaper, across multiple pages, across each other, growing like unruly vines. They consumed columns on two, three, or four pages before ending somewhere in the deep recesses of the paper.

The early days of the *Agri-News* saw stories and entertainment and illustrations mingling on each page, vying all at once for a reader's attention; beckoning to her to follow a meandering path down column after column. Whether the result of a conscious design choice or a subconscious sense of what a newspaper ought to look like, issues of the *Agri-News* from the winter and spring of 1939 gestured toward the broadsheet papers of the late nineteenth and early twentieth centuries, unconcerned with efficiency and hierarchy, laying out a world for readers to explore. Hand-drawn column lines gave visual boundaries to stories, but the newsprint itself crossed those boundaries time and again. The original form of the *Agri-News* was somewhat backward-looking, perhaps even skeptical of the project of organizing news.

The paper's seven-page issue dated February 16, 1939 is an excellent example of the pre-modern jumble. The front page features the headline, "New Camp Council Approves Constitution." What follows on page one is a one-sentence description of the Thursday evening meeting at which "the Camp Constitution was read and approved," followed by the constitution's Preamble, and the first sentence of Article I. To the right of this main story is an illustration of a monkey. Below the monkey are two announcements: one about the camp's dog policy, the other a reminder not to put hot ashes in garbage cans. The additional front-page items are a brief poetry section titled "Food 4 Thot," an article about the camp's welfare exchange (an organization staffed and led by camp residents for the distribution of aid to needy families in and beyond camp), and an essay by Reverend F. E. Klein on "The Values that Endure."

All of these items, excepting "Food 4 Thot," flow onto later pages. The announcements continue on page two, alongside the concluding paragraph of the welfare exchange story and a schedule of "Services for Sunday" placed by the Society of Missionary Men and Women. A list of the paper's staff hangs in the upper left-hand corner of page two. A short joke is nestled into the lower right. The dominant item on the page is a signed article about the United Cannery, Agricultural Packing, and Allied Workers of America (UCAPAWA) that describes the labor movement as America's only hope "if the fate of Germany is to be averted." The author, Bud Fisher, called readers to "wake up" and "live as human beings and not like dogs," before announcing that UCAPAWA locals 250 and 281 would be hosting two "Old Fashion Box Supper[s]."

The final item in the aforementioned "Announcements" section, positioned in the lower left-hand corner of page two, is another reminder about Protestant services, this one submitted by J. R. Kummerfeld, a local preacher associated with the Christian and Missionary Alliance.

> Do not forget the rousing good Church meeting again this Fri in the Recreation Hall. There will be a lively song service, including solos, duets, trios, quartets and instrumental numbers. If you sing give us a chance to hear it. Remember the surprise period for the children. This Fri. the egg will talk to us [sic] and we will sing more choruses. Also a short sermon from the Bible. Everyone is invited, and bring your neighbor.

Kummerfeld's announcement was far more substantive than the simple schedule submitted by the Society of Missionary Men and Women, which announced Sunday School for February 19, a "Preaching Service" on the subject "Signs of Christ's Coming," and an evening event called simply "Pictures" focusing on "The Millennium." In addition to all of this, a brief item submitted by camp resident Mildred Searcy inquired about a watch that she lost in Unit 2's wash tubs.

The remaining pages of the February 16 issue feature Reverend Klein's essay on Christian values ("There is possitively [sic] no lasting profit if a man would strive only to gain material riches or gain."), competing with the full text of the camp constitution, a report on recreational activities, a reflection on the benefits of burning one's pent-up energy, and a call to "shake off the gloom of Old Man Winter and really get out and enjoy ourselves." There is hard and soft news, reporting on "Society" and a column called the "Crying Post" where camp residents can address complaints to the manager.[13]

Subsequent issues of the *Agri-News* from the spring and early summer of 1939 have a similar layout and a similar feel. The headline usually reports on a development within the camp. The work of the camp welfare committee is also frequently front-page news. Bud Fisher contributes a regular pro-union column for page two. Each week the final page of the paper is devoted to comics.

Other items, like their authors, come and go from one week to the next. There was no Protestant theologizing and no mention of Protestant services in the February 23 and March 2 issues. Both reappeared, however, on March 9 with another essay by Reverend Klein, this one titled "The Peace Christ Gives," and an item on page four titled "Church,"

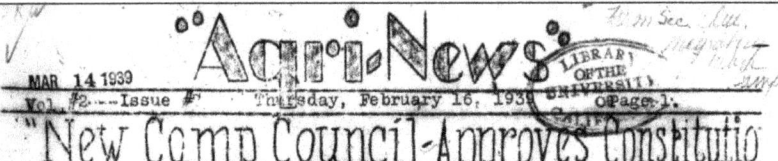

Agri-News

Vol. #2 --- Issue #   Thursday, February 16, 1939   Page 1.

New Camp Council Approves Constitution

At the first Meeting of the New Council, Thursnite the Camp Constitution was read and approved and reads as follows: Preamble.

We the people of the U. S. Farm Workers Camp, located at Shafter, Calif., in order to form a Democratic self-government, establish justice, insure peaceful relations among ourselves and with others, promote the general welfare, and take part in the privileges and responsibilities given us by the Constitution of our Country, the United States of America, do ordain and establish this Constitution for the Camp.

Article I
Section 1. Legislative powers.
All legislative powers shall be vested in a Camp Council, which shall consist of two men and two women elected from each of the six camp units
(cont. page 3. col. 1 and 2)

"VALUES THAT ENDURE"
by. Rev. F. E. Klein
"""
Text: "For what is a man profited, if he shall gain the whole world, and lose his own soul? Or what shall a man give in exchange for his Soul. Matt. 16:26

The Lord Jesus Christ spoke these words to His disciples. He had just told them of His high mission that He must go to Jerusalem to be offered up as the "Lamb of God, which taketh away the sin of the world." That was the purpose for which He had come into the world, to die the atoning death on the cross, as a substitute for us, that we might be free from the power of sin. Peter greatly resents the idea and begins to
(cont.page 3. col. 3)

"FOOD 4 THOT"
I've Always noticed Great Success,
Is mixed with trouble more or less,
And it's the man that does the best,
That gets more kicks than all the rest.
****
I always Argy that a Man
Who does the best he Can,
Is plenty good enough to suit, This lower Mundane Institute.

"WELFARE EXCHANGE"
The Welfare Exchange did not hold their regular weekly meeting this week but nevertheless the ladies have gone right ahead with the regular work and a lot has been accomplished this week. Only emergency orders were taken care of and arrangements are being made to dispose of the shoes as soon as they have been checked and sorted.

The Welfare ladies have been very busy this week and several of them have visited the County Camp and have reported that there were much greater needs there than here in our Camp.
(cont. page. 2. Col. 2)

"ANNOUNCEMENTS"
All Dogs in Camp, MUST BE TIED. The whole Camp is under Quarantine for Rabies under the County Health Law. This must be enforced.

Any loose Dogs found in Camp will be caught and tied and will be turned over to the Police Dept. to be disposed of.

These are orders from the County Health Dept.
C. E. Barry.
"""""""
The Management has acquired new trash cans Please do not dump hot ashes in with the trash but use the can that is marked for ashes only.
(cont. page 2. col.1)

Front page, *Agri-News*, February 16, 1939.

Vol. #2 --- Issue #7   Thursday, February 16, 1939   Page 2

PUBLISHED BY THE CAMPERS OF THE SHAFTER FARM WORKERS CAMP..........
WEEKLY...............
....STAFF....
Supervisor, Charles Evans.
Advisors, Baxter McCombs
           John J. Dobson
SOCIETY   Mrs. Duke
           Mrs. McCaig
REPORTERS
    Wauldene McElroy
    Viola Luker
LOVE LORN ADVICE
    Aunt Bella.
****

"ANNOUNCEMENTS"(cont)
Miss Heller wishes to announce that there will be no regular Sewing Classes on Fri., but she will be at the Camp on Mon., Tues. and Fri. during the week and help any ladies she can.
The regular cooking class is on Tues. 6:30PM
****
If anyone knows about someone finding a watch in the wash tubs of Unit #2 will you please see Lot 204 or return it to Mildred Searcy.
****
Do not forget the rousing good Church meeting again this Fri. in the Recreation Hall. There will be a lively song service, including solos, duets, trios, quartets and instrumental numbers. If you sing, give us a chance to hear it. Remember the surprise period for the children, this Fri. the egg will talk to us and we will sing more choruses.
Also a short sermon from the Bible. Everyone is invited, and bring your neighbor.
    J. R. Kummerfeld.

"UNITED-CANNERY-AGRICULTURE-PACKING-ALLIED"
"WORKERS OF AMERICA"
"The establishment of a facist dictatership in U. S. A. would undoubtedly assure a retrogression from which civilization might not recover for ages and from which it would certainly not recover for many years. I know of only one means of insuring our safety--the workers of America must find self-expression in economic, in Social, and in political matters. Labor to us extends from the unskilled industrial and agricultural workers throughout the so-called white-collar groups, including technicians, teachers, professional groups, newspaper employees, and others. If the fate of Germany is to be averted from this Nation, we must and we shall secure a strong, well organized disciplined and articulate labor movement."
Fascism comes to power as a party of attack on the revolutionary movement of the proletriat, on the masses of the people who are in a state

"WELFARE"(cont.)
The regular meeting of the Ladies Welfare will be held Mon. at 7:00 P.M. Mrs. Webb, Mrs. Ledbetter and helpers made a lovely quilt and raffeled it at the Dance Sat. nite. Due to such a short time for making the quilt and selling tickets only 17 chances were sold. At the next meeting the ladies will decide what to do with the 85¢ made on the quilt.
    Ladies Welfare.
****
"SERVICES FOR SUNDAY"
           Feb. 19, 1939
Sunday School--10:00 AM
Preaching Service
           11:00 AM
Subject: "Signs of Christ's Coming"
Pictures: 7:00 P.M.
Subject: The Millennium.
All are cordially invited to these services.
Society of Missionary Men and Women.

of unrest; yet it stages its accession to power, as a "revolutionary" movement against the people on behalf of the "whole Nation" and for the "salvation" of the Nation. Facism is a most ferocious attack by capital on the toiling masses. Folks wake up. Don't stand and let these parisites destroy our rights to live as human being. and not like dogs. Think! don't be fools, help us and help yourselves.
Don't forget our meetings: #250 has its Old Fashion Box Supper next Fri. nite at 7:00 P.M. #281 has their regular meeting Thurs. night at 7:00 P.M. at the White Spot.
    So, Long.
    Bud Fisher.
****
Andy: You'll never ge rich talking to yourself.
Oliver: I get plenty of exercise tho.

Page two, *Agri-News*, February 16, 1939.

submitted by the Society of Missionary Men and Women, which informed camp residents of the schedule for the coming Sunday's "Divine Services." The Society was, again, hosting Sunday school, a "Preaching Service," and another evening picture presentation, this time the topic was "Court Week in Heaven."

These early issues of the *Agri-News* are full of news. What they lack is an organizing logic. The *Agri-News* maps a world where the quilt raffle sponsored by the Busy Bee Girls, a list of newly-arrived camp residents, and a joke about grandpa's gray hair belong side-by-side on the same page. These items are related in printed space like strangers sharing a taxi. They have in common a desire to get somewhere—out to a readership—and a conveyance—page six of the *Agri-News*—but little else. After a while, this approach to news presentation can become familiar. One adapts to the serpentine lay-outs and the heterogeneous content; one can even discern patterns in the placement of a few elements. But like the people by and for whom it was published, the *Agri-News* is a newspaper in motion. It is disheveled and somewhat unpredictable.

In the summer of 1939, a new camp manager arrived in Shafter. Ray Mork had been transferred from the Indio camp in June of 1939 as a replacement for Charles Barry. Mork arrived in the San Joaquin Valley with his wife Helen, their daughter Betty May, and his emphasis on cleanliness, order, and sobriety.

Mork announced his arrival in the pages of the *Agri-News* with the first of many weekly letters. Mork let readers know that he was going to "get around and get acquainted with each of you," but since there were "over a thousand people" living in the camp, he also encouraged residents to introduce themselves. "I want you to understand," he wrote, "that I am here to work with you and to help you make this camp a nice place to live. So if you have any suggestions or anything on your mind, please don't be bashful about coming up and talking to me." Being bashful, it turns out, was not Mork's style. Readers of the *Agri-News* learned this as Mork turned his attention to the state of the camp.

> There isn't any use beating around the bush about it, cause right now this camp is filthy. Why, I don't know. I know darn well you folks who live here don't want it to be dirty. This morning as I made a trip around camp,

I saw paper, plums [?], matches, cigarette packages and all kinds of junk scattered around camp, by the utilities buildings, around the tent platforms. I saw pails of garbage almost alive with flies. I saw in the kitchens bread and old clothes scattered around.[14]

Mork committed himself publicly to the project of "running a camp" that was "a nice place to live for you folks." His "two important rules . . . first, cleanliness and second, no drunks," were connected to his overall goal of order in the camp. Ironically, this message of introduction and of a commitment to "change these things" opened on the front page, spilled onto the second where it was chopped into three different parts including Mork's signature, and ended on page three, where his signature appeared again. In other words, there was significant dissonance between the form and the message of Mork's first letter to his new camp.

From the very next issue forward, the form of the *Agri-News*, like the state of the camp, began to change. Beginning on July 1, 1939, columns, though not disposed of entirely, became far less common on the first pages of the paper. Mork's letter, a report on the camp inspection, and an article about camp rules dominated whole pages, from the left margin to the right. There was a new sheriff in town and a new form to the news.

Changes to the format of the paper that were initiated in the July 1 issue became the new norm under Ray Mork's management of the camp. The entire paper became less crowded. Over time, articles covering other aspects of camp life, e.g., "Council Minutes," "Nursery School News," "Clinic News," "Boxing," "Young People's Club News," and "Vaudeville," appeared either across the entire page, from margin to margin, or in a more spacious, two-column format. The paper still included some three-column pages, but the logic of these more crowded pages was clearer, their layout less haphazard.

In the September 1, 1939 issue, the first of these three-column pages, page five of the paper, includes the camp's schedule of activities for the week, a recipe, a note from the editor, and a pro-union letter titled "If Jesus Should Visit Our Camp": ("Remember, it was the poor and humble among whom Jesus worked healing, teaching, and feeding.") The second three-column page, page ten, includes gossip from around the camp as well as poetry and some jokes.

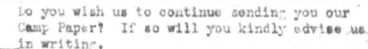

Do you wish us to continue sending you our Camp Paper? If so will you kindly advise us in writing.
Thanks

Shafter Farm Workers Community.

"GRAND OPENING OF SEWING AND IRONING ROOM"

long looked for opening of the Sewing and Ironing Room took place Wednesday 23rd from 4 to 6 PM.
a nifty room we have; everything newly painted, a brand new linoleum floor ng, eight new ironing boards attached to the walls all newly covered; with sockets for the irons and Oh,-irons for each board and four of those brand new.

he opposite wall are our six sewing machines and with the new electric lights just right, it will sure be a pleasure to work in such a well lighted room.

ers are making up for lost time, busy as bees trying to get their sewing done e children before school. And those ladies that depended on the irons certa late being able to use the new room again, for so many had no means other tha row irons and ironing boards from the neighbors.

Busy Bee girls and the Welfare Ladies helped at the opening. Plenty of coolade okies were served to the many who visited during this time.

wish to extend our sincere thanks to the individuals who gave so generously of time, to make this opening the success that it was. We hope the Mothers will keep the young children out of this room so that we can keep the irons and machines in good order.

Front page, *Covered Wagon News*, 1 September 1939.

Shafter, California Friday September 1, 1939.

Saturday's Inspection

Well folks, that man is here again. In my absence of about four or five weeks, I see where many changes have taken and are taking place in camp. All of them are toward improvement, a better camp and a better home for all of us. That is a very healthy sign. I remember something that a smart man once told me some few years ago, and being a young fellow I most of the time keep my mouth shut and my ears open to the advice of smart people; this man told me that a camp never stands still, it either is going up hill or down hill, that is it is either improving or growing worse, and I think that is right. This camp is certainly getting better. Without question the camp areas today are cleaner that they have ever been since my arrival here in June. By cleaner I mean less paper and garbage scattered around. That is a pat on the back for all you good people, not because I said so, but because we saw a job in camp that had to be done, we called it to your attention and you went ahead and did and are doing it. Before I left here about five weeks ago for some reason the areas around the utility buildings were always pretty dirty. It always seemed funny to me that forty families grouped around each utility building couldn't keep such a small peice of ground clean. Today those same areas are very clean. It was very good to see the dirt and rubbish swept in nice neat piles around some of the buildings. Whoever did these good jobs should have finished it, by picking up the rubbish piles and deposit them in the trash barrels. All the Unit Areas were very clean as far as paper and rubbish were concerned. There are still some wood piles in several of the units which could be much straighter and cleaner. Because some of the units are being painted and families are moving around no judgement can be made as to the best unit. This will have to be withheld until all the work is completed. In the Navy they scrub, paint and swat flies; in the Army they scrub, paint, pick papers and swat flies, at the Shafter camp we do all these.

MICHAEL P. BRUICK
Assistant Camp Manager

Clinic News

Dear Campers; August 29, 1939.

As this is my first contribution to our paper I am not going to give you a health talk. Instead, I am just going to say Hello and I am glad to be here.

Through Miss Pimentel's kindness in introducing me around I have already met quite a few of you. The rest will have to introduce themselves. Just stop up and say howdy. I'm Bill Jones or Jane Brown or whatever your name might be. That way we'll all get acquainted fast.

With your help I want to make this the healthiest camp of the lot so please don't hesitate in coming to me with your health problems.

Your nurse,

Mrs Bramsen

Mrs. Bramsen

WONDERFUL

An old farmer and his wife were attending church one hot Sabbath day. The windows were open, and the noisy chorus of the crickets was distinctly audible. In due course the choir sang an anthem, and the old man, a music lover, listened enraptured. At its conclusion he turned to his wife and whispered;
"Ain't that glorious and divine, Mirandy?"
"Yes," she answered; "and to think that they do it all with their hind legs!"

Three months after Ray Mork's arrival, the name of the Shafter camp newspaper changed without comment or explanation from the *Agri-News* to the *Covered Wagon News*, subtly directing the readers' attention away from their current vocation and socio-economic position, and connecting their displacement, even their deprivation, to a powerful American mythology.[15] Instead of being loaded with headlines and the opening sentences of stories and announcements, the front page bore the paper's new name, a large illustration, and a single announcement, in this case "Grand Opening of Sewing and Ironing Room." The drawing—more or less stable for the run of the paper—juxtaposed scenes from 1859 and 1939, the former a covered wagon pulled by a team of four horses, ostensibly making its way through the American West, the latter a somewhat ramshackle automobile carrying passengers along a similar route, destination: California.

By the spring of 1940, the *Covered Wagon News* had firmly established its layout and its new aesthetic, presenting readers with a front page that ennobled migrant identity, constructed camp community, and showcased migrant creativity. The front page of the March 31, 1940 issue, along with the illustration featuring the prairie schooner and the jalopy, presented readers with a poem, "America: Our Country," written by camp resident Ada Hilton Davies. Her lyrical cry for economic justice concludes:

> America, America, Beloved country, Free
> At last from poverty, from that old need
> To crush the many that the few may be
> Their masters. From that grim incentive freed,
> All men shall feel their brotherhood, and grow
> Like him they crucified so long ago.[16]

The front page of the *Covered Wagon News* laid claim to and sanctified American belonging. The second page reported on camp residents' arrivals and departures, but was dominated by the minutes from the camp council meeting, which recorded conversations about scheduling a showing of the movie *The Grapes of Wrath*, and a motion, which passed, to buy a six-month subscription to the *Kern Daily Herald*. Page three of the paper was devoted entirely to the camp's schedule for the

"Covered Wagon News"

Shafter Farm Workers Community

AMERICA OUR COUNTRY!

America one day shall truly be
  Our country, really ours, who dig the earth
For coal and iron, who sail the ships at sea,
  And harvest fruit and grain and cotton, worth
An emperor's ransom. We, whose hands and brains
  Create all wealth, all goods and service, we
The eager workers who produce the grains
  That make the nation great, shall make it free,
one day, from hunger, fear, and clutch of greed,
  From hate, the spawn of privilege unearned,
and from the crime of war, for all our need
  America shall meet. When we have turned
The mighty wheel again, and cast the bell
  Of liberty in contours of Today,
And turned its music to the rise and swell
  Of a hundred million voices, we shall say
And sing it to the stars, "America,
  America! Beloved country! Free,
At last from poverty, from that old need
  To crush the many that the few may be
Their masters. From that grim incentive freed,
  All men shall feel their brotherhood, and grow
    Like him they crucified so long ago."

By Ada Hilton Davies

Front page, the *Covered Wagon News*, 31 March 1940.

(5) VOL. III ISSUE NO. 13 SHAFTER GOVERNMENT CAMP'S WEEKLY NEWS SUN. MARCH 31/40

Cont. from page four

Borned with death in our system.

that is why so few people care to talk to and with God, they are separated from God, they are separated from God, dead to him, don't understand His language. Listen, there is one voice that can give life to the dead, that is Christ's. "I am the resurrection and the life, he that believeth on me though he die, yet shall he live". "And you did he quicken make alive when you were dead through your trespasses and sins". How? "For by grace have you been saved through faith; and that not of yourselves, for it is the gift of God". Listen, when you look to God in faith, and say with all your heart, "I do accept Christ as my Saviour, the one who took my place on the Cross that I might live," Ho gives you ETERNAL LIFE, you then become united with God's family, you can then talk God's language, He will galk to you. While you may yet have to face a physical death, the power of spiritual death will be broke,. Do not you want this etc eternal life now?

ALBERT F. NIKKEL

****

YOUR COMMUNITY CHURCH SERVICES

COME! Bring the family.

10:00 A.M. SUNDAY SCHOOL

11:00 A.M. CHURCH SERVICE

Recreation Hall

3:00 P.M. SING— Home talent
especially invited.

6:30 P.M. Evening Service

at
CENTER BUILDING

REV. PAUL PIETSCH
REV. ALBERT F. NIKKEL

****

WEEKLY LETTER FROM YOUR CAMP MANAGER:

I think we certainly received a splendid welcome at the Visalia Camp, at least fifty went on the trip, and each of us were served two splendid meals. To the folks at the Visalia camp, let me again give our thanks.
The trip was fine, excepting one thing, a couple of the boys had to get drunk, it seems they probably disgraced the rest of you a little. The play was better even than it was at Arvin, all the acts were fine, I know the crowd there enjoyed every bit of it. We made a clean sweep of the athletic events. Won both soft ball games as well as the Basketball game, the boys at Visalia said they hadn't had much practice. We hope we can get some return games. I suggested that both Visalia and Arvin, bring teams here the same day and make a real day of it. Its a fine thing, this friendly meeting and competition between the camps. The Shafter Camp has been losing some families the last few days, many of them going to the potato district at Edison, same however have gone north for the fruit.
There are quite a few who are behind in work rent, that should come up and get the hours worked. A ain let me remind those on FSA that no credit will be given for work done on the grant work orders until camp hours are worked. First work orders should be through about the fourth of April. There are some strange rumors going the rounds in camp about working out grants. The grant office has assured me that all in camp that

Cont. on page (6)

week, listing forty-nine separate happenings by day and time. Of these forty-nine, six were related to Protestant worship, and four of those were organized by erstwhile "Camp Pastor" Paul Pietsch. The entire right half of page three advertised the "Sound Movie" scheduled for the next two Saturdays, *Early to Bed* on April 6th and *Heart of Atlanta* on April 13th.

The *Covered Wagon News* of March 31, 1940 is a paper fully transformed. It is organized and uncrowded. The division between items is unmistakable. Even when a story runs from one page onto the next, as happened with a brief sermon from Paul Pietsch's associate Albert F. Nikkel, and also with Ray Mork's weekly letter to camp residents, following the text is as simple as turning the page.

The clear divisions within the paper served another purpose as well. The reformatted *Covered Wagon News* mapped a community where there was no confusion between and among categories of life and types of authority. Beginning with Nikkel's sermon and a clear reminder of the times for "Your Community Church Services"—meaning those led by Pietsch and Nikkel—and continuing on through the "Weekly Letter from Your Camp Manager," a brief statement from the "Camp Fire Girls," and submissions from camp librarian Mildred Dykeman, camp nurse "Nurse Crain," and nursery school supervisor Opal Butts, camp society is obviously segmented, authority over and in each realm clearly differentiated. Although the paper is not divided into stand-alone or sealed-off sections, one can easily discern the beginning and the ending points for the sport and recreation section, the home and health section, and a section on camp events.

The jumble and the clutter of the *Agri-News* of winter and spring 1939 have been chased from the pages. There may be other things going on in the camp and in the world, the format of the *Covered Wagon News* says, but this is our map, this is our America. Nearly every week of the *Covered Wagon News*' run while Ray Mork managed the camp featured these same firm lines, clearly differentiating realms of life and leaving no doubt as to the type of expertise that mattered most in each realm.

Migrant voices had an important role to play within this framework. But as the *Covered Wagon News* moved toward and settled into a more modern presentation of camp news, the place for migrant voices became more defined. While the camp manager discussed the state of camp life, the director of recreation wrote official reactions to a children's play, and the camp nurse advised readers on matters of health, cleanliness, child birth, and child rearing, the migrants wrote poetry, shared jokes, and dished gossip. In other realms of camp life, specialists spoke loudest and most consistently.

The structures of this discursive environment are important to keep in mind as we consider the explicitly Protestant content of the camp newspapers and Protestant dominance of their pages. The structures created by the layout of the newspaper set the terms for a reader's understanding of her camp community. Minimalist Protestant sensibilities were built into those structures. In many ways, minimalist Protestantism built those structures. Protestantism was often a prominent presence in the papers' pages, but its prominence and its social force were mitigated structurally.

Not coincidentally, the same was true with respect to migrant voices, which entered the paper through poetry, through gossip, and through the minutes of camp council meetings. When there were eruptions from within the camp and those eruptions found their way into the paper, there were familiar locations for them and pre-set rationales for their placement in the papers' pages.

Protestantism as Camp News

All of the religion that appeared in the pages of the camp newspapers was Protestant. But the types of Protestantism that appeared were not all identical theologically, nor were they of the same discursive type. The different types of Protestant discourse published in the camp papers—chronological, poetic, and homiletical or sermonic—created expectations as to where Protestantism ought to be and how it should influence the world.

Chronological Protestantism

The camp newspaper was the primary venue for announcing schedules, for placing them "on the map" for readers, and thus authorizing and legitimating them. The pages of the camp paper also placed news of events and their scheduled times alongside other items, organizing time, knowledge, and awareness for its readers. The camp paper was, in other words, the main instrument of a chronological Protestantism. By chronological Protestantism, I mean the demarcation of time with the structures of Protestantism and the demarcation of Protestantism with the structures of time. Chronological Protestantism placed the sacred on the community map and, in so doing, perpetuated the idea that the overwhelming majority of space and of time was not only not sacred, but was untouched by the hand of Protestantism.

As we have seen, during the year 1939, the layout of the *Agri-News / Covered Wagon News* evolved from something rather haphazard to a look and structure that more closely approximated a modern newspaper. Throughout this transition, it gave space to chronological Protestantism and developed a more consistent and efficient approach to announcing camp schedules. Scheduled worship appears at the bottom of page two in the February 16th issue, only to vanish and be replaced by a "Movie Program" on February 23rd. In both issues, these are the only scheduled events announced outside the context of a longer article. The former schedule of "Services for Sunday" promised "Sunday School" and "Preaching Service" on Sunday morning, with "Pictures" in the evening. The "Movie Program" announced such films as *Oxwelding* [sic] *for Profit*, *America's High Spots*, and *Lip Reading*, to be shown on Wednesday and Sunday nights.

Over the course of the spring and early summer months, editors began extracting events from longer articles, grouping them together, and creating a weekly schedule—one spot where camp residents could turn for guidance on structuring their time. They also placed that schedule near other items—new recipes, new jokes—and created a category of knowledge, call it optional knowledge, for readers to consider, to choose from, or to ignore altogether. The "Program for the Week" in the August 11, 1939 issue of the *Agri-News* is long and diverse. Worship services scheduled for Sunday and Monday compete for space with the camp council meeting, roller-skating, dancing, and boxing. This hybrid schedule appears on page five of the paper alongside the announcement for "Sound Movies," and on the same page as recipes for "Raisin Pie" and "Cream of Tomato Soup," and a blatantly racist joke.

By March of 1940, the schedule of events had grown so dramatically that Protestant worship and other Protestant gatherings—held Sunday morning and evening, Tuesday evening, and Friday evening—though

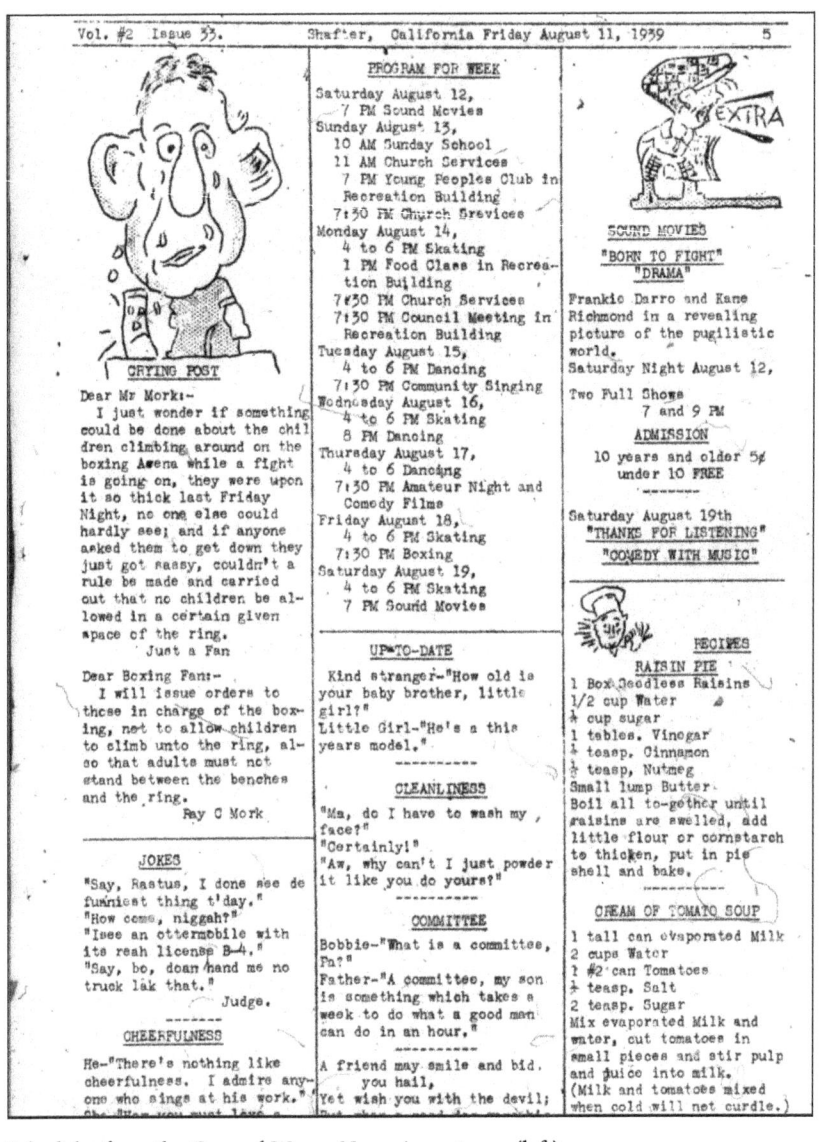

Schedules from the *Covered Wagon News*, August 1939 (left).

Vol. #3 Issue No. 8   Shafter, California Sunday February 25, 1940.   3

"PROGRAM FOR WEEK"

Sunday February 25,
  11 to 5:30 PM Athletics
  10 AM Sunday School in Center
  (The following is Rev Paul J Pietsch,
  Camp Pastor's schedule for the day)
  10 AM Bible School Classes for all ages
  in Recreation Building
  11 AM Church Services in Center Bldg.
  3 to 4 PM Hymn Singing in "   "

  6:30 PM Church Services in Center Bldg.
Monday February 26,
  11 to 5:30 PM Athletics
  9 to 11 AM Welfare Clothes
  2 to 4 PM   "   "
  9 to 4:30 PM Woodcraft
  8 to 4 PM Sewing in Recreation Bldg.
  3 to 6 PM Tiny Tots Club ages 6 to 12
  2 to 8 PM Library
  7 PM Council Meeting
  7 PM Boy Scouts in Center Building
Tuesday February 27,
  9 to 4:30 PM Woodcraft
  11 to 5:30 PM Athletics
  8 to 4 PM Sewing in Recreation Bldg.
  9 to 5 PM Woman's Club in "   "
  3 to 6 PM Art & Crafts by Mrs Austin
  4 to 6 PM Busy Bee girls over 12 years
  2 to 8 PM Library
  7 PM YPC in Recreation Building
  7 PM Church Services in Center Bldg.
Wednesday February 28,
  9 to 4:30 PM Woodcraft
  11 to 5:30 PM Athletics
  8 to 4 PM Sewing in Recreation Bldg.
  3 to 6 PM Tiny Tots Club ages 6 to 12
  2 to 8 PM Library
  7:30 PM Welfare Meeting in Clinic
  8 PM Dancing
Thursday February 29,
  9 to 4:30 PM Woodcraft
  11 to 5:30 PM Athletics
  8 to 4 PM Sewing in Recreation Bldg.
  4 to 6 PM Busy Bee girls over 12 years
  9 to 11 AM Welfare Clothes
  2 to 4 PM   "   "
  2 to 8 PM Library
  7 PM Amateur Night also Sound Movies
Friday March 1,
  9 to 4:30 PM Woodcraft
  11 to 5:30 PM Athletics
  8 to 4 PM Sewing in Recreation Bldg.
  10 to 5 PM Woman's Club in "   "
  3 to 6 PM Tiny Tots Club ages 6 to 12
  2 to 8 PM Library
  4 PM Weekday Bible Class by Rev Pietsch
  7 PM Boxing and Wrestling
Saturday March 2,
  11 to 5:30 PM Athletics
  4 to 6 PM Busy Bee girls over 12 years
  6:30 and 8 PM Sound Movies

Calling all Campers:—
Don't forget the first
Movie starts at 6:30 PM
promptly.

SOUND MOVIES

For Saturday March 2nd

"TROPIC HOLIDAY"

"COMEDY WITH MUSIC"

Bob Burns – Martha Rahe – Dorothy Lamour

Come see Martha Rahe as a bull-fighter,
you'll get a good laugh.

Two Full Shows

    6:30 and 8 PM

ADMISSION

10 years and older 5¢; under 10 FREE for
first show only. Second show 5¢ for both
children and adults. Please do not ask
to go in or out of the building, during
the showing of the pictures.

Saturday March 9th

"SING YOU SINNERS"

"COMEDY WITH MUSIC"

Note:—The doors for the Saturday Movies
will be open at 6 PM show to start at
6:30 PM promptly, doors will stay closed
during the show. The siren will sound
for the second show between 8 and 8:15 PM

****

Thursday February 22nd
    "TIGERS OF THE DEEP"
    also
    "ROUND THE WORLD IN SONG"

Schedules from the *Covered Wagon News*, March 1940 (right).

present, are harder to make out. They have been reduced on the page, surrounded by a list that includes athletics and woodworking, library and tiny tots, sewing, welfare clothes distribution, and amateur night. Larger on the page and more prominent on the camp's map are the weekly movie offerings, which for March 2nd and 9th were the musical comedies *Tropic Holiday* and *Sing You Sinners*.

The *Agri-News* and the *Covered Wagon News* presented a regularized, routinized chronological Protestantism with increasing precision in the years 1939 and 1940. Regular Protestant worship was not, however, the only form of Protestant worship that made news. From the early days of the paper, editors also made space on the map for additional news—an itinerant ministry that stopped to evangelize and entertain; a group wanting to explain what potential attendees could expect from their services.

These special notices and announcements were also features of chronological Protestantism. Editors set them apart from the regular program, drawing a reader's attention to the deviation from familiar patterns and shaping expectations of the events themselves. The June 17, 1939 issue of the *Agri-News* announced on its front page the arrival in camp of "The Pilots of the Cross Quartet," consisting of first tenor Wayne Roberts, second tenor Dale McCully, first bass Dick Hjorth, and second bass Herb Williams. All four were students from the Bible Institute of Los Angeles. "We are working in the Camps up and down the San Joaquin Valley," the article quoted them as saying. "In the morning we hold classes for the children and in the evening conduct open air meetings with the aid of the Loud Speaking System."

Another deviation from familiar chronologies in the Shafter camp, albeit a more frequent one, came in small announcements submitted by the Society of Missionary Men and Women and, sometimes, by a member of the society, J. D. Thom, describing the worship services they had planned. These announcements were placed apart from the main "Program of the Week" and were usually more substantive. On June 24, 1939, the paper notified camp residents that the Society would "present a real, tangible, model of the Tabernacle which Moses erected in the wilderness" to all who would join them in the Center Building at 8pm on Sunday, June 25th. As summer waned, the Society promoted a "Lecture With Beautiful Pictures" in the Center Building on September 10th at 7:30 pm, on the topic "'The Mark of the Beast.' What is it? Who is the beast and what is his mark?" J. D. Thom, who signed the announcement, noted, "Everybody is heartily invited to come and help sing and play."

It is hard to know just how the Society of Missionary Men and Women fit into the life of the Shafter camp. They appear to have represented the Seventh-Day Adventist tradition, and to have garnered at best tepid support among camp residents. With the format of the paper as a guide, though, we can say that they, like the Pilots of the Cross Quartet, were being placed on the camp landscape as more of a side interest than a main feature. Their events were out of the ordinary, not part of the "Program of the Week." Their chronology became familiar by virtue of repetition—Sunday evening, 7:30—but remained spatially "other" in the pages of the *Agri-News*.

Poetic Protestantism

If chronological Protestantism cultivated a particular orientation toward time and its intersection with the practice of faith, poetic Protestantism expressed in verse something of the ideas migrants developed about the divine within and without scheduled worship. Poetic Protestantism appeared on the front page of camp papers. It sometimes took over a paper's dedicated poetry page. It could also be found stashed in the corner of a page dominated by prosaic concerns. Migrants often submitted original work, but occasionally sent in more famous poems—"In Flanders Fields," for instance—or the lyrics of a favorite hymn. Some authors signed their work. Some assumed pen names. Some wrote briefly. Others chose a longer format.[17]

Poetic Protestantism in the camp papers provides a rich account of migrant theologies and religio-political commitments. It demonstrates, to quote scholar of religion Robert Orsi, that "popular theology was practiced with considerable fervor and verve" in the camp papers. Migrants expressed divergent theologies through their poetry, and put into their own words their expectations of the divine and of the world.[18]

Taken together, their work is a remarkable record of the creative energies that can be loosed when a community under stress cultivates an active culture of performance—in the community center—and receives regular encouragement to literary expression—in the newspaper. Migratory farm workers were certainly not the first displaced, impoverished people to turn to poetry as a way of speaking of and to God. Indeed, poetic religion seems a common by-product of such circumstances. Poetry has been both an accessible and a compelling way of sharing belief, emotion, and experience.

In thinking through the significance of poetic Protestantism to the camp newspapers, it is important to keep two countervailing truths in view. The first is that poetic Protestantism was doing important work for both the writers and the migrant community. In writing poetry to be published for and read by their camp community, migrants, to borrow again from Orsi, "not only discovered who they were but constituted themselves as well."[19] That process of discovery and community creation involved giving voice to nostalgia for lives left behind, expressing anger at the people and the structures that frustrated their plans, and daring hope for better, more faith-filled lives.

The second truth is that poetic Protestantism was part of a broader lyrical, poetic production that camp papers generally separated from "hard news" and commentary in their pages. Often, poetic Protestantism appeared alongside other types of poems on pages dedicated to cultural expression. How exactly readers encountered these poems is impossible to know, but the structures of the paper may well have worked to limit and to direct their influence.

To explore this subject in greater depth, we can focus on five signed poems from three camp papers (Shafter, Arvin, and Indio), published in 1939 and 1940. Each poem tells a different story of past, present, and future. Each projected a migrant voice and its theological perspective into the public square for consideration. The first was written by Shafter camp resident Othra Gonderman, who put pen to paper in late 1939 to reflect on the appeal of farm life. The result, an untitled fusion of nostalgia for place, life, and God, landed on the front page of the last issue of the *Covered Wagon News* for that year.

Gonderman opened her poem with a warning. To those who "don't like to see new turned earth," to smell fresh hay, or to experience new life, she wrote: "folks you'ed better stay away." She turned then to those, like her, who loved and longed for the sights and smells of the farm.

> The farm is a wonderful place to live,
> Where our thoughts can be our own

> Where our heavenly Father will guide us
> Through fields, thru pastures and home
>
> Our work all done in the evening
> We enjoy a few hours of rest
> From a day we have spent at farm labor
> Guided by the one who knows best.

The middle stanzas of Gonderman's poem do not praise agricultural work in general. The affection they express is for agricultural life built on the foundation of farm ownership or tenancy. Gonderman writes as one alienated not just from a place, but from a way of living that was comfortable and God-directed. She and her readers are not just spatially remote from "the farm," they are existentially remote as well. The Shafter camp, whatever its benefits, does not provide the same restful end to a day's work or the comfort of God's hand guiding one across familiar terrain. She concluded her poem by writing of her God:

> He is with us when we wake in the morning
> And He stays with us all through the day
> He knows our needs, our wants, and our cares
> And he hears every prayer that we pray.[20]

This final stanza presents a theology that on its surface is reassuring. But when read with the rest of the poem, ambiguity and perhaps even mournfulness surface. The ambiguity arises not from Gonderman's portrayal of the divine. Her words are clear enough. But hanging over the closing lines is the question of whether the God she describes is a god of the "fields ... pastures, and home" that she left behind, or if His reach extends to the here and now of the government camp and migratory farm labor. If God's knowledge of "our needs, our wants, and our cares" was indeed specific to a place or to a lifestyle she knew in the past, what does this say about her relationship to God in December of 1939? Is her longing for the life she recalls so fondly also a longing for a God who once heard her prayers? Is this poem of exile also a poem of alienation from the divine?

The ambiguity of God's presence in Gonderman's poem contrasts with the clear presence of Jesus in Ruby Massey's poem from January 1939, "A Talk With Jesus." Writing from Indio camp, platform #439, Ms. Massey told of, or more accurately spoke to, a Jesus who listens closely as she laments the fallen state of the world. Massey's message for her savior is bleak.

She confesses first that the most basic practices of her faith have become a challenge:

> Sometimes, Dear Lord, it's hard to pray,
> I want to think some other way
> Sometimes this precious Holy book
> Is sealed to me when in I look.

Too distracted for prayer, not inspired to read scripture, Massey struggles to find a spiritual foothold. Her separation from Protestant practices is part of a broader experience of separation from social relations, which tempts her to isolate herself even more. She continues, "My trials and troubles here below, / It seems they're more than friends must know / I want to steal far, far away, / As tho I would know no dreary day." Up to this point, Massey's poem is deeply personal. The struggles and the emotions she describes are her own. She does not pinpoint a cause or a particular circumstance that has nudged her toward this state. It seems, instead, to be atmospheric, a mood that has settled over her like a fog.

As she writes on, Massey conveys a more expansive sense of crisis. Though she feels alone and isolated and unable to practice Protestantism fluently, her situation is of a piece with developments in houses of worship and the social order to which they are connected.

> The churches aren't what they used to be
> Neither is the neighbor as we can see
> Pride has crowded out that spiritual life
> And is causing confusion, disappointment and strife.
> We see the lost souls drifting down.
> To eternities punishment they are bound.

The world and so many of the people moving through it are in deep spiritual trouble, Massey tells her Jesus. Everything seems to be going to hell. Yet her vision also includes a ray of hope. She concludes her poem with a call to transformative action expressed in the lines, "Oh, why do we wait for others to go? / When we know we all have seed to sow."[21] The key to restoring that which has faltered—the spirit of prayer, Bible reading, a sense of community, the churches themselves—is to act, to spread the word, to make disciples of the nations; or perhaps, just to make disciples of the family in the next tent over. And just as important as these outward-directed actions is an awareness of the theology implied by the title (and the central act) of Massey's poem. Regardless of the scope, scale, and intensity of difficulties, solutions and comfort emerge through "a talk with Jesus."[22]

"Thine be the Dominion," published by Joseph August in the *Covered Wagon News* in early 1940, looks past conversations with the divine and forward to a world in which Christ reigns supreme. The redemption August describes has a strongly political dimension to it. And, as one might expect, August's politics include a clear accounting of the good and the bad, which is how he begins the poem, "'We have no king but Caesar,' / The jeering nobles cried. / Our king is Christ of Galilee / Whom then they crucified."

This juxtaposition of the vicious and the virtuous animates the entire work. Those who embrace Caesar as their leader embrace violence as their means, and blind themselves to the true nature of power. "So many throne[s] have crumbled! / The Caesar turned to dust, / But he lived on forever, / The king in whom we trust." The implications of following Christ and turning from Caesar were surely many for Joseph August, but war was at the forefront of his thinking in January of 1940. The wars unleashed by modern Caesars had exhausted the world, August wrote. Earthly rulers had shown themselves to be unrelenting in their violence. "The world is over weary / Of wars that will not cease! / And now, as then, the Caesar[s] / Have failed to bring us peace." Christ, on the other hand, would not disappoint.

> Oh Christ! Our King eternal
> Come to rule and Reign,

> To end earths desolation,
> Her terrors, and her pains.[23]

August's millennial vision addressed a reality, world war, that may have felt distant to some camp residents in 1940, but was bearing down on them quickly. And though calling on Christ to bring about systemic, top-down change, August's poetic Protestantism was not without its personal message. Those who follow Jesus truly and faithfully, he argues, show their allegiance to Him by turning from war.

In his poem, "Christ, Our Life," published in the Arvin camp's *Tow Sack Tattler* on November 29, 1939, migrant Ollie W. Huffman disengaged from the downward-spiraling world that drew the attention of Ruby Massey and Joseph August. He wrote instead of the event that mattered most to him: Christ's intervention on behalf of sinners. He opened his poem with praise for his Jesus and for the work accomplished through his death.

> Oh Jesus Christ what value thee
> To shed thy Blood on Calvery's [sic] tree
> To free the lost, a man like me.
> And to you, Christ, my thanks shall be.

The benefit that Christ worked in history was not measured by the presence or absence of earthly peace, but rather by the freedom his death made possible for "a man like me." Huffman's poem was not all praise, though. He included words of concern for those who did not appreciate Christ's gift, such as an acquaintance who "said some time ago, / 'away from church a hunting go / Is much more joy than church you know.'" Rather than rallying to redeem this lost man, or praying for Christ to make himself known to the sinner, Huffman seemed content to let him go to hell on his own, and to express sadness for any man who joined untold millions and chose hunting (or the horse shed, or a few extra hours of sleep) over church, "About that man I often grieve / Who calls on God, but don't believe."[24] He closed with a message for the *Tow Sack Tattler*'s readers:

> Eternal life we can receive,
> But this I know if we achieve

And never more ourselves deceive
In Jesus Christ we must believe.[25]

Against a backdrop of political, economic, and social turmoil, Huffman used verse to draw with special clarity the line between the saved and the lost, and, arguably, to lower the stakes involved in crossing it. The path to eternal life, he emphasized, requires both belief in Jesus Christ and the forethought to schedule one's hunting outings so that they don't interfere with worship.

The different understandings of Jesus and his meaning for humanity that shaped the poetic Protestantism of Ruby Massey, Joseph August, and Ollie Huffman presupposed a connection between Jesus and the common person. Migrant poet Jack Bays wrote to readers of the *Covered Wagon News* in February of 1940 that this connection was strictly a thing of the past. But on his way to arguing that something had gone horribly wrong in the relationship between Jesus and common folk, he wrote first of how things had been. Bays opened his poem "Kidnappers of Jesus" with the stanzas.

> With soothing words the Master came to those of low estate
> And like the men of God before he scorned the rich and great.
> Down through the years His host has been the crushed and poor and sad.
> They've loved and held Him in their hearts, the only friend they had.

Bays then turned abruptly to the injustice brought about by the wealthy. Painting them in villainous hues, he accused the rich of "shut[ting] [Jesus] in and driv[ing] the poor away" to the cynical end of "mock[ing] Him as you did of old with wealth and rich array," and the demonic end of breaking up a divinely-arranged friendship between Jesus and the poor. Bays concluded his poem with livid verse.

> What right have you to claim our Lord and so blaspheme His name?
> How dare you drive away the poor by boasting such a claim!
> To win the public favor and make your profits sure,
> You've taken Jesus from His own, the meek and lowly poor.[26]

"Kidnappers of Jesus" is a striking poem, though much of it is not surprising. There was more than enough reason for Bays's anger, and he was not the first to direct that anger up the class hierarchy. What is striking in Bays's work is the absence of a vision of reconciliation, a return of Jesus to right the wrongs. Indeed, Bays doesn't even allude to a reordering of history. There are no soothing words about the world to come, no promise of rekindling the embers of love between Jesus and the marginal. Was the coalition that had planned and executed the "kidnapping of Jesus" powerful enough to hold him forever? Was there, in Bays's view of the world, no hope for redemption?

These poems, written by migrants living in different camps and shaped by diverse histories and Protestant traditions, show a level of theological engagement that may well have surprised those who described the migrants as uncultured, unsophisticated, and in need of civilization. They show, too, that there was no one way in which migrants made theological sense of their world. Some expressed nostalgia, some anger; others confessed feelings of disorientation or hopes for an apocalypse.

What all of the poems named, some more quietly than others, was a feeling of alienation: alienation from the land, from religious practice, from a world rightly ordered, from consensus about the demands of Protestant faith. Poetic Protestantism was a way for camp residents to give voice to experiences of exile, wandering, and betrayal; it was a way for migrants to address, for themselves and for their community, the experience of living hungry and poor and remote from the places and the ideas that once provided comfort.

Poetic Protestantism was a regular presence in camp newspapers, along with many other types of poetry: humorous limericks, political verse, hymns of protest, odes to lost love. And because these poems often appeared together on a page, mapped into the same creative/cultural region of the camp, it is useful to consider this broader poetic output as a body. What work was done by publishing theological poems like "God is at the Anvil" and love poems like "Once I Had a Sweetheart" in the same newspaper, and by locating them in particular spaces?[27]

On occasion during 1939 and the first half of 1940, and consistently in the months of August through November of 1940, the *Covered Wagon News* published a poem on its front page. It appeared beneath the masthead image, described above, that juxtaposed the covered wagon and the automobile. Some of these poems were unquestionably theological in orientation. Others celebrated the camp more generally. Othra Gonderman's ode to farm life, Joseph August's "Thine be the Dominion," and the above-mentioned "God is at the Anvil," appeared in this spot, each one making a front-page argument for the Protestant orientation of the camp community. A poem titled "Success" fronted the November 2 issue ("It's doing your job the best you can / And being just to your fellow man. . . . It's figuring how and learning why / And looking forward and thinking high.") having been preceded in that space by poems such as "How Did You Die," "The Table Set for Two," and "Our Camp."[28] These poems focused less on the divine, and more on the human community, its dynamics, and its values.

Beginning on November 23, 1940, the poems gave way to narrative dedications honoring individuals or groups whose work strengthened and sustained the community. The first dedication was made to two brothers, Raymond and Harvey Montgomery, who "volunteered their services in the defense of their country and their democracy." The dedication noted that they were the first two from the camp to join the military and expressed the hope that "by being prepared you may scare war away from us."[29] The editors dedicated subsequent issues to, among others, "our library and our librarian," (12/7/40) "the Camp Council," (12/14/40) "Mr. Mork and Mr. Spencer," (12/21/40), and to the camp nursery school and its staff (1/4/41).

The point of these front-page statements, the theological and the non, the lyrical and the prosaic, was to acknowledge the forces at work in migrants' lives and to express awareness of and appreciation for them. They establish the camp as a community with its own values: God-aware, individualist, grateful, and where part of being a good neighbor is awareness of the work and the place of the "people in the neighborhood."

Poetic Protestantism published elsewhere in the paper conveyed a different message. There were, of course, the messages of the poems themselves. Ollie Huffman warned men not to turn their backs on church. Ruby Massey described a broad religious decline and nudged individual readers to righteous action. Jack Bays decried the cooptation of Jesus by the wealthy and lamented, presciently, the permanence of this captivity. But it seems that a different kind of message might have been on the page as well. When the *Covered Wagon News'* "Poets Page" contained the hymn "Abide With Me" as well as compositions such as "Only a Dog," and "What a Man," the editors were not just filling space. They were managing a genre, perhaps hoping to create a cultural sensibility. They and their paper were arguing that poetic Protestantism was a sub-category of "the poetic" rather than as a sub-category of "the Protestant." It was, in other words, the poetry of poetic Protestantism rather than its theological sensibilities that made it worthy of notice.

Homiletical Protestantism

Homiletical Protestantism in camp papers was less theologically diverse than poetic Protestantism. Newspaper sermons were written most often by semi-official camp pastors who, by force of theological argument and frequency of publication, created a sort of Protestant mainstream in the government camps. The volume of their prose combined with the layout of the paper to shrink other religious identities and to push them to the margins, sometimes literally. These mainstream messages, while edifying to some, did not please everyone. In rare but colorful instances, homiletical back-talk troubled the consensual, communal Protestantism that camp officials favored.

Homiletical Protestantism was common in the pages of the *Covered Wagon News*. In most cases the authors were clergy working in and around the camps. Reverend F. E. Klein contributed to the *Agri-News* occasionally in the later winter and early spring of 1939. The frequency of Protestant sermons in the *Covered Wagon News* increased late in 1939 and into 1940, particularly in the months following Reverend Paul Pietsch's self-affiliation with the Shafter camp. An article in the paper's October 21, 1939 edition titled "Sunday Night Church" announced "Rev. Pietsch will move his family to Shafter in the near future" and that he would be conducting "non-denominational services" and would also offer, "free of charge, weddings, funerals etc." The author argued that, because Pietsch was "working on so many things in the interest of camp folks," readers should "come and welcome him this Sunday evening."

Pietsch returned to the camp and to the pages of the *Covered Wagon News* in February 1940. This time he contributed a hybrid introduction and exhortation that began, "I was very much pleased to see such a fine attendance in the Recreation Hall last Sunday. There were 76 present. Let's try to make it 100 this time." Those wondering what it might mean to join Pietsch for worship found an answer in his brief introductory homily.

> I am an ordained Baptist Minister, but I am not here to try to make Baptists out of any of you. My job is to tell you, as the scripture . . . that he was buried and that he rose again the third day according to the scripture. I believe the entire Bible is the word of God, revealed to show man his lost condition and God's remedy for that condition. Again I say I have "no creed but Christ" and "no books but the Bible." . . . I am here not to make church members, but to be a friend and help you to know the friend of [the] friendless, the Lord Jesus Christ, whose I am and whom I serve.[30]

Reverend Pietsch wrote again the following week. His words, which appear just beneath recreation director Ethel Dilts's description of the amateur night play, provided a more robust accounting of his theology, and suggested that attendance at his previous service had not had the gender balance he desired. "[Won't] more of you men come along and help us make these community service[s] a credit to our camp[?]" Pietsch wrote further, reminding those who knew, informing those who did not, that the Bible was full of "Wonderful Promises." He began his accounting of those promises with "Salvation God's Gift."

> For by grace are you saved through faith, and that not of yourselves. It is the gift of God. Eph. 2.8. How wonderful a plan! Some of us could not have salvation if it were not a gift. Christ gave his life so it might be free to us.

Pietsch wrote next of "Forgiveness of Sins."

> When we take God's gift of salvation and receive the Lord Jesus Christ into our lives our sins are forgiven, for we read in Eph. 1:7 "In whom we have redemption through his blood [the] forgiveness of sins, according to the riches of his grace."
>
> God is providing us with salvation and forgiveness of sins through the blood of Christ shed on Calvary Cross.

> Oh the love that drew salvation plan
> Oh the Grace that brought it down to man,
> Oh the mighty gulf that God did span,
> At Calvary.

Reverend Pietsch concluded his message by asking his readers "honestly" if they had "taken God's gift of salvation" and if they were "trusting in the Blood of Christ? If you are, your sins are forgiven."[31] He signed the column, "Your Camp Pastor."

In his exegesis and presentation of Ephesians, Pietsch performed a classic Protestant vanishing act. He made himself disappear as an interpreter of the text and made other possible interpretations vanish as well. What remained, he claimed, was "no creed but Christ. No books but the Bible."

Shortly after writing these two columns in February of 1940, Reverend Pietsch handed the weekly writing job to his assistant pastor, Reverend Albert E. Nikkel. Nikkel made his debut in the Easter edition of the *Covered Wagon News*, with a "Sunday Sermon" reflecting on the parallels between new life springing from dead seeds and Christ's resurrection. Two weeks later, Nikkel offered another sermon, with a darker presentation of death and the consequences of sin. "With few exceptions, every babe is born to die, to die physically," he wrote, "Within every human body there are two forces at work, one the force of life, of construction, of building the body tissues, the other, the force of destruction, of death, tearing down the body tissues." The tearing down of body tissues was not Reverend Nikkel's focus any more than the sowing of actual seeds had been.

> We are thinking of another "Death Process" that is working in the life of every man, woman and child. In fact he is born with this, that is SIN. God said to Adam, who giving him orders regarding the tree of the knowledge of good and evil—"for in the day that thou eatest thereof, thou shalt surely die." Adam and Eve did not die a physical death the day they ate of the forbidden fruit, they did die an immediate spiritual death, that is they were separated from God.

Nikkel could promise nothing against "physical death," but he assured readers who would "look to God in faith, and say with all your heart,

'I do accept Christ as my savior, the one who took my place on the cross that I might live,'" that the "power of spiritual death [would] be broken."[32]

In June of 1940, Arthur Nikkel passed the torch to Ed Schellenberg, who identified himself as "Acting Camp Pastor," and who wrote on in the spirit of his immediate predecessors. His homilies were full-page (or nearly so) compositions bearing titles such as, "What is Truth," "Trusting God," "What Have We in Christ," "The Book That Never Grows Old," and "The Temptations of Christ," in which he wrote, "the scriptures say that he was tempted in all points like as we are, but was without sin." Schellenberg continued, "This last statement is important.... Things become a temptation to us because of our sinful inclinations, because of our sinful nature which finds pleasure in sin. Christ had a sinless nature, but never the less sensed temptation." He then moved to quiet the doubters, the critics, or the merely confused. "It is not for us to try and understand all the things in the scripture, but it is for us to believe all things in scripture. Understanding increases with time and study and seeking Gods guidance patiently and in a trusting way."

In a concluding paragraph that shared page space with ads for "Diane Beauty Shop" and Frank Russel's "Blacksmithing and Welding" business, Acting Pastor Schellenberg returned to the topic of understanding and empathy, "In Christ we have one who understands. He has been 'through the mill,' and can really feel with us and knows what we need."[33]

In his sermon of August 24, 1940, "James and the Horse," Schellenberg retold the story of James, a "good man" who "always kept the law." (The source of the story at the heart of the sermon was "a little book called 'Come Home Gospel Stories.'") James, Schellenberg wrote, "had a good job as coachman with a fine Christian master," and was often the focus of his master's efforts to convert him. He resisted because he "knew better.... He kept the law and what more was needed." The horse enters the story when James's master offers it as a reward if James "can keep the law for half an hour," a challenge that James readily accepts.

James's master locks him in the hay loft, apparently out of reach of temptation, and then returns after a half hour. When James descends from the loft, his master asks him how he passed the time. "Oh, I was just thinking," James replies. "What were you thinking?" his master asks. And then James's dream of a "fine brown horse" (not to mention eternal life) begins to unravel. "Why to tell the truth sir, I was just thinking that as you're as good as to give me the horse, maybe you would let me have the old saddle too, for you see sir, the horse is not much use without a saddle."

"Oh James, James," his master replies, "I am sorry to say that I cannot even give you the horse. The law says that 'Thou shall not covet' and you were coveting all the time you were in the loft. You have not kept the law for even half an hour, much less all your life."[34] With the racialized subject of James humbled, horseless, and theologically mistaken, Pastor Schellenberg steps forward to explain the deeper meaning of the story for his readers.

> By the works of the law shall no man be saved. There always have been two extremes. The one is that works produce salvation. Then there is no place for works and we can live as we please. Neither one is right. Both are dangerous. The Truth of the matter is that salvation produces good works. The man who claims to be saved and lives a life of sin bears false testimony. He had better check in to that. He has not been borned [sic] again. Of a true Christian it is said in the scripture, For it is God that worketh in you both to will and to do according to his will. Philippians 2:13.

It was not good enough to be good. The true Christian sought forgiveness of sins and a cleansing of "all unrighteousness," and then gave thanks to God who "has made all things possible that we may enjoy continuous fellowship with him."

If Pastor Schellenberg ever wondered whether camp residents read his printed homilies, the answer was not long in coming. The next issue of the *Covered Wagon News* included an "Answer to James and the Horse" signed by "A Camper." This sermon-like rebuttal, which consumed a page and a half, was accompanied by a note from the editor, which read, "the above article is not advocated by the paper but is the opinion of a camper" and reminded readers that "we are glad to print the views of the readers as long as they do not contain heresy or slander."[35]

But from the perspective of the author of "Answer to James and the Horse," the paper had in fact printed heresy. Pastor Schellenberg was "a Christian," the author acknowledged, but she/he also found "the attempt that he made to prove that that the law cannot be kept was very flimsy indeed, not realizing the purpose of the ten commandments." The author then devoted a dense page and a half to describing moments from the Hebrew Bible and the New Testament that supported the position that keeping God's law was the defining characteristic of righteousness. Abraham and Noah, the Psalmist and Isaiah, and Jesus himself testified to this.

> Surely Christ himself was as good as most of us streamlined Christians, yet he, in order to live a victorious life was compelled to keep the commandments. Listen to his own words, John 15:9–10. As the father hath loved me so have I loved you; continue in my love, if you keep my commandments ye shall abide in my love, EVEN AS I HAVE KEPT MY FATHER'S COMMANDMENTS AND ABIDE IN HIS LOVE.[36]

The force of this passage, "A Camper" argued, was "that there is only 1 law for the entire universe of God. Christ was very familiar with this law, even from creation he was confronted with the preachers of lawlessness in his days." "A Camper" then called modern-day preachers of lawlessness "liars" possessed of "carnal mind(s)," and accused them of misleading the people into "enmity against God."

By way of conclusion, "A Camper" drew a straight line from "James and the Horse" to the work of the great deceiver. "Full well I know that it is Satan's constant effort to misrepresent the character of God (which his law only can reveal) the nature of sin, and the real issues at stake in the great controversy." Five pages further into the *Covered Wagon News*, Pastor Schellenberg's sermon based on a young man's story of redemption appeared under the title "The Bag of Beans."

"A Camper's" direct challenge to Pastor Schellenberg was barely a memory when another sermon, this one signed by "Dessie Farmer," appeared in the paper's pages on September 7, 1940. Farmer's sermon, "How to Find the True Way to Heaven," opened by sounding the alarm over "false doctrines" and "departures from the faith," "seducing spirits" and "hypocrisy" as described in 1 Timothy. Farmer then called camp residents to look to the "holy ghost" in these days of upheaval: "It is going to take the holy ghost power in our own lives . . . to be able to stand against the wiles of the devil. The holy ghost is a part of the whole armor [of] God. He is our comforter in time of trouble."

True believers should repent their sins "humbly before Jesus," she wrote, but soon thereafter turn to the holy ghost and find their "sweet rest." Holy ghost people, Farmer continued, would be known by one sign:

> Tongues is Bible evidence of having received the holy ghost [acts, 10:44–47]. Here in part of the verses "on the gentiles was poured out the gift of the holy ghost, for they heard them speak with tongues and magnify God." You see that was the sign that they had received the holy ghost for it says, for they heard them speak in tongues. . . . Some say that the speaking in the tongues was just for the apostles, but read acts, 2:38–40, for the promise is unto you and your children and to all that are afar off.[37]

Farmer added proof texts from Acts and from the Gospel of Mark in support of "tongues," but advised readers, "Don't just seek tongues but seek God for a close walk with him and walk in all the light that he gives you and he will give you more." She also urged camp residents to study scripture themselves "with much earnest prayer to God," in order to weather the storms of the age. She concluded, "In these times we need all the power that we can get and because of false prophets read Tim 1 4–12," and then quoted 2 Timothy, "Study to show thyself approved unto God, A workman that needeth not to be ashamed rightly dividing the word of truth." Pastor Schellenberg's printed sermon for the week, a reflection on the constancy of Jesus, was titled, "Always the Same." It was his last submission.

The presence of these two dissenting sermons in the pages of the *Covered Wagon News* brings into focus three important truths. First, the homiletical Protestantism that dominated the paper for much of its run, while central to the paper, was one voice among others in the camp. Not all theological particularities—Protestant perfectionism, Pentecostalism—dissolved in the camp's allegedly non-denominational ecosystem.

Second, these few but strong voices challenge the non-denominational, "no creed but Christ" pose struck by camp pastors Pietsch, Nikkel, and Schellenberg. While these men may have seen themselves as operating apart from doctrinal constraints, ritual traditions, institutional structures, and other hamstringing qualities of historic denominations, they were most certainly operating out of a tradition of scriptural interpretation and assumptions as to the contours of a properly Christian life. As much as they (and the camp staff) might have wanted to obscure their particularities and to paint their theology as simple Protestantism, mere Christianity, dissenters from this dominant homiletical Protestantism exposed its theological and interpretive investments. Sermons in the camp's Protestant mainstream conveyed a strong understanding of human depravity, which many Protestants from Holiness traditions would contest. They also rejected the necessity of baptism in the Holy Spirit, not to mention Pentecostal understandings of speaking in tongues as uniform evidence of Spirit baptism.

Finally, voices from the paper's margins help to expose and refute implicit claims to historical and geographic expansiveness in the words of the official camp pastors. Lessons and anecdotes, chapters and verses, framed and hemmed in by the printed page, pretended to speak from beyond it. You are like all Christians and all Christians are like you, the camp newspaper's homilies regularly asserted. This time and this place are like all times and all places in the eyes of God. "A Camper" and Dessie Farmer begged to differ.

Another instance of dissent surfaced in the March 30, 1940 issue of the Indio camp's *Migratory Clipper*. Homiletical Protestantism in the *Migratory Clipper* had a similar flavor to that of the *Covered Wagon News*. It denied any act of scriptural interpretation and encouraged a robust turnout whenever worship was happening.

H. T. Feathergill, who claimed the title of "Superintendent" of camp church activity, wrote regularly to the *Migratory Clipper* in a column titled "March of the Church." Feathergill blended homiletical and chronological Protestantism, giving space to messages and to schedules, reporting on attendance, exhorting camp residents to turn out in even greater numbers. He did not present full sermons, but in the March 30, 1940 issue he noted that the message for the week would be "The Continuing Task," and would describe the "privilege we have [of] witnessing for Christ wherever we go." He also promoted an upcoming meeting to be led by "Brother Miller" who would be "preaching the grand old truths of the old-time gospel. May God bless him."

Three weeks later, Feathergill wrote energetically, attempting to draw readers into his community of practice and "plain" scripture presentation.

> There are many folk in the camp, no doubt, who have been used to going to Sunday school and church, and have just got out of the habit and sort of hesitate to start again. Come on folks; the Lord needs your help in his work, and you need Him and the fellowship of His people. We have no ax to grind no dogma to hammer on, no denomination to push at you, no collections to make, but we do have the Bible and the Father, Son and Holy Spirit, and teach and preach "The Way, the Truth, and Life."; The Book, the Blood, and the Blessed Hope. A Church in the Camp, by the camp and for the camp means a great deal to the camp, so give it your support by your presence.[38]

What was there for any Christian to lose? The truth wasn't only clear and unadulterated, it came free of cost and free of pressure. Supporting this Protestant community was an act of support for the camp as well.

It seems that camp resident O. V. Owens did not like the direction in which the church was marching. In the March 30, 1940 issue of the *Migratory Clipper*, he called for an about-face in a sermon titled, "Behold, I come quickly," a reference to Revelation 22:12, "And behold, I come quickly; and my reward is with me, to give every man according as his work shall be." Owens did not hold back in his interpretation and application of "Bible truth" to the world as he saw it. He opened his sermon with a list of the troubles abroad in the land and in the world: wars, assassinations, "world conference failures, suicides of eminent persons, flights into voluntary exile of the horde of gigantic syndicates . . . financial difficulties everywhere." He then summarized the global situation for readers: "It becomes apparent that this poor world is reeling to and fro like a drunkard." The upheavals of the present and the recent past were only the beginning. This drunkard world was in for one whale of a hangover. Owens continued, "Without wishing to be sensational we wish to state on unfailing authority that an event is yet to occur which will give the world its greatest shock. The shock will consist in the sudden and complete disappearance of millions of its choicest inhabitants."

Owens was not referencing the persecution and murder of Jews in Europe or the deadly violence of the global war, then in its seventh month. His eyes were on heavenly actors and disappearances of a different sort. "The disappearance will be of such a mysterious nature that it will seem as though the earth has opened its mouth and swallowed them. However the reverse will be the case. Heaven will have opened its doors to receive them."

Owens and the camp residents who shared his reading of the moment were prepared to be ridiculed as "old fogies." They were ready for "experts" to describe this disappearance as "a natural phenomena." But, he insisted, scripture and God had their back. "What I say unto you, I say unto all. Watch."[39]

The extent to which Owens's message filled camp residents' hearts with expectation or led them to turn their eyes heavenward is a mystery. But Owens returned in print the following week to catalog and interpret the "signs" that indicated so clearly that "the coming of the Lord is right at hand." He saw signs in nature: "pestilences and fearful sights." He saw signs in religious developments: "some shall depart from the faith, giving heed to seducing spirits and doctrine of devils." But Owens devoted the most space in this letter to "economic signs." The sign, he wrote, "[that] probably concerns and effects us most is the tragic unemployment situation which is causing untold suffering throughout the intire world," including, as Owens knew quite well, California's agricultural interior. Were these circumstances difficult? Yes they were. Were they surprising? Owens thought not.

> [W]e were told hunreds of years before Christ was born that this would be for in Zach 8–10 we read "For therefore these days (Restoration of Israel) there was no hire for man, nor any hire for beast." To me this is moast significant and enough to make anyone stop and think. Then we have the great [mer]gers and chain stores everything merging into one, it would seem, which is undoubtedly clearing the way for the great superman the anti-Christ who will be the supreme head of all business, governments, etc. on this world for a short period of time (Rev 13–16) God does not approve of the merger system for in his word he declares, "woe unto them who join house to house, field to field, till there be no place alone in

the midst of the earth"..... And we do know that practically all the wealth today is in the hands of few men.[40]

While many voices across the state and the nation were calling workers and labor organizers agents of anti-Christian communism, the prophet O. V. railed against corporate injustice and anti-Christian greed. Their damnation, he shouted from the pages of the *Migratory Clipper*, had been promised centuries before Christ.[41]

The circumstances that brought O. V. Owens to the tent platforms of the Indio Migratory Farm Labor Camp and the precise contours of his daily life are hard to make out. What is absolutely clear is the extent to which he theologized not just his circumstances but also the larger narratives of global turmoil to which they were connected. What could it all mean? The poverty, the suffering, the violence, the landlessness, the injustice, the absence of a clear way out?

It meant, in short, that the end was near. It meant that the righteous would soon be plucked up like so many ripe melons and would rise above "the farm strikes, mob outbreaks, and financial difficulties" to "meet the lord in the air."[42] It meant that Owens's reading of scripture, his notion of what scripture was, his understanding of how history worked, and his vision of God were all true. Not only would O. V. Owens's sufferings soon end—his lack of a permanent place and a stable living be resolved eternally—but he and those who believed like he did would be vindicated. It was time, he told readers of the *Migratory Clipper*, to "plead the blood."[43]

At one level, there is nothing remarkable about Owens's sermons in the *Migratory Clipper*. In their reading of history and God's role in it, they map onto an apocalyptic strain in American Protestantism that dates to the Puritans of Massachusetts Bay Colony and can be found coursing through the words of Nat Turner, the actions of Adventist founder William Miller, the visions of John Brown, and the transAtlantic phenomenon that was the Scofield Reference Bible.

Yet apocalyptic thought is indeed remarkable. Apocalyptic imaginings do not exist apart from contexts, and are emphatically *not* morally neutral. For all of its predictions of the workings of cosmic history to come, apocalyptic thought is always situated in a present, shaped by a place, and articulated by a person enmeshed in circumstance and experience. Apocalyptic prophets render the microcosmic macrocosmic. They teach God to speak the local dialect. And the narratives that they relate involve righteous and unrighteous, heroes and villains, winners who win once and forever and losers for whom it would be better had they never been born.

Apocalyptic discourse is not a discourse that accommodates nuance and compromise. It is hard wired to obliterate these things. Without questioning the sincerity of apocalyptic beliefs, we can note their appeal among women and men who imagine themselves as wronged or marginalized by earthly powers, but not truly wrong or justly marginal. Apocalyptic visionaries look forward—as O. V. Owens did—to a righting of the wrongs, a centering of the margins, and a whole glorious heap of punishment for those currently standing on the wrong side of cosmic history.[44]

Visions of the end have much to tell us about lives in a moment. O. V. Owens's visions are no exception. Owens's apocalypticism has a distinctively agricultural flavor, with strong hints of a migrant's frustration with the agro-economic order of Depression-era California. Owens wrote from within the Indio Migratory Farm Labor Camp, a space set aside for those who had lost their places on the land and in society, men and women who had traded what was left of disintegrating lives for the promise of something more. What most got back in return was hunger, sickness, and humiliation. The fortunate among them found income that moved with the harvest and communities that wanted their labor, then wanted them gone.

O. V. Owens's sermons also have odd qualities that evoke Indio (and even Oklahoma) more than they do Los Angeles or Pasadena. Four times in the space of seven sentences in his second homily (Second O. V.?) Owens uses the word "earth." It is not a definitive marker of an agricultural prophet, to be sure, but it is also not a usage one would expect to find in the writings of someone unconcerned about or disconnected from "earth."

Moreover, the specifics of his usage suggest an earth that has agency: "it will seem as though the earth has opened its mouth and swallowed them"; "myriads of bodies which were resting in mother earth will be missing at the same moment." Owens's earth is the earth of the ancients, it is a being and a thing. More to the point, it is the kind of being that can swallow or disgorge, rise up or lie down, strike or nurture, punish or reward. The apocalyptic prophets of California's urbanized coast wrote of ideas and movements, empires and their rulers. While these things mattered to O. V. Owens, he made sure that the earth, too, was an actor.

When Owens asked his fellow camp residents if they could not discern the signs of the times, and then, following an age-old pattern, provided them with a list, he included "farm strikes" and "financial difficulties" and, in a dramatic departure from more urbane prophets, described the conglomeration of business interests and the merging of corporate entities as counter to the will of God. The satanic, communistic "collectivization" on which prophets from Biola and other urban institutions looked in such horror does not seem to have concerned Owens directly. He saved his anger for the powerful businesses that were consolidating their assets and growing ever more powerful. These developments were, to him, evidence that "the great superman the anti-Christ" would soon rule the world.

Yet rather than confine himself to the rich imaginary of Revelation with its beasts and lambs, harlots and blood, Owens (re)turns to the fields of the prophets of Israel, citing Isaiah: "woe unto them that join house to house, that lay field to field, till there be no place alone in the midst of the earth" and referencing Micah 2:2, "Woe to you . . . you want a certain piece of land, or someone else's house (though it is all he has); you take it by fraud and threats and violence."

These are the prophecies and the scriptures of a man deeply immersed and yet placeless in a system of industrial agriculture. The world he condemns is a world in which lands and homes—all that people had and, quite possibly, all they would ever have—had been taken by an angry earth and by unscrupulous lenders, leaving God-fearing women and men suddenly destitute. It is a world whose threats and violence and fraud keep migrants moving, landless, and, in the case of O. V. Owens at least, pleading the blood and looking to God to bring the whole damn thing to an end.

These dissenting sermons brought fire to the pages of the camp papers which, while familiar in poetic Protestantism, was uncommon in the homiletical tradition. They show that the editors of the *Covered Wagon News* and the *Migratory Clipper* were willing to cash the checks they had written to all camp residents offering space for material that did not injure individual residents or the reputation of the camp. The homilies themselves reveal that characterizations of the modern newspaper as a map and not a mirror are valid. There was more going on in terms of belief and practice than the camp papers accounted for regularly. And the newspapers, taken as a body, reveal the subtle power of print both to make public and to bury dissenting voices.

These three dissenting authors, "A Camper," Dessie Farmer, and O. V. Owens, appeared a total of four times in two camp papers. Those papers brought out fifty-two issues each year for roughly three years each, and the voices that were heard much more frequently were those of a mainstream homiletical Protestantism. They were not part of each issue, but the voices that established themselves as fixtures of the camp's map spoke with the confidence of the modern religious specialist, and with the faith that Protestantisms that strove to make news or be newsworthy would marginalize themselves.

Reforming Government Camp Protestantism

Back north in the Shafter camp, the *Covered Wagon News* saw a merger of its own. Just two weeks after Dessie Farmer made her case for Pentecostal truth and Pastor Schellenberg published his last sermon, the paper featured its first-ever religion page, a single page on which one could find most of the chronological, poetic, and homiletical Protestantism published in a week. The authors and compilers of this Protestant content, and the likely architects of its consolidation, were the new "Camp Pastor and Wife," Chris and Reba Ummel.

The top of the new page featured a passage from scripture—for their September 28, 1940 debut, it was 1 Chronicles 16:11, "Seek the Lord and His strength, seek His face continually." Just below was a schedule of "Sunday Service" for September 29, including Bible School at 10, Morning Worship 11–11:45, an "Old Time Sing" 2–3 in the afternoon, and "Evening Worship" 7–8pm. The page also announced "Week day services" for Friday, October 4, consisting of "Bible Story Hour[s]" for "primary" and "junior" children, 3–4 and 4:30–5:30, respectively.[45] Having established a chronology, the Ummels offered an invitation to worship.

> We extend a cordial welcome to all who feel the need of Christ; to those who are burdened; to those who need comfort in sorrow; to those who wish to serve; to those who disire christian Fellowship. We are here

to exalt the risen Savior, the Lord Jesus Christ, and to make Him precious [to] you—that is our joy.[46]

Unlike previous camp pastors, the Ummels avoided long-form sermons, opting instead for short statements, stories, poems, illustrations, puzzles, and theological quips to convey their message. But the message was very much in the spirit of the camp's mainstream homiletics, particularly when it came to the essence of Protestant Christianity. They wrote in the October 5, 1940 issue.

> To become a Christian is not to turn over a new leaf, it is not to do the best we can, it is not to join a church, it is not to try to keep the law, but to RECEIVE A PERSON, the Lord Jesus Christ, (John 1:12) When we know him as our personal Savior, then he is all in all to us.[47]

Protestantism was not a matter of keeping the law. Holy Spirit baptism was not a required credential for the heaven-bound. The essence of Protestantism was to "receive a person."

This consolidation of Protestant content brought with it a narrowing of theological possibilities, a washing out of parts of the camp's Protestant map. Gone from the *Covered Wagon News* was the mournful exilic theology of Othra Gonderman and the revolutionary poetics of Jack Bays. In place of these angular voices came a more predictable poetic Protestantism, one that shunned ambiguity and anger. Its task was to praise and to encourage readers to praise. As an expression of this "streamlined Christianity," the Ummels deployed the hymn "He Giveth More Grace" under the title "God Never Fails Us."

> He giveth more grace when the burdens grow greater.
> He sendeth more strength when the labors increase.
> To added affliction he addeth his mercies.
> To multiplied trials his multiplied peace.
>
> When we have exhausted our store of endurance.
> When our strength has failed ere the day is half gone.
> When we reach the end of our hoarded resources
> Our Father's full giving is only begun.

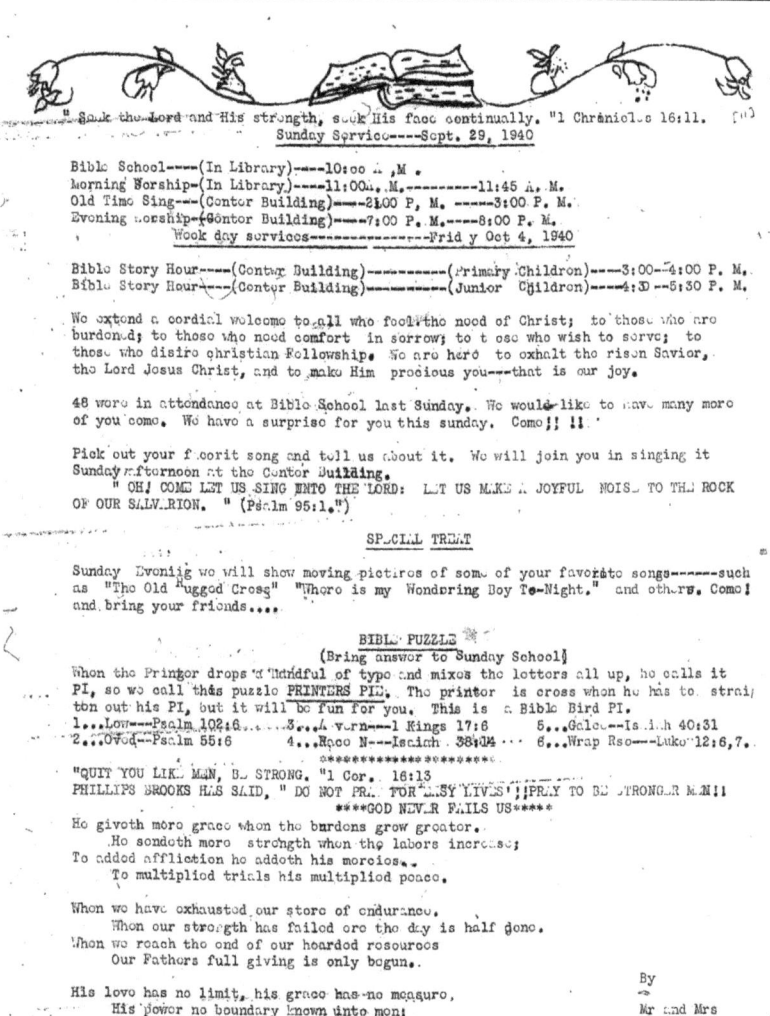

Two of the Ummels' pages, *Covered Wagon News*, 28 September 1940.

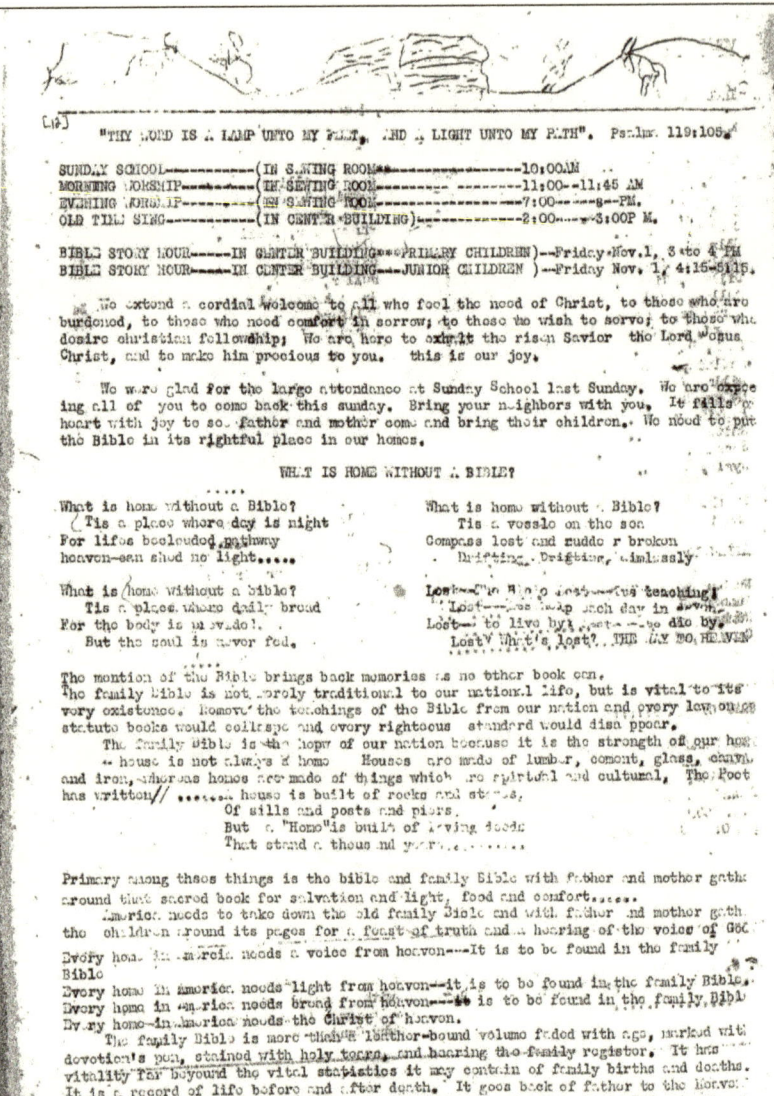

Two of the Ummels' pages, *Covered Wagon News*, 24 October 1940.

On page five of the same issue, Floyd P. Harvey published a poem, "The Death of My Babies," describing a fire that took the lives of his son and daughter. He explained in verse that the family had been gathered to celebrate a birthday, "But God had planned it different."

> The trailer house was like a furnace
> The fire red as coals
> The firemen tried to reach them
> By cutting great big holes.
>
> But the babies spirits had left them
> No more to cry and mourn.
> They had left this sinful world
> And in a new one they were born.

Though there is no record of an interaction between Mr. Harvey and the Ummels, one can imagine him taking issue with the idea that any combination of grace, mercy, and peace was worth the affliction of losing his children in a fire.

The weekly papers of the federal migrant camps mapped a homiletical Protestantism that assumed and performed consensus. This map presented a truth that was always only partial. Within the gates of the government camp, Protestantism had many faces, many bodies, many histories. Expressions of Protestantism that rose from the migrants themselves pull back the curtain on consensus and drag the ethereal, de-historicized Protestantism down into the fertile dirt of California's agricultural interior, not to mention the muck of Protestant controversies old and new. The venue in which these disputes were staged, however, worked to limit their escalation and made their characterization as "disputes" itself something of a fiction.

In newspapers dominated by official voices and characterized by differentiation among the realms of society, there was little acknowledgement of alternative points of view, much less any true back-and-forth. The angular anti-modernism of Dessie Farmer and O. V. Owens thrived in other arenas. In the pages of the *Covered Wagon News* and the *Migratory Clipper*, they took their place alongside more subdued homilies, diverse poetics, and chronologies inscribed with predictability and respectability. The modern camp newspaper quietly but surely sought to modernize the antimodern.

Yet the lay homilies and poetry preserved in the papers' pages remind us, to borrow from J. Z. Smith, that map is not territory. They remind us, too, that territoriality, chronology, and other affixing, anchoring forces are a challenge—perhaps the most profound challenge—not only to modernity and minimalist forms of Protestantism, but also to Protestantisms with non-denominational pretensions. "A Camper," Dessie Farmer, and O. V. Owens are lost to history. History was, however, not lost on them. They wielded it like a cudgel in a fight that they weren't going to win, but that they felt called to fight for themselves, their God, and quite possibly for migrants who could not or would not write their beliefs themselves.

They also provide clues to a more robust culture of Protestant practice than the papers showed regularly. Given the form of the newspaper and the ideological work that it quietly accomplished, we should not be surprised to find migrants looking to other spaces for the expression of more satisfying theologies.

7

The Gate, Revisited

The gate, the point at which migrants entered a government camp and crossed from one type of life to another, one kind of space to another, symbolized more than just relief from a life of filth and vulnerability. It was also symbolic of two disciplinary regimes, the behavioral discipline of living within the camp system's communal norms and the religious discipline of worshiping within its Protestant norms. This meaning of the gate comes into focus as individuals and families who did not respond to either type of discipline pass back through the gate and out of the camp, in search of other communities.

Evidence of these disciplinary programs and of their effects on the moral and religious lives of migrants comes from two sets of sources. The first is the documents generated by camp councils and camp managers related to the removals of what Ray Mork described as "a certain type of family" from the community.[1] These memos and minutes and reports describe the circumstances under which the camp community threw up its hands and threw out a member, and the system-wide response to these unredeemable residents.

The second is a dissertation completed in June of 1944 by James Bright Wilson, a graduate student in the University of Southern California's School of Religion.[2] Wilson's dissertation, a blend of ethnography, sociological analysis, and critique, described the Protestant lives that migrants pursued on both sides of the camp gate, and also captured something of the attitudes that reformers harbored toward the migrants' Protestantisms. Wilson helps us understand what types of Protestant communities migrants sought outside the gate, what they found unfulfilling about the camp's Protestant offerings, and what more comfortably-situated Californians saw when they looked at fundamentalist and spirit-filled migrants.

These documents show that camp system officials used the power of their offices and the power of communal judgment to try to make migrants live in conformity with the values of the camp program, which camp officials regarded as the values of modern society. These efforts bore fruit, to be sure. But life beyond the gate and worship in spaces outside the gate offered alternate paths and counter-communities for those who found the price of living and worshipping inside the gate to be too high.[3]

Looking at the gate in this way also underscores the importance of other places and structures in a federal migrant camp. Spaces such as the tent platform and the sanitary unit matter for the physical presence they gave to camp norms. Decisions not to conform to those norms were made in and around these spaces and sometimes in direct response to them. The convergence of space and ideology created an atmosphere in which departures from prescribed or expected practice acquired enhanced meaning. The elevation of hygiene and sanitation to a spiritual discipline and the creation of a space, the sanitary unit, for the practice and performance of cleanliness made transgressions against the sanitary unit more than just carelessness, more than bad form. The establishment of a standard space and time for the practice of Protestantism, the regular dissemination of those standards through the camp paper, and the enactment of those standards in and around the community center, made those who wanted something different into dissenters and misfits.

The theme of coercion or "social control" has run through much of this book and becomes more explicit in this final chapter. Camp officials discussed with each other the limits of their power to shape migrant life and their desire for more power over them. Incentives are important, they wrote, but so is punishment. Wilson, a graduate student with close ties to the Methodist Church and a taste for Social Gospel theology, lamented the fact that religious leaders in California's Central Valley controlled migrants through fear of eternal punishment, and structured religious education around incentives. They are adept, he wrote disapprovingly, at using Protestantism as social control.

What is most illuminating in revisiting the gate with ideas of discipline in mind is not just that an emphasis on discipline shaped the camp system's approach to social and religious life, not just that conservative Protestant approaches to discipline often ran parallel to camp system approaches to discipline. What is most illuminating is that the seminary-trained, sociologically-minded PhD student, James Bright

Wilson, conducting field research around the camps and in churches and ministries beyond the camp gate, did not notice (or did not mention) this parallel. This blind spot, willful or not, points to the larger erasure of the Protestant outlines within which communal norms were articulated and lived out. The vision of reform work running through Wilson's study was common among New Deal reformers, and helps us to situate the camps, their staff, and their residents in the religious history of the United States.

The Architecture of Eviction

A gate functions differently depending on one's position and direction of movement relative to it. And a gate has an inherent, structural power to limit; the deeper work that it does depends largely on how a person feels about what lies beyond it. A gate functions differently, too, depending on the forces, common or uncommon, leading a person toward it.

Movement in and out of a government camp gate was often driven by common forces. Migrants arrived with ripening crops and departed with the close of the harvest. Editors of the camp paper, in cooperation with the camp office, regularly reported who had come and who had gone. This was a human gesture in an economic environment that tried to erase migrant humanity. Editors used the paper to say, "Welcome. We see you," or "Good bye. We will miss you."

The May 27, 1939 edition of the Shafter camp's *Agri-News*, for example, listed twenty-four "New Campers," among them J. A. Jones, Dennis L. Hoggartt, Marion G. Vanzandt, and Floyd B. Williams, with the note "We welcome all of you and hope that your stay with us will be pleasant and prosperous." The August 4, 1939 edition of the same paper announced a set of departures, "Mr. and Mrs. Alexander and family, Mr. Grady Phillips and son Alex, Mr. Grub and son Jessie all left Tuesday afternoon for Tulare to look for work in the peaches. We wish them good luck."[4]

Once established in the camp, residents passed through the gate constantly. In good times, when work in the cotton fields, the apricot orchards, or the pea fields was plentiful, most adults left camp in the morning to labor and returned in the early evening to rest. In harder times, daily comings and goings were in search of work, or relief, or some way to stretch financial, physical, and spiritual resources just a bit farther. For nine months out of the year, school-age children made their way out of the gate each day to attend local schools, to learn to let insults roll off their backs, to accept tepid welcomes as the price of lukewarm lunches. The children returned each afternoon more educated, and also wiser to the ways of the world.

The gate was a common place. It was a space that one might move through without a second thought. It is this understanding of the gate that I think camp officials sought to instill in residents. In their eyes, the camps were not quite the gated communities of late twentieth-century privilege or the suburban developments fed by postwar prosperity and racial tribalism, but neither were they wholly unlike them in their spatial, social, and aesthetic logic. We live inside. They live outside. We mark our insider-ness by looking and behaving according to rules, spoken and not. We are the ones who can move fluidly from outside to inside, inside to outside.

Some migrants arrived more or less suited to this type of communal life, pre-wired to value a tidy lawn, a clean tent, and a potty-trained child. Some were longer-term projects, taking time to adjust to new surroundings, learn new practices, and build resistance to unacceptable but not-quite-dormant desires. There were also those for whom rehabilitation did not work, for whom redemption was fleeting—if it had ever taken hold in the first place. These were the migrants who did not belong and who could not stay.

When perseverance failed and a migrant returned to the drink, showed a stubborn propensity for volcanic interactions with neighbors, or refused to take a turn cleaning the sanitary unit, she would be called before the camp council. The council considered the case from all sides and then passed judgment on the accused, usually naming what was already clear to the community: the migrant and her family were unfit for life in the government camp. They were then ordered by the council to vacate their tent platform and to leave. This was not the same as a legal eviction, but it usually functioned in the same way. In these circumstances, departing through the gate was a ruling of unfitness, a judgment passed on sins that could not be hidden or cleansed. From the moment a migrant family passed through the gate to join the camp community, the possibility hung in the air that transgressions would force them back out.

This was the message of a letter written by the Shafter camp's manager, Charles Barry, that he titled "Revocable Camp Permit," and placed on the front page of the *Agri-News* on May 13, 1939. In the letter, Barry quoted at length from the permit that camp residents were required to sign: "the GOVERNMENT, at its option, may revoke said permit and privilege granted thereby at any time, by giving three days' written notice delivered or addressed to the CAMPER at his above-designated place of residence. Immediately upon the expiration of such notice, the CAMPER shall quietly and peacefully remove from the premises and surrender possession thereof."[5]

The legal authority on which the camp council acted to rid their community of transgressors and misfits was, in a word, flimsy. In most cases, the council relied, as did the manager of the camp, on the weight of accusation, conviction, and shame to do the purging work. And most expulsions from the camp were completed with little resistance. Some condemned residents chose to wait a while, perhaps wanting to show up the censorious council or the tyrannical manager. But even the most ornery and stubborn usually felt their banishment and decided to pass through the gate one last time, making it a site of communal discipline and public punishment.[6]

To depart through the gate by force of eviction was to arrive at pariah status vis-à-vis the camp system as a whole, to be looked upon by the system as a contaminant. Once the ruling came down from the council and a family departed, the camp manager was to add them to a list of migrants unwelcome in any federal migrant camp. The longer the camp system existed, the longer the list of unfit families became. A few entries from the list of families who departed the Shafter camp under less than honorable circumstances give a sense of the sins and the sinners.

> Doster, Marion F., owes $28.30 to Camp Fund, owes 37 hours work. Arrested for stealing. Will not keep promises.
> Hudson, Norman F., owes $.60 to [Camp Fund], owes 6 hours work. Drinker. Did not check out. Maliciously cut holes in Government tent.
> Franks, Jess M. owes $3.00 to [Camp Fund]. Family split up for drinking.
> McClanahan, Jay, says he never worked in camp and never will—definitely a trouble maker.

Enloe, Marion, did not check out, moved out during nite, trouble maker, dirty, will not work.

Good, Elmer, Did not check out, was ordered before council for immoral conduct, but left.

And then there were "Ring, Thomas A." and "Cummings, Clyde E.," both of whom owed money to the camp fund, but who set themselves apart as transgressors when they both, either in cooperation or inspired at different times by the same malign spirit, "emptied [the] toilet commode [into the] isolation unit laundry." Their entries in this roster of the damned offer no further comment. What more was there to say?

As this list demonstrates, camp residents were capable of all kinds of sins, banal and spectacular. But what landed the overwhelming majority of migrants on the camp system's blacklist was not an egregious transgression, but a covenantal violation of a more basic sort. The most frequently enumerated sins were not drinking, gambling, "immoral conduct," or dumping a bucket of shit into the laundry, but rather failure to pay debts to the camp fund and failure to work out one's required hours—two per week—cleaning and maintaining the camp. Such forgetful or dismissive conduct revealed a lack of concern for rules, for reputation, and for the moderating force of a respectable community.

Those who could not keep these basic requirements of the camp covenant revealed themselves as incapable of meeting the standard of camp communal life. Even those who had advanced to life in the garden homes were not immune from these basic lapses. A form reporting "Gaston, Charles E." as having been "dispossessed" of the garden home that he occupied with his family of five, noted confidentially, "Mr. Gaston failed to care for the property or to utilize the Garden to advantage; He was un-cooperative in community activity; allowed his rent to accumulate." When camp manager Spencer Bisby withdrew the Gaston's rental contract on the last day of September of 1938, the family owed seven months' rent, or sixty-one dollars. The gate reminded all camp residents of the covenant into which they had entered and of the cost of breaking it.[7]

Yet these lists are not just catalogues of iniquity. As historian Perry Miller argued in his mid-century analysis of Puritan divines and their public discussion of colonists' moral failings, discussions of sin and social degradation often function in multiple ways. One can interpret them simply as records of a people's bottomless capacity for transgression, chronicles of lapses both surprising and foretold. In the eyes and hands of some camp program administrators, the list of sins and sinners was simply that. But the rosters may also have had a more positive, even constructive meaning to them. A list of those to be kept out of camp testified simultaneously to the virtue of those who were in. It said not just that those within the gates were *not* sinners of the type listed, but also that they knew sins when they saw them and knew precisely what to do in response. The people in the camp were a disciplined people, and they knew how to discipline others. At the same time that the gate gave material and spatial expression to expulsion and exclusion, it reinforced communal notions of virtue, self-governance, and discipline.[8]

Eviction is a means to achieve separation between those who are unable or unwilling to keep the terms of a covenant and those who are. Its relatives in the world of institutional Christianity include the ban, excommunication, and disfellowshipping, all of which involve a determination that a person is no longer fit to claim membership in the community. The desire to achieve separation of the fit from the unfit was an important aspect of the camp program from the beginning. Recall Tom Collins's description of the exodus that half of the residents of the Marysville squatter camp undertook in the summer of 1935, when they learned that the federal government would be assuming control of the space and implementing a communal reform program. These subjects valued what they saw as freedom over the promise of a more intentional community. Better in Collins's eyes that they move along than remain and derail the camp experiment.

Echoes of that larger, original culling are present in manager Ray Mork's letter in the Shafter camp's *Agri-News* on July 1, 1939. Published with the headline, "Changes Mind About Entering Camp After Reading Rules," the letter told the story of a migrant man and his family who entered the Shafter camp and were in the process of registering, when the camp security guard / manager's assistant read them the rules of camp life. "Don't know what it was in the rules that scared them," Mork wrote, "but they dident [*sic*] stay long after they heard them."[9] The gate and the prospect of the discipline within had done their work preemptively.

Discipline and the gate are inextricable, one from the other. Not surprisingly, the manager who wrote most frequently and colorfully about the importance of discipline in the camp, Ray Mork, was also the manager who advocated most energetically for the manager to possess the power of summary eviction. He wanted the consequence of stubborn resistance to the reforming program of the camp to be swift, dramatic, and—to borrow a word from Harry Drobish's description of the camp's themselves—demonstrational.

Mork spent a great deal of time in the summer of 1940 chewing on the problem presented by misfits, and thinking through what he and his superiors might do to solve it. His report for May of 1940 described the situation and what he perceived as the solution. "I believe more effort should be made," he wrote, "to eliminate a certain type of family from our camps. Certain families that leave here will not be readmitted." Some would face this exclusion because "they do not seek agricultural work but wish only to get cash or grocery grants." Given that the camp program was specifically for agricultural workers and that those in other lines of work were routinely required to move on, Mork's plan makes sense.

He was troubled, though, by another type of migrant, those "trouble makers . . . who do not conform to community and cooperative life." He elaborated:

> For the benefit in the long run of the people we care for as well as our program, I think that we should encourage discipline and set high standards of citizenship in the camp, this will require a more systematized camp program as well as greater supervision, supervision with enforceable discipline. This in the line of recreation, home management, as well as ordinary camp cleanliness and order.[10]

The time had arrived, Mork proclaimed, to be more demanding when it came to compliance with the camp's model of modern, virtuous living made present in the tent platform, the sanitary unit, and the community center. Those who were on board and wanted to stay on board had nothing to fear. Those who resisted or backslid and transgressed should be shown the gate.

Mork became more strident in the summer heat. In his monthly narrative report for June 1940, which marked his one-year anniversary as manager of the Shafter camp, Mork informed Raul Hollenberg, assistant director of the Farm Security Administration's Region IX, that the regional office was being neglectful, and that their neglect would have far-reaching consequences. "The one important problem that the regional office has failed to solve is the eviction problem," Mork wrote. "In a letter received from the regional office to-day, the statement was made that failure to evict cannot possibly break down camp morale or the manager's authority. We who have worked with southwestern farm workers of course realize that such isent the case."

If the manager and the council did not have the legal power to force someone off of their tent platform and out of the camp, Mork argued, the integrity of the entire project was in jeopardy. It was part and parcel of a culture that took seriously the business of redemption. "[H]elping workers," Mork continued, "[can] not be done necessarily by soft words and indulgence, but rather through discipline." He wrote on:

> Taking people of very low standards, with a history of shacks, dirt floors, extreme individualism, sloth, extreme superstition, and trying over night to make them ideal citizens in an ideal community has been a problem that could hardly be solved with only pleading and organization. If we have been successful we have been lucky, because at no time have [managers] in the field had a tangible power of discipline.

Mork wanted "tangible discipline in the form of a workable eviction proceeding" for those deemed too fallen to be saved. "Self-discipline" was an important part of the formula, but, he insisted, "there must be discipline, from the top" as well. There was no question in Mork's mind as to the form that "discipline, from the top" ought to take. The camp needed a legally articulated and exercisable power to throw recalcitrants and troublemakers out on their asses. The gate needed to be an even more vivid marker between the saved and the damned.[11]

Eviction was a problem in theory. Because government camps were federal property, local authorities had very limited ability to intervene. As Mork explained it, in order to compel a family to leave by force of law, he had to present a case of misuse of federal property to a federal magistrate or a US attorney, a process that could take months. In practice, however, evictions and departures driven by the camp council's judgments were quite common and effective. If, however, someone wanted to resist and to linger in a community that had asked them to leave, the wheels of justice would turn slowly, far too slowly for Ray Mork.

Where Mork went beyond his fellow managers, at least on paper, was in wanting to take action against not only those who sinned boldly, but also against those who caused trouble in more subtle ways. People could behave themselves well enough, he argued, and still not belong. "For instance," he offered, "a family is causing trouble in camp, yet does nothing tangible such as get drunk or disturb the peace for which legal action can be taken and the camp committee orders the manger to move the family out. The family may understand the manager's predicament and refuse to move." In other words, Mork was worried that he would look weak and ineffectual against families who stayed within agreed-upon behavioral lines, but proved difficult for other reasons. And he felt certain that he was not alone in this concern. "Such a situation is bound to arise some time in each camp and when it does and the manager is helpless to carry out the camp committee's orders, the morale and discipline of the camp is bound to fall. . . . [Even] if the time involved in evicting a family could be lowered to fifteen days, it would help a lot."[12]

Mork documented his frustrations in the summer of 1940, but they were not new either to him or to the camp system. The force of many of his public statements in the papers of his former camp at Indio and his current camp at Shafter was that camp residents who were not reforming and improving were regressing; that the drunk, the dirty, and the disruptive were a menace not just to themselves and to their families, but to the larger community as well. The sooner these misfits could be made to pay for their resistance to the gospel of the good neighbor, and the sooner they could become examples for other residents, the better for everyone involved.

Mork illustrated his point with a story, conveyed to Regional Director Lawrence Hewes, in his monthly narrative report for October 1940. He had recently taken a chance on a family that had caused problems in two previous camps. "I wanted to try and help them become good citizens," he wrote, "I have had success in a number of such instances. I am failing in this case, however." He was fairly certain that the camp council would vote to evict the family. That's where things might get complicated.

> Then comes the almost impossible job of moving them out, it will have to be done by trickery, it isent practical or sensible to wait for government procedure . . . as their staying in camp only points out to the campers the helplessness of the camp council as well as the camp management. . . . If we had a procedure whereby families could be evicted quickly, there would be no fear of letting in problem families, for if the trial failed, they could be promptly evicted. As it is the camp black list grows larger and larger.[13]

Put differently, those who most needed the redemption available in the government camp also needed the threat of damnation hanging low over their heads. Without the fear of losing everything that the camp offered, the bad apples would just rot and rot and spoil the entire bushel.

* * *

The gate also functioned to discipline unruly Protestantism. This was a constructive project, and one with a longer timeline. For most of the life of the federal camp system, the reform program involved a sustained catechesis, an attempt to rewire the religious circuitry of migrants. The goal was not to turn the migrants' Protestantism off, but rather to redirect at least some currents toward other concerns and to make the circuitry more reliable.

This rewiring was not about theology exactly, though theological differences between camp residents and between migrants and camp staff were significant. Camp managers showed themselves to be quite accommodating of a Protestantism in the camps that was pietistic, conservative, and anti-modernist. The rewiring, the disciplining, was about cultivating proper and restrained Protestant practice and converting migrants to the belief that the truest forms of Protestantism and religion (all but synonymous to reformers and migrants alike) were polite and restrained.

Among the unwashed, the starving, the desperate, and the racially indistinct, camp program officials saw unmoored and unruly Protestant practice. They saw unrestrained and unreasoned Protestant belief. The civilizing program within the gate was meant in part to subdue those practices and to subject those beliefs to the reducing and limiting power of differentiated authority and a community humming with secular interests. Georgie Nunn, whose term as Tom Collins's housekeeper led to a great deal of condescending commentary from Collins and his associates, is an example of what this looked like in practice.

Georgie Nunn also helps crystalize aspects of the camp program that might otherwise pass unnoticed. Her life as a young pentecostal evangelist drew condescension. Her tendency to talk too much and to treat domestic spaces as porous drew Collins's direct intervention with a job offer. Collins celebrated her domestication through her marriage to Noah, and their eventual purchase of a Chevrolet, visible evidence of her connection to and placement in the earthly realm. He had helped her make strides toward a disciplined Protestantism, a faith that did not call uneducated, uncredentialled young women to lives of aggressive soul-saving and dependency on the donations of others; a faith that did not require direct experiences of the divine or constant seeking after such experiences.[14]

The archives of the camp program indicate that this program of re-wiring, like the program of behavioral disciplining, had its successes. The gate functioned reasonably well as a tool of Protestant discipline. The social ecosystem of the camps trained religious desires and practices by limiting options for worship, and by making them regular, routine events.

The result was a communal Protestant life with a particular look and feel. This life fit well into the camp program, even validated it, by staying in the narrow lane of worship, Bible study, and hymn sings, and by tracking and measuring success numerically. Much of the success or failure of a program of Protestant worship depended on the demeanor of the pastor and migrants' perceptions of his commitment to them. But the success or failure of a particular ministry didn't matter as much as the cultivation of an expectation that successes and failures would happen at a designated time and in an advertised place.

I have found no record of a camp resident being evicted or even considered for eviction because of the form of Protestantism that she or he practiced. The camp council had the authority to permit or forbid ministers and ministries access to the camp, but camp managers and program authorities gave wide berth to camp residents' beliefs, not wanting to infringe on their First Amendment rights. Undisciplined

Protestantism did not go unnoticed among camp residents, however, and occasionally drew a reprimand from the camp council or the camp manager. Minutes from the April 2, 1938 meeting of the Arvin camp council, recorded by camp resident Earl Stone, noted "Church activities in tents at late hours was reported keeping some of the campers from sleeping. Motion was carried that after 9:30 P.M. quietness should be obtained." Whether or not that motion was applied to the worship lives of camp residents, it is at least clear that the nine elected council members hoped to discipline some forms of Protestantism for the good of the community.[15]

Another incident took place in the Firebaugh camp in March of 1942. Manager Conrad Reibold described it in a letter to Regional Assistant Director, Harvey Coverley.

> [R]esidents in the community called upon management to stop a disturbance and noise being created at approximately 10:50 P.M. on the night of March 17th. This disturbance was evidently a religious service being conducted in Metal Shelter A5.1 occupied by Mrs. W. M. Harris and family. About eighteen adult persons were in attendance in her living quarters and services were being conducted by a preacher living outside of this Farm Workers Community. The preacher as well as residents have on two previous occasions been advised and told by the management—request to hold a particular denominational service must be made through the Community Council.

Reibold's action prompted camp resident W. H. Matthews to complain to the camp program hierarchy, "When he told them to stop, he also told her that if she held any more Services, she would have to move. Making a person move on account of Church Services sounds like dictatorship to me."

The official response, written by Harvey Coverley, reminded Mr. Matthews that "the right of religious freedom means freedom of worship, but this right must be exercised in such a way as not to disturb public peace. When an individual exercises his right of freedom of worship in such a way as to disturb the public peace, he or she, although retaining the right of freedom of worship, must exercise the right under conditions and at times satisfactory to the community at large."[16]

The relative rarity of disciplinary or corrective action connected to religious practice does not, of course, indicate the absence of a disciplinary program. The camp environment made little space for undisciplined Protestantism, seeking both to locate Protestant worship predictably in space and to convert camp residents to a regular Protestant chronology.

A disciplinary program for Protestant practice situated within a broader program of modernization and civilization can be difficult to see. But one account shows how strong the connection among social, cultural, and Protestant reform could be. In July of 1936, Arthur Lundin paid a visit to the Arvin camp to observe the camp operation, to meet camp residents, and to get a sense of what it might mean to serve as a camp manager, a job for which he seems to have been under consideration. He compiled his notes and submitted an eleven-page report of his experiences on July 26, 1936.[17] The report is a familiar mix of admiration and condescension toward the migrants. Lundin praised camp residents: "As a group their morality is the highest. Frankness and honesty are characteristic," but he also made clear that, good as these people were, they needed the reform and the rehabilitation that he and others hoped to provide. They have about them, he wrote, an uncivilized, premodern innocence, an "unbelievable" "thoughtfulness" that makes "the people seem almost childlike at times, as indeed they are."[18] They were, he wrote, "rapidly loosing [sic] . . . qualities essential to reliable citizenship" such as "pride and confidence." To be "worthwhile," the camp program had to be "more than a palliative."

Lundin noted as well that work remained to be done in repairing and modernizing the social lives of camp residents. He described the scene at a Saturday night dance:

> On the night of July 4 the floor was packed by over 500 people. Three instruments usually furnished the music, a violin, a guitar, and 'bones.' Both "square" and "round" dances are played with emphasis on the square dance. The music is typical hill-billy music . . . plaintive, closely akin to negro music. It was like a page out of an old book, or a reenactment of a saga to hear the music and to see the migrants throw themselves with abandon into the dance. . . . The performance, to one familiar with it, is like a native celebration. The "round" dances have been introduced to urbanize the people.[19]

Lundin connected the work of disciplining these racialized, indigenized, stubbornly rural subjects to the disciplining of Protestant practice when he turned to a discussion—brief but loaded—of a "mendicant" who "slipped into camp unseen" one afternoon and "unsuccessfully attempted to start a meeting." He wrote nothing of the itinerant preacher other than that she was sneaky and a failure. He focused instead on the disciplined way that campers reacted to the presence of this antimodern temptress. "Money that used to be given to the roving mendicants is now being used for clothes and food and other tangibles."

Lundin also described one woman in particular "who had refused to have anything to do with the preacher." Camp manager Tom Collins approached the woman after the evangelist had departed. "She proudly showed him two pairs of silk stockings and some underwear which she had lately bought for herself. Not long back this woman was giving her money to the mendicants in an effort to better her family's lot."[20]

Before her encounter with the government camp, this migrant woman did not understand that round dances were more civilized than square, or that silk stockings, underwear, and food were the surest way to "better her family's lot." Living inside the gate taught her these things, and taught her also to avoid religious beggars who snuck around selling snake oil and trafficking in pre-modern, magical thinking. Camp life was moving her away from performances that were "like a native celebration," that featured tunes "akin to negro music," and that otherwise threatened to trap participants in some arrested state. Camp life set her firmly on a path that elevated ritual consumer practices—the purchase of silk stockings and new underwear—and not only frowned upon "giving . . . money to the mendicants," but told so-called mendicants that they did not belong.

The government camp needed to be more than a palliative, and where Protestantism was concerned, the camp program sought not only to change migrants' definitions of palliation, but to reform their Protestant longings to fit more neatly into modern society.

Protestant Departures

We have seen, so far, the work that the camp program did in its attempt to reform migrants like the woman Arthur Lundin met in the Arvin camp and "her kind." That program of reform met them at the gate and in the camp office, and followed them through a federally-established world, structured to improve them, civilize them, and redeem them.

At this point, though, we are going to follow the "mendicant" whom Lundin encountered, out of the camp and into the Protestant communities that served migrants beyond the gate. Doing so builds a wider sense of the Protestant worlds in agricultural California and illuminates more clearly the work of the camp program vis-à-vis Protestant practice. To achieve what they believed was right and true, managers and administrators had to work on and against people and dynamics over which they exercised little actual control.

The mendicant to whom Arthur Lundin referred in his report of July 1936 did not appear out of thin air. Her challenge to the disciplinary program of the camp was no lark. She slipped into the camp because she knew that she was likely to find an audience there for her preaching. She represented a vibrant, charismatic Protestant culture beyond the gate, leaders of which wanted to draw migrants into their houses of worship and open-air meetings.[21]

This culture expressed multiple antitheses of the disciplined ideal present within the camps. It was ecstatic, not staid; spontaneous, not regulated; divisive and particular, not unifying and general; it was supernatural and often body-centered, not scientific and intellectualized. It argued, too, for an understanding of values and community that placed strong claims on participants, drawing them outside the gate physically for worship, but also and importantly drawing them out of the gate for their sense of community membership and social connection.[22]

This alternative source of meaning and devotion lives in the shadows of the camp program's archives. It appears in the invasive mendicant, in a log entry from the Arvin camp recording a visit from "Rev. Wysong, Travelling [sic] evangelist," in invitations to worship published in the camp paper, and in moments of loss and grief marked by Protestant clergy from outside the gate.[23]

The lack of extended bureaucratic reporting or commentary on these alternative Protestantisms beyond the gate can be read in at least two ways. The first is that they did not fit the reporting template of the camp manager and other staff members, and therefore did not register in their consciousness. There was plenty going on within the gate, plenty of

Apostolic Faith church near Blythe, California, 1936.
Photograph by Dorothea Lange. *Church near Blythe, California*. August 1936. Courtesy of Library of Congress. https://www.loc.gov/item/2017763155/.

Protestant activity for a manager to follow and record without adding unsolicited information to the weekly or monthly reports. The second possible explanation involves a more willful ignorance. Houses of Protestant worship beyond the gate were competitors to the camp program's project of reform. They were also witnesses to the limits of the camp program in achieving its goal of a modernized, socialized, rational, civilized migrant. Best, perhaps, not to acknowledge this challenge and to hope that it would go away.

Fortunately, as we have seen, a University of Southern California PhD student named James Bright Wilson took enough interest in the Protestant lives of agricultural migrants to study them closely. His dissertation, "Religious Leaders, Institutions, and Organizations Among Certain Agricultural Workers in the Central Valley of California," allows us to access the religious environments that existed beyond the reach of camp discipline. It also provides an extended look at how an analyst from an educational and political space similar to that of the camp managers and program administrators made sense of migrants' religious choices.

James Bright Wilson conducted the majority of his field research in the late summer and early fall of 1942. Those months, he wrote, "were spent by the writer in traveling from Marysville to Bakersfield for the purposes of observation and interviewing." He was working during the later stages of the camp program, but his research coincided with a critical annual period for the harvest. July, August, and September cover the "peak" of the "fruit and grape harvest" and the transition to Kern County's massive cotton harvest. It is a busy time in the Sacramento and San Joaquin Valleys, which gave Wilson ample opportunity to talk with agricultural workers, Protestant leaders, government officials, and more settled local residents. In all, Wilson conducted "about five hundred interviews" before returning to Los Angeles to do follow-up interviews, and to write. While still in the field, though, Wilson cast his net widely.

> The time was divided as evenly as possible between auto and trailer camps which are operated by private citizens . . . government camps for agricultural workers, such as the one at Arvin; grower-owned camps . . . and settled communities of agricultural workers which have appeared on the fringes of most valley towns, Olivehurst near Marysville and Airport Community at Modesto, being striking illustrations.[24]

His wanderings also brought him to the Shafter, Woodville, Firebaugh, and Thornton camps, and given the proximity of the Yuba City and Ceres camps to Olivehurst and Hughson—towns in which he observed Pentecostal worship services—it is likely that he visited these camps as well. Even if he did not enter each of them, he certainly encountered hundreds of women and men whose lives had been touched by the camp program.

Wilson's dissertation is not about the government camps per se. Rather, he directed his scholarly eye toward Protestant leaders and institutions, toward the way they interacted with "agricultural workers," and toward the question of Protestantism as social control. In what ways did the Protestant ministries that operated in the Central Valley work on and work with migratory farm workers? How did they draw them in, convince them to keep attending services, get them to believe what they were preaching, and to reach deep into shallow pockets for donations? In pursuit of answers, Wilson talked with women and men who worked inside and outside the government camps. He also talked with those who had observed camp religious life and had a thing or two to say about it.

James Bright Wilson was not, of course, a *tabula rasa*. His background offers some intriguing parallels to the experiences of the migrants among whom he conducted research, as well as some experiences that set him apart from them. Wilson was a relatively recent arrival to California when he began his research. Born in Chattanooga, Tennessee in 1911, he attended Chattanooga Central High School, Tennessee Wesleyan College in Athens, Tennessee, and then Marysville College, just outside of Knoxville. He graduated from Marysville in 1936, but not before spending three years as a Methodist pastor in the Holston Conference of the United Methodist Church, covering eastern Tennessee and adjacent regions of Virginia and Georgia. Wilson then attended seminary at Garrett Biblical Institute in Evanston, Illinois, from which he graduated in 1939, before heading west and beginning work on his PhD at the University of Southern California.[25]

James Bright Wilson was a man on the move, but in contrast to the migrants, his kind of movement was polite, clean, acceptable—a sign of promise and progress rather than of failure and erosion. He was already a highly-educated, credentialed Methodist when he began his graduate studies in sociology and religion. He had pastored churches in western Appalachia, been elected and ordained as a deacon, and gone to one of the Methodist Church's premier seminaries. On the way from Tennessee to California, he also acquired an affinity for the Social Gospel, a type of trans-denominational Protestantism that sought to reform economic and industrial structures and practices, and that took social reform to be the essence of the Christian message.

Wilson had many grounds for critiquing the Protestant messages he heard among the migrants. The absence of a declared Christian solution to the exploitation of agricultural workers and other laborers was a consistent concern of his. This concern and others that he articulated in his dissertation came, I believe, from a place of genuine affection for the migratory farm workers among whom he conducted his research.

Whether or not he felt a close connection to the rural poor, his early life and pastoral experience positioned him well to see goodness in the women and men working on California's industrial farms. Whether or not he had encountered aggressive Protestant competitors in Tennessee, his deep commitment to Methodism likely inclined him to skepticism when faced with religious entrepreneurs, particularly those who focused their efforts on the vulnerable.

While engaged in his fieldwork, Wilson had extended interactions with some of the figures we have already met. He interviewed former manager of the Arvin camp Fred Ross. He interviewed managers Ray Mork, Conrad Reibold, and Milen Dempster. He interviewed Chris and Rheba Ummel, who had become fixtures of the Shafter camp community under the auspices of the Migrant Gospel Fellowship. But few figures in this book loom as large in Wilson's dissertation as Reverend Paul Pietsch, founder and leader of the Migrant Gospel Fellowship. Pietsch occupied Wilson's spotlight for an entire chapter, representing one type of "religious leader" at work in agricultural California.

It is worth spending some time with Wilson's description of Paul Pietsch, not only as a way of backfilling Pietsch's story, but also as a way of demonstrating how James Bright Wilson's gaze operated and how it shaped his project. Wilson told the story of Protestantisms in California's Central Valley, but he told that story from a particular point of view, evaluating various ministries, ministers, and movements against the form of Protestantism—socially-engaged Methodism—that he knew best. Wilson was seldom derisive as he wrote, but he did occasionally abandon scholarly objectivity (or the pretense thereof) to drive home points about good and bad Protestantism. His prose is more subtle in some moments than in others but, on the whole, his leanings are not difficult to discern.

The Reverend Paul Pietsch

The chapter of Wilson's dissertation devoted to Reverend Paul Pietsch and his Migrant Gospel Fellowship opens by noting that Pietsch "has had a varied career."[26] Unlike Wilson, who spent his first three decades in schools and in the ministry, Pietsch had held jobs in radio repair, sales, and law enforcement, while also serving as a Baptist pastor.

Sunday service at the Victory Through Christ Society, Dos Palos, California, 1938. Photograph by Dorothea Lange. *Sunday morning revival of the Victory through Christ Society. Dos Palos, California.* June 1938. Courtesy of Library of Congress. https://www.loc.gov/item/2017770687/.

During a period of service as assistant pastor of First Baptist Church in Riverside, California, Wilson continued, Pietsch developed the idea for a ministry focused on migratory farm laborers.

In 1939, he struck out on his own to launch the Migrant Gospel Fellowship. Pietsch based his operation in Turlock, California, fifteen miles southeast of Modesto, where he found support from the local chapter of the Christian Businessman's Committee. His first foray into migrant ministry focused on the FSA migrant camp at Westley, about twenty-two miles west of Turlock. Reverend Pietsch embodied many traditions of "plain folk" Protestantism. He was a multi-vocational preacher with an entrepreneurial spirit, a cozy relationship with self-described Christian businessmen, and a hard theological edge.[27]

After three years of toil, recruitment, itinerancy, word-of-mouth promotion, and prayer, his Migrant Gospel Fellowship grew to include thirty full-time "workers" in the field, distributed across California, Oregon, and Arizona. Each was supported by donations from churches or private donors. Careful budgeting does not seem to have been a priority for the fellowship. Pietsch explained his approach to Wilson. "Just a few friends keep me in the field. One Sunday School class sends seven dollars per month, another sends five, and I get a little here and a little there. It is strictly a faith work. . . . I've received fifty-six cents from the [migrant] people in two years. We discourage them from giving for they need the money."[28]

But one man's faith work is another man's alarm bell, a fact that Wilson conveyed with a quote from a clergyman in Turlock, who recalled, "When Pietsch first came here I asked him in an open meeting of ministers and Christian businessmen just how he intended to finance his work." When Pietsch responded, "The Lord will provide," the frustrated questioner pointed out that "the Lord provides for the birds but still they have to get out and scratch for it."

In his first pages focused on Paul Pietsch, Wilson situated him among the multi-vocational, the peripatetic, and those with questionable finances. Pietsch had taken an idea and made it into reality. He had convinced thirty other Protestant evangelists to share in his work. But he remained something other than a serious, established minister. Pietsch scratched and clawed and proved that skepticism over his financing was misplaced. He built his ministry and his fellowship without the support of a denomination or a mission board. But this independence meant that he remained reliant upon the generosity of others. He remained, in short, a mendicant.

Wilson described Pietsch and his missionary fellowship as "strict fundamentalist[s]." That this was Pietsch's disposition as well as his doctrinal stance came through as Wilson wrote further that Pietsch gave the impression "that his beliefs alone are correct, and people who disagree or oppose him are anathematized." Not by any stretch an apostle of interfaith understanding, Pietsch reportedly looked at keeping fellowship with a rabbi as an un-Christian act, and was convinced "that only certain churches were Christian and that only these churches should be allowed to work in camps."[29] The struggle in the mission field had multiple fronts for Pietsch. He was fighting to win souls to his fellowship and fighting to defeat illegitimate Protestants. Asked about the relationship of his ministry to broader social and economic issues, Pietsch responded,

> Our Gospel is to the individual based on the Word. We preach Christ and Him crucified. We are not trying to meet the need of these people in any other field, ours is strictly a Scriptural approach. When it comes to labor unions or political questions, we hear no evil, speak no evil, do no evil. . . . We will take care of our own and let the economists work on theirs. We are not trying to tell Uncle Sam how to get the people out of these camps. As long as they are there we will take the Gospel to them.[30]

To do more than preach the Gospel was to run afoul of the Gospel. Pietsch's Migrant Gospel Fellowship was not going to expand its mission or its vision. That was not what true Christians did.

Inside the gate of a federal camp, the Migrant Gospel Fellowship acted in a disciplined fashion. It was more inclusive, systematic, and bureaucratic. Its workers even adopted incentives to encourage camp residents, children especially, in their Protestant education. Wilson recounted that children involved in the Daily Vacation Bible School program run by the Migrant Gospel Fellowship receive "a five dollar Scofield Bible or a week at a Bible Club Camp" if they learn "three hundred and fifty-two verses."

The statistics collected by Chris and Rheba Ummel and their "aides" in the Shafter camp paint an impressive picture of participation. "We enrolled over six hundred children who memorized over six thousand passages of scripture. In the government camp we had an enrollment of two hundred and fifty-seven with an average daily attendance of one hundred and seventy-three. Eighty-seven had a perfect attendance, while twenty-eight missed only one day."[31] Pietsch and his fellow missionaries concluded that "results were not as good" in the absence of these incentives, and so they kept offering them.

In his analysis, Wilson lamented that, rather than cultivate true interest and true knowledge, the missionaries used incentives and rote memorization. "The emphasis appears to be on quantity and not quality of work. . . . An historical perspective with modern interpretations is completely absent. It is apparently assumed that the children know the various shades of meaning which [the] words [sin, sinner, saved, heaven, hell born again, blood of Jesus, etc.] connote."[32]

Pietsch won praise from Wilson for his work among migrant camp residents, particularly his promotion of their financial interests. Wilson related a story from the Shafter camp, where residents had opened a "small cooperative store, fourteen by sixteen feet." Pietsch joined the coop advisory board, which drew the ire of the local business community and led to him and "others connected with the enterprise [being] labeled 'Communists.'" In the face of an attempted boycott of the store, Pietsch stood up to the merchants and pointed out their hypocrisy. "I told [them] that they were always yelling that the poor migrants never tried to help themselves and now they were crabbing about even a feeble effort in that direction. They didn't like it, and along with some church people, were just about ready to chase me out of town."

In spite of this show of support for the migrant's economic independence, Pietsch claimed not to have any aspirations to rescue the migrants from poverty, or to reform the agricultural system that exploited them. While inside the gate, he balanced his desire to connect with and support the migrants against his claim to "preach only Christ and Him crucified."

The Migrant Gospel Fellowship's successes were due in part to the support Pietsch found among camp managers. Conrad Reibold, manager of the Firebaugh camp, described Migrant Gospel Fellowship missionaries to Wilson as "indefatigable workers" who made immediate contact with new arrivals to the camp, and returned frequently for visits. A fellow manager confessed, "Pietsch's workers seem to be doing a pretty good job in our camp. I know they spend more time here than anyone else would."[33] Inside the gate, the contentiousness fell away, the hard edges softened, and bureaucracy blossomed. Though not accomplished statisticians, Migrant Gospel Fellowship workers took pains to track numbers and generate regular reports that testified to their progress.[34]

Wilson admired Pietsch's energy and his work ethic, but he had his concerns as well. The first of these was the extent to which "a fear-reward basis" formed the core of the Fellowship's approach to "teaching and preaching." "Fear of hell if bad habits are continued, lucrative rewards in heaven if a change of life is affected. The future life, either in its good or bad aspects dominates their thinking. Present welfare . . . is largely ignored."[35] The upshot of this other-worldly focus in doctrine and homily was that the Social Gospel had no place in the Migrant Gospel Fellowship and that, true to their word, "the sole purpose of the leaders [was] to win souls." Wilson continued, "The assumption is maintained . . . after the people are 'saved,' the Lord will take care of them."

In addition to the lack of a critique of "the industrial character of California agriculture," Wilson was bothered by the exclusivist stances of Pietsch and his group, their "holier than thou attitude," and their separation from "established churches" and churches with "more liberal views" in the area. This self-segregation was offensive to Wilson on its face. But it was also problematic in terms of the Protestant lives of converts. Raising a concern that dates at least to the 1740s in New England, Wilson wrote, "Since the Fellowship is largely at variance with the established churches, many of their 'converts' never enter the activities of any church. Only those churches which are 'sound' in theology receive consideration, and often such churches are not within reach of the workers . . . the 'born again' drift about at will without pastoral care." Women and men set adrift on the land by circumstances beyond their control were now being set up to live their Protestant lives unmoored as well.[36]

In truth, migrants had little difficulty connecting with Protestant communities that the Migrant Gospel Fellowship deemed sound in camps where the Fellowship was active. The Migrant Gospel Fellowship demonstrated quite an ability to develop long-term relationships in the camps, visiting a camp at least twice a week. How well Pietsch's Fellowship fared outside the gate is harder to know. But their regular presence in the camp says a lot about the discipline of the Migrant Gospel Fellowship. They were out of line theologically with many of the camp managers and with camp program leaders, and their divisive spirit and rigid fundamentalist positions were not exactly the stuff of communal harmony. And yet they were welcome. They related well to the migrants. They focused on worship. And they kept their theological weapons holstered.

In closing his chapter on Reverend Paul Pietsch, Wilson wrote like the scholar cum Methodist deacon that he was. Pietsch deserved praise for what he had built. But what he had built ought not obscure who he was. Paul Pietsch knew how to play nice when it served his interests. In the end, though, he was a troublesome figure. "In theology, in hostility to those holding a different view, in enthusiasm for the work, in appeal to fear and reward, and as a form of social control with those contacted, the members of the Fellowship have some similarities to Pentecostal ministries."[37]

And nobody did undisciplined Protestantism quite like the pentecostals.

Among the Undisciplined

When James Bright Wilson turned his attention to pentecostalism among migrant workers in California, he did so with a mix of fascination and dismay. Some of the admirable qualities of the Migrant Gospel Fellowship were present among the pentecostal leaders, though not as strongly present. The negative qualities of Pietsch and his ministry were among them too, amplified to deafening levels. Wilson devoted a chapter to "The Pentecostal Sects and the Agricultural Workers," combining interviews, observation of worship services, theory, and critical reflection. He had ample material in all of these categories. Pentecostal worship services abounded in agricultural California. And pentecostal leaders and laity were not shy. The only thing they liked as much as speaking in tongues, was speaking about their experiences.

What motivated pentecostals, and why people were drawn to them, were questions that called out to Wilson for theoretical responses. And, of course, alarm at the proliferation of "Pentecostal sects" fueled myriad critiques of their leaders, their theology, and the women and men who allowed themselves to be drawn in.

Before taking his readers into the strange world that his ethnographic observations would describe, Wilson wrote extensively of the history of church-type and sect-type bodies in Christianity, drawing on the theologian and theorist Ernst Troeltsch, and expanded this analysis to churches and sects in the United States. The factors driving the continuing atomization of Protestantism, he argued, included revivalism and the frontier, war and depression, "doctrinal controversies and dynamic leaders."[38]

What Wilson termed "the Pentecostal revival" was thus another manifestation of historical and social dynamics long apparent within Christianity and within American Protestantism. There were, however, distinctive characteristics of the pentecostal revival, aspects that made it remarkable, even unique. Wilson pointed to the drama of their origin story, centered on the Azusa Street revival, and to the pentecostal "pattern" of combining speaking in tongues with faith healing.

He also wrote of the mainstream Protestant concern with the missionary success of pentecostalism. Quoting Elmer T. Clark, who wrote on small sects in the *Christian Advocate* and in a 1937 book *The Small Sects in America*, Wilson alerted his readers. "These sects are increasing constantly. The recent religious census listed fifty-eight denominations that were unheard of ten years ago. They are flourishing in every rural and industrial area, drawing the disinherited poor into their folds by multiplied thousands. The problem of the small sect is becoming home missions problem No. 1."[39] Churches such as the "Apostolic Overcoming Church of God," the "Pentecostal Holiness Church," and the "Pilgrim Holiness Church" reported growth rates ranging from sixty to six hundred percent. Most present to Wilson, though, was the Assemblies of God, which, he wrote, had "witnessed a phenomenal development and is perhaps the most aggressive group among the agricultural workers in the Central Valley."[40]

As he pondered the factors contributing to the growth of these Protestant bodies and their appeal to agricultural workers, Wilson summoned the voices of pentecostal leaders and worshippers themselves. "A large percentage . . . were members of Pentecostal churches in their home states," he wrote, but many others "changed loyalties." "I used to belong to the Baptists, but left them after I got the full light on baptism of the Holy Ghost," said Mrs. Roy Williams of Yuba City. Oma Ellis, a pentecostal evangelist in nearby Marysville, indicated that Mrs. Williams's "full light" shone forth from a profound experience that was deeply appealing to followers. "People from other churches come into our movement because they feel like they get a deeper experience. They get the blessing of God where they had grown cold."[41]

Assemblies of God pastor Donald Weston did not disagree with Oma Ellis or Mrs. Roy Williams, but he—and, in turn, Wilson—noted that

"Gospel Bus" in Kern County, California, 1938.
Photograph by Dorothea Lange. *Sunday morning, Kern County, California. Many Texans, Oklahomans, Arkansans are settling in this country. Their cultures and forms of religious expression are being transferred with them.* November 1938. Courtesy of Library of Congress. https://www.loc.gov/item/2017770790/.

class divisions and local attitudes toward the migrants were powerful forces as well:

> Most of the ones who were loyal Baptists and Methodists in the southwest, upon coming to California, usually drop these ties. If they go to a house of worship it is to a center of people of their own walk [of] life and not to older denominational churches. They feel they are not wanted in

the denominations that nurtured them back home. They say the churches are above them so they practically become outcasts.⁴²

Wilson added that even some Nazarene churches lost migrants to the pentecostal churches "due to [the] higher social and economic status of the Nazarene people." The pentecostal churches pulled migrants in with the experiences they offered, their familiarity, and the communal identity that they created. But migrants were also pushed, as Weston noted, by the haughtiness of more established churches in the Central Valley. Elsewhere in his dissertation, Wilson offered ample evidence that this was the case. He described the half-hearted ministries that some local churches undertook in the camps. "The minister never became part of the people, they came [to the camp] only in time to preach a sermon and left immediately. No minister would be seen again until the following Sunday."⁴³ One Methodist minister working near Olivehurst told Wilson that a church in Marysville "invited me to a service and told me to bring some of these people, but they quickly added, 'Not too many of them.' You see," he explained, "in one breath they gave me an invitation and in the next breath they cancelled it. I didn't go."⁴⁴

Growth and goodness were not the same thing in Wilson's eyes, though, and whether or not Methodists and Presbyterians were arrogant and unwelcoming, the disorder that characterized pentecostalism remained regrettable. Everything from the spaces they occupied, to the qualities of their leaders, to the worship services themselves cast shadows across the pentecostal revival in agricultural California, darkening perceptions of its effect on those swept up in it.

Pentecostalism was a subject of study for James Bright Wilson. It was also, to borrow from Elmer Clark, "problem No. 1." At the root of the problem was the extent to which pentecostalism challenged and shunned modernizing programs, from the way it understood leadership, to its all-encompassing claims on believers; from the financial models on which it operated, to the frenzy of its services, pentecostalism dismissed the architecture of modernity as irrelevant. In the pentecostal view, discipline—other than the obedience required by pentecostal leaders—was a hindrance to righteousness put in place by Satan himself.

Pentecostal Church, Salinas, California, 1939.
Photograph by Dorothea Lange. *Migrants from the Southwest bring their institutions with them. Greenfield, Salinas Valley, California.* April 1939. Courtesy of Library of Congress. https://www.loc.gov/item/2017771859/.

Camp managers had long been aware of the migrants' taste for pentecostal worship, and worked to keep pentecostal ministries out of the camp's practical Protestant mainstream. Wilson encountered this sentiment in interviews with camp managers Milen Dempster and Conrad Reibold, and with former manager Fred Ross. He summarized these conversations: "As a rule, Pentecostal ministers are forbidden to conduct services in government camps due to their noise and excessive length."[45]

In the course of his research, Wilson learned also that camp staff were concerned about the social effects of pentecostalism and the extent to which pentecostal faithful shunned the broader reform effort. "Pentecostal people," Wilson wrote, "will not participate in planned activities such as recreational or educational programs." He then quoted a leader of Modesto's labor movement, R. M. Thompson, who said out loud what camp program officials usually whispered: "We've had some trouble with these holy rollers. They have screwy ideas. Some of them don't want to belong to any organization and will quit their jobs rather than join the union. Their preachers won't let them belong to any organization but their own. That can be a glorified racket."[46] And it wasn't only government camps and labor unions that wanted pentecostals to keep their distance. Wilson noted also that "owners of private camps and ranchers had found them to be a nuisance" and had in some cases forbidden worship entirely rather than risk the disruption.[47]

Pentecostalism was perceived by many to be an undisciplined and disordering faith, incompatible with social order in general and with many local visions of the social order. It required undivided loyalties. It was too physical, too emotional. And it posed specious challenges—but challenges that needed to be answered—to leadership, to credentials, and to authority more broadly.

The undisciplined nature of migrant pentecostalism was evident to Wilson in its leadership, long on charisma and short on education, which used a surplus of the former to malign the latter. As Nettie Lawrence, leader of a house church in Olivehurst, not far from Yuba City and its government camp, told Wilson, "I've never been ordained. Have never conducted a funeral or a wedding. The Lord didn't call me to bury people or marry them. He called me to preach the Gospel."[48]

The fact that Reverend Everett Stewart was preaching at all was proof to the world that something miraculous was at work in his church, or so the Reverend said. At the outset of a revival in Modesto in August of 1942, Stewart told those present that he needed their help.

> I want you good people to pray for me as I attempt to preach. I'm not an educated man. I'm just an old Oklahoma plough boy. I've eat about

as many beans and black-eyed peas and watermelon and rosen ears as anybody. Someone asked me once if I ever had a course for preachers and I told them the only course I ever had was to bury my head in this old book . . . and study. I never went a day beyond eighth grade so if there's preachin' here tonight the Holy Ghost will have to do it.[49]

In his encounters with these and other pentecostal leaders, Wilson discerned a pattern. "Very few Pentecostal ministers advance beyond the elementary school," he explained, and "they frequently take pride in this fact, attributing any superior knowledge which they deem themselves as possessing, to the Holy Ghost." In drawing a tight connection between themselves and the Holy Ghost, they claimed a wide-ranging, un-credentialed, extra-institutional authority. Moreover, they frequently directed this authority against credentials and institutions, depicting both as not only unnecessary, but also as worldly and corrupt. Wilson detected more than a hint of envy in this posture. "It is a tendency to discredit those things which one cannot secure. Since the established churches have high educational standards for those seeking ministerial credentials, many men who cannot qualify enter the ranks of the Pentecostals." Put another way, if pentecostal evangelists were any smarter, they wouldn't be pentecostal evangelists.

Wilson recognized, though, that in emphasizing their limited education and in discrediting trained, credentialed ministers, pentecostal leaders were shoring up a different kind of credential, that of being "one of us" to the migrants, of coming from "home folks" and speaking "the language of the people." Simple dress and simple living bolstered this credential, creating a bond between evangelist and migrant. The effects of this bond concerned Wilson. It was clear that the migrant faithful listened to pentecostal preachers. It was also clear that preachers' messages to the migrants inhibited progress toward better, healthier, more stable lives, that they used their charismatic authority to sow doubt about modern medicine, and to soften up congregants for financial exploitation.

The healing dimension of the pentecostal message was a significant source of concern for Wilson. As we have seen, camp staff worried about the introduction and spread of contagious diseases inside the camp by those who adopted the pentecostal position that prayer and faith were the only healing tools a Christian needed. For their part, some migrants were concerned that to choose life in the camp was to choose a compromised version of their pentecostal faith. Wilson confirmed that he found "many instances in which Pentecostal devotees have refused the services of a physician," choosing instead to rely on the supernatural.

Reverend C. B. Sanderson, leader of a pentecostal congregation in Olivehurst, described the stakes involved in making this choice. "We don't need to go to a doctor. To go see one of them shows people ain't got faith in God. . . . God is our great physician. He can heal. I was healed of tonsillitis while I was preachin' a sermon one night. Healed instantaneous."[50] Reverend Sanderson's belief was no outlier. Mary Edgar of Modesto testified to Wilson, "I've been healed by the power of God more times than I could tell. Two years ago I was healed of internal cancer. I didn't do anything but pray and trust God. If I'd done anything else I might not have been cured." She added by way of conclusion, "It was wonderful." Modern medicine wasn't only the wrong way to achieve healing. In the pentecostal world, it was a marker of insufficient faith.[51]

Wilson was also bothered by the practice of tithing, which he believed to be harmful to the migrants' financial health. In his experience attending pentecostal worship services, he learned that tithing was pentecostal leaders' preferred way of funding their ministries, and was treated by nearly every preacher as a sign of true righteousness. "Tithing is a frequent theme of Pentecostal ministers, often entire sermons being devoted to it. . . . The people are encouraged to tithe in order to be 'one hundred percent Christians,' 'to get the full blessing,' 'to set an example to the sinners,' 'to be square with God so He will prosper you.' . . . All the arts of oratory and salesmanship are employed to break down resistances, to build up favorable thinking and feeling within the hearers."[52] The ministers who discussed tithing with Wilson made their position clear.

> I don't like to be on a salary basis. A man who has a set salary has nothing to look forward to. Whereas fer me, every time I git a new person comin' [steady] and givin' that means more fer me. It gives me a feelin' that I should work harder. The more people tithin', the more I git. I like it that way.[53]

Another spoke of tithing in a more theological register, "We believe it and we preach it. Can't have the victory in your soul without it. If you take part of the Bible, you've got to take all of it." The "mendicants" may have struggled to find a foothold in the RA/FSA camps, but in Wilson's view they were filling their coffers outside the gate while also working to shift migrants' values away from material wealth toward spiritual riches. Pentecostal leaders often demanded the former and were more than happy to promise the latter.[54]

Wilson found pentecostal leaders and the faithful eager to invert the values that they saw around them and to argue that poverty in this world meant little compared to eternal wealth in the next. The faithful, he wrote, "are comfortingly told" that they should "patiently endure" and that "deliverance from this vale of tears will some day arrive." One worshipper told Wilson, "It ain't what's in this life, it's what we are goin' to do in the next life that counts. I'm waitin' for that."[55] A woman whom Wilson interviewed in Hughson, not far from the federal migrant camp at Ceres, recounted a more visceral reaction when she encountered fellow migrants who did not share her disdain for the things of this world. She was in the sewing room of the Ceres camp, along with a number of others.

> Most of the women wasn't holiness women and had on paint and powder and short sleeves. My arms would hurt from just lookin' at them. I had to tell them about it, testify. That's the way the Lord used me. They said they couldn't see how it would make my arms hurt just watchin' them.... The Lord didn't teach in his Word fer us to use lipstick and rouge and finger nail polish. That's all of the devil.[56]

Mrs. Casey concluded, "You don't see full consecrated people wear stuff either." In Wilson's eyes this restructuring of values and desires was disingenuous. "Self denial usually has to do with things naturally desired, but which are beyond attainment." Others, Wilson wrote, called this "a slave morality."[57] This racializing characterization, and the insinuation that the pentecostal faithful surrendered their freedom as no (white) American should, obscures another transgression against the camp program. Mrs. Casey claimed to have used an informal gathering in the camp's sewing room for the purpose of evangelizing her camp neighbors. Prompted by "the Lord," she told those who had gotten dressed that morning and put on some make-up that those acts were sinful and that they were in the thrall of the devil. This sort of undisciplined behavior confirmed suspicions—Wilson's and the camp staff's—about the problems pentecostals caused in community.

As critical as Wilson's view of pentecostal thinking about leadership, medicine, and money was, his view of pentecostal worship was just as harsh. The irrationality and the impulsiveness that offended his sensibilities when he considered pentecostal approaches to modernity found their source in the chaotic, delirious, uncivilized performances that masqueraded as worship services.

Wilson based his analysis of pentecostal worship on observations in numerous churches, most notably the Pentecostal Holiness Church in Olivehurst, the Pentecostal Church and the Jesus Name Only Pentecostal Church, both in Modesto, and the Full Gospel Mission in Hughson. These were all venues for "emotionally-charged" services, as opposed to the more staid worship services that characterized the Assemblies of God. The former, Wilson described as "marked by wild frenzy from beginning to end"; the latter he called "semi-formal."

Not surprisingly, he believed that the "motive back of the entire [pentecostal] service is to get people aroused" and noted that "appeal is never made to the intellect." Repetitive music, fervent prayer and testimony, a minister who "harangues his hearers with great vigor for an hour or more," and physical manifestations such as "jerks" and "tongues" were the notable features of these services, "the regular religious 'diet' of many agricultural workers."

To Wilson's credit, he recorded quite a few specifics of the service at the Pentecostal Holiness Church in Olivehurst, allowing the humanity of the worshippers onto the pages of his dissertation. He quoted directly from prayer requests and testimonies that poured forth on a "hot Saturday evening in July." Some were brief eruptions. Others were longer and more scripted.

MAN: Pray for all who are unsaved. Pray for me.
MAN: Pray for my boy who has to be driving all day tomorrow. Pray that God will drive the wheel.

WOMAN: My sons are backsliders. Let's pray for them.

WOMAN: I'm glad I'm saved, sanctified, and have the Holy Ghost. I feel tonite like pressin' on. I want your prayers tonite that I may serve God. You can't please people. I've quit tryin' to do that. I want to please God.

WOMAN: I wouldn't exchange what I've got in my soul for anything in this old world. I've got peace in my soul.

MAN: I want the love of God in my heart to move on closer. I need your prayers.[58]

Wilson then described a guitar player, a woman, leading the hymn singing, and providing vocal cues and stimulation to those gathered. "The guitar player began another chorus which told about 'the glory of the Lord comin' down,'" he wrote, "She said, 'If you believe the glory of the Lord is comin' down don't sit out there like you are dried up. Amen.'"

Up to this point, the worship service, though certainly more interactive than Wilson preferred personally, was legible, even sympathetic. A congregation gathered to express their vulnerabilities, to pray for strength, and to give thanks for blessings. The music, informal as it was, established a mood. The song leader leaned on people to participate. It was a common scene. But religious chaos and a rupture of understanding between observer and observed were just a shout away.

After the prayer and testimony came to an end "the leader asked the congregation to stand and raise their arms over their heads. All talked in unison and were quite incoherent."[59] It was then that two more women carried the Pentecostal Holiness Church of Olivehurst into the next phase of worship with preaching and exhortation. The first was Sister Hazel, whom Wilson described as "approximately thirty years of age, fat, and neatly dressed." She took the "sixth chapter of the book of Jeremiah" as her text and began her portion of the service by "pray[ing] loudly and fervently that sinners might be saved." Sister Hazel preached,

> Sinners do you know you are nearer to facin' your Creator now than you were a year ago? He says over there in the Bible, "Come unto me all ye that are weary and heavy laden and I will give you rest." I tell you tonight

it pays to stand in the old paths. It may be called old fashioned, but it will git you into heaven. If you walk in the broad way you will land in hell.

A second woman, whom Wilson did not name, picked up the message from there and gave embodied evidence of its truth.

> Let us all say tonight "I will bear my cross until he sets me free." I feel the power of God from the top of my head to the bottom of my feet. Glory to Jesus. [She broke out in tongues]. Let us follow the message Sister Hazel gave us tonight and it will lead us to glory. Thank God, the old time Gospel is still good. I am not ashamed to walk in the old paths.

Wilson reported that the woman "talked in tongues again in the midst of loud screaming on the part of all," and that when she wasn't speaking in tongues, she "constantly shouted, 'Glory to God. Hallelujah.'"[60] Not long after, another woman "stood in the aisle with raised hands saying, 'Bless the holy name of Jesus. She spoke in tongues and presently, a man did likewise." By the time worshippers filed out at 10:55 pm—following a brief attempt at a faith healing—the service had become far less legible, its participants far less sympathetic. Pentecostal services could begin normally enough, but they quickly ran off the rails.

Though he gave prominent place to the service in Olivehurst, Wilson also recorded scenes from "Pentecostal services which were even more emotional" in other Central Valley towns. These included a service run by Pastor Ernest Adams of the Pentecostal Church in Modesto, who preached, "A lot of the world thinks we're crazy. They can't understand what we are doin'. Bless the Lord we are not crazy, we have the real thing," and a "rotund woman" testifying at the Jesus Name Only Pentecostal Church in Modesto, "If you want to git a thrill, git the Holy Ghost and quit goin' to shows and dances. Glory to God." As he watched this Jesus Name Only service come to a close, "a lively chorus was repeated many times while people danced, shouted, spoke in tongues . . . [and] a man stood with outstretched arms giving violent jerks for fifteen minutes."

At the Full Gospel Mission in Hughson, Wilson wrote, a "visiting minister" who was "a carpenter by trade" and was helping to lead a revival "many times . . . departed from his discourse giving vent to a flow of incoherent words of a deep guttural nature, accompanied by jerking of his body" and spent another five minutes saying only "Praise the Lord, Glory to God. Amen. Hallelujah." The pastor of the Full Gospel Mission, Clarence Muston, punctuated another service by exclaiming, "Them mansions in the sky is what we are livin' fer, ain't it?"[61]

In summarizing what he described as a "typical Pentecostal service," Wilson listed several elements: "informality, congregational participation, appeal to the emotions, Biblical allusions, use of figurative language, warning to sinners, indication of rewards to Christians, references to being slandered by 'outsiders,' use of simple language, securing attention by being loud, repetition of the familiar, belief in the controlling power of God, manifestations of faith in divine healing, its length, and the like."[62] But what Wilson the sociologist saw as arguably the most important characteristic was the creation and perpetuation of a sense of counter-community, the "recognition on the part of these religionists that the average person views them as being peculiar." He wrote further, "they make capital of this fact, it being used as a source of pride, and . . . doubtless a means of securing attention."[63]

Pentecostals were not wrong. People, including many within the camp system, found them peculiar. Some residents of Central Valley communities said pentecostal churches were better described as "crazy house[s]"; one called them "just plain goofy" and compared them unfavorably to "Negro churches back home" whose members "were not as crazy as these people." One local observer commented, "People in Africa jump and carry on like this." Another, upon observing a pentecostal worship service said, "They were all standing and shouting like wild Indians."[64] The words "crazy" and "goofy" came from observers other than Wilson, but he did not disagree.

Toward the end of his analysis of pentecostalism among the migrants, he wrote, "There are certain similarities . . . between the experiences of the mentally ill and the phenomena of pentecostal religion," later adding that because of the communities pentecostals formed "the disordered state of the mentally ill is . . . usually avoided."[65] This concession from Wilson, that pentecostals weren't always nuts, is an all-but-transparent cover for his feeling, shared by many around him and in California's agricultural interior, that pentecostal teachings and practices were dangerous and degenerative, that their Protestantism was not the good

Protestantism that balanced, sane, responsible, white Americans ought to embrace. In many, if not all of its manifestations, pentecostalism served as a form of social control, inhibiting freedoms, slowing progress, and undermining much-needed programs of reform.

James Bright Wilson was an academic, a reformer, and an optimist. There is no question that he saw pentecostalism as disordered, exploitative, and wrong. Yet it is also clear that he saw it as a problem that could be solved. From what he had seen, pentecostalism took hold among the poor, the "emotionally starved," and the overly mobile. The key to pulling souls out of this miasma of deception, division, and prophetic foolishness was to shore up their financial situation, settle them down, and situate them in meaningful, durable communities. Some of this was already happening as pentecostal "sects" matured into pentecostal "denominations."[66] But without systemic changes to the world that kept punishing the poor for their poverty, the "economically disinherited" would continue to seek out these degenerate Protestant "refuges of the poor."[67] Wilson explained,

> The life of the agricultural workers is . . . drab and monotonous. At the close of day or on week-ends, many of them are ready for some sort of emotional excitement—drunkenness, hair-raising movies, or thrills in a religious service. Their diversions, including their form of religions expression, sustains a close correlation to the social and economic environment in which they live. In turn, by diverting attention from these conditions, their religion tends indirectly to sanction. A more refined expression of the emotions through better movies, travel, reading, concerts, and the like is beyond their reach. But psychological release can be had through "rousements" of various kinds: shouting "Amen," "Praise the Lord," and "Hallelujah." Two or three hours of sustained enthusiasm brings about a state of physical relaxation. In short, religion becomes a way of escape.

Safety valves for pent-up emotion and frustration, being shared among a large group of migrants, fostered a "consciousness of community," and a "we-feeling," which in turn enhanced the migrant's "sense of personal significance." The lesson that migrants took from the experience of pentecostal worship was that "they count," that "God has chosen them."[68] If, however, "more refined expression of the emotions" or some better form of recreation were within the migrants' reach, perhaps this whole house of cards built by charlatans and carnival barkers would blow down and be carried away on the winds of modernity.

* * *

James Bright Wilson's perspective, both as scholar and as progressive clergy member, clearly shaped the data he recorded and the way he presented it. The information that he gathered and wrote on is of great value, to be sure. It captures voices—Oma Ellis, Nettie Lawrence, Clarence Muston—that would otherwise have become inaudible. It is, at the same time, sculpted to make a point and to feed a narrative of cultural and religious superiority.

Wilson undertook a study of religious leaders and institutions among "certain agricultural workers" in California's Central Valley. He defined his study strictly and deliberately. He had regular interactions with camp managers, staff, and residents. But he did not think of them as part of a system, much less as belonging to the category of "religious leaders and institutions." Wilson's definition of religion was broader than most. He considered it a Christian calling to work for industrial reform and to support the cause of workers. But he did not think of the work New Deal reformers undertook in the camps as religious. And it would be unfair to expect him to make such a connection.

Some sociologically-minded scholars had been thinking about actions, attitudes, and institutions outside of the ecclesiastical as related to or manifestations of the religious (neither Emile Durkheim nor Max Weber appear in Wilson's footnotes), but Wilson was very much of his era in considering churches—mostly Protestant churches—as the site of religion, and every space that was not a church as a space of and for the secular.

Yet on closer examination of Wilson's work, descriptions, and critiques, and of the work of the federal migrant camps, this "church" vs. "not a church" dichotomy becomes harder to sustain. Indeed, sticking to it as devoutly as Wilson did obscured some instructive and perhaps uncomfortable parallels. Recall that Wilson praised Paul Pietsch and the Migrant Gospel Fellowship for being present, dedicated, and accessible to camp residents, and at the same time developed a full-throated critique of their approach to religious education and of their attempts to control the behavior of their followers. Their approach to discipline, he concluded, was rooted in fear. Believe differently and you will be cut off from the fellowship. Die outside the fellowship and you will be damned. In the view of the Migrant Gospel Fellowship, properly disciplined Christians believed and lived by the official statement of faith and did not deviate.

Wilson was also put off by the Fellowship's use of incentives to convince children to learn Bible verses. If they did as they were told and studied and learned, they would receive rewards (a new Bible, a trip to a Bible camp) otherwise beyond their reach. Migrant Gospel Fellowship workers swore by these methods. They generated results. But Wilson worried that children were attending and learning not for the love of Protestantism, but in order to get rewards. Pentecostals were equally committed to a vision of community that required certain beliefs and practices. They were no strangers to the use of fear and incentive to steer the faithful toward proper actions and attitudes.

Camp managers working within the migrant camp system used the promise of community, stability, and cleanliness to bring the lost and the wandering into their camps. They used incentives—contests, prizes, status, the promise of a better house—to encourage migrants to learn modern ways, interact with modern technologies, and accept the burdens of a modern civil society. And when those incentives were not enough, when migrants who had signed their name to a "revocable camp permit" violated the rules of the camp and showed themselves to be undisciplined, they used ostracism and eviction to cast them out.

In his critiques of the Migrant Gospel Fellowship and of "the Pentecostal revival," Wilson noted repeatedly and disapprovingly their use of Protestantism for social control and called into question the permanence of gains won through manipulation. For their part, Ray Mork and many other camp managers were happy to have the Migrant Gospel Fellowship around. Under Mork's tenure as camp manager at Shafter, first Paul Pietsch and then Chris Ummel were allowed to call themselves "camp pastor" and to use the camp newspaper to promote their ministries. First Pietsch and then the Ummels provided clerical oversight of the camp's annual Christmas service. Mork may well have seen the Migrant Gospel Fellowship as fellow travelers of a sort, emphasizing saving work, deploying incentives strategically, speaking regularly of the wages of sin. Both were committed to working among the migrants and both were committed to the idea that the path to redemption was precise and demanding.

Mork and many others working within the camp system showed their theological cards even more in their active discouragement of pentecostalism in the camps. James Bright Wilson wrote this critique and his support of it into his dissertation. The camps gave that critique an architecture, a space. Camp residents were a people apart, but their apartness consisted in a commitment to a structured, ordered, social life in a world that worked relentlessly to deny them that right.

The spirit that moved through the camp, holy or not, was a civic spirit, a domestic spirit, a modern spirit. Touched by that spirit, people who had been dirty and unsanitary cleaned their bodies and used flush toilets. Touched by that spirit, people who had lived under branches and tarps and disintegrating cardboard set up tents on wooden platforms, kept their space clean, and aspired to something more. Touched by that spirit, people gathered to govern, to dance, to listen to each other play music, to play baseball, and to attend church. Touched by that spirit, migrants helped one another to eat, to heal, to mourn. This spirit moved those who accepted it to turn from those who disrupted this vision of community and to be suspicious of those who, like the pentecostals, found belonging through another spirit.

The federal camp system reflected the humanitarian concerns of a number of New Deal reformers. Harry Drobish and Irving Wood, Paul Taylor and Omer Mills, Rexford Tugwell and Jonathan Garst, Tom Collins, Fred Ross, and Ray Mork. Camp staff, from Millie Delp and Mary Sears to Opal Butts and Roy Carter, worked at the intersection of humanitarian impulse and human desperation, bringing a vision of intervention and redemption to life.

We could look at their work and the efforts of hundreds of others, admire it, and write it into history without regard for its religious dimensions. We could watch the individual migrants and the migrant families leaving through the camp gate and see the simple exhale of a transient community. But not all who left the camp did so for the same reasons. Not all left with reputations and prospects intact. Some had transgressed, been judged and forced out. Some had to leave, albeit temporarily, to pursue a form of Protestantism judged by camp managers

Collins and Eddy, Mork and Ross, Dempster and Reibold, to be undisciplined, destabilizing, and a threat to the community.

The combination of humanitarianism and exclusion, uplift and condescension, has a long history in North American Christianity, both in explicitly Christian missionary contexts and in putatively secular reeducation and assimilation programs sponsored by the federal government. The RA/FSA migratory farm labor camps were a combination of these, as is often the case in humanitarian efforts that cross cultural and religious boundaries. Their efforts to be "more than palliative" began and sometimes ended with the belief that the migrants were a decent but backward people desperately in need of modernization. Camp managers and staff, and bureaucrats within the camp program hierarchy, did not question the assumption that the people who needed their help were in some way—in many ways—flawed. They became committed evangelists for modernity, strongly encouraging and, at times, demanding conformity to their lived ideals. Some reformers were more subtle than others, but all had the same end in mind: a remade, civilized migrant; a proper, disciplined, white American.

It is not surprising that camp managers had profound concerns about pentecostalism among the migrants and sought to keep it on the other side of the gate. Many observers before them worried about the effect of the revivalistic "frenzy" on social order and on the psychological well-being of participants. Pentecostals' theological and ritual innovations only increased these concerns about instability, sexual energy, and exploitation. Wilson gave voice to these concerns repeatedly in his dissertation. They dot the archives of the camp program as well.

Christian missionary work in North America has frequently occurred across the imagined lines of race, with European-descended Protestants and Catholics reaching out and, in their eyes, *down* to help, to lift up, to educate. The absence of a firm color line between missionaries and the missionized in the migrant camps might have raised camp managers' expectations as to what they could achieve, but at the same time it amplified concerns in the face of missionary failures of all types. When camp residents were slow to embrace modern hygiene, domestic order, or round dances over square dances, racializing rhetoric was never far behind. "Negro music," "native celebrations," and other non-white activities afflicted these people and limited their advancement; slave morality and superstition kept them in thrall, unable to ascend quickly to modern, American whiteness. Protestantism wrongly imagined and applied could clearly have this effect too, while also raising questions about the whiteness of its practitioners.

Whether reducing them to "wild Indian" shouts and "African" jumping and carrying on, convincing them that invisible powers could heal them, or conning them out of their hard-earned pay, pentecostalism both hindered and undid reform. The gate created a boundary of discipline for Protestant practice. Those who crossed it to worship outside the camp on Sundays, or on any other day, raised questions, at least among the reformers, about the strength of their grip on modernity.

So, why did they go? Why did some migrants turn their backs on the disciplined Protestantism of the camp and give bodily expression to their dissent? James Bright Wilson thought of the migrants' pursuit of Pentecostalism as a "means of escape." He was writing in a generally Marxist register and thinking of those undisciplined services he observed as fantasy spaces, spaces cordoned off from the real world and populated by people fleeing its hard economic and social truths. Rather than remain in the realm of reality and work on solutions to society's problems, they pushed through a gate and into a world that allowed them to think either that problems were not problems, or that natural problems had supernatural solutions ("I was healed of tonsillitis.... Healed instantaneous.").

This was a gate that most camp staff would have locked if they could have. When migrants and camp residents entered these alternate worlds, they heard and believed messages that hurt them, that stalled their progress. When pentecostal leaders pushed their way through the gate and into the camp, they sowed division, disturbed peace, and took money that destitute migrants needed to nourish themselves and their families. Pentecostalism was, to Wilson, to Collins, to Mork, a distraction, a racket, an opiate.

Wilson was likely correct that migrants were drawn to pentecostal communities as an escape, that passing through the camp gate and through the doors of the Pentecostal Holiness Mission led them away from the harsh realities of California agriculture. But passing through the camp gate and connecting with a pentecostal fellowship was not only an escape from reality. It was also an escape from the government camp.

For all of the material stability and access to modern facilities that the camps provided, they also traded heavily in social, cultural, and religious norms, and used a range of mechanisms for social control. They were animated by the assumption that many migrants were an inferior type: simple, gullible, childlike, and that camp staff were well positioned to educate, elevate, and civilize them.

The message of pentecostal worship, as Wilson inadvertently demonstrated, was quite different. To the extent that it emphasized brokenness, it emphasized a shared brokenness. To the extent that it emphasized social order, it reminded worshippers that the last could be first. To the extent that it emphasized community, it was a community given life through ecstatic worship and otherworldly experiences rather than a relentless focus on order, on dirt, and on the body.

Passing through the gate and leaving the camp could indeed be an escape, and perhaps it involved some degree of magical thinking. But it was also and importantly a flight from a community that required forms of discipline at odds with pentecostal practice. From the pentecostal perspective, the gate was a marker, as Mork intended it to be, between the saved and the damned. But, contra Ray Mork, the saved were the ones turning their backs on camp discipline, embracing pentecostal counter-community, and spending a few hours not trying to "please people" but instead trying to "please God."

Migrant worshippers found, in pentecostal gathering places, spaces where they could speak and be heard, where they were not treated as outsiders and projects. They also found an affective experience that fulfilled in a world that deprived and deprived, and then deprived some more. Describing the feeling associated with speaking in tongues and its various manifestations in her family, Mrs. Casey—whose arms had begun to hurt while looking at women in short sleeves in the Ceres camp sewing room—told Wilson:

> When you git the Holy Ghost you jist commence rollin' and stirrin' inside. You jist feel glad all over, you shore do. When you git to feelin' that way you know you've got somethin' you can't give up and you want to tell the world about it. It's real, praise God, I know it's real.
>
> Every one of my girls has been filled with the Holy Ghost. Gloretta is nine. She got stammerin' lips but never did speak in tongues plain. Her

lips would move and her tongue too but I reckon she never did git fur enough along so the Lord could speak to her clear, or else she didn't git yielded to Him.

My oldest girl is thirty-three. She got the baptism fourteen years ago. Her husband and all his folks kind of pulled agin her. She had an awful hard time.... She just growed cold, let the devil cheat her out of the blessin'.... They come out here from Texas two years ago and since then got a re-fillin' right in her own home. Her husband was filled at Turlock the other night. He spoke in tongues fer an hour and fifty-five minutes.[69]

Was she deluded? Had she been taken for a ride? Or was she expressing a wisdom that comes from the experience of losing everything? Did she have to be a fool to call these feelings real and to rejoice when her children reaffirmed them? Or was she actually pursuing valuables that she believed this world could not repossess or reduce to dust?

It was, in the end, possible for people like Mrs. Casey to live inside the gate when it came to domestic and sanitary arrangements, and simultaneously to look outside of it for ultimate meaning. And it was understandable, for those who wanted to understand, that a displaced people would be skeptical of belief systems that directed them to embrace a world into which they poured so much, and that gave so little back.

Epilogue

The Camp, Reimagined

Migratory farm labor camps were spaces of transition and movement, comings and goings. Residents stayed for as long as the work would sustain them, and then moved on. Staff joined a camp and then left or got transferred. New structures were built. Old ones were renovated or removed. Change was a part of camp life.

In November of 1942, Warren Engstrand's time as manager of the Brawley camp came to an end. Devoted manager and diligent record keeper that he was, Engstrand took time in his final days to write a narrative report for the month of November. There was quite a bit about his report that was conventional for the genre and the season. He noted that planning was underway for the camp's annual Christmas celebration. Local religious groups had offered their support for the party. Each child in camp would receive "a small present." The camp council, as usual, was doing the bulk of the planning. Engstrand also noted that some camp residents were contemplating "slight revisions to the Constitution" and that "wages for row crop labor [had been] set at 50 cents per hour at a hearing the early part of the month." He added that fifty cents per hour was "considerably lower than the prevailing wage in the San Joaquin Valley."

These sentences could have been lifted from any November report since the Brawley camp opened in 1937. Engstrand's words speak to the rhythms of time and longing, to the liturgical pattern of camp life.

The rest of his report, however, narrates quickly-advancing changes. "The Community has had a variable but rather large amount of Mexican workers resident since November 21," he wrote. "They appear to be accommodating themselves very well. We have provided a cooking and heating stove for each tent house. In addition, each tent house is equipped with one double bed and one single bed sufficient for three occupants." Engstrand noted that the Mexican camp residents had been cold the first few nights, but that with more straw for their mattresses and more blankets to cover them, the situation was sure to improve.

The Bracero Program, established through an agreement between Mexico and the United States in the spring of 1942, brought mostly young, mostly single men to the United States to provide agricultural labor. Though it was a national program, its largest impact was in California. Within California, its largest impact was in the Imperial Valley.

The influx of braceros was, as Engstrand wrote, transforming the Brawley camp. Tent platforms once used to house white families were being reconfigured for groups of single Mexican men. The camp, once run for white migrants was now, he reported, turning them away to make room for the newly contracted work force. He did not want to minimize "the great importance" of the Bracero Program, but Engstrand also wondered if "preserving a portion of our original mission to provide housing for domestic agricultural workers" might be possible. And he worried both about the "hardship" that would result if the Brawley camp were designated "exclusively for Mexican labor" and the "unpleasant feeling of being discriminated against" that would develop among the white workers being kept out.

Warren Engstrand concluded his final report as manager of the Brawley camp by writing about spaces and sanitation. "In a very practical sense, on the other hand, we must calculate the problems that would inevitably arise from close association of single Mexicans and American families. Likewise, there would only be one utility building for all." He closed with an update, "The water shortage has been corrected."[1]

The next report from Brawley, penned by Engstrand's successor Glen Trimble, noted that the camp now consisted of "two largely separate communities," one made up of an unspecified number of white residents, the other comprising "150 Mexican Nationals" brought in under the Farm Labor Transportation Program. According to Trimble, the Mexican contingent was already organizing for self-government and had been "of considerable help in dealing with the sanitary and disciplinary problems."

They were also making good use of the community center, crowding in for "an extensive educational program" consisting of two classes taught in Spanish four times per week, and gathering for "three

Spanish-talkie films" obtained by Trimble from the Motion Picture Society of the Americas. Most evenings there were "tables and chairs" in the community center "for reading and letter writing." The braceros also interacted with local churches to plan a Christmas celebration.[2]

The changing demographics of the Brawley camp were tied to the changing demographics of the agricultural work force, which were tied to labor shortages, which were tied to the world war. Many white migratory farm workers followed long-thwarted dreams of prosperity out of the fields, out of the camps, and into the military-industrial complex. Developing concerns about a lack of farm labor led the US government to look toward Mexico and to establish the contract labor program that would provide nearly two decades worth of answers to the question on the mind of every California grower: Who is going to harvest my crops?

The braceros, like the white migrants before them, encountered concerns about their level of civilization and their embrace of the modern. Historian Deborah Cohen writes, "the [bracero] program not only had modernization as an explicit goal rather than an incidental outcome, which both [the United States and Mexico] supported; this modernization was built around human transformation through migration." Signing up to leave Mexico and work in the United States, "the quintessential place of the modern," meant that one was also, in theory at least, signing up to be "transformed" into a modern subject.

In some cases, the braceros encountered architectures, like those of the Brawley camp, built with conversions to modernity in mind. Cohen explains that the nature and the configuration of the spaces these men occupied shaped the ways that they saw themselves as Mexicans, as men, and as workers. She observes further that some camp managers, perhaps Warren Engstrand and Glen Trimble, took it as their mission to instill in the Mexican men new bodily sensibilities and new social patterns. One bracero camp manager noted that newly-arrived residents showered "once a week" at most, but "after a man had been here [for a while], he insists on having his shower every day."[3] Whether this embrace of one ritual of modern hygiene was enough to establish the bracero body as "clean" in the eyes of white California, it seemed to some observers to be a sign of progress.

Not every RA/FSA camp became a space of shelter, sanitation, and community for the braceros. Some were sold to private buyers. Some reverted to local government control. Others were knocked down. Beginning in 1942, the Farm Security Administration's end-of-year report shifted its coverage of the migrant camp program from its role in improving the lives of migrants to "the "liquidation of resettlement projects" and the transfer of "all nonfarm projects . . . to the Federal Public Housing Authority."[4] In most cases, this marked the end of the RA/FSA camp program.

But federal involvement with camp spaces and their logic of gathering, missionizing, and even redeeming continued. For Dust Bowl migrants who were not content to serve in "the agricultural army," federal migrant camps gave way to military training camps. Eligible and physically-fit migrants moved from Arvin, Brawley, Indio, and Shafter to military installations across the country. In these camps, they encountered an indoctrination and catechesis more explicit, rigid, and intense than anything that confronted them inside the migrant camp gate. These camps demanded a different kind of conversion. They spoke of rank and routine, of obedience and duty, of subordinating individual identities and aspirations to the collective need. They sought to impart what one Imperial Valley radio program called a "rock-ribbed faith" that the nation was worth serving and the war was worth fighting.[5]

For Americans who looked too much like the enemy in the Pacific, those of Japanese descent, government camps also loomed large in the war years. Though longer established on the land than the Dust Bowl refugees, Japanese Americans found themselves stripped of their belongings and their rights and detained in internment camps in the name of national security. These spaces spoke to those who lived in them of the precariousness of belonging in America, the ways that ancestry, ethnicity, and religion could be weaponized, and the power of the federal government to set the terms of citizenship.[6] They offered Japanese Americans a coerced redemption, which required enduring multiple injustices as a demonstration of loyalty.

Each of these camps spoke to those who lived in and around them of American essentials, American values, American community. In doing this, each camp also sent messages about the deficiencies of its residents vis-a-vis an American ideal and what, if anything, they could do to improve themselves. These are important messages for historians of religion in America to think about, whether in colonial New England, the Oklahoma Territory, Depression-era California, Guantanamo Bay, Cuba, or Texas's Rio Grande Valley. They are especially important messages for scholars interested in those who left a comparatively light imprint in the written record. What did America want then, and what does it want now, from these men, women, and children? What do their interactions with the structures around them tell us about their religious lives and their faith in America?

The spaces that people inhabited, the forces that made themselves felt through those spaces, and the ways that people rethought and rechoreographed their lives in response, expose important truths about how religion and secularism are constructed in and through modern life. Given the number of times in the history of North America that civil and ecclesiastical powers have gathered people in enclosed communities for observation, instruction, conversion, and control, we do well to think carefully about government camps and other spatial assertions of righteousness, and to work to connect them and the voices of those who experienced them to the stories of America's religion as imagined, constructed, and lived.

ACKNOWLEDGMENTS

There were moments in the past twelve years when I wondered if I would finish this book. There were moments when I was sure that I couldn't.

The fact that it is now as done as any book ever is, is testament to the value of listening to the people who encourage you, letting a project change if it needs to, and just putting one foot in front of the other, or, more appropriately, one word after another.

The beauty of a project that spans so many years is that it has been helped along by so many people and institutions. The latter include the University of Illinois, Urbana-Champaign, my professional home since 2005, and the many centers and institutes on its beautiful campus that have facilitated my work. These include the Center for Advanced Study; the Humanities Research Institute; the Office of the Vice Chancellor for Research and Innovation; the Campus Research Board; the History, Philosophy, and Newspaper Library; and the School of Literatures, Cultures, and Linguistics. I am especially grateful to Masumi Iriye, Antoinette Burton, Craig Koslofsky, Maria Gillombardo, Carol Symes, Celestina Savonius-Wroth, Antony Augoustakis, and Elena Delgado, for their generosity and support.

I would also like to thank the John Simon Guggenheim Foundation, the Louisville Institute, and the Young Scholars in American Religion program at IUPUI for their fellowship awards and diverse ways that each supported this project. All three provided me with time to think about and to work on this book. All three also provided validation that this idea had merit, which was, at different times and for different reasons, the bit of fuel that kept it moving forward. I hope that I have created something worthy of the creative traditions that each institution has curated so well over the years.

I could not have done any of this without the help of the excellent people at the Bancroft Library at the University of California, Berkeley; and the National Archives and Records Administration, Pacific Region, in San Bruno, California. Early research trips to look through archives at Sonoma State University and Fuller Theological Seminary, though less central to the final project, were nevertheless generative and made pleasant by helpful librarians and archivists. I have also had wonderful research help along the way from University of Illinois graduate students Sarah Jackman, Joshua Young, and Hannah Ellingson.

I have been incredibly fortunate in my career to have advisors, teachers, and mentors who are both thoughtful scholars and wonderful people. The guidance and encouragement that I have received from Catherine Brekus, Tracy Fessenden, Clark Gilpin, Phillip Goff, Martin Marty, David Price, and Judith Weisenfeld shapes me every day. I am thankful, too, for the friends who have listened, questioned, and helped in more ways than they know. The world is richer and I am able to navigate it better because of John Carlson, Nancy Castro, Jed Esty, Adam Freed, Jim Hansen, Lilya Kaganovsky, Kip Kosek, Rick Layton, Eduardo Ledesma, Kathryn Lofton, Rajeev Malik, William Munro, Erik Owens, Brent Plate, Rob Rushing, Renée Trilling, and Gillen Wood.

For years now, a small group of friends who study the religious history of the United States has gathered one day prior to a major conference to read and comment on works in progress, and to eat and be together. This group, which has included Heather Curtis, Tracy Fessenden, Jennifer Graber, Alison Greene, Kip Kosek, and Kathryn Gin Lum, has read and commented on more parts of this book than it has parts. I cannot thank these friends enough for the gifts of their time, attention, and ideas. Even in the depths of a global pandemic and in the midst of life's myriad other challenges, Heather, Tracy, Jen, and Alison found time to read, comment, and suggest. Your friendship means the world to me. Thank you.

The process of making a book out of a manuscript is not simple. The people at New York University Press have, however, made that process delightful. I am especially grateful to senior editor Jennifer Hammer and to the editors of the North American Religions series, Tracy Fessenden, Laura Levitt, and David Watt for their vision and their enthusiasm. Through the generosity of the press, I was also able to work with Constance Rosenblum to refine the manuscript. Her careful attention to my prose made this a better book.

I am so fortunate to have the loving and supportive family that I have. My wife Meredith has been there from what feels like the beginning, encouraging, celebrating, and supporting, all while building her own remarkable career and being an amazing mother to our girls. She is the foundation on which all of this is built, the necessary precondition for this book and this career. I also have a brilliant, funny, hard-working extended family, whose love and patience means so much. Thank you Mom, Greg, Kip, Jen, Sarah, Tom, Jane, Sue, Marnie, and Peg. You are wonderful and I love you.

I took my first research trip for this project in 2009. Of the many things that were different about that world than this one, the one that knocks me sideways is that my daughters, Sophia, Charlotte, and Beatrice, were then nine, six, and three years old, respectively. As I write these acknowledgements, they are twenty-two, nineteen, and sixteen—beautiful, brilliant, and flourishing in ways that I never dared dream. Of all of the things I've done in life, being your dad is my favorite. You are awesome. This one's for you.

NOTES

INTRODUCTION

1 Thomas Collins to Irving Wood, March 14, 1936, "Kern Migratory Labor Camp, Report for week ending March 14, 1936," Folder 9 "Kern / Arvin," Carton 77, Irving Wood Papers [hereafter referred to as IWP]; Bancroft Library, University of California, Berkeley. The information on J. A. Wall is on page ten of Collins' sixteen-page report.
2 "Executive Order: Establishment of the Resettlement Administration," April 30, 1935, Carton 2; Harry Drobish Papers [hereafter referred to as HDP], Bancroft Library, University of California, Berkeley.
3 "Tentative Program of the Division of Rural Rehabilitation in California ERA," April 27, 1935, IWP, Folder 6, Carton 77.
4 Ibid., 8–9.
5 Ibid., 8. Walter Stein, *California and the Dust Bowl Migration*, 147–159.
6 Major works on Euro-American Christian missions and Native peoples in North America include Ramon Gutierrez, *When Jesus Came, the Corn Mothers Went Away: Marriage, Sexuality, and Power in New Mexico, 1500–1846*; James Axtell, *The Invasion Within: The Contest of Cultures in Colonial North America*; Linford Fisher, *The Indian Great Awakening: Religion and the Shaping of Native Cultures in Early America*; Jennifer Graber, *The Gods of Indian Country: Religion and the Struggle for the American West*; the dynamics that these authors examine are present as well in a related historiography of North American Protestant missions, examples of which included Nayan Shah, *Contagious Divides: Epidemics and Race in San Francisco's Chinatown*; Nathaniel Deutsch, *Inventing America's Worst Family: Eugenics, Islam, and the Fall and Rise of the Tribe of Ishmael*; and Evelyn Brooks Higginbotham, *Righteous Discontent: The Women's Movement in the Black Baptist Church, 1880–1920*.
7 Arthur Lundin, a young employee of the Resettlement Administration, used this phrase in a report that he filed from the Arvin camp in 1936. Arthur A. Lundin, Untitled, 26 July 1936, Corporations (Prior 7-1-40), RF-CF-16 (25) 620, Arvin Box 20, Coded Administrative Camp Files [1933–1945], Record Group 96 [hereafter referred to as RG96], National Archives and Records Administration [hereafter referred to as NARA]–Pacific Region (San Bruno). All subsequent citations to the camp files in Record Group 96 conclude with the camp name and box number.
8 New Deal reformers were, in many ways, playing an old song in a new key. Observers of the First and Second Great Awakenings had recoiled at the social

and physical effects of revivalistic worship, critiquing all of those involved quite harshly. Closer to the reformers' historical moment, F. M. Davenport and W. E. B. Du Bois expressed concern about the persistence and the meaning of revivalism. See F. M. Davenport, *Primitive Traits in Religious Revivals* (1905) and, more subtly, W. E. B. Du Bois, *The Souls of Black Folk* (1903).

9. Ray Mork to Laurence Hewes, December 2, 1940; RR CF 27 918-02 (4); Shafter Box 46.
10. Clarence Glacken, "Report of a Visit to the Resettlement Camp at Arvin," 14 August 1936; Arvin General (Prior 7-1-1940), RF-CF-16 (25) 789, Arvin Box 21.
11. Wallace Best, *Passionately Human, No Less Divine: Religion and Culture in Black Chicago, 1915–1952*; Kate Bowler, *Blessed: A History of the American Prosperity Gospel*; Anthea Butler, *Women in the Church of God in Christ: Making a Sanctified World*; Joel Carpenter, *Revive Us Again: The Reawakening of American Fundamentalism*; Peter R. D'Agostino, *Rome in America: Transnational Catholic Ideology from the Risorgimento to Fascism*; Leonard Dinnerstein, *Antisemitism in America*; Robert Orsi, *Thank You, St. Jude: Women's Devotion to the Patron Saint of Hopeless Causes*; Matthew Avery Sutton, *Aimee Semple McPherson and the Resurrection of Christian America*; Judith Weisenfeld, *Hollywood Be Thy Name: African American Religion in American Film, 1929–1949* and *New World A' Comin': Black Religion and Racial Identity During the Great Migration*.
12. Robert Handy, "The American Religious Depression, 1925–1935."
13. Lloyd D. Barba, "California's Cross: A Cultural History of Pentecostalism, Race, and Agriculture." Barba makes this point with regard to the term "pentecostal" in his study of Mexican and Okie Pentecostals in California's Central Valley. See also Barba, *Sowing the Sacred: Mexican Pentecostal Farmworkers in California*.
14. Stein, *California and the Dust Bowl Migration*; James N. Gregory, *American Exodus: The Dust Bowl Migration and Okie Culture in California*; Carey McWilliams, *Factories in the Field: The Story of Migratory Farm Labor in California*.
15. I am indebted to Darren Dochuk's influential *From Bible Belt to Sunbelt: Plain-Folk Religion, Grass Roots Politics, and the Rise of Evangelical Conservatism*.
16. Roland Curran, "The Central Valley Project and Its Place in the War Program," quoted in James Bright Wilson, "Religious Leaders, Institutions and Organizations among Certain Agricultural Workers in the Central Valley of California," 28.
17. Ibid., 28.
18. Alison Collis Greene, *No Depression in Heaven: The Great Depression, the New Deal, and the Transformation of Religion in the Delta*, 6.
19. Barba, *California's Cross*, 15–19; 69–71.
20. Colleen McDannell, *Picturing Faith: Photography and the Great Depression*, 20–21.
21. Kathryn Lofton, *Consuming Religion*, Introduction.
22. Dochuk, 13.
23. The definitive work on early pentecostalism is Grant Wacker, *Heaven Below: Early Pentecostals and American Culture*. See also Butler, *Women in the Church of God*

in Christ and Sutton, *Aimee Semple McPherson and the Resurrection of Christian America*.
24 Many documents written by camp program leaders make this point. See in particular Eric Thomsen to Jonathan Garst, August 3, 1936, Arvin General (Prior 7-1-40) RF-CF-16 (25) 789, Arvin Box 21.
25 Ibid.
26 Jackson Benson, "'To Tom, Who Lived It': John Steinbeck and the Man from Weedpatch," and "An Afterword and an Introduction"; John Michael Coburn, *The Gospel According to John (Steinbeck)*.
27 "Whitfield Winsey, M.D., A Pillar of Nineteenth Century Baltimore's Black Elite," Maryland State Archives (website), accessed February 21, 2023, https://msa.maryland.gov/msa/stagser/s1259/121/6050/html/11424000.html.
28 Coburn, 3–25; Collins' birth certificate is included in Coburn as Appendix 1; Collins' WWI draft card is available at: https://www.familysearch.org/ark:/61903/1:1:KZ84-BLQ, accessed October 15, 2022.
29 Maureen Fitzgerald, *Habits of Compassion: Irish Catholic Nuns and the Origins of New York's Welfare System, 1830–1920*.
30 Charles Philipps Papers, Archives of the Archdiocese of San Francisco; Dorothy Day, *The Long Loneliness*; Jay P. Dolan, *The American Catholic Experience: A History from Colonial Times to the Present*.
31 Collins, "Report for week ending August 22, 1936 and August 29, 1936," 6; July–August 1936, RF-CF-918-01, Arvin Box 23.
32 See Talal Asad, *Formations of the Secular: Christianity, Islam, Modernity*; Tracy Fessenden, *Culture and Redemption: Religion, the Secular, and American Literature*; John Lardas Modern, *Secularism in Antebellum America*; Chad Seales, *The Secular Spectacle: Performing Religion in a Southern Town*; Winnifred Fallers Sullivan, *The Impossibility of Religious Freedom*; and Charles Taylor, *A Secular Age*.
33 Lofton, *Consuming Religion*, chap. 4.

1. THE GATE

1 Harry Drobish and Irving Wood to L. M. Canady, June 7, 1935, Kern County SERA [Rankin Tract] [Migrant Camp] [1935], 028 General Correspondence, Box 10.
2 See Stein, 167. Walter Stein alluded to both conversion and more generic transformations as key aspects of the camp program when he wrote, "While they strove to break cultural habits they termed 'degraded,' which had been engrained in the Southwest for generations, they also attempted to instill in their wards new patterns of social and political behavior, which should convert them into model citizens of a model community sculpted by committed young liberals."
3 William L. Hudson to Harry E. Drobish, March 25, 1936, 028 161-Public Relations, Speeches, General Correspondence Box 30. Citations are to the enclosure Hudson sent Drobish, "Remarks by Harry E. Drobish."
4 "Dedication Program: Marysville Migrants Camp, Harry E. Drobish, Chairman, October 12, 1935," Carton 2, HDP.

5 Stein, 158. He wrote, "The ditch bank settlements increased markedly the potential danger from epidemics of typhoid, malaria, or tuberculosis which, once started, might spread from the Okies to the resident Californians."
6 McWilliams, *Factories in the Field*, chap. 13–14.
7 McWilliams, *Factories in the Field*; Stein, chap. 1; Gregory, *American Exodus*, chap. 2.
8 See Stein, 39–44. "The irony of their situation," Stein wrote, "was that California's pittance seemed munificent in contrast with wages of tenant shares in [the Okies'] home state."
9 McWilliams, *Factories in the Field*.
10 "Prominent Kern Men Injured in Outbreak," transcription from the *Fresno Bee*, 11 October 1933, Folder 7, Carton 77, IWP.
11 McWilliams, *Factories in the Field*, 219–224.
12 Pelham B. Glassford to Imperial County Board of Supervisors, June 23, 1934, Folder 1, Carton 77, IWP.
13 McWilliams, 211.
14 Simon J. Lubin, J. L. Leonard, and Will J. French, "Report to the National Labor Board," February 11, 1934, Folder 6, Carton 77, IWP.
15 Ibid.
16 Glassford Report, Enclosure #3, "Example of the results of intimidation," Folder 1, Carton 77, IWP.
17 Glassford to Imperial County Board of Supervisors, June 23, 1934.
18 Stein, 59.
19 Clarence Glacken, "Brawley Site Report," October 9, 1936, RF-CF-16-201-2, Brawley Box 9.
20 Drobish to Frank McLaughlin, March 15, 1935, Folder 7, Carton 77, IWP.
21 Ibid.
22 Stein, 154.
23 Drobish, "Operation of Camps for Migrants in California Agriculture: (Statement Prepared for Walter E. Packard to be forwarded to Washington.)" August 3, 1935, HDP, Carton 2.
24 W. L. Smith to Garst, February 24, 1937 and Garst to Smith, March 1, 1937; 028 General Suggestions, California, Kern County [1937–1942], RG 96, General Correspondence, 1935–1945, Box 2, NARA—Pacific Region (San Bruno). Subsequent citations to RG 96 General Correspondence files will conclude with the county name and, where relevant, the date range.
25 John Thomson to Garst, December 7, 1937, 028 General Suggestions, California, Kern County [1937–1942].
26 Richard Perrott, "Brawley Site, Social and Economic Survey of RA Migrant Camp Site at Brawley, 1936," RF-CF-28-201-02, Brawley Migratory Labor Camp, 7/1/40–6/30/41, Brawley Box 9.
27 Richard Perrott to Omer Mills and Irving Wood, March 17, 1936, RF-CF-16-200, Brawley Land Acquisitions, Brawley Box 9.

28 Charles Barry to Omer Mills, March 17, 1938, RF-CF-16-434, Brawley Reports, Brawley Box 9.
29 Undated notes marked "Never Sent," Folder 2, Carton 2, HDP. Surrounding documents indicate that these notes date from the summer of 1935.
30 See Stein, 156–157. "Region IX was also subjected to hostility from legislators who saw in the migratory labor camps a cynical attempt to subsidize California's large farms."
31 "Who Advocates Force and Violence," 233 *Flash*, August 17, 1936; Carton 2, HDP. Word reached the Arvin camp of Briggs's tirade against migrants in August of 1936. According to Collins, "The Camp Committee . . . highly resented the clippings" and supported "turning the paper over to an attorney." Collins, "Report for the weeks ending August 8 and August 15, 1936," July—August 1936, RF-CF-918-01, Arvin Box 23.
32 Ibid.
33 Drobish to George Nickel, June 11, 1935, Kern County SERA Rankin Tract, Migrant Camp, 028 Suggestions—General Correspondence, 1935-1936, Box 10.
34 Jonathan Garst to R. G. Tugwell, March 14, 1936, "Exhibit 'A' Social and Economic Justification," Section III, A and Section VII, A, 3, "Arvin, California Migrants' Camp. Reg. IX, State—California," RF-CF-16 703; Arvin Box 20. Drobish is not listed as an author of the report, but the language is his.
35 Garst to John Thomson, April 21, 1938, 028 General Suggestions, Kern County [1935-1942].
36 On March 26, 1936, Harry Drobish gave a talk at the First Congregationalist Church in Petaluma, California titled "Fruit Tramps: California's Big Agricultural Problem." 161—Public Relations—Speeches, Box 30, RG96, NARA—Pacific Region (San Bruno).
37 "Remarks by Harry E. Drobish," enclosed in William L. Hudson to Drobish, March 24, 1936, 161—Public Relations—Speeches, Box 30. Hudson had forwarded a transcript of the talk to Drobish for him to edit.
38 "Guide to the Harry Everett Drobish Papers," Online Archive of California, https://oac.cdlib.org/findaid/ark:/13030/tf896nb3gx/, accessed 16 May 2022.
39 "Remarks by Harry E. Drobish."
40 Ibid.
41 The sources are slightly ambiguous as to who described the benefits of the federal camp to the audience gathered October 12, 1935. The text was written by Tom Collins, a cover sheet says that he presented it, and the text itself would make little sense if presented by someone else. The version of the program that I have, however, lists Collins as present but not as a speaker.
42 Mensing, "Inspection of the Arvin Migratory Labor Camp, RF-CF-25, Kern County, California," Arvin Administration (7-1-40) RF-CF-16(25) 100, Arvin Box 18. Mensing wrote of Collins, "He stated that most of these people were bewildered and amazed at the facilities provided for them at the camp some of which were a completely new experience for them."

43 Collins, "The Human Side in the Operation of a Migrants Camp: An Address by Thomas Collins at the California Conference on Housing for Rural Workers and The Dedication Exercises of the Marysville Migrants Camp of the Resettlement Administration, October 12, 1935, Marysville, California," Folder 7, Carton 77, IWP.
44 This language is fully in line with Protestant opinions about the outdoors, exercise, and recreation developed in the United States from the 1880s forward. See Evan Berry, *Devoted to Nature: The Religious Roots of American Environmentalism*.
45 Stein, 42, 90. Walter Stein wrote briefly of the Hoover Ranch and "rumors" of its underhanded labor practices.
46 "Notes: Low-Cost Houses," July 1936, Carton 2, HDP.
47 Collins to Drobish, "Report for the Week ending April 18, 1936," Folder 9, Carton 77, IWP.
48 Collins to Drobish, "Report for the Week ending May 30, 1936," Folder 9, Carton 77, IWP.
49 Charles Eddy to Wood, "Marysville, Calif., Week ending January 18, 1936," Folder 4, Carton 77, IWP.
50 Ibid., "Marysville, Calif., Week ending January 25, 1936."
51 Collins to Drobish, "Report for the Week ending January 25, 1936," Folder 9, Carton 77, IWP.
52 Collins, "The Human Side in the Operation of a Migrants Camp."
53 William Mercer to camp program officials, August 1940, Brawley Migratory Labor Camp, 7/1/40–6/30/41, RR-CF-28-912-06, Brawley Box 10.
54 "Memorandum for Mr. J. C. Henderson, Chief, Migratory Labor Section," November 25, 1940, Brawley Migratory Labor Camp, 7-1-40-6-30-41, RRCF 28 201–0, Brawley Box 9.
55 Collins to Drobish, "Report for the Week ending December 28, 1935," Folder 9, Carton 77, IWP.
56 Ibid.
57 Ibid., January 18, 1936; February 29, 1936.
58 Ibid., March 21, 1936.
59 Ibid., January 25, 1936.
60 Ibid.
61 Robert Orsi, *Thank You, St. Jude*.
62 Eddy to Wood, "Marysville, Calif., Week ending April 18, 1936," Folder 4, Carton 77, IWP.
63 Collins to Drobish, "Report for the week ending June 27, 1936," Folder 9, Carton 77, IWP.
64 Ibid.

2. THE OFFICE

1 Lofton, *Consuming Religion*, chapters 2, 9, and 10. Kathryn Lofton's treatment of offices and corporate cultures as significant locations for and expressions of religion in American life intersects with and enriches my thinking throughout this chapter.

2 Norman Corse, "Arvin Migratory Labor Camp Weekly Report, Week Ending 6-12-37," and "Arvin Migratory Labor Camp Weekly Report, Week Ending 5-29-37," Arvin Reports—Weekly (Prior 7-1-40) RF-CF-16 (25) 183–07, Arvin Box 19.
3 Max Weber, *Economy and Society*, 241; see also excerpts from *Economy and Society* in *The Protestant Ethic and the Spirit of Capitalism with Other Writings on the Rise of the West*, 417.
4 "Remarks by Harry E. Drobish," enclosed in William L. Hudson to Drobish, March 24, 1936, 161—Public Relations—Speeches, Box 30.
5 Hazel K. Peterson, "Office Procedure, Routine, and Forms," 161, State Office, Speeches, March 1938—January 1939, General Correspondence, Box 30.
6 "Instructions to Camp Managers," August 1, 1935, 1, Folder 7, Carton 77, IWP.
7 Ibid., 2.
8 Ibid., 1.
9 See Bederman, *Manliness and Civilization: A Cultural History of Race and Gender in the United States, 1880–1917*.
10 "Instructions to Camp Managers," August 1, 1935, 1.
11 Ibid., 3.
12 Ibid.
13 Ibid.
14 Ibid.
15 Ibid., 5.
16 Ibid., 4–6.
17 Wood to Collins, February 5, 1936, Arvin Reports—Weekly (Prior 7-1-40), RF-CF-16(25) 183–07, Arvin Box 19.
18 Wood to Collins, May 29, 1936, Arvin Appointments, Invitations, and Meetings, (Prior 7-1-40), RF-CF-16 (25) 030, Arvin Box 18.
19 Garst to Rexford Tugwell, May 28, 1936, Arvin Camp, General, Arvin Box 18.
20 Stein, 154. Stein describes the RA/FSA as one of the most assailed agencies of the New Deal. "With the possible exception of the writers' and actors' projects of the WPA, no New Deal agency sustained more severe congressional criticism than RA-FSA."
21 Walter Stein and James Gregory discuss Collins and his work. See Stein, 166; and Gregory, 108. See also Benson, "'To Tom, Who Lived It': John Steinbeck and the Man from Weedpatch," and "An Afterword and an Introduction"; and Coburn, "The Gospel According to John Steinbeck," 3–25.
22 Collins, "Report for week ending February 29, 1936," 32, Folder 9, Carton 77, IWP.
23 Collins, "Report for weeks ending May 16 and May 23, 1936," 8, Folder 9, Carton 77, IWP.
24 Mensing, "Inspection of the Arvin Migratory Labor Camp, RF-CF-25, Kern County, California."
25 Ibid., 2.
26 Ibid., 7.
27 Ibid., 6.

28. Ibid., 6–7.
29. Ibid., 8.
30. Collins wrote of his effort to distribute these pamphlets in Collins, "Weekly Report for Week Ending January 25, 1936," Arvin Migratory Labor Camp, January 1936, (7-1-40) RF-CF-16 918–01, Arvin Box 22.
31. Mensing, "Inspection of the Arvin Migratory Labor Camp, RF-CF-25, Kern County, California," 7.
32. Joe E. Schoales, "Inspection of the Arvin Migratory Labor Camp, RF-CF-26, Kern County, California," February 24, 1937, 5, Arvin Administration (7-1-40) RF-CF-16 (25) 100, Arvin Box 18. Unless otherwise noted, subsequent quotations from Schoales are from this report.
33. Ibid., 8.
34. Ibid., 1.
35. Ibid., 1, 10.
36. Ibid., 10.
37. Ibid., 1.
38. Ibid., 2.
39. Eric Thomsen to Robert Hardie, March 13, 1937, Arvin Statistics (Prior 7-1-40), RF-CF-16(25) 180, Arvin Box 19.
40. Hardie to Thomsen, March 18, 1937, Arvin Statistics (Prior 7-1-40), RF-CF-16(25) 180, Arvin Box 19.
41. For reflections on RA/FSA attitudes toward Mexican, Filipino, and other non-white migrants, see Stein, 44–47; Collins, "The Human Side in the Operation of a Migrants Camp"; and Collins to Thomsen, October 12, 1935, Arvin Investigation and Selection, (Prior 7-1-40), RF-CF-16 (25) 550, Arvin Box 20.
42. Nellie Porter to Collins, August 7, 1936 and Collins to Thomsen, August 10, 1936, both in Arvin Public Relations (Prior 7-1-40) RF-CF-16(25) 160–169; Arvin Box 19.
43. Thomsen to Nellie Porter, August 14, 1936, Arvin Public Relations (Prior 7-1-40) RF-CF-16(25) 160–169, Arvin Box 19.
44. Ibid.
45. Ibid.
46. Ibid.
47. Ibid.
48. Collins to Thomsen, August 15, 1936, Arvin Camp 000 [+033], Arvin Box 18.
49. "Migratory Camp Director Describes Migrant Labor," undated newspaper clipping, Arvin Public Relations (Prior 7-1-40) RF-CF-16(25) 160–169, Arvin Box 19.
50. M. A. Gifford to Thomsen, February 24, 1937, Arvin Public Relations (Prior 7-1-40) RF-CF-16(25) 160–169, Arvin Box 19.
51. Mensing, 6–7.
52. Collins, "Weekly Report for Week Ending February 29, 1936," Folder 9, Carton 77, IWP.
53. Collins, "Weekly Report for Week Ending January 26, 1936," Folder 9, Carton 77, IWP.

54 Ibid., "Weekly Report for Week Ending May 9, 1936."
55 Ibid., "Weekly Report for Week Ending June 20, 1936."
56 Ibid., "Weekly Report for Week Ending February 29, 1936," 52.
57 Drobish, Personal notes, "Low Cost Houses," July 1936, Carton 2, HDP; and Collins, "Report for the weeks ending July 11 and July 18, 1936," July–August 1936, RF-CF-918-01, Arvin Box 23.
58 Drobish, Personal notes, "Low Cost Houses," July 1936, Carton 2, HDP.
59 "Minutes, Arvin Camp Committee Meetings," July 13, 1936, Arvin Appointments, Invitations and Meetings, (Prior 7-1-40) RF-CF-16 (25) 030, Arvin Box 18. Drobish asked his secretary to transcribe the minutes and to preserve the original spelling, grammar, and capitalization.
60 Collins, "Reports for the weeks ending July 11 and July 18, 1936," July–August 1936, RF-CF-918-01, Arvin Box 23.
61 Ibid.
62 Ibid.
63 Collins, "Report for the week ending June 6, 1936," Folder 9, Carton 77, IWP.
64 Collins, "Reports for the weeks ending July 11 and July 18, 1936," July–August 1936, RF-CF-918-01, Arvin Box 23.
65 Collins, "Report for the week ending September 5, 1936" and "Report for the week ending September 19, 1936," Sept. 1936, RF-CF-918-01, Arvin Box 23.
66 Collins to Drobish, July 7, 1936, Carton 2, HDP.
67 Charles Wollenberg, "Introduction," in Steinbeck, *Harvest Gypsies: On the Road to the Grapes of Wrath*.
68 For further reading on the relationship between Tom Collins and John Steinbeck, see Jackson Benson, "'To Tom, Who Lived it,'" and "An Afterword and an Introduction"; and John Michael Coburn, "The Gospel According to John Steinbeck."
69 John Steinbeck, *The Grapes of Wrath*, 78.
70 Ibid., 210–211.
71 Ibid., 211–212.
72 Ibid., 308–9. David Hall, in *Worlds of Wonder, Days of Judgment*, writes eloquently of the early modern belief, shared by New England Puritans, in the connection between a woman's moral standing and her ability to deliver a healthy baby. See Hall, 72–77, 80–84, 101, 111–112.
73 Ibid., 320–21.

3. THE TENT PLATFORM

1 RA/FSA policy was to limit the amount of time that a migrant family could stay in any one camp to one year. The records show that there were occasional exceptions to this policy, but the seasonal nature of agricultural work made it unlikely that a family would be able to settle in one place for twelve months or more.
2 Examples of domestic evangelism abound in North American religious history. Two particularly well-crafted histories that touch on the subject are Graber, *The Gods of Indian Country* and Fessenden, *Culture and Redemption*.

3   Rauschenbusch, *Christianity and the Social Crisis in the 21st Century*, 222–23.
4   Leonard, *Illiberal Reformers: Race, Eugenics, and American Economics in the Progressive Era*.
5   Shah, *Contagious Divides*, 106.
6   Ibid., 107.
7   Thomas A. Tweed, *Crossing and Dwelling: A Theory of Religion* (Cambridge, MA: Harvard University Press, 2008), 85. Tweed discusses this metaphor throughout chapter four of Crossing and Dwelling.
8   Steinbeck, *The Grapes of Wrath*, 33, 38.
9   Ibid., 52.
10 Ibid., 88.
11 Ibid., 82.
12 Tweed, 104–105.
13 Ibid., 103.
14 United States Department of Agriculture, *The Farm Security Administration*.
15 Ibid., 31.
16 Ibid.
17 Clara Thompson to Garst, May 6, 1938, 161—Speeches, March 1938–January 1939, General Correspondence, Box 30.
18 Ibid. Quotations are from enclosure 1, Sue Taylor, "Home Management Plans with Rehabilitation Families."
19 Frederick Soule to Mrs. Kenneth (Blanche) Premo, April 15, 1938, 028 Tulare County [1935–42], General Correspondence, Box 5.
20 Steinbeck, *The Grapes of Wrath*, 317–318.
21 Collins, "Report for Weeks Ending July 25 and August 1," July–August 1936, RF-CF-918-01, Arvin Box 23.
22 Collins to Eric Thomsen, April 2, 1937, RF-CF 16(27) 912–034 Camp Funds, Shafter Box 46.
23 Ibid.
24 Ibid.
25 For an excellent account of American humanitarianism in the late nineteenth and early twentieth centuries, see Curtis, *Holy Humanitarians*.
26 Deutsch, *Inventing America's Worst Family*; Leonard, *Illiberal Reformers*.
27 Paul Taylor to Jonathan Garst, November 1, 1937, 028 Suggestions—General 1935–38 [MISC], Box 5, RG 96, NARA Pacific Region (San Bruno).
28 "Rules and Regulations of the Yuba City Migratory Labor Camp," enclosure in Frank Iusi to Lawrence Hewes, July 24, 1940, CF 34-934-02-935, Yuba City Migratory Labor Camp [MLC] 7/1/40–6/30/41, Yuba City Box 67; also *Migratory Clipper*, 16 December 1939, 2.
29 "Arvin Camp Ordinances," enclosure in Myer Cohen to Iusi, April 17, 1942, RR-CF-34-101 Yuba City MLC, 7/1/41, Yuba City Box 64.
30 Iusi to R. W. Hollenberg, December 12, 1940, RR-CF-34 918-02, Yuba City MLC 7/1/40–6/30/41, Yuba City Box 67.

31 Mork to Omer Mills, December 30, 1937, CF-26-918, Coachella Property Operation and Disposition, Indio Box 41.
32 Mork to Mills, September 11, 1937, CF-26-918, Coachella Property Operation and Disposition, Indio Box 41.
33 Mork to Hewes, December 2, 1940, RR CF 27 918-02 (4), Shafter Box 46.
34 Mork to Hewes, October 29, 1940, RR CF 27 918-02 (4), Shafter Box 46.
35 *Covered Wagon*, 10 December 1938, 2.
36 *Covered Wagon*, 17 December 1938, 2.
37 *Covered Wagon*, 29 March 1939.
38 *Indio Migratory Worker*, vol. II, no. XXIV, 26 August 1939.
39 Ibid., vol. II, no. XXV, 2 September 1939.
40 *Tow Sack Tattler*, 29 September 1940.
41 Mork to Harvey Coverley, December 30, 1940, RR CF 27 918-02 (4), Shafter Box 46.
42 Author unknown, "Case Histories," State Office-161-Speeches, March 1938–June 1938, General Correspondence, Box 30.
43 Ibid.
44 Collins to [Hewes], "Monthly Narrative Report, Winter Migratory Labor Camp December 1940," December 30, 1940, RR-CF-33 919-02, Winters MLC 7/1/40–6/30-41, Winters Box 60; Iusi to Harvey Coverley, October 1, 1941, RR-CF-34 918-02, Yuba City MLC 7/1/41, Yuba City Box 67.
45 *Tow Sack Tattler*, 29 September 1939, 1.
46 Gene Nicholson, "Monthly Narrative, Brawley Farm Workers Community, May 3- June 3," June 4, 1942, RR-CF-28-918-02, Brawley MLC, 7/1/42, Brawley Box 11.
47 Taylor to Garst, November 1, 1937, 028 Suggestions General, 1935–38 [Misc], Box 5.
48 Guy Griset, "Open Letter to Indio Migratory Labor Camp," August 1, 1940, RR-CF-26 918-02, Indio MLC Monthly Narrative Reports and Clippings, Indio Box 41.
49 Glen Trimble to R. B. Moore, December 5, 1942, RR-CF-28-911-04, Brawley MLC 7/1/42, Brawley Box 10.
50 "United States Department of Agriculture, Farm Security Administration, Indio Housing Project," CF 26 912-912-06, Indio Box 41.
51 Hauke, "A Progress Survey of Twenty Families Living in the Labor Homes of the Yuba City Migratory Labor Camp, Yuba City, California, for the Year 1940," RR-CF-34 911-042, Yuba City MLC, 7/1/41, Yuba City Box 66.
52 Hauke, "A Progress Survey of Twenty Families Living in the Labor Homes of the Indio Migratory Labor Camp, Indio, California, for the Year 1940," RR-CF-26 911-042, Indio MLC, Indio Box 4.
53 Hauke, "A Progress Survey of Thirty-Three Families Living in the Labor Homes of the Shafter Migratory Labor Camp, Shafter, California, for the Year 1940," RR-CF-27 911-042, Shafter Box 46.
54 Collins, "Report for week ending February 8, 1936," 21, Folder 9, Box 77, IWP.
55 *Tow Sack Tattler*, 24 November 1939, 4.

56 *Migratory Clipper*, 9 December 1939, 6, 4.
57 Ibid., 6 January 1940, 6.
58 Ibid., 10 February 1940, 3, 4.
59 *Happy Valley People's Word*, 25 January 1941, 1.
60 Ruth Coe to Myer Cohen, April 9, 1942, RR-CF-34 Yuba City MLC, 7/1/41, Yuba City Box 68.
61 Iusi to Harvey Coverley, March 10, 1942, RR-CF-34 918–02, Yuba City MLC, 7/1/41, Yuba City Box 67.
62 Milen Dempster to Cohen, April 9, 1942, RR-CF-34 Yuba City MLC, 7/1/41, Yuba City Box 68; Coe to Cohen, April 9, 1942.
63 Dempster to Cohen, April 9, 1942.
64 Ibid.
65 Collins to Wood, Report for weeks ending July 25 and August 1, 1936, 4, Folder 9, Box 77, IWP.
66 Iusi to Hewes, December 12, 1940, RR-CF-34 918–02, Yuba City MLC 7/1/40–6/30/41, Yuba City Box 67.

4. THE SANITARY UNIT

1 Mensing, "Confidential Report: Inspection of the Arvin Migratory Labor Camp, RF-CF-25, Kern County California," July 15, 1936, 4.
2 "Constitution," RR-CF-28-101, Brawley MLC, 7/1/41, Brawley Box 8. The text appears in Article I, Section 2. Original capitalization.
3 *Tow Sack Tattler*, 17 November 1939.
4 Douglas, *Purity and Danger: An Analysis of the Concepts of Pollution and Taboo*, 2.
5 *Indio Migratory Worker*, vol. I, no. 2, 7 December 1938, 4.
6 Douglas, 2.
7 Drobish to L. M. Canady, June 7, 1935, 028 Kern County SERA [Rankin Tract] [Migrant Camp], General Correspondence, Box 10.
8 William L. Hudson to Drobish, March 25, 1936, 028 161-Public Relations—Speeches February 1936, Box 30. William L. Hudson, Assistant Executive Secretary of the club, sent Drobish the text of his speech for editing.
9 There are dozens of similar reports in the files, dating from 1936 to1942. Perrott wrote in the midst of Resettlement Administration attempts to determine where to establish permanent migrant camps. "Alameda Co. is the second [county] in the state in production of peas. . . ." Pea fields were concentrated in the southern part of the county "from San Leandro in the north to the [county] line in the south."
10 Drobish Commonwealth Club address in William L. Hudson to Drobish, March 25, 1936.
11 "Dedication Program, Marysville Migrants Camp, October 12, 1935," Carton 2, HDP.
12 Imperial County Ordinance No. 8, RF-CF-16–130 Brawley Personnel, Brawley Box 8.

13 Voyle, *The Settler Sea: California's Salton Sea and the Consequences of Colonialism*; see also greetingsfromsaltonsea.com, accessed October 18, 2022.
14 Charles A. Clark and Glacken, "Brawley Site, Social and economic survey of RA migrant camp site at Brawley, 1936," RF-CF-16-201-2, Brawley Box 9.
15 Imperial County Ordinances No. 8 and 101, RF-CF-16–130 Brawley Personnel, Brawley Box 8.
16 Clark and Glacken, "Brawley Site, Social and economic survey. . . ."
17 T. T. Miller, "Brawley Migrant Camp Area, Oct. 10–36, Check of Migrants. Brawley Area," RF-CF-200, Land Acquisitions, Brawley Box 9.
18 Clark and Glacken, "Brawley Site, Social and economic survey . . ."
19 Supplementary information on the racial and religious diversity of the Imperial Valley prior to 1942 comes from the Imperial Valley Historical Society's Pioneers' Park Museum, which I visited in November of 2015. www.pioneermuseum.net.
20 Clark and Glacken, "Brawley Site, Social and economic survey . . ."
21 Ibid.
22 New Deal officials used each of these terms to describe the Mexican presence in Brawley.
23 Ibid.
24 These thoughts were not Glacken's alone. See Garst to W. W. Alexander, February 12, 1937, RR-CF-16–913 Brawley, Attitude Towards Project, Brawley Box 10. Garst wrote to the head of the RA making a final appeal for funds to build the Brawley camp. "Most field workers now on ditch banks are white stop Mexican families in general permanent slum dwellers El Centro Brawley stop."
25 Mork to Raul Hollenberg, June 25, 1940, CF-27 Shafter 918–02 (3), Shafter Box 46.
26 Collins to Edward Rowell, October 25, 1938, Brawley, Public Relations, RF-CF-16–160, Brawley Box 25.
27 Ibid.
28 Coverley, "Investigation of Housing Conditions of Stable and Migratory Agricultural Labor, Coachella Valley, Riverside County, California," March 7, 1935, 10, Folder 6, Carton 7, IWP.
29 Ibid., 9.
30 Ibid., 6–7, 8.
31 Ibid., 9.
32 Ibid., 2.
33 Ibid., 3, 6, 8.
34 Coverley, "Investigation of Housing Conditions of Stable and Migratory Agricultural Labor, Coachella Valley, Riverside County, California," March 7, 1935, 10.
35 H. M. Beaumont, "The Operation of Imhoff Tanks."
36 Ibid. Beaumont advised his audience and readers about the challenges of maintaining Imhoff tanks. "The satisfactory operation of Imhoff tanks requires intelligent and conscientious supervision founded on a thorough understanding of the purposes of the tank and the fundamental principles involved." For a contemporary description of Imhoff tanks, see https://sswm.info/taxonomy

/term/3799/imhoff-tank, and Tilley et al., *Compendium of Sanitation Systems and Technologies*.
37. Frederick Soule to Congressman Clarence Lea, January 15, 1937, 028—General Suggestions—California, Butte County [1936–1941], Box 2.
38. Burton Cairns to C. G. Gillespie, June 24, 1937, RF-CF-27-762, Shafter Box 45.
39. Gillespie to Cairns, July 6, 1937, RF-CF-27-762, Shafter Box 45.
40. Cairns to Gillespie, June 23, 1937, RF-CF-16-762 Brawley Sewer System, Brawley Box 10.
41. Richard Whitehead to Arthur Crenshaw, January 31, 1937, RF-CF-16-762 Brawley Sewer System, Brawley Box 10.
42. Cairns to Gillespie, July 14, 1937, RF-CF-16 Winters 762 Sewage System, Winters Box 59.
43. C. F. Baughman to Garst, June 4, 1938, RF-CF-27-762 Sewage Systems, Shafter Box 45. See also Arthur Siemers to Edward Rowell, July 8, 1938, CF-27 912-06/913-07 Shafter, Shafter Box 46.
44. Omer Mills to Charles Barry, December 7, 1937, RF-CF-16-100 Brawley Administration, Brawley Box 8.
45. "Resolution: Imperial County Farm Labor Council," May 12, 1936, 028—General Suggestions—California—Imperial County, 1936–1942, General Correspondence, Box 2. See also "Petition to Governor Frank F. Merriam," RF-CF-16-913 Brawley, Attitude Toward Project, Brawley Box 10.
46. Collins to Eric Thomsen, March 1, 1937, RF-CF-16-789-02 Brawley General, Brawley Box 10.
47. Gillespie to Garst, December 21, 1937, RF-CF-16-789-02 Brawley General, Brawley Box 10.
48. Garst to Gillespie, January 27, 1938, RF-CF-16-789-02 Brawley General, Brawley Box 10.
49. Collins, "Report for the week ending March 14, 1936," 16, Folder 9, Box 77, IWP.
50. Collins, "Arvin Migratory Labor Camp, Report for the weeks ending August 8, 1936 and August 15, 1936," 15, RF-CF-918-01 July–August 1936, Arvin Box 23.
51. Collins, "The Human Side in the Operation of a Migrants Camp."
52. Collins, "Report for Week Ending January 11, 1936," 2, RF-CF 918-01 January 1936, Arvin Box 22.
53. Iusi to Hollenberg, June 4, 1940, RR-CF-34 918-02 Yuba City MLC, Yuba City Box 67.
54. *Happy Valley People's Word*, 25 January 1941, 4.
55. Collins, "Report for Week Ending December 28, 1935," RF-CF-16 918-01 Arvin Weekly Reports, 1935, Arvin Box 22.
56. Collins, "Kern Migrants Camp, Report for week ending February 8, 1936," 15, Folder 9, Box 77, IWP.
57. Iusi to Coverley, December 1, 1941, RR-CF-34-762 Yuba City M.L.C, 7-1-41, Yuba City Box 66.
58. Frank J. Doyle to Coverley, December 12, 1941, RR-CF-34-762 Yuba City M.L.C, 7-1-41, Yuba City Box 66.

59 Elizabeth Davisson to Addie Swapp, February 28, 1942, RR-CF-28–761 Brawley MLC 7/1/41, Brawley Box 10.

5. THE COMMUNITY CENTER

1 Collins to Wood, January 11, 1936, RF-CF-16 918–01 Arvin Migratory Labor Camp, Jan. 1936, Arvin Box 22.
2 Collins, "Report for the week ending February 8, 1936," RF-CF-16 918–01 Arvin Migratory Labor Camp, Feb. 1936, Arvin Box 22.
3 Wood to Collins, December 5, 1935, RF-CF-16 (25) 030 Arvin Appointments, Invitations, and Meetings (Prior 7-1-40), Arvin Box 18.
4 The history of Protestant intersections with recreation and exercise has been told in multiple monographs over the past three decades. See Bederman, *Manliness and Civilization*; Berry, *Devoted to Nature*; and Putney, *Muscular Christianity: Manhood and Sports in Protestant America, 1880–1920*.
5 Lincoln, *Holy Terrors: Thinking about Religion after September 11*.
6 See Berry, *Devoted to Nature*, and Lofton, *Consuming Religion*.
7 Collins, "Report for week ending February 22, 1936," Arvin, February 1936, RF-CF-16 918–01, Arvin Box 23.
8 Ibid.
9 Rauschenbusch, 338–339.
10 "Recreation," *Weed Patch Cultivator*, October 21, 1938, 1.
11 Bederman, *Manliness and Civilization*; Berry, *Devoted to Nature*; Putney, *Muscular Christianity*.
12 Collins, "The Human Side in the Operation of a Migrants Camp."
13 Collins, "Report for the week ending July 11, 1936 and July 18, 1936," RF-CF 918–01 July–August 1936, Arvin Box 23.
14 Collins, "Report for the week ending February 22, 1936," RF-CF-16 918–01 February 1936, Arvin Box 23.
15 Mary K. Davies, "Nursery School," January 6, 1942, RR-CF-34 918–02 Yuba City MLC 7/1/41, Yuba City Box 67.
16 For further discussion of the convergence of moralism and coercion in American policy and governing philosophy, see Leonard, *Illiberal Reformers*.
17 Charles Barry to R. W. Hollenberg, June 16, 1939, RF-CF 16 (27) 912–034 Camp Funds, Shafter Box 46.
18 "Minutes of Council Meeting, Saturday, April 2, 1938," RF-CF-16 (25) 620 Arvin Corporations (prior 7-1-40), Arvin Box 20.
19 Mork to John Henderson, August 22, 1939, encl. "Camp Permit," RF-CF-27 100 Administration, Shafter Box 43.
20 Wacker, *Heaven Below: Pentecostals and American Culture*. As Wacker has shown, "this condition" of denying the existence of "leisure" was characteristic of early Pentecostals and of other apocalyptic Protestants. Evangelical Protestant suspicion of theater has particularly deep roots.
21 Collins, "Report for the week ending February 22, 1936."

22 Mensing, "Inspection of the Arvin Migratory Labor Camp, RF-CF-25, Kern County, California."
23 Collins, "Report for week ending March 14, 1936," Folder 9, Box 77, IWP.
24 Collins, "Report for the week ending September 5, 1936," RF-CF-918–01 Sept. 1936, Arvin Box 23.
25 Ibid.
26 Ibid.
27 Ibid.
28 "Noted Woman Honors Indio Migratory Labor Camp," *Covered Wagon News*, 14 January 1939, 1. Mork appears to have drawn on some of Sanger's materials in writing the article, which, though clearly written in his voice, is also attributed to Sally M. Huffel of Washington, DC.
29 "Camp Citizens See Religious Picture 'Golgotha,'" *Covered Wagon*, 18 February 1939, 1.
30 Robert Brown to Hollenberg, December 1, 1939, RF-CF-16–918 Brawley, Reports, Brawley Box 11.
31 Griset to Hollenberg, March 5, 1940, CF 26 918 Monthly Narrative Reports, Indio Box 41.
32 Griset to Hollenberg, April 4, 1940, CF 26 918 Monthly Narrative Reports, Indio Box 41.
33 *Migratory Clipper*, 4 November 1939, 4.
34 Ibid., 6.
35 *Migratory Clipper*, 11 November 1939, 5; 18 November 1939, 7; 2 December 1939, 8.
36 *Migratory Clipper*, 11 November 1939, 5.
37 *Tow Sack Tattler*, 28 October 1939, 8.
38 *Tow Sack Tattler*, 17 November 1939, 10.
39 *Tow Sack Tattler*, 24 November 1939, 8.
40 "Minutes of Council Meeting, Saturday, April 2, 1938," RF-CF-16 (25) 620 Arvin Corporations (prior 7-1-40), Arvin Box 20.
41 *Migratory Worker*, 26 November 1938, 1; *Indio Covered Wagon*, 7 January 1939, 3.
42 *Weedpatch Cultivator*, 21 October 1938, 1.
43 Mork to Hewes, September 20, 1940, CF-27 935 Camp social questionnaire, Constitution, Shafter Box 46.
44 "Migratory Labor Camp Weekly Report: Shafter, California," January 6, 13, 20, 27, February 3, 10, 17, 1940, CF-27 918–01 Shafter, Shafter Box 46.
45 Iusi, "Monthly Narrative Report for July 1940," August 11, 1940, RR-CF-34 918–02 Yuba City MLC 7/1/40–6/30/41, Yuba City Box 67.
46 Robert Allen to Coverley, "Monthly Narrative Report for April 1941" and "Monthly Narrative Report for July 1941," RR-CF 33 919–02 Winters MLC 7/1/40–6/30/41, Winters Box 60.
47 *Arvin Cultivator*, 7 April 1939, 2.
48 *Migratory Clipper*, 21 January 1939, 5.
49 Sutton, *Aimee Semple McPherson and the Resurrection of Christian America*.

50 Rheba Ummel, *Almost Sixty Years of Miracles*, unpublished memoir, Shafter Historical Society. Unless otherwise noted, all information on the Ummels' lives and ministry is derived from Rheba Ummel's memoir.
51 George Marsden, *Fundamentalism and American Culture*; Sutton, *American Apocalypse*; Dochuk, *From Bible Belt to Sunbelt*.
52 Wilson, "Religious Leaders, Institutions and Organizations among Certain Agricultural Workers in the Central Valley of California," 363–64.
53 Wilson, 375.
54 Throughout the Depression, the *King's Business*, published out of the Bible Institute of Los Angeles, featured writings condemning the New Deal, among many other earthly concerns, and prophesying the end of times. See Ebel, "'In Every Cup of Bitterness, Sweetness': California Christianity and the Great Depression"; and Matthew Avery Sutton, "Was FDR the Antichrist? The Birth of Fundamentalist Antiliberalism in a Global Age."

6. THE PAPER

1 *Migratory Worker*, 26 November 1938, 1.
2 Ibid.
3 John Nerone and Kevin Barnhurst, *The Form of the News*.
4 This chapter also incorporates insights from Benedict Anderson, *Imagined Communities*; Taylor, *A Secular Age*; Fessenden, *Culture and Redemption*; Curtis, *Holy Humanitarians*; Orsi, *Thank You, St. Jude*, and my own *Faith in the Fight*.
5 Stein, *California and the Dust Bowl Migration*, and Gregory, *American Exodus* also draw on the camp newspapers.
6 Nerone and Barnhurst, 39.
7 Ibid., 12.
8 Ibid., 10.
9 Ibid., 9.
10 There are numerous mentions in the camp papers of migrants having access to larger circulation newspapers, including the *Kern Daily Herald*, the *Bakersfield Californian*, the *Fresno Bee*, the *Riverside Enterprise*, the *Los Angeles Examiner*, and the *San Francisco Chronicle*. When the *Covered Wagon News* announced the opening of the new library in camp, it mentioned that "the daily papers" would be available "for your convenience." *Covered Wagon News*, 15 September 1939, 1.
11 *Covered Wagon News*, 11 November 1939. Mork published a similar passage in the Indio camp paper, also called the *Covered Wagon* at the time. See the *Covered Wagon*, 18 March 1939, 3. It reads, in part, "To every one that reads this paper, I wish to point out that it is not edited by any one connected with the Government. The paper is put out by the camp committee, democratically elected by all residents of the camp. Like every one else that lives in camp I contribute an article or two each week, to which I sign my name, whether it is printed or not is up to the editor."
12 "The Covered Wagon Speaks," *Covered Wagon News*, 10 February 1940, 11.

13 This distinction, though often murky, is common in media studies. For a discussion of these categories, see Carsten Reinemann, James Stanyer, Sebastian Scherr, and Guido Legnante, "Hard and Soft News: A review of concepts, operationalizations, and key findings," *Journalism* 13, no. 2 (11 November 2011): 221–239.
14 *Agri-News*, 24 June 1939, 1, 2.
15 The name change happened with the September 1, 1939 issue.
16 *Covered Wagon News*, 31 March 1940, 1.
17 For example, the *Covered Wagon News* printed "Abide with Me" on its "Poets' Page," 10 August 1940.
18 Orsi, *Thank You, St. Jude*, xvii.
19 Ibid.
20 Othra Gonderman, untitled, *Covered Wagon News*, 30 December 1939, 1.
21 Ruby Massey, "A Talk With Jesus," *Covered Wagon* (Indio), 14 January 1939, 3.
22 See Greene, *No Depression in Heaven* for a discussion of the meaning-making power of declension narratives in Depression-era Protestantism.
23 Joseph August, "Thine Be the Dominion," *Covered Wagon News*, 27 January 1940, 1.
24 See Hall, *Worlds of Wonder, Days of Judgment* for a deeper historical discussion of the phenomenon of "horse shed Christians."
25 Ollie Huffman, "Christ, Our Life," *Tow Sack Tatler*, 29 November 1939, 2.
26 Jack Bays, "Kidnappers of Jesus," *Covered Wagon News*, 10 February 1940, 11.
27 *Covered Wagon News*, 10 August 1940, 1.
28 *Covered Wagon News*, 5 October 1940, 12 October 1940, 19 October 1940.
29 *Covered Wagon News*, 23 November 1940, 1.
30 "Letter from Rev. Pietsch," *Covered Wagon News*, 3 February 1940, 3.
31 "A Word from Your Pastor," *Covered Wagon News*, 10 February 1940, 11.
32 "Borned with Death in Your System," *Covered Wagon News*, 31 March 1940, 4.
33 "The Temptations of Christ," *Covered Wagon News*, 20 July 1940, 8.
34 "James and the Horse," *Covered Wagon News*, 24 August 1940, 3.
35 Such a disclaimer never accompanied camp pastors' homilies.
36 "Answer to 'James and the Horse,'" *Covered Wagon News*, 31 August 1940, 3.
37 "How to Find the True Way to Heaven," *Covered Wagon News*, 7 September 1940, 4.
38 "Camp Church and Sunday School," *Migratory Clipper*, 20 April 1940, 2. Emphasis in the original.
39 *Migratory Clipper*, 30 March 1940.
40 Ibid., 6 April 1940.
41 See Greene, *No Depression in Heaven*, chap. 2, for a discussion of similar varieties of apocalypticism in Memphis and the Delta.
42 *Migratory Clipper*, 30 March 1940.
43 Ibid., 6 April 1940.
44 These were characteristics of other California apocalypticisms roughly contemporaneous with Owens's. Writers for the *King's Business*, published out of Los

Angeles, saw signs of the end times everywhere in the 1930s. In the empires of Russia, England, Japan, and Italy, they saw the kings of the north, south, east and west (respectively) described in the book of Daniel. When they looked closer to home, they saw communists and collectivists of any stripe serving as agents of the adversary, preparing for a final struggle. Charles Fuller, broadcasting out of Los Angeles, was far less specific when it came to naming the signs, but was no less convinced that the fight was on between the forces of faith and the forces of infidelity, that resistance to his radio program and the growth of atheism and collectivism in America were evidence of Satan's activity, and that Jesus would soon return in glory to cast down the unrighteous and the infidel.

45 *Covered Wagon News*, 28 September 1940, 11.
46 *Covered Wagon News*, 28 September 1940, 11.
47 *Covered Wagon News*, 5 October 1940, 7.

7. THE GATE, REVISITED

1 Mork to Hollenberg, 1 June 1940, CF-27 Shafter 918-02 (3), Shafter Box 46.
2 Wilson, "Religious Leaders, Institutions and Organizations Among Certain Agricultural Workers in the Central Valley of California." Lloyd D. Barba also makes use of Wilson's work in his dissertation "California's Cross: A Cultural History of Pentecostalism, Race, and Agriculture."
3 See Barba, "The Dust District: Okies, Authority, and the Hard-liner Transformation of California Pentecostalism," in Barba, Johnson, and Ramírez, eds. *Oneness Pentecostalism: Race, Gender and Culture*; and Dochuk, *From Bible Belt to Sunbelt*.
4 *Agri-News*, 27 May 1939, 1–2; 4 August 1939, 8.
5 *Agri-News*, 13 May 1939, 1–2. Capitalization in the original.
6 Foucault, *Discipline and Punish*.
7 "Withdrawals from Homes, Farms, Etc.," 30 September 1938, RF-CF-16 (25) 918 Arvin Reports (Prior 7-1-1940), Arvin Box 22.
8 Perry Miller, "Errand into the Wilderness."
9 *Agri-News*, 1 July 1939, 4.
10 Mork to Hollenberg, 1 June 1940, CF-27 Shafter 918-02 (3), Shafter Box 46.
11 Mork to Hollenberg, 25 June 1940, CF-27 Shafter 918–02 (3), Shafter Box 46.
12 Mork to Hollenberg, undated, RF-CF-27-789-02 Shafter General, Shafter Box 45.
13 Mork to Hewes, 29 October 1940, RR CF 27 918–02, Folder 4, Shafter Box 46.
14 Barba, "The Dust District."
15 "Minutes of Council Meeting, Saturday, April 2, 1938," Arvin Corporations (prior 7-1-40), RF-CF-16 (25) 620, Arvin Box 20.
16 Conrad Reibold to Harvey Coverley, 29 March 1942, Firebaugh, Box 13; W. H. Matthews to "United States Department of Agric," Farm Security Administration, March 20, 1942, Firebaugh, Box 13; Harvey Coverley to W. H. Matthews, 24 March 1942, Firebaugh, Box 13.
17 Arthur A. Lundin, "Observations made during stay at Arvin Migratory Labor Camp, July 10 to July 17, 1936," 26 July 1936.

18 Lundin, Untitled, 26 July 1936, RF-CF-16 (25) 620 Arvin Corporations (Prior 7-1-40), Arvin Box 20.
19 Ibid.
20 Ibid.
21 Barba, "The Dust District."
22 Dochuk, *From Bible Belt to Sunbelt*.
23 Collins to Wood, 11 January 1936, "Report for Week Ending January 11, 1936," Folder 9, Box 77, IWP.
24 Wilson, 45.
25 Biographical information on Wilson comes from a wide range of sources including school and church records, yearbooks, alumni publications, and local newspapers. See in particular "Wilson Victor in Bates Meet," *The Highlander*, 18 May 1935, 1, https://archive.org/details/Highland_Echo_1925-1936/page/n693/mode/2up, p. 1179; "Alumni News," *The Garrett Tower* (August 1943), 5, https://collections.carli.illinois.edu/digital/collection/uni_tower/id/2003/rec/5; and *Journal of the Southern California-Arizona Annual Conference, the Methodist Church* (1944), 39, https://archive.org/details/journalofsoutheroooometh_q7s2, accessed October 19, 2022.
26 Wilson, 356.
27 Dochuk, *From Bible Belt to Sun Belt*.
28 Wilson, 359.
29 Ibid., 365.
30 Ibid., 366.
31 Ibid., 378.
32 Ibid., 382.
33 Ibid., 374, 380.
34 Ibid., 371. Wilson included as "Figure I" in his chapter on Pietsch a copy of the "Migrant Gospel Fellowship Weekly Summary Report," a spreadsheet for tracking activities from "Home Visits" and "Hospital [Visits]," to people "Restored to Fell[owship]" and the number of "Colportage Books" distributed.
35 Ibid., 380–381.
36 Ibid., 382.
37 Ibid., 382.
38 Ibid., 240.
39 Ibid., 243.
40 Ibid., 243.
41 Ibid., 250–251.
42 Ibid., 251.
43 Ibid., 452.
44 Ibid., 346.
45 Ibid., 289.
46 Ibid., 316.
47 Ibid., 289.

48 Ibid., 249.
49 Ibid., 254–255.
50 Ibid., 264.
51 Bowler, *Blessed: A History of the American Prosperity Gospel.*
52 Wilson, 270.
53 Ibid, 271.
54 Ibid., 272.
55 Ibid., 261.
56 Ibid., 263.
57 Ibid., 263–264.
58 Ibid., 276–277.
59 Ibid., 278.
60 Ibid., 278–279.
61 Ibid., 284.
62 Ibid., 281.
63 Ibid., 288.
64 Ibid., 290–291, 310.
65 Ibid., 317.
66 Ibid., 307.
67 Ibid., 292.
68 Ibid., 301.
69 Ibid., 268.

EPILOGUE

1 Warren Engstrand to Myer Cohen, November 28, 1942, Brawley Migratory Labor Camp 7-1-42, RR-CF-28-918-02, Brawley Box 11.
2 Glen Trimble to Myer Cohen, January 2, 1943, Brawley Migratory Labor Camp 7-1-42, RR-CF-28-918-02, Brawley Box 11.
3 Deborah Cohen, *Braceros: Migrant Citizens and Transnational Subjects in the Postwar United States and Mexico*, 3, 118.
4 *The Annual Report of the Farm Security Administration, 1942–43*, 8, 22–24.
5 Elizabeth Davisson to Addie Swapp, December 21, 1941 (Enclosures include "Radio Script" titled "Farm Flashes, KXO El Centro, California, December 18, 1941"), "Brawley," RR-CF-28-918-02; Brawley and Ceres, Box 28.
6 Duncan Ryūken Williams, *American Sutra: A Story of Faith and Freedom in the Second World War* (Cambridge, MA: The Belknap Press of the Harvard University Press, 2019).

BIBLIOGRAPHY

ARCHIVES / COLLECTED PAPERS

Coded Administrative Camp Files [1933–1945], Record Group 96, National Archives and Records Administration, Pacific Region, San Bruno, California.
Harry Drobish Papers, Bancroft Library, University of California, Berkeley.
Charles Philipps Papers, Archives of the Archdiocese of San Francisco.
Irving Wood Papers, Bancroft Library, University of California, Berkeley.

CAMP NEWSPAPERS

Agri-News (Shafter)
Arvin Cultivator (Arvin)
Covered Wagon News (Shafter)
Indio Covered Wagon (Indio)
Happy Valley People's Word (Indio)
Migratory Clipper (Indio)
Migratory Worker (Indio)
Tow Sack Tattler (Arvin)
Weedpatch Cultivator (Arvin)

SECONDARY SOURCES

Anderson, Benedict. *Imagined Communities: Reflections on the Origin and Spread of Nationalism.* London: Verso, 1983.
Asad, Talal. *Formations of the Secular: Christianity, Islam, Modernity.* Stanford: Stanford University Press, 2003.
Axtell, James. *The Invasion Within: The Contest of Cultures in Colonial North America.* New York: Oxford University Press, 1985.
Babb, Sonora. *Whose Names Are Unknown.* Norman: University of Oklahoma Press, 2004.
Barba, Lloyd D. "California's Cross: A Cultural History of Pentecostalism, Race, and Agriculture." PhD diss., University of Michigan, 2016.
———. *Sowing the Sacred: Mexican Pentecostal Farmworkers in California.* New York: Oxford University Press, 2022.
Barba, Lloyd D., Andrea Johnson, and Daniel Ramírez, eds. *Oneness Pentecostalism: Race, Gender and Culture.* University Park: Pennsylvania State University Press, 2023.
Barnhurst, Kevin and John Nerone. *The Form of the News: A History.* New York: The Guilford Press, 2001.

Beaumont, H. M. "The Operation of Imhoff Tanks." *Sewage Works Journal* 1, no. 2 (January 1929): 211–217.

Bederman, Gail. *Manliness and Civilization: A Cultural History of Gender and Race in the United States, 1880–1917*. Chicago: University of Chicago Press, 1995.

Benson, Jackson. "'To Tom, Who Lived It': John Steinbeck and the Man from Weedpatch," and "An Afterword and an Introduction." *Journal of Modern Literature* 5, no. 2 (April 1976): 151–194.

Berry, Evan. *Devoted to Nature: The Religious Roots of American Environmentalism*. Berkeley: University of California Press, 2015.

Best, Wallace. *Passionately Human, No Less Divine: Religion and Culture in Black Chicago, 1915–1952*. Princeton: Princeton University Press, 2013.

Bowler, Kate. *Blessed: A History of the American Prosperity Gospel*. New York: Oxford University Press, 2013.

Butler, Anthea. *Women in the Church of God in Christ: Making a Sanctified World*. Chapel Hill: University of North Carolina Press, 2012.

Carpenter, Joel. *Revive Us Again: The Reawakening of American Fundamentalism*. New York: Oxford University Press, 1997.

Coburn, John Michael. "The Gospel According to John Steinbeck." MA Thesis. Georgetown University, 2011.

Cohen, Deborah. *Braceros: Migrant Citizens and Transnational Subjects in the Postwar United States and Mexico*. Chapel Hill: University of North Carolina Press, 2011.

Curtis, Heather. *Holy Humanitarians: American Evangelicals and Global Aid*. Cambridge, MA: Harvard University Press, 2018.

D'Agostino, Peter R. *Rome in America: Transnational Catholic Ideology from the Risorgimento to Fascism*. Chapel Hill: University of North Carolina Press, 2004.

Day, Dorothy. *The Long Loneliness*. New York: HarperOne, 2009.

Deutsch, Nathaniel. *Inventing America's Worst Family: Eugenics, Islam, and the Fall and Rise of the Tribe of Ishmael*. Berkeley: University of California Press, 2009.

Dinnerstein, Leonard. *Antisemitism in America*. New York: Oxford University Press, 1995.

Dochuk, Darren. *From Bible Belt to Sunbelt: Plain-Folk Religion, Grass Roots Politics, and the Rise of Evangelical Conservatism*. New York: W. W. Norton and Company, 2010.

Dolan, Jay P. *The American Catholic Experience: A History from Colonial Times to the Present*. Garden City, NY: Doubleday and Company, 1985.

Douglas, Mary. *Purity and Danger: An Analysis of Concepts of Pollution and Taboo*. London: Ark, 1984.

Ebel, Jonathan H. "'In Every Cup of Bitterness, Sweetness': California Christianity and the Great Depression." *Church History: Studies in Christianity and Culture* 80, no. 3 (September 2011): 590–599.

———. "Reforming Faith: John Steinbeck, the New Deal, and the Religion of the Wandering Oklahoman." *The Journal of Religion* 92, no. 4 (October 2012): 527–535.

Egan, Timothy. *The Worst Hard Time: The Untold Story of Those Who Survived the Great American Dust Bowl*. New York: Houghton Mifflin Company, 2006.

Fessenden, Tracy. *Culture and Redemption: Religion, the Secular, and American Literature* Princeton: Princeton University Press, 2006.

Fisher, Linford. *The Indian Great Awakening: Religion and the Shaping of Native Cultures in Early America*. New York: Oxford University Press, 2014.

Fitzgerald, Maureen. *Habits of Compassion: Irish Catholic Nuns and the Origins of New York's Welfare System, 1830–1920*. Urbana: University of Illinois Press, 2021.

Foucault, Michel. *Discipline and Punish: The Birth of the Prison*. New York: Vintage Books, 1995.

Galbraith, John Kenneth. *The Great Crash, 1929*. Boston: Houghton Mifflin, 1997.

Graber, Jennifer. *The Gods of Indian Country: Religion and the Struggle for the American West*. New York: Oxford University Press, 2018.

Greene, Alison Collis. *No Depression in Heaven: The Great Depression, the New Deal, and the Transformation of Religion in the Delta*. New York: Oxford University Press, 2016.

Gregory, James N. *American Exodus: The Dust Bowl Migration and Okie Culture in California*. New York: Oxford University Press, 1989.

Gutierrez, Ramon. *When Jesus Came, the Corn Mothers Went Away: Marriage, Sexuality, and Power in New Mexico, 1500–1846*. Stanford: Stanford University Press, 1991.

Hall, David D. *Worlds of Wonder, Days of Judgment: Popular Religious Belief in Early New England*. Cambridge, MA: Harvard University Press, 1990.

Handy, Robert. "The American Religious Depression, 1925–1935," *Church History* 29, no. 1 (March 1960): 3–16.

Higginbotham, Evelyn Brooks. *Righteous Discontent: The Women's Movement in the Black Baptist Church, 1880–1920*. Cambridge, MA: Harvard University Press, 1994.

Lange, Dorothea and Paul Schuster Taylor. *An American Exodus: A Record of Human Erosion*. New York: Reynal and Hitchcock, 1939.

Leonard, Thomas C. *Illiberal Reformers: Race, Eugenics, and American Economics in the Progressive Era*. Princeton: Princeton University Press, 2017.

Lincoln, Bruce. *Holy Terrors: Thinking about Religion after September 11*. Chicago: University of Chicago Press, 2002.

Lofton, Kathryn. *Consuming Religion*. Chicago: University of Chicago Press, 2017.

Marsden, George. *Fundamentalism and American Culture*. New York: Oxford University Press, 1980.

McDannell, Colleen. *Picturing Faith: Photography and the Great Depression*. New Haven: Yale University Press, 2004.

McWilliams, Carey. *Factories in the Field: The Story of Migratory Farm Labor in California*. Berkeley: University of California Press, 2000.

Miller, Perry. "Errand into the Wilderness." *The William and Mary Quarterly*, Third Series 10, no. 1 (Jan., 1953): 4–32.

Modern, John Lardas. *Secularism in Antebellum America*. Chicago: University of Chicago Press, 2011.

Orsi, Robert. *Thank You, St. Jude: Women's Devotion to the Patron Saint of Hopeless Causes*. New Haven: Yale University Press, 1996.
Putney, Clifford. *Muscular Christianity: Manhood and Sports in Protestant America, 1880–1920*. Cambridge, MA: Harvard University Press, 2003.
Rauschenbusch, Walter. *Christianity and the Social Crisis in the 21st Century*. Edited by Paul Rauschenbusch. New York: HarperOne, 2007.
Seales, Chad. *The Secular Spectacle: Performing Religion in a Southern Town*. New York: Oxford University Press, 2013.
Shah, Nayan. *Contagious Divides: Epidemics and Race in San Francisco's Chinatown*. Berkeley: University of California Press, 2001.
Stein, Walter. *California and the Dust Bowl Migration*. Westport, CT: Greenwood Press, Inc., 1973.
Steinbeck, John. *The Grapes of Wrath*. New York: Penguin Books, 2006.
———. *Harvest Gypsies: On the Road to the Grapes of Wrath*. Berkeley: Heyday Books, 1988.
Sullivan, Winnifred Fallers. *The Impossibility of Religious Freedom*. Princeton: Princeton University Press, 2005.
Sutton, Matthew Avery. *Aimee Semple McPherson and the Resurrection of Christian America*. Cambridge, MA: Harvard University Press, 2007.
———. *American Apocalypse: A History of Modern Evangelicalism*. Cambridge, MA: Belknap Press of Harvard University Press, 2014.
———. "Was FDR the Antichrist? The Birth of Fundamentalist Antiliberalism in a Global Age." *Journal of American History* 98, no. 4 (2012): 1052–1074.
Taylor, Charles. *A Secular Age*. Cambridge, MA: Belknap Press of Harvard University Press, 2007.
Tilley, Elizabeth Anne et al. *Compendium of Sanitation Systems and Technologies*, rev. 2nd ed. City unknown: EAWAG, updated 2016. https://www.researchgate.net/publication/241276067.
Tweed, Thomas A. *Crossing and Dwelling: A Theory of Religion*. Cambridge, MA: Harvard University Press, 2008.
Ummel, Rheba. *Almost Sixty Years of Miracles*. Unpublished memoir, Shafter Historical Society.
United States Department of Agriculture. *The Annual Report of the Farm Security Administration, 1942–43*. Washington, DC: US Government Printing Office, 1944.
———. *The Farm Security Administration*. Washington, DC: US Government Printing Office, 1941.
Voyle, Tracie Brynn. *The Settler Sea: California's Salton Sea and the Consequences of Colonialism*. Lincoln: University of Nebraska Press, 2021.
Wacker, Grant. *Heaven Below: Early Pentecostals and American Culture*. Cambridge, MA: Harvard University Press, 2003.
Watkins, T. H. *The Hungry Years: A Narrative History of the Great Depression in America*. New York: Henry Holt and Company, 1999.
Weber, Max. *Economy and Society*. Berkeley: University of California Press, 1978.

———. *The Protestant Ethic and the Spirit of Capitalism with Other Writings on the Rise of the West*. 4th ed. Translated and introduced by Stephen Kalberg. New York: Oxford University Press, 2009.

Weisenfeld, Judith. *Hollywood Be Thy Name: African American Religion in American Film, 1929–1949*. Berkeley: University of California Press, 2007.

———. *New World A' Comin': Black Religion and Racial Identity During the Great Migration*. New York: New York University Press, 2018.

Williams, Duncan Ryūken. *American Sutra: A Story of Faith and Freedom in the Second World War*. Cambridge, MA: The Belknap Press of the Harvard University Press, 2019.

Wilson, James Bright. "Religious Leaders, Institutions and Organizations among Certain Agricultural Workers in the Central Valley of California." PhD diss., Graduate School of Religion, University of Southern California, 1944.

INDEX

Page numbers in *italics* indicate photographs

"Abide with Me" (poem), 310
activism, 39–42, 44–45, 51
Adams, Ernest, 365
advertisements, 295, 313, 340
African Americans, 23, 44, 195, 366, 371–72
agriculture: agricultural society, 184–85; Associated Farmers, 24–26; in California, 12, *13*, 14, 34, 43–44, 49, 53, 80–81, 109, 191–200; cotton industry and, 211, 224; culture of, 137–38; after droughts, 2; economics of, 5; to Farm Bureau, 34–35; fertilizer for, 185, 208, 211; to FSA, 136–37; in Great Depression, 36, 266, 321; harvesting, 189, 202–3; in Imperial Valley, 191–92, 212–13; industrial farms, 348; labor in, 39–40, 55–56, 129–30, 165–67, 354; management of, 96; migration and, 24–25, 124–28; picking and, 53–54; politics of, 302–3; to RA, 123; in San Joaquin Valley, 346; in US, 4–5, 137
Agri-News, 278–80, 282–85, *286*, *287*, 288–89, 300–301, 331–33. *See also* newspapers
alcohol, 231–32, 237–38
Allen, Robert, 258–59
"America" (Davies, A. H.), *292*, *293*
American Civil Liberties Union, 39
American Legion, 34–35
Ames, George, 202
Andrews, Alonzo, 38

anthropology, 8–9, 63, 117, 184–85
apocalyptic discourse, 319–22, 402n44
Apostolic Faith church, *345*
architecture, 9–10, 35–36
Arizona, 104, 271–72, 350
Arkansas, 1, 18, 100–101, 104, 133; culture of, 140–44, 171; Indio Migratory Farm Worker's Camp and, 175–76; migration from, 168; stereotypes of, 214
"Arkies Welcome" (Burns), 175–76
Arvin Migratory Farm Labor Camp: authority at, 150–51, 158–59; children at, 215; Collins, T., at, 22, 25, 56, 70, 72, 77–78, 83, 169, 179–80, 389n31; community centers at, 241–42; culture at, 227–28; family in, 100–101; gates to, 31–32, *32*; guards at, 261; history of, 1–2, 8, 21, 38–39; labor and, 38, 108; Lundin at, 342–44; management at, 82, 116; Marysville Migratory Farm Labor Camp and, 186–87, 214; "New Clean Up Schedule" for, 217–18; newspapers at, 184, 275; population of, 68; to RA, 103; recreation at, 233; reputation of, 95, 98; sanitary unit at, *10*
Asad, Talal, 223–24
Associated Farmers (organization), 24–26
"As the Feller Sez" (Ross), 219–21
August, Joseph, 305–7, 309
Auguston, John, 171–74

authority: at Arvin Migratory Farm Labor Camp, 150–51, 158–59; bureaucracy and, 83–84, 88–89, 107–8; of Collins, T., 214; in community, 339–40; for dehumanization, 127–28; in family, 154–55; of FSA, 200, 210, 337; of Garst, 98, 212–13; for gates, 57–66, 76–79; in government camps, 185–86; in humanitarianism, 370–71; legal, 333; of management, 82–83, 86–87, 97–107, 219, 375–79; in migration, 191–200, 329–30; of Mork, R., 309; in RA, 93–95, 115, 210; at Shafter Migratory Farm Labor Camp, 208–9, 335; in US, 102

Bakersfield, California: conditions in, *146*, *188*, *276*; culture of, 8, 68, 99, 113–15, 144–45, 276
Baptists, 11, 18, 146, 196, 268, 311, 348–49, 355–57
Barnhurst, Kevin, 280–81
Barry, Charles, 47, 49, 212–13, 221, 238, 288, 333
Baughman, C. F., 211–12
Bays, Jack, 307–10, 324
Beaumont, H. M., 206–7, 397n36
behavior: of children, 218–19; in Christianity, 368–69; in community, 219–23; ordinances for, 150–51, 214–15; racism and, 223–24
Behold the Man (film), 247, 249, 273
Biggs, Claude V., 50–51
Bisby, Spencer, 334
Blythe, California, *345*
Boylston, C. E., 40
Boy's and Girl's Club, 252
Bracero Program, 376–77
Bramlett, Eddie, 263–64
Brawley Migratory Farm Labor Camp: conditions in, 46–47, 49, *148*, 199, 212–13, 226; gender in, 164; management of, 196; policy at, 183; racial diversity at, 197; religion at, 252; sanitary units at, 376–77; sanitation at, 209–10; Shafter Migratory Farm Labor Camp and, 207–8
Breeden, William, 40
"The Broken Wheel" (Taylor, S.), *139*
Brown, John, 320
Brown, Robert, 252
bureaucracy: authority and, 83–84, 88–89, 107–8; to Drobish, 186–87; in FSA, 138, 140, 170; in government camps, 80–86, *81*, *83*; hierarchies in, 64; ideology and, 149–50; in management, 86, 93–97, 186–91; of New Deal, 127–28; in politics, 3–4, 107–15, 124–28, 186–91, *187*, *188*; in scholarship, 17; Tugwell in, 96
Burns, George, 175–76

Cairns, Burton, 207–13, 221–22, 226
California: agricultural society, 184–85; agriculture in, 12, *13*, 14, 34, 43–44, 49, 53, 80–81, 109, 191–200; Blythe, *345*; culture of, 4, 11, 34–35, 41–42, 51–52, 201–5, 223–24, 376; Department of Public Health, 34–35, 207, 210; Dos Palos, *349*; economics of, 14–15; environment of, 192–93; FSA and, 18, 222–23; government camps in, 11–12, *13*, 14–16, 153; in Great Depression, 5–6, 136, 184, 199; homelessness in, 138, 140; Housing and Immigration Commission, 39; Human Habitation in, *45*; humanitarianism in, 147; Imperial Valley of, 20, 38–39, 40–41, 170, 191–92, 212–13; industrial farms in, 348; in literature, 29–30; Mexico and, 38, 196–98; migration to, 18, 50–51, 55–56, 96, 100–101; during New Deal, 2–3, 9; Oklahoma and, 104; politics in, 32–33, 95, 112–13; poverty in, 132–33; Protestantism in, 17; RA in, 231–32; reform in, 137; religion in, 321–22; reputation of, 123, 124–28; Salinas, *358*; San Joaquin Valley to, 1–2, 12, 14,

24, 30; SERA in, 31, 34, 68–69; State Relief Administration, 170; "Tentative Program of the Division of Rural Rehabilitation, California," 5. *See also specific topics*

camps. *See specific topics*

Canada, 168

canning, 168

capitalism, 3, 16, 27, 50

Carter, Roy, 261

Catholicism: in Mexico, 146; missionaries for, 130–31; orphanages in, 22–24; priesthood in, 23; Protestantism and, 11, 15, 197; rituals in, 117; in Spain, 6; theology of, 26; in US, 118; women in, 76

Central Valley (California). *See specific topics*

charisma, 83–84, 123

children: at Arvin Migratory Farm Labor Camp, 215; Auguston on, 172–73; behavior of, 218–19; Boy's and Girl's Club, 252; Children's Welfare Committee, 163–64; cleanliness of, 155, 159–60, 191; in culture, 110–11; education of, 154, 221; family and, 143–44; in government camps, 101–2, *148*, 332; in migration, 59–60, 104, 144–46, *145*; in newspapers, 262–63; nursery school for, 236–37, 257; from Oklahoma, *149*; parents and, 235–36; in poverty, 68; psychology of, 70; quality of life for, 61–62; recreation for, 295–96; sanitary units for, 218; washing hands, *216*; women and, 60–61, 164–65; in Yuba City Camp, 236–37

Chinese immigrants, 36, 131–32

"Christ, Our Life" (Huffman), 306–7

Christianity: behavior in, 368–69; Catholicism, 127–28, 198; Christian Businessman's Committee, 349–50; Church Services, 252–53, *254*, 255–59, 261–68; entertainment in, 248–49; excommunication in, 335; housing to, 131; in literature, 126; marriage in, 266; Migrant Gospel Fellowship, 265, 268–72, 348–54, 368–70; missionaries in, 285, 371–72; movements in, 232–33; New Deal and, 368; philosophy and, 112; poetry in, 324, 327; politics and, 319–20; psychology of, 115; race in, 136; scholarship on, 347–48; Scofield Reference Bible, 266–67, 320, 351; social dynamics of, 355; social living in, 174; theology of, 230; in US, 24, 401n54

Christianity and the Social Crisis (Rauschenbusch), 232

Church Services, 252–53, *254*, 255–59, 261–68

Clark, Charles A., 196–99

Clark, Elmer T., 355, 357

class, 20, 111–12

cleanliness: of children, 155, 159–60, 191; to Collins, T., 176; competitions for, 174–75; discipline and, 151–60; of family, 156; in government camps, 169–76; to missionaries, 176–81; in newspapers, 215–21, 284, 288–89; ordinances for, 192–200; record-keeping of, 178–79; at Yuba City Camp, 177–78

Coachella Valley, *187*, 201–5

Coe, Ruth, 176–79

Cohen, Deborah, 377

Cohen, Myer, 178

Collins, Edith, 23

Collins, George, 23

Collins, Thomas: alcohol and, 237–38; at Arvin Migratory Farm Labor Camp, 22, 25, 56, 70, 72, 77–78, 83, 169, 179–80, 389n31; authority of, 214; cleanliness to, 176; Coe and, 178–79; on community, 212–13, 233–35, 239–40; on culture, 116–17; Drobish and, 83–84, 123; early life of, 22–23; for government camps, 57–66; leadership of, 77, 97–100, 120, 242–43; marriages of, 23–24;

Collins, Thomas (*cont.*)
at Marysville Migratory Farm Labor Camp, 57–58, 221–22; to Maudlin, 102–3; Mensing and, 101–2; on Mexicans, 145–46; migration and, 24–26, 115–16, 119, 140–44, 343; Mork, R., and, 177; Nunn, Georgie, and, 340; Porter and, 113–14; on poverty, 235–36; RA and, 1–2, 68, 79, 98; record-keeping by, 120–23; religion to, 73–76, 106–7, 231, 240–42, 335; reputation of, 19, 21, 26–27, 98–99, 124–28, 189–90, 389n42; Rowell and, 200; secularism to, 118; Steinbeck and, 21; Wood and, 94–95, 227–28, 233–34, 241–42
Collins, Thomas David, 263–64
Collins, Walter, 103
colonialism, 6, 130–31, 334–35
Colorado, 18
Colorado River, 192–93
Comer, Ernest, 233
communism/"communist," 39, 50, 213, 272, 320, 322; "Communists," 352
community: activism in, 39–40; at Arvin Migratory Farm Labor Camp, 241; authority in, 339–40; behavior in, 219–23; Collins, T., on, 212–13, 233–35, 239–40; culture of, 85; dialogue, 314–23; faith in, 304–5; family and, 7, 166–67, 179–80; FSA Department of Community and Family Services, 176; Golden Rule in, 171; to Good Neighbors committee, 119–20; in government camps, 9–10, 173–74; housing in, 41–42, 65–66; ideology of, 52–53, 63–64; management of, 176–81; in modernity, 28–29; morality in, 203; in newspapers, 295; politics of, 34–35; poverty in, 204–5; in Protestantism, 329–30; psychology of, 283, 369; race and, 375–77; religion in, 33, 102; social centers for, 256–57; songs, 242–46

community centers: culture at, 301–2; entertainment in, 227–28, 231–34, 241–50, 250, 251, 255, 259; films in, 376–77; in government camps, 227–30, 229, 237–41, 250, 251, 250–53, 254, 255–59, 260; missionaries in, 260–69; philosophy of, 241–50; recreation at, 231–37, 235; religion and, 269–73
contaminants, 212–23, 216, 217
Corse, Norman, 103–6
cotton industry: agriculture and, 211, 224; culture of, 331–32; economics of, 80, 98, 108–9, 242–43, 246, 346; labor in, 45–46; picking in, 185–86; in US, 12, 14, 36–37, 45–46; women in, 162–63
Covered Wagon News, 290, 291, 292, 293, 294, 295–300, 298, 299, 307–17, 322–24, 325, 326. *See also* newspapers
Coverley, Harvey, 19, 72, 201–5, 225, 341
Craig, Fred, 238
culture: of agriculture, 137–38; alcohol in, 231–32, 237–38; of Arkansas, 140–44, 171; at Arvin Migratory Farm Labor Camp, 227–28; of Bakersfield, 8, 68, 99, 113–15, 144–45, 276; of California, 4, 11, 34–35, 41–42, 51–52, 201–5, 223–24, 376; children in, 110–11; Collins, T., on, 116–17; of community, 85; at community centers, 301–2; of cotton industry, 331–32; cultural values, 223–24; discipline in, 344; of Dust Bowl, 18, 27, 146–47; evangelism in, 6–7, 11; gambling in, 239; geography and, 133; in government camps, 27–30, 156, 401n10; of Great Depression, 36–37, 64, 66–75, 67, 69, 73, 131; of Imperial Valley, 20, 38–39; of Indio Migratory Farm Worker's Camp, 151, 185, 321; Irish Americans in, 145; leadership in, 86–87; literature and, 124–28; of migration, 19–20, 65–66, 68–69, 69; modernity in, 279–80; moral environments in, 174; of Oklahoma, 127–28;

of pentecostalism, 11, 18–19, 27, 30, 316–17, 371–74; picking, 37–38, 46–47; of Protestantism, 241–50, 366–67; of revivals, 15, 19, 122, 251, *349*, 354–60; of San Joaquin Valley, 168–69, 268, 300; social control in, 330–31; social forces in, 6; social purity, 191–200; Steinbeck in, 44–45; of US, 29–30, 50–57; after World War I, 12, 14; of World War II, 318–19
Cummings, Clyde E., 334
Curran, Roland, 12, 14

Darby, John Nelson, 267
Davenport, F. M., 385n8
Davies, Ada Hilton, 292, *293*
Davies, Mary K., 28, 236–37
Davila, Delfino, 38
Davisson, Elizabeth, 163–64, 224–26
Day, Dorothy, 24
"The Death of My Babies" (Harvey), 327
dehumanization, 10, 127–28
Delp, Millie, 28
democracy, 115, 140
DeMort, Fred, 264
Dempster, Milen, 177–78, 348, 358–59
Department of Labor, 102
Department of Public Health, California, 34–35, 207, 210
Deutsch, Nathaniel, 147–48
Dilts, Ethel, 311
discipline: cleanliness and, 151–60; in culture, 344; evictions and, 238, 336–39; in migration, 331–36; in Protestantism, 340–43; psychology of, 330–31; scholarship on, 345–46. *See also* gates; Pentecostalism
discourse: apocalyptic, 319–22, 402n44; in evangelism, 62–63; of Protestantism, 10–11; public, 160, 171; in religion, 62, 229–30, 314–23
diversity, 15, 197, 272, 397n19
Dochuk, Darren, 19

domestication, 136–38, *139*, 140–50, *145*, *146*, *148*, *149*
domestic instruction, 163–64
domesticity, in migration, 143–44
domestic righteousness, 174–75
domestic sin, 130–31, 150–60
Doster, Marion F., 333
Douglas, Mary, 184–85, 191, 202, 224
Drobish, Harry: bureaucracy to, 186–87; Collins, T., and, 83–84, 123; discipline to, 336; on family, 119; Garst and, 52; on ideology, 55–56; on labor, 53–54; leadership of, 43, 49, 201, 207; on migration, 65, 71; Nickel and, 51–52; picking to, 54–55; RA to, 4–6; reputation of, 109; Roosevelt and, 4–5; on sanitary units, 56–57, 189–90; Tugwell and, 3, 5; Wood and, 21, 190
Du Bois, W. E. B., 385n8
Dunham, J. H., 103
Dust Bowl: culture of, 18, 27, 146–47; history of, 42, 378; migration during, 8, 12, 123; New Deal and, 3; Protestantism in, 30; refugees from, 6–7
Dykeman, Mildred, 295
Dykes, Sam, 106

Eastton, Sherman, 103, 105
economics: of agriculture, 5; banking, 212–13; Barry on, 47, 49; business, 55–56; of California, 14–15; of capitalism, 3; Christian Businessman's Committee, 349–50; of cotton industry, 80, 98, 108–9, 242–43, 246, 346; family, 161; in government camps, 119–20; of Great Depression, 18; hierarchies in, 200; of labor, 36, 114; of land use, 98–99; of migration, 73–74; during New Deal, 49; in San Joaquin Valley, 375; of Wall, 1–2
Eddy, Charles, 68–69, 77, 94
Edgar, Mary, 361
editors, of newspapers, 275, 279–83, 289, 297, 300, 309–10, 314, 322

education: of children, 154, 221; in government camps, 202–3; immigration and, 132; lectures, 300–301; in migration, 114; nursery school, 236–37, 257; poverty and, 7; religion in, 250–52, 257; Sunday School, 250–52, 297
Edwards, Robert, 201, 205
electoral politics, 182–83
"Eleven Cent Cotton" (song), 242–43
Ellis, Oma, 355, 368
Emerson, Marie, 259
engineering, 206–12, *209*
England, 6
Engstrand, Warren, 375–77
Enloe, Marion, 334
entertainment, 227–28, 231–34, 241–50, *250*, *251*, *255*, 259, 283–84. *See also specific topics*
ethnicity, 15
Europe, 6, 130, 163, 226, 318–19
evangelism: in culture, 6–7, 11; discourse in, 62–63; ideology of, 59–60; migration and, 78; poverty and, 62; in Protestantism, 15, 19; psychology of, 144–46; tradition of, 28, 33, 52–53
evictions: discipline and, 238, 336–39; gates and, 331–36; in Protestantism, 339–43
excrement, 189, 193–95, 199–200, 206, 210, 221–22, 224
extra-legal violence, 41

family: in Arvin Migratory Farm Labor Camp, 100–101; authority in, 154–55; in "The Broken Wheel," *139*; children and, 143–44; cleanliness of, 156; community and, 7, 166–67, 179–80; Drobish on, 119; economics, 161; FSA Department of Community and Family Services, 176; gender in, 168; housing for, 59–66, *73*, 133–36; in labor, 70–71; leadership in, 165–66; in migration, 18, 33, 133–36, *149*, 182–83; Mork, R., on, 329; orphanages and, 26; in poverty, 68–70; in Progress Surveys, 167–68; to RA, 108–9; race therefore, and, 15; religion and, 132–33, 172–73; services, 177–78; at Shafter Migratory Farm Labor Camp, 333–34; on tent platforms, *148*
Farm Bureau, 34–35
Farmer, Dessie, 315–17, 323, 327–28
Farmersville Migratory Farm Labor Camp, *73*
farming. *See* agriculture
Farm Labor Transportation Program, 376
Farm Security Administration (FSA): agriculture to, 136–37; authority of, 200, 210, 337; bureaucracy in, 138, 140, 170; California and, 18, 222–23; Department of Community and Family Services, 176; gender to, 160–61; hierarchies in, 153; leadership of, 72; literature, 160; modernity to, 281; policy, 393n1; politics of, 377–78; Progress Surveys by, 167–68; RA and, 2–3, 15–16, 19, 44, 57–58, 80–86, *81*, *83*, 147, 186; reputation of, 272
Feathergill, H. T., 317–18
Federal Migrant Camps. *See* government camps
films: in community centers, 376–77; for migrants, 228–29, 247–49, 297, 376–77; about migration, 21–22; in newspapers, 292, 295, 297, 300
"Filthy Human Beings" (Mork, R.), 156
Firebaugh Migratory Farm Labor Camp, 17, 165, 341, 352
Fisher, Bud, 284–85
Ford, John, 21
Franks, Jess M., 333
free speech, 340–41
Frick Ranch, 74
FSA. *See* Farm Security Administration
Fuller, Charles, 267, 402n44

gambling, 239
Garst, Jonathan: authority of, 98, 212–13; Drobish and, 52; opinions of, 397n24; Packard and, 21; for RA, 45–46; Taylor, P., and, 149–50; Tugwell and, 95
Gaston, Charles E., 334
gates: to Arvin Migratory Farm Labor Camp, 31–32, *32*; authority for, 57–66, 76–79; evictions and, 331–36; to government camps, 31–33, *32*, 329–31, *349*, *356*, *358*, 370–74; in migration, 66–75, *67*, *69*, *73*; to Mork, R., 336–39; philosophy of, 34–40, 50–57; to Pietsch, 348–54; poverty and, 41–47, *45*, *48*, *49*; Protestantism and, 343–48, *345*; punishment with, 354–61, *358*; religion and, 339–43; Wilson and, 361–70
gender, 160–62, 164, 168
Germany, 163
Gifford, M. A., 114–15
Gillespie, C. G., 207–13, 226
Glacken, Clarence, 8, 19, 42, 196–99
Glassford, Pelham, 38–41
God. *See specific topics*
"God is at the Anvil" (poem), 308–9
"God Never Fails Us" (poem), 324, 327
Golgotha (film), 247, 249, 273
Gonderman, Othra, 302–4, 309, 324
Good, Elmer, 334
Good Neighbors committee, 119–20
government camps: architecture of, 35–36; authority in, 185–86; bureaucracy in, 80–86, *81*, *83*; in California, 11–12, *13*, 14–16, 153; children in, 101–2, *148*, 332; Church Services in, 252–53, *254*, 255–59, 261–68; cleanliness in, 169–76; in Coachella Valley, *187*, 201–5; Collins, T., for, 57–66; community centers in, 227–30, *229*, 237–41, *250–51*, 250–53, *254*, 255–59, *260*; community in, 9–10, 173–74; conflict in, 157–58; culture in, 27–30, 156, 401n10; danger in, 191–200; to Department of Public Health, 34–35; domesticating in, 136–38, *139*, 140–50, *145*, *146*, *148*, *149*; domestic filters in, 165–69, *166*; economics in, 119–20; education in, 202–3; entertainment in, 227–28, 231–34, 241–50, *250*, *251*, 255, 259, 283–84; family services in, 177–78; gates to, 31–33, *32*, 329–31, *349*, *356*, *358*, 370–74; in *The Grapes of Wrath*, 124–28; hierarchies in, 210–11; history of, 1–7; Home Centers in, 164; homelessness and, 147; home management in, 160–65; homiletical Protestantism in, 316–23, 327–28; humanitarianism in, 57–58; illness in, 73–75, 388n5; libraries in, 295, 309; migration into, 66–75, *67*, *69*, *73*; missionaries in, 6, 9; Mork, R., on, 150–60; newspapers and, 50–51, 113–14, 274–79, *276*, *277*, 283–85, *286*, *287*, 288–89, *290*, *291*, *292*, *293*, *294*, 295–96; Packard on, 43–44; philosophy of, 50–57, 86–97, *89*; politics of, 97–107, 401n11; poverty in, 46–47, *48*, *49*; property in, 106; Protestantism in, 231–37, *235*, 323–24, *325*, *326*, 327–28; racism in, 195; records from, 42; recreation in, 141, 241–50, 269–73; reform of, 31; regional directors of, 338–39; religion in, 7–11, *10*, 31–33, *32*, 76–79, 107–15, 196–97, 368–69; reputation of, 45–46, 115–23, *121*, 215–21; sanitary units in, 186–91, *187*, *188*, 397n36; scholarship on, 17–27, *22*, *25*, 375–79; showers in, *217*; tent platforms in, 129–33, 135–36; theology in, 125; women in, 343–44. *See also specific topics*
Grapes of Wrath (film), 292, 295
Grapes of Wrath (Steinbeck), 21, 29–30, 81, 124–28, 134–35. *See also specific topics*

Gray, R. M., 202–3
Great Depression: agriculture in, 36, 266, 321; California in, 5–6, 136, 184, 199; culture of, 36–37, 64, 66–75, 67, 69, 73, 131; economics of, 18; exploitation in, 146–47; history of, 11–12; New Deal and, 28–29; newspapers during, 401n54; politics in, 11–12, 13, 14–16, 223–24; race in, 130; refugees in, 44; religion in, 11–12, 15; secularism in, 27–30
Greene, Alison Collis, 12, 15
Gregory, James, 12
Griset, Guy, 252
Grub, Jessie, 331
Guam, 23

Hall, G. Stanley, 236
Handy, Robert, 11
Hardie, Robert, 103–8, 113–15, 238
Harvey, Floyd P., 327
Harvey, Gerald, 40
Heinrichs, Sarah, 271
Henderson, J. C., 72
Heo, Angie, 8–9
Hernandez, Dolores, 38
Hewes, Lawrence, 338–39
Hildebrand, George, 274–75
Hildebrand, Roy, 274–75
Hjorth, Dick, 300
Hoggartt, Dennis L., 331
Hollenberg, Raul, 337
Home Centers, 164
homelessness, 132–36, 138, 140, 147
home management, 160–65
homiletical Protestantism: apocalyptic discourse in, 319–22; in government camps, 316–23, 327–28; in newspapers, 310–16, 325, 326
Hood, Marvin, 238
Hooser, A. A., 103
Hoovervilles. *See specific topics*
Hopkins, Annie, 22–23

housing: ad hoc shelters, 147; in Brawley, California, 46–47; in "The Broken Wheel," *139*; to Christianity, 131; in Coachella Valley, 201–5; in community, 41–42, 65–66; domestic filters, 165–69, *166*; engineering for, 206–12, *209*; for family, 59–66, 73, 133–36; hierarchies in, 165–66; homelessness, 132–33; home management, 160–65; immigration and, 112; in Imperial Valley, 170; in Indio Migratory Farm Worker's Camp, 167; at Marysville Migratory Farm Labor Camp, 176; in migration, 43–44, 63–64, 71–72; in philosophy, 56–57; psychology of, 133–36; to RA, 54; Riverside Title Company for, 204; in Shafter Migratory Farm Labor Camp, *166*; squatters camps, *48*, *146*, 146–47
Housing and Immigration Commission, 39
Hudson, Norman F., 333
Huffman, Ollie W., 306–7
humanitarianism: aid in, 204; authority in, 370–71; in California, 147; management and, 115–23; migration and, 78–79, 204–5; philosophy of, 57–59, 78–79; politics of, 138; theology and, 59
human waste. *See* sanitary units
Hunter, Charles, 103
hygiene. *See* illness; sanitary units

ideology: bureaucracy and, 149–50; of Communism, 50; of community, 52–53, 63–64; Drobish on, 55–56; of evangelism, 59–60; of Marysville Migratory Farm Labor Camp, 66; of New Deal, 107, 125–26; in newspapers, 279–80; philosophy and, 173–74; in poetry, 292; of politics, 58, 96–97; in Protestantism, 328; psychology and, 50–57, 362–63, 366–67; of record-keeping, 107–15; of religion, 85–86, 120–23; righteousness, 150–60; theology and, 353; of US, 378–79

illness: cleanliness and, 151–60; in government camps, 73–75, 388n5; to Metropolitan Life Insurance Company, 102; in migration, 78–79, 187–89, 205; nurses, 295; reports on, 82; sanitary units and, 73–75, 191–200; in theology, 77, 117
Imhoff tanks, 206–13, *209*, 225, 397n36
immigration, 42, 112, 132
Imperial Valley, 20, 38–39, 40–41, 170, 191–92, 212–13
Indio Migratory Farm Worker's Camp: Arkansas and, 175–76; culture of, 151, 185, 321; housing in, 167; labor at, 168–69; *Migratory Clipper* at, 173–74, 252–53, 261–63, 317, 320–22, 327; Mork, R., at, 151–52; newspapers and, 171, 261–64; office at, *81*; Shafter Migratory Farm Labor Camp and, 338
Iusi, Frank, 151–52, 176–77, 180, 214, 224–25, 258

Jack, Clyde, 40
Japan, 163, 224–25, 378
Jefferson, Thomas, 240
Jesus Christ. *See specific topics*
Johnson, Charles E., 204
Jones, J. A., 331
Jones, Philo, 40
Jones, T. P. B., 201, 204–5
journalism. *See* newspapers
Judaism, 11, 318–19

Kansas, 18, 266–68
"Kidnappers of Jesus" (Bays), 307–8
Kirkpatrick, C. W., 162
Klein, F. E., 284–86, 310
Kruger, E. G., 38
Kummerfeld, J. R., 285

labor: in agriculture, 39–40, 55–56, 129–30, 165–67, 354; Arvin Migratory Farm Labor Camp and, 38, 108; in cotton industry, 45–46; Department of Labor, 102; Drobish on, 53–54; economics of, 36, 114; family in, 70–71; homes, 168; at Indio Migratory Farm Worker's Camp, 168–69; from Mexico, 46–47, 375–76; National Labor Board, 38–39; in New Deal, 138; politics of, 51, 64–65; poverty and, 144–47; to RA, 43; racism in, 41–42, 198–99; sanitation and, 199–200; strikes, 37; women in, 62–63; WPA for, 68–70, 233, 252, 257, 391n20
labor camps. *See* government camps
Lange, Dorothea, 149, 201–2
Lascellos, Phillip, 253, 255
Lawrence, Nettie, 359, 368
League of Women Voters, 114–15
lectures, 300–301
legal authority, 333
leisure. *See* recreation
Leonard, Thomas, 147–48
libraries, 295, 309
Lincoln, Bruce, 230
literature, 21, 29–30, 81, 124–28, 134–35
livestock, 14, 138, 193–95
Lofton, Kathryn, 390n1
Lubin, Simon J., 38–39
Lundin, Arthur, 342–44, 385n7

management: of agriculture, 96; at Arvin Migratory Farm Labor Camp, 82, 116; authority of, 82–83, 86–87, 97–107, 219, 375–79; Barry in, 333; of Brawley Migratory Farm Labor Camp, 196; bureaucracy in, 86, 93–97, 186–91; of community, 176–81; Coverley in, 341; home management, 160–65; humanitarianism and, 115–23; leadership in, 87–88, 103, 130; missionaries and, 169–76; Pentecostalism to, 358–59; policy, 182–84; politics of, 80–81, 370–71; psychology of, 151–60; in RA, 87–89; reputation of, 103–7; Ross in, 216–17; of sanitary units, 201–5; at Shafter

management (*cont.*)
  Migratory Farm Labor Camp, 337; tent platforms and, 148, 164; Thomsen in, 107–15; Wood and, 86–88, 90–92, 111
marriage, 121–22, 142–43, 266
Marysville Migratory Farm Labor Camp: Arvin Migratory Farm Labor Camp and, 186–87, 214; Collins, T., at, 57–58, 221–22; Eddy on, 77; history of, 34–38; housing at, 176; ideology of, 66; leadership of, 68; migration to, 56–59; religion in, 116–17; reputation of, 50, 72; squatters camps at, 178
Massey, Ruby Nell, 256–57, 304–7
Matthews, W. H., 341
Maudlin, Thomas, 102–3
Maurin, Peter, 24
McClain, Joseph, 152, 157–58, 253, 255, 261–62
McClanahan, Jay, 333
McCully, Dale, 300
McDannell, Colleen, 15–16
McGuire, P. A., 253
McKenzie, James, 106
McPherson, Aimee Semple, 264
McWilliams, Carey, 35, 37
Means, Nancy Duvall, 23–24
media. *See* newspapers
media scholarship, 280–81, 402n13
Mensing, Herbert, 98–105, 107, 110, 182, 241
Mercer, William, 70–71
Methodists, 11, 72–73, 347–54, 357
Metropolitan Life Insurance Company, 102, 119
Mexico: California and, 38, 196–98; Canada and, 168; Catholicism in, 146; Glacken on, 42; to Imperial Valley, 41; labor from, 46–47, 375–76; racism against, 196, 376–77; reputation of, 145–46; US and, 375–77
Migrant Gospel Fellowship, 265, 268–72, 348–54, 368–70

migration: activism and, 41–42, 44–45; agriculture and, 24–25, 124–28; from Arkansas, 168; authority in, 191–200, 329–30; to California, 18, 50–51, 55–56, 96, 100–101; children in, 59–60, 104, 144–46, *145*; Collins, T., and, 24–26, 115–16, 119, 140–44, 343; culture of, 19–20, 65–66, 68–69, *69*; discipline in, 331–36; domesticity in, 143–44; Drobish on, 65, 71; during Dust Bowl, 8, 12, 123; economics of, 73–74; education in, 114; evangelism and, 78; excrement in, 189, 193–95, 199–200, 206, 210, 221–22, 224; family in, 18, 33, 133–36, *149*, 182–83; films about, 21–22; gates in, 66–75, *67*, *69*, *73*; into government camps, 66–75, *67*, *69*, *73*; in *The Grapes of Wrath*, 81, 134–35; health in, 154; housing in, 43–44, 63–64, 71–72; humanitarianism and, 78–79, 204–5; illness in, 78–79, 187–89, 205; to Marysville Migratory Farm Labor Camp, 56–59; migrant Protestantism, 124–28; to missionaries, 111–12; politics of, 107–8; poverty in, 138, 140; psychology and, 27–28, 114–15, 169–76, 236, 362, 372–73, 375–79; to RA, 396n9; race and, 144–47; racism and, 109; reform and, 51–52; registration in, 90–93; religion on, 176–81; scholarship on, 29; self-government in, 99; settling after, 136–38, *139*, 140–50, *145*, *146*, *148*, *149*; to Shafter Migratory Farm Labor Camp, 211–12; social repair in, 227; in US, 89; women in, 67–68, 118, 161–62, 243–45; to Yuba City Camp, 180
Migratory Clipper, 173–74, 252–53, 261–63, 317, 320–22, 327. *See also* newspapers
migratory farm labor camps. *See* government camps
Migratory Worker. *See* newspapers
Miller, Bob, 242–43

Miller, James A., 253, 264
Miller, Perry, 334–35
Miller, T. T., 196
Miller, William, 320
missionaries: for Catholicism, 130–31; in Christianity, 285, 371–72; cleanliness to, 176–81; in community centers, 260–69; in government camps, 6, 9; management and, 169–76; migration to, 111–12; in newspapers, 284; in politics, 109–10; psychology of, 351–52; Society of Missionary Men and Women, 284–85, 288, 300–301; Ummel family and, 264–73
Missouri, 18, 104, 133
modernity: civilization in, 7, 223–26; community in, 28–29; in culture, 279–80; to FSA, 281; medicine in, 361; philosophy in, 387n2; photography in, 15–16; Protestantism in, 30; religion in, 28, 79, 186, 322–23; scholarship in, 17–18; in US, 190
Montgomery, Harvey, 309
Montgomery, Raymond, 309
Montgomery, W. L., 40
moral environments, 174
moral fitness, 131
morality, 203, 313–14, 334–35
Morgan, Clifford, 106
Mork, Betty May, 288
Mork, Helen, 288
Mork, Ray: authority of, 309; Collins, T., and, 177; Delp and, 28; on entertainment, 247–50; on family, 329; gates to, 336–39; on government camps, 150–60; interviews with, 348; Iusi and, 180; leadership of, 172, 216–17, 239, 295, 373, 401n11; newspapers and, 238, 281–82; policy of, 335; record-keeping by, 264–65, 268–69; religion to, 176, 257, 265–66, 272–73, 369–70; reputation of, 8, 27; at Shafter Migratory Farm Labor Camp, 199–200, 288–89; on tent platforms, 160; theology and, 246–47, 370
music, 242–46, 300. *See also specific topics*
Muston, Clarence, 366, 368

National Labor Board, 38–39
Native Americans, 39, 47, 134, 198, 372
Nerone, John, 280–81
"New Clean Up Schedule" (Ross), 217–18
New Deal: activism for, 51; agents, 223–24; bureaucracy of, 127–28; California during, 2–3, 9; Christianity and, 368; Dust Bowl and, 3; economics during, 49; Great Depression and, 28–29; ideology of, 107, 125–26; labor in, 138; philosophy of, 31, 222, 272; politics of, 20–21, 200, 391n20; race in, 197–98; reform during, 16, 20, 127–28, 261, 385n8; reputation of, 147; technology in, 226; in US, 11, 81–82; WPA, 68–70, 233, 252, 257, 391n20
Newman, J. W., 202, 204
newspapers: at Arvin Migratory Farm Labor Camp, 184, 275; children in, 262–63; chronological Protestantism in, 296–97, 298–99, 300–301; cleanliness in, 215–21, 284, 288–89; community dialogue in, 314–23; editors of, 275, 279–83, 289, 297, 300, 309–10, 314, 322; entertainment in, 283–84; films in, 292, 295, 297, 300; government camps and, 50–51, 113–14, 274–79, 276, 277, 283–85, 286, 287, 288–89, 290–91, 292, 293–94, 295–96; during Great Depression, 401n54; homiletical Protestantism in, 310–16, 325, 326; ideology in, 279–80; Indio Migratory Farm Worker's Camp and, 171, 261–64; maps in, 281–82; missionaries in, 284; Mork, R., and, 238, 281–82; philosophy of, 156, 279–83, 401n10; poetic Protestantism in, 301–10; poetry in, 275–76, 282–83, 327–28; policy in, 331, 333; poverty in, 144–45; Protestantism in, 277–79,

newspapers (*cont.*)
284–85; public discourse in, 171; reform in, 173–74; religion in, 252–53, 256, 275, 285; Sunday School in, 297; tent platforms in, 169–70, 174–76; theology in, 323–24, *325*, *326*, 327–28
Nichols, C. H., 256
Nichols, Filander, 238
Nicholson, Gene, 164–65
Nickel, George, 51–52
Nikkel, Albert F., 295, 312–13, 316–17
No Depression in Heaven (Greene), 12
Nunn, George, 119–20
Nunn, Georgie, 27, 103, 119–25, *121*, 127–28, 140, 142, 340
nursery school, 236–37, 257
nurses, 295

Oklahoma, 1, 18, 100–101, 133, 168; California and, 104; children from, *149*; culture of, 127–28; Protestantism in, 124; race and, 42; reputation of, 29–30
Olsen, Laverne, 271
ordinances: for behavior, 150–51, 214–15; for cleanliness, 192–200; punishment and, 207, 218–19; racism in, 195
Oregon, 271–72, 350
organizations, for reform, 34–35
orphanages, 22–24, 26
Orsi, Robert, 301
"Our Camp" (poem), 309
Owens, O. V., 28, 318–23, 327–28

Packard, Walter, 21, 43–44
parents, 235–36
Patterson, Elsie, 202–3
pentecostalism: culture of, 11, 18–19, 27, 30, 316–17, 371–74; stereotypes of, 126–27, 140, 340, 346; theology of, 354–55, 361–70, 399n20; Wilson on, 357–61, *358*
Perkins, Alva Joe, 154
Perkins, Antha Lula, 154
Perrott, Richard, 188–89, 396n9

Peterson, Hazel K., 85–86
Philipps, Charles, 24
Phillips, Alex, 331
Phillips, Grady, 331
philosophy: anthropology and, 63; Christianity and, 112; of community centers, 241–50; of democracy, 115, 140; of gates, 34–40, 50–57; of government camps, 50–57, 86–97, *89*; housing in, 56–57; of humanitarianism, 57–59, 78–79; ideology and, 173–74; in modernity, 387n2; moral fitness, 131; of New Deal, 31, 222, 272; of newspapers, 156, 279–83, 401n10; of RA, 281; of racism, 47, 49; of recreation, 141; religion and, 51–52, 378–79; in US, 97–98
photography, 15–16
picking: agriculture and, 53–54; in cotton industry, 185–86; culture, 37–38, 46–47; to Drobish, 54–55; racism in, 36–37; sanitation and, 184–86; in San Joaquin Valley, 37
Pickle, Vester, 28
Picturing Faith (McDannell), 15–16
Pietsch, Paul, 265, 268–72, 295, 310–12, 316–17, 348–54, 368–69
Pixley uprisings, 38
play. *See* recreation
playgrounds, 60–61
poetic Protestantism, 301–10
poetic religion, 301–2
poetry, 275–76, 282–83, 292, 324, 327–28. *See also specific poems*
policy, 113, 182–84, 331–35, 393n1
politics: of agriculture, 302–3; bureaucracy in, 3–4, 107–15, 124–28, 186–91, *187*, *188*; in California, 32–33, 95, 112–13; Christianity and, 319–20; of community, 34–35; electoral, 182–83; of FSA, 377–78; of government camps, 97–107, 401n11; in Great Depression, 11–12, *13*, 14–16, 223–24; of humanitarianism, 138; ideology of, 58, 96–97; of labor, 51,

64–65; of livestock, 193–94; of management, 80–81, 370–71; of migration, 107–8; missionaries in, 109–10; of New Deal, 20–21, 200, 391n20; of ordinances, 192; public discourse in, 160; of RA, 52; religion and, 115–23, *121*; of self-government, 145–46; of SERA, 68–69; social forces in, 180–81; theology and, 34, 172–74, 272; in US, 27–28
Porter, Nellie, 109–14
poverty: in California, 132–33; children in, 68; Collins, T., on, 235–36; in community, 204–5; debt in, 169; education and, 7; evangelism and, 62; family in, 68–70; gates and, 41–47, *45*, *48*, *49*; in government camps, 46–47, *48*, *49*; labor and, 144–47; in migration, 138, 140; in newspapers, 144–45; psychology of, 332; race and, 38–39; theology and, 17; tithing and, 361–62; in US, 41
prejudice, 20
Premo, Blanche, 138, 140
Presbyterians, 11, 132, 198
privatization, 377–78
privies. *See* sanitary units
Progressive movement, 231–32
Progress Surveys, 167–68
Prohibition, 231–32
property, 106, 218, 377–78
Protestantism: apocalyptic discourse in, 319–22; in California, 17; Catholicism and, 11, 15, 197; charisma in, 123; chronological, 296–97, *298*, *299*, 300–301; Church Services, 252–53, *254*, 255–59, 261–68; community in, 329–30; culture of, 241–50, 366–67; discipline in, 340–43; discourse of, 10–11; in Dust Bowl, 30; evangelism in, 15, 19; evictions in, 339–43; faith in, 171; gates and, 343–48, *345*; in government camps, 231–37, *235*, 323–24, *325*, *326*, 327–28; identity with, 27; ideology in, 328; leadership in, 346–47; Methodism and, 348–54; migrant, 124–28; Migrant Gospel Fellowship, 265, 268–72, 348–54, 368–70; in modernity, 30; in newspapers, 277–79, 284–85; in Oklahoma, 124; pentecostalism and, 357; poetic, 301–10; to RA, 7; recreation and, *250*, *251*, 250–53, *254*, 255–59, *260*, 390n44, 399n20; reform in, 229–30, 342; at Shafter Migratory Farm Labor Camp, 264–65; Society of Missionary Men and Women, 284–85, 288, 300–301; theology of, 3, 237–41, 262; unruly, 339; in US, 127; Wilson on, 347–48. *See also* homiletical Protestantism
psychology: of children, 70; in Christianity, 115; of community, 283, 369; of dehumanization, 10; of discipline, 330–31; in evangelism, 144–46; in homelessness, 132–36; of housing, 133–36; ideology and, 50–57, 362–63, 366–67; of management, 151–60; migration and, 27–28, 114–15, 169–76, 236, 362, 372–73, 375–79; of missionaries, 351–52; of poverty, 332; of registration, 129; in religion, 352–53; of revivals, 3, 6–7, 60, 63, 84, 125, 371, 385n8; Steinbeck on, 134; of theology, 304–8
punishment, 207, 218–19, 238, 354–61, *358*. *See also* discipline
Puritanism, 6, 52–53, 334–35, 393n72
purity, 191–200, 206–12, *209*
Purity and Danger (Douglas), 184–85

RA. *See* Resettlement Administration
race: in Christianity, 136; of Collins, T., 23; community and, 375–77; family and, 15; in Great Depression, 130; history of, 147–48; Irish Americans, *145*; migration and, 144–47; Native Americans, 39, 47, 134, 198, 372; in New Deal, 197–98; Oklahoma and, 42; poverty and, 38–39; to Presbyterians, 198; racial diversity, 197, 397n19; religion and, 20, 101, 130–31; in US, 115

racism: against African Americans, 366, 371–72; behavior and, 223–24; in government camps, 195; against immigration, 42; in labor, 41–42, 198–99; against Mexico, 196, 376–77; migration and, 109; in ordinances, 195; philosophy of, 47, 49; in picking, 36–37; in US, 26, 147–48

Rainier, Jack, 154

Rauschenbusch, Walter, 131, 232

record-keeping: by Barry, 221; of cleanliness, 178–79; by Collins, T., 120–23; gender in, 161–62; ideology of, 107–15; by Mork, R., 264–65, 268–69; registration and, 106–7; regulation and, 214–15; scholarship from, 19–20; from Shafter Migratory Farm Labor Camp, 272

recreation: advertising for, 275–76; for children, 295–96; at community centers, 231–37, 235; in government camps, 141, 241–50, 269–73; limits of, 260–69; philosophy of, 141; Protestantism and, 250, 251, 250–53, 254, 255–59, 260, 390n44, 399n20; religion and, 237–41

reform: in California, 137; of government camps, 31; history of, 37, 131–32; migration and, 51–52; during New Deal, 16, 20, 127–28, 261, 385n8; in newspapers, 173–74; organizations for, 34–35; in Protestantism, 229–30, 342; by RA, 223; religion and, 323–24, 325–26, 327–28, 343–47, 345; for sanitary units, 59, 104–5, 111

refugees, 6–7, 44

registration, 23, 90–93, 105–7, 129

Reibold, Conrad, 341, 348, 352, 358–59

religion: in anthropology, 8–9, 117; bad, 142–43; of Baptists, 11, 18, 146, 196, 268, 311, 348–49, 355–57; at Brawley Migratory Farm Labor Camp, 252; in California, 321–22; Church Services, 252–53, 254, 255–59, 261–68; class and, 111–12; to Collins, T., 73–76, 106–7, 231, 240–42, 335; Communism and, 320, 322; in community, 33, 102; community centers and, 269–73; conflict in, 74–75; discourse in, 62, 229–30, 314–23; domestic sin in, 130–31, 150–60; in education, 250–52, 257; ethics of, 53–54; family and, 132–33, 172–73; gates and, 339–43; Gospel Bus, 356; in government camps, 7–11, 10, 31–33, 32, 76–79, 107–15, 196–97, 368–69; in Great Depression, 11–12, 15; history of, 6; ideology of, 85–86, 120–23; in Imperial Valley, 40; to Iusi, 258; leadership in, 84; marriage and, 121–22, 142–43; in Marysville Migratory Farm Labor Camp, 116–17; of Methodists, 72–73; Migrant Gospel Fellowship, 265, 268–72, 348–54, 368–70; on migration, 176–81; in modernity, 28, 79, 186, 322–23; morality in, 313–14; to Mork, R., 176, 257, 265–66, 272–73, 369–70; music and, 242–44, 300; in newspapers, 252–53, 256, 275, 285; philosophy and, 51–52, 378–79; to Pietsch, 265, 268–72, 295, 310–12, 316–17, 348–54, 368–69; poetic, 301–2; politics and, 115–23, 121; psychology in, 352–53; to RA, 88; race and, 20, 101, 130–31; recreation and, 237–41; reform and, 323–24, 325, 326, 327–28, 343–47, 345; religious conflict, 256; religious diversity, 397n19; religious identity, 18–19; sanitation and, 197–98, 223–26; sects in, 355; secularism and, 6–8; sin in, 311–12; Society of Missionary Men and Women, 284–85, 288, 300–301; in US, 11–12, 13, 14–16, 27–30, 390n1; Wilson on, 329–31; women in, 340. *See also specific religions*

Resettlement Administration (RA): agriculture to, 123; Arvin Migratory Farm Labor Camp to, 103; authority in,

93–95, 115, 210; in California, 231–32; Collins, T., and, 1–2, 68, 79, 98; diversity in, 272; to Drobish, 4–6; employees of, 42; family to, 108–9; FSA and, 2–3, 15–16, 19, 44, 57–58, 80–86, *81*, *83*, 147, 186; Garst for, 45–46; hierarchies in, 72–73; housing to, 54; labor to, 43; leadership in, 35–36; management in, 87–89; migration to, 396n9; philosophy of, 281; policy, 113, 393n1; politics of, 52; privatization with, 377–78; Protestantism to, 7; reform by, 223; religion to, 88; to Roosevelt, 3–4; scholarship on, 8, 37; SERA and, 31; staffing for, 24; surveyors for, 196; violence to, 61; Weller for, 50–51

revivals: culture of, 15, 19, 122, 251, *349*, 354–60; psychology of, 3, 6–7, 60, 63, 84, 125, 371, 385n8; stereotypes of, 30, 75, 77, 101, 115, 281, 369

Richardson, Ralph, 263

Ring, Thomas A., 334

Riverside Title Company, 204

Roberts, Wayne, 300

Roosevelt, Franklin, 3–5

Ross, Fred, 152, 158–59, 203, 216–17, 358–59

Rowell, Edward, 200

"Rural Rehabilitation Camps for Migrants," 5

Russel, Frank, 313

Ryan, John, 24

Salinas, California, *358*

Sanderson, C. B., 253, 361

Sanger, Margaret, 246–50, 273, 400n28

sanitary units: architecture of, 9–10; at Arvin Migratory Farm Labor Camp, *10*; at Brawley Migratory Farm Labor Camp, 376–77; for children, 218; cleanliness of, 153–54; Drobish on, 56–57, 189–90; in government camps, 186–91, *187*, *188*, 397n36; hygiene in, 64; illness and, 73–75, 191–200; management of, 201–5; near Bakersfield, *188*; reform for, 59, 104–5, 111; in San Joaquin Valley, 221; sewage for, 206–12, *209*; at Shafter Migratory Farm Labor Camp, *183*, *185*; shelter and, 2; technology in, 182–86, *183*, *185*, 223–26; water contaminants in, 212–23, *216*, *217*; water for, 144, 206–12, *209*

San Joaquin Valley: agriculture in, 346; to California, 1–2, 12, 14, 24, 30; culture of, 168–69, 268, 300; economics in, 375; picking in, 37; reputation of, 44, 124, 288; sanitary units in, 221

Schellenberg, Ed, 313–17, 323

Schoales, Joe E., 103–7, 110

scholarship: bureaucracy in, 17; on Christianity, 347–48; on discipline, 345–46; on government camps, 17–27, 22, 25, 375–79; media, 280–81, 402n13; on migration, 29; in modernity, 17–18; on RA, 8, 37; from record-keeping, 19–20; on registration, 105–6; on SERA, 34; on theology, 301; from Wilson, 345–47

Scofield Reference Bible, 266–67, 320, 351

secularism, 6–8, 27–30, 118

self-government, 99, 145–46

SERA. *See* State Emergency Relief Administration

settling, 136–38, *139*, 140–50, *145*, *146*, *148*, *149*

sewage, 206–12, *209*

Shafter Migratory Farm Labor Camp: *Agri-News* at, 278–80, 282–85, *286–87*, 288–89, 300–301, 331–33; authority at, 208–9, 335; Brawley Migratory Farm Labor Camp and, 207–8; *Covered Wagon News* at, 290, *291*, *292*, *293*, *294*, 295–300, *298*, *299*, 307–17, 322–24, *325*, *326*; entrance, *67*, *89*; family at, 333–34; history of, 45, 144; housing in, *166*; Indio Migratory Farm Worker's Camp and, 338; labor homes in, 168; leadership in, 151–52; management at,

Shafter Migratory Farm Labor Camp (*cont.*)
  337; migration to, 211–12; Mork, R., at, 199–200, 288–89; Protestantism at, 264–65; record-keeping from, 272; recreation at, 257; sanitary units at, *183*, *185*
Shah, Nayan, 131
sin. *See specific topics*
Sing You Sinners (film), 300
slavery, 54–55
The Small Sects in America (Clark, E. T.), 355
Smith, J. Z., 328
Smith, Leo, 34
Smith, W. L., 45
Snow, E. J., 238
social centers, 256–57
social control, 330–31
social forces, 6, 180–81
social purity, 191–200
social repair, 227
Society of Missionary Men and Women, 284–85, 288, 300–301
Soule, Frederick, 113, 138, 140
Spoehward, Rosetta, 18, 28, 170–71, 174–75
sports. *See* recreation
squatters camps, 48, *146*, 146–47, 178
State Emergency Relief Administration (SERA), 31, 34, 68–69
State Relief Administration, 170
Stein, Walter, 12, 42, 387n2
Steinbeck, John, 21, 29–30, 44–45, 124–28, 134
Stephens, Jess, 103
Stephens, Noah, 120–22, *121*, 340
stereotypes: of pentecostalism, 126–27, 140, 340, 346; of revivals, 30, 75, 77, 101, 115, 281, 369; in US, 127, 140, 213–14
Stewart, Everett, 359–60
Stock Market Crash (1929), 18
Stone, Earl, 341

Subia, Pedro, 38
Sunday School, 250–52, 297
supervision. *See* management
Swapp, Addie L., 225

"A Talk With Jesus" (Massey), 304–5
Taylor, Paul, 149–50, 165, 201–3
Taylor, Sue, 137–38, *139*
technology: history of, 15–16; Imhoff tanks, 206–13, *209*, 225, 397n36; in New Deal, 226; in sanitary units, 182–86, *183*, *185*, 223–26; for sewage, 206–12, *209*
"Tentative Program of the Division of Rural Rehabilitation, California," 5
tent platforms: family on, *148*; in government camps, 129–33, 135–36; management and, *148*, 164; Mork, R., on, 160; in newspapers, 169–70, 174–76. *See also specific topics*
Texas, 18, 100–101, 104, 133, 168
theology: in art, 303; of Catholicism, 26; of Christianity, 230; in government camps, 125; humanitarianism and, 59; ideology and, 353; illness in, 77, 117; Mork, R., and, 246–47, 370; in newspapers, 323–24, 325–26, 327–28; of pentecostalism, 354–55, 361–70, 399n20; politics and, 34, 172–74, 272; poverty and, 17; of Protestantism, 3, 237–41, 262; psychology of, 304–8; scholarship on, 301
"There is a New Star in Heaven Tonight" (Richardson), 263
"Thine be the Dominion" (August), 305–6, 309
Thom, J. D., 300–301
Thomas, William, 37–38
Thompson, R. M., 359
Thomsen, Eric, 107–15, 144
Thomson, John, 46, 52
tithing, 361–62
Titsworth, R. L., 103
Trimble, Glen, 376–77

Troeltsch, Ernst, 354
Tropic Holiday (film), 300
Tugwell, Rexford, 3, 5, 95–96
Tulare Migratory Farm Labor Camp, 229, 235, 250, 260, 278
Turner, Nat, 320

Ummel, Chris, 264–73, 323–24, *325*, 326, 327, 348, 351, 369–70, 401n50
Ummel, Rheba, 264–73, 323–24, *325*, 326, 327, 348, 351, 369–70, 401n50
United States (US): African Americans in, 366, 371–72; agriculture in, 4–5, 137; American Legion, 34–35; apocalyptic discourse in, 402n44; authority in, 102; Bracero Program in, 376–77; capitalism in, 50; Catholicism in, 118; Chinese people in, 131–32; Christianity in, 24, 401n54; class prejudice in, 20; Communism in, 39, 272, 352; cotton industry in, 12, 14, 36–37, 45–46; culture of, 29–30, 50–57; Europe and, 163; free speech in, 340–41; history of, 15–16; ideology of, 378–79; Irish Americans, *145*; Jews in, 11; Mexico and, 375–77; migration in, *89*; modernity in, 190; National Labor Board, 38–39; New Deal in, 11, 81–82; philosophy in, 97–98; politics in, 27–28; poverty in, 41; Progressive movement in, 231–32; Prohibition in, 231–32; Protestantism in, 127; race in, 115; racism in, 26, 147–48; religion in, 11–12, *13*, 14–16, 27–30, 390n1; stereotypes in, 127, 140, 213–14; Stock Market Crash in, 18; urban centers in, 36; in World War I, 12, 14, 23; in World War II, 163, 224–26, 318–19, 378; WPA, 68–70, 233, 252, 257, 391n20
University of Chicago, 8
US. *See* United States

Vanzandt, Marion G., 331
Victory Through Christ Society, *349*

violence, 39–41, 61
Visalia Migratory Farm Labor Camp, *209*, 216, 217, 219, 235, 250, 251, 254, 260

Wall, J. A., 1–2, 18
water, 144, 191–200, 206–12, *209*, 212–23, 216, 217. *See also specific topics*
Weber, Max, 82–83
Weedpatch Cultivator. See newspapers
Weller, Frank, 50–51
Wells, Elmo, 263–64
Wells, Mary Alice, 263–64
Weston, Donald, 355–57
"What's the Wrong Way to Whip the Devil" (song), 245
White, Lynn T., 34
"Why Do You Bob Your Hair Girls" (song), 243–44
Williams, Floyd. B., 331
Williams, Roy, 355
Wilson, James Bright: gates and, 361–70; on pentecostalism, 357–61, *358*; on Pietsch, 348–54; on Protestantism, 347–48; on religion, 329–31; scholarship from, 345–47
Winters Migratory Farm Labor Camp, 258–59, 271
Winthrop, John, 53
women: in Catholicism, 76; children and, 60–61, 164–65; in cotton industry, 162–63; domestic instruction for, 163–64; in government camps, 343–44; in labor, 62–63; in leadership, 162–63; League of Women Voters, 114–15; in migration, 67–68, 118, 161–62, 243–45; in pentecostalism, 373–74; Presbyterians, 132; in Puritanism, 393n72; in religion, 340
Wood, Irving: Collins, T., and, 94–95, 227–28, 233–34, 241–42; Coverley and, 201–2; Drobish and, 21, 190; management and, 86–88, 90–92, 111; Taylor, P., and, 201–3

Works Progress Administration (WPA), 68–70, 233, 252, 257, 391n20

World War I, 12, 14, 23

World War II, 163, 224–26, 318–19, 378

WPA. *See* Works Progress Administration

Yuba City Camp, 69, 167–68, 177–78, 180, 236–37, 271

ABOUT THE AUTHOR

JONATHAN H. EBEL is Professor in the Department of Religion at the University of Illinois, Urbana-Champaign. A past recipient of a John Simon Guggenheim Foundation fellowship, Ebel is the author of *G.I. Messiahs: Soldiering, War, and American Civil Religion* and *Faith in the Fight: Religion and the American Soldier in the Great War*.